Appalachian Whitewater

The Northern States
Fourth Edition

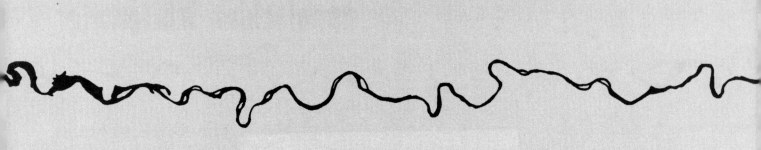

Appalachian Whitewater

The Northern States

FOURTH EDITION

The Premier Canoeing

and Kayaking Streams

of Maine, New Hampshire,

Vermont, Massachusetts,

Connecticut, New York,

Pennsylvania, Maryland, and

West Virginia

John Connelly
Ed Grove
John Porterfield
Charlie Walbridge

Menasha Ridge Press
Birmingham, Alabama

Published by Menasha Ridge Press
Distributed by The Globe Pequot Press
Fourth edition, first printing
Printed in the United States of America

Library of Congress Cataloging-in-Publication Data:
Appalachian whitewater. The Northern States: the premier canoeing and kayaking streams of Maine, New Hampshire, Vermont, Massachusetts, Connecticut, New York, Pennsylvania, Maryland, and West Virginia / John Conelly ... [et al.].—4th ed.
        p. cm.
    Includes bibliographical references and index.
    ISBN 0-89732-380-7 (alk. paper)
    1. Canoes and canoeing—Appalachian Mountains—Guidebooks. 2. Appalachian Mountains—Guidebooks. I. Connelly, John 1956-

GV776.A55A67 2001
797.1'22'0974—dc21

                                                        00-068364

Cover photo © Tim Brown, 1999
Cover design by Grant Tatum
Book design and river ornaments by B. Williams & Associates

Editor's Note: There were many people who helped get this book into print. Thanks go to Donald E. Williams, Carol Engel, Peter Engel, Jim Michaud, Charlie Wilson, as well as members of the Merrimac Valley Paddlers and the Berkshire Chapter of the AMC.

Menasha Ridge Press
P.O. Box 43673
Birmingham, Alabama 35243
(800) 247-9437
www.menasharidge.com

Contents

The Appalachian Mountain System

To appreciate the variety of whitewater opportunities described in this guidebook, it is good to begin with a brief discussion of Appalachian geography. The Appalachian Mountain system extends from the Gaspé Peninsula in Quebec, Canada, southwestward 1,500 miles to northern Georgia and Alabama. Only 80 miles wide in its northernmost reaches, the mountain range broadens to a considerable 350 miles in the south. Elevations vary from 300 feet above sea level at the far eastern edge of the range to lofty peaks exceeding 6,000 feet. New Hampshire and North Carolina have many of the highest mountains, and the highest peak in the range is Mount Mitchell in North Carolina, with an elevation of 6,684 feet.

The Appalachian Mountains are seldom considered in their entirety. Explored, settled, and named by people from different nationalities over more than a hundred years, the Appalachians are more familiar to most of us when discussed in terms of component subranges. Extending southwest from Quebec and Maine are the White Mountains with their Presidential Range containing Mount Washington, the highest peak in the northeastern Appalachians at 6,288 feet, well above treeline at this latitude. Just west of the White Mountains are the Green Mountains, which become the Berkshires in Massachusetts. Covering parts of Vermont, Massachusetts, and Connecticut, the Green Mountains attain their highest elevations in Vermont, where summits range from 2,000 to 4,000 feet. Both the Green and the White Mountains are beautifully forested and embellished by spectacular highland lakes, a legacy of their history of glaciation.

Northwest of the Hudson River in New York are the Adirondacks, and to the west, the Catskills. A long plateau carved by many rivers runs southwest from the Catskills. This feature is known as the Allegheny Plateau in the north and as the Cumberland Plateau in the south. The Allegheny Plateau runs from the Mohawk Valley in New York to southeastern Kentucky. The Cumberland Plateau encompasses much of southeastern Kentucky, east-central Tennessee, and northeastern Alabama. For the most part the Allegheny Plateau, which contains the Catskills and the Pocono and Allegheny Mountains of Pennsylvania and northern West Virginia, is more rugged and mountainlike than the sandstone ridges of the Cumberland Plateau.

The Blue Ridge Mountains begin in southeastern Pennsylvania and extend south to northeastern Georgia and northwestern South Carolina. To the immediate west of the Blue Ridge are the Cumberland Mountains of western Virginia, the Pisgah, Bald, and Black Mountains of North Carolina, and the Unicois, containing the Great Smoky Mountains, in North Carolina and Tennessee. These ranges boast some of the highest summits in the Appalachian system, as well as some of the greatest diversity of plant and animal life. Trees that are typical of northern states, such as spruce, birch, hemlock, and fir, grow on many of these southern mountaintops.

The Blue Ridge and its adjacent ranges are separated from the Allegheny and Cumberland Plateaus to the west by a series of river valleys known collectively as the Great Appalachian Valley. Beginning in the north with the St. Lawrence River valley and moving southwest, the Hudson River valley in New York, the Kittatinny valley in New Jersey, the Lebanon and Cumberland valleys in Pennsylvania and Maryland, the Shenandoah valley in Virginia, the Tennessee valley in Tennessee, and the Coosa valley in Georgia and Alabama all combine to form the Great Valley. While some sections of the Great Valley are broad and verdant, much consists of long, narrow, steep parallel ridges.

Born of powerful upheavals within the earth's crust and forged by the relentless force of moving water on the surface of the continent, the Appalachians are among the oldest mountains on earth. Yet, old as the mountains are, some of the rivers within the Appalachian system are older. Northeast of the New River in Virginia, the major Appalachian rivers flow into the Atlantic Ocean, sometimes through dramatic passages called water gaps. Southwest of the New, however, the rivers (with only a couple of exceptions) flow to the Ohio River. During the faulting and folding which thrust the mountains up, these ancient west-flowing rivers were blocked in their course to the prehistoric sea which once covered mid-America. During the ensuing millennia, these rivers sculpted the landscape of the eastern United States, carving new routes to the sea and in the process creating the spectacular canyons and gorges which make the Appalachians a joy to the whitewater boater.

Water is, of course, the cutting agent, and the Appalachians generally have an abundance of this resource. Owing in part to its elevation, the Appalachian system receives an abundance of rainfall, exceeded in the United States only along the northwest Pacific coast. Much of the annual rainfall, averaging 69 inches a year over most of the system, comes in great downpours. The brevity of these downpours, coupled with the steep gradient of many streams, accounts for water levels changing radically in very little time.

There is enough whitewater in the Appalachians to last the most avid paddler a lifetime. Many smaller streams are only occasionally runnable, but the larger ones, as well as those which are dam-controlled, are runnable year-round. Level of difficulty ranges from the splashy and scenic Class I to the virtually unrunnable. Throughout, the scenery is often spectacular, and river travel is frequently the only means of enjoying a true wilderness environment in the heavily populated eastern U.S.

Stream Dynamics

Understanding hydrology—how rivers are formed and how they affect our activities—is at the very heart of paddling. To aid the paddler, we discuss the effects on paddling of seasonal variations of rainfall, water temperature, and volume, velocity, gradient, and stream morphology.

The most basic concept about water that all paddlers must understand is, of course, the hydrologic or water cycle, which moves water from the earth to the atmosphere and back again. Several things happen to water that falls to the earth: it becomes surface runoff that drains directly into rivers or their tributaries, or it is retained by the soil and used by plants, or it may be returned directly to the atmosphere through evaporation, or else it becomes groundwater by filtering down through subsoil and layers of rock. About 40 percent of each year's rainfall runs either directly into the streams or through the ground and then into the streams, and seasonal variations in the flow levels of watercourses are based on fluctuations in rainfall.

Local soil conditions have a great deal to do with stream flow, as do plant life, terrain slope, ground cover, and air temperature. In summer, during the peak growing season, water is used more readily by plants, and higher air temperatures encourage increased evaporation. The fall and winter low-water periods are caused by decreased precipitation, although since the ground may be frozen and plant use of water is for the most part halted, abnormally high amounts of rain, or water from melting snow, can cause flash floods because surface runoff is high—there's no place for the water to go but into creeks and rivers. Though surface runoff is first to reach the river, it is groundwater that keeps many larger streams flowing during rainless periods. Drought can lower the water table drastically. Soil erosion is related to the surface runoff—hilly land in intensive agricultural use is a prime target for loss of topsoil and flash flooding, as are areas where road building, other construction, or intensive logging is taking place.

The Water Cycle

The earth's water moves in a never-ending cycle from the atmosphere to the land and back to the atmosphere again. Although approximately 97 percent of the earth's water is contained in the oceans, with most of the remainder in ice caps, glaciers, and groundwater, atmospheric water and water in streams is what most concerns us. Atmospheric moisture flows constantly over the Appalachians, and the amount that falls on the region now is much the same as it was when only the Indians worried about dried-up springs and floods.

Beginning the cycle with the oceans, which cover some 75 percent of the earth's surface, the movement of the water follows these steps (see Figure 1):

1. Water from the surface of the oceans (and from the lands between) evaporates into the atmosphere as vapor. This water vapor rises and moves with the winds.
2. Eventually, either over the ocean or over the land, this moisture is condensed by various processes and falls back to the earth as precipitation. Some falls on the ocean; some falls on the land, where it becomes of particular concern to people.
3. Of the rain, snow, sleet, or hail that falls on the land, some runs off over the land, some soaks down into the ground to replenish the great groundwater reservoir, some is taken up by the roots of plants and is transpired as water vapor, and some is again evaporated directly into the atmosphere.
4. The water that flows over the land or soaks down to become groundwater feeds the streams that eventually flow back into the oceans, completing the cycle.

The key steps in this great circulation of the earth's moisture are evaporation, precipitation, transpiration, and stream flow. All occur constantly and simultaneously over the earth. Over the Appalachian river basins, the quantities in any part of the cycle vary widely from day to day or from season to season. Precipitation may be excessive or may stop entirely for days or even weeks.

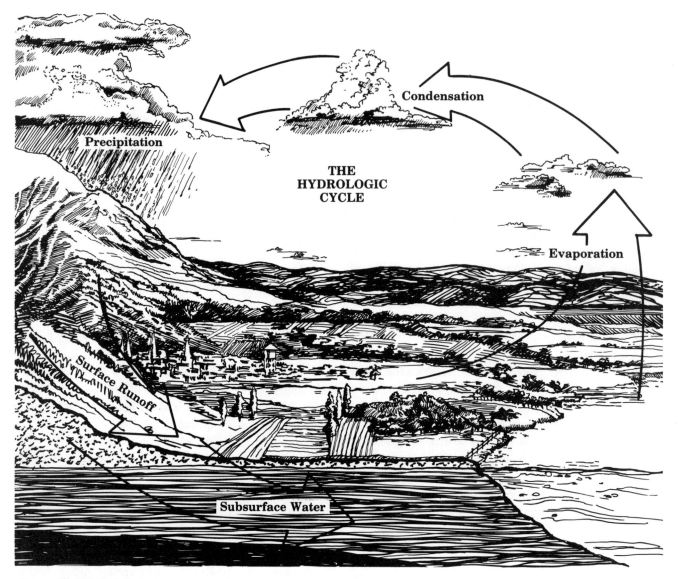

Figure 1. The Hydrologic Cycle

Evaporation and transpiration demands are low in winter but high in July and August. Stream flow depends on the interrelation of these processes.

Climate in the Appalachians

The mountains generally have cooler and wetter climates than neighboring low-lying elevations, with mean temperature dropping approximately 3°F per 1,000-foot rise in elevation. The effects of mountains on air flow make the relation between elevation and precipitation a variable one. The dependence of temperature and precipitation on elevation plays an important role in determining the plant and animal life found in the area.

Water Temperature

Water temperature is another important factor to be considered by paddlers because of the obvious dangers of encountering cold water when they aren't prepared for it.

Surface water temperatures tend to follow air temperatures. Generally, the shallower the stream or reservoir, the closer the water temperature will be to the air temperature. Streams in the Appalachians show a wide variation in temperature throughout the year, ranging from a low of 32°F in winter to a high of about 88°F on some days in July, August, and early September. Streams also show a daily variation: the smaller the stream, the greater the variation, with the least variation occurring in large rivers. The Tennessee River may change only one or two degrees in a day, while changes in a small stream can be almost equal to the range in the day's air temperature.

Coal-burning steam plants, other non-hydroelectric power generation plants, and industrial users may influence the water temperature in some rivers through thermal discharges. Usually, the added heat is lost within 20 miles downstream from the discharge point, but this heat loss depends on the amount of water used, the temperature of the wastewater, the size of the discharge stream, the air temperature, and other factors.

Stream Evolution and Morphology

Often, someone new to boating will fix an inquisitive stare at a large boulder in midstream and ask, "How in blazes did that thing get in the middle of the river?" The frequency of being asked this and similar questions about the river has prompted us to include in this book a brief look at river dynamics, which is basically the relationship between geology and hydraulics, or, expressed differently, what effect flowing water has on the land surface and, conversely, how the land surface modifies the flow of water.

We all know that water flows downhill, moving from a higher elevation to a lower elevation and ultimately flowing into the sea, but contrary to what many people believe, the water on its downhill journey does not flow as smoothly as we might imagine the water in our home plumbing flows. Instead, to varying degrees, depending on the geology, it has to pound and fight every inch of the way, squeezing around obstructions, ricocheting from rock to rock, and funneling from side to side. Almost any river's course is tortuous at best, because the land was there first and is very reluctant to surrender to the moving water. Therefore it does so very slowly and grudgingly. In other words, the water must literally carve out a place in the land through which to flow. It accomplishes this work through erosion.

There are three types of moving water erosion: downward erosion, lateral erosion, and headward erosion. All three represent the wearing away of the land by the water. Downward erosion is at work continuously on all rivers and can be loosely defined as the moving water's wearing away the bottom of the river, eroding the rocks of the river bottom, allowing the river to descend deeper and deeper into the ground. A graphic example of downward erosion in its purest form is a river that runs through a vertical-walled canyon or gorge. The resistance of the rock forming the canyon walls here has limited erosion to the sides. Down and down the river cuts without proportional expansion of its width. A gorge or canyon is formed this way.

Most of the time, however, two and usually three kinds of erosion are working simultaneously. When the water, through downward erosion, for example, cuts into the bottom of the river, it encounters geological substrata of varying resistance and composition. A layer of clay might overlay a shelf of sandstone, under which may be limestone or even granite. Since the water is moving downhill at an angle, the flowing water at the top of a mountain might be working against a completely different type of geological substratum than the water halfway down or at the foot of the mountain. Thus, to carve its channel, the water has to work harder in some spots than in others.

Where current crosses a seam marking the boundary between geological substrata of differing resistance to erosion, an interesting phenomenon occurs. Imagine that upstream of this seam the water has been flowing over sandstone, which is worn away by the erosive action of the current at a rather slow rate. As the current crosses the seam, it encounters limestone, which erodes much faster. Downward erosion wears through the limestone relatively quickly while the sandstone on top remains little changed over the same period. The result is a waterfall (see Figure 2). It may be only a foot high, or it may be 100 feet high, depending on the thickness of the layer eaten away. The process is complete when the less resistant substratum is eroded and the water again encounters sandstone or another equally resistant formation. The evolution of a waterfall by downward erosion is similar to covering your wooden porch stairs with snow so that from top to bottom the stairs resemble a nice snowy hill in the park, with the normal shape of the stairs being hidden. Wood (the stairs) and snow can both be eaten away by water. Obviously though, the water will melt the snow much faster than it will rot the wood. Thus, if a tiny stream of water is launched downhill from the top of

Figure 2. Downward Erosion: Waterfalls

Drawing by K. Jackson

the stairs, it will melt through the snow quickly, not stopping until it reaches the more resistant wood on the next stair down. Through a similar process, erosion forms a waterfall in nature.

Once a waterfall has formed, regardless of its size, headward erosion comes into play. Headward erosion is the wearing away of the base of the waterfall. This action erodes the substrata in an upstream direction toward the headwaters or source of the stream, thus it is called headward erosion. Water falling over the edge of the waterfall lands below with substantial force. As it hits the surface of the water under the falls, it causes a depression in the surface that water from downstream rushes to fill in. This is a hydraulic or hole. Continuing through the surface water, the falling current hits the bottom of the stream. Some of the water is disbursed in an explosive manner, some deflected downstream, and some drawn back to the top where it is recirculated to refill the depression made by yet more falling current. A great deal of energy is expended in this process, and the ensuing cyclical turbulence, which combines with bits of rock to make an abrasive mixture, carves slowly away at the rock base of the falls. If the falls are small, the turbulence may simply serve to smooth out the drop, turning a vertical drop into a slanting drop. If the falls are large, the base of the falls may be eroded, leaving the top of the falls substantially intact but precariously unsupported. After a time, the overhang thus created will surrender to gravity and fall into the river. Thus we see one way that huge

boulders happen to arrive in the middle of the river. Naturally the process is ongoing, and the altered facade of the waterfall is immediately attacked by the currents.

Lateral erosion is the wearing away of the sides of the river by the moving current. While occurring continuously on most rivers to a limited degree, lateral erosion is much more a function of volume and velocity (collectively known as discharge and expressed in cubic feet per second, cfs) than either downward or headward erosion. In other words, as more water is added to a river (beyond that simply required to cover its bottom), the increase in the volume and the speed of the current causes significant additional lateral erosion, while headward and downward erosion remain comparatively constant. Thus, as a river swells with spring rain, the amount of water in the river increases. Since water is noncompressible, the current rises on the banks and through erosion tries to enlarge the riverbed laterally to accommodate the extra volume. Effects of this activity can be observed every year following seasonal rains. Even small streams can widen their beds substantially by eroding large chunks of the banks and carrying them downstream. Boulders and trees in the river are often the result of lateral erosion undercutting the bank.

Through a combination of downward erosion, lateral erosion, and meandering, running water can carve broad valleys between mountains and deep canyons through solid rock. Downward and lateral erosion act on the terrain to determine the morphology (depth, width, shape,

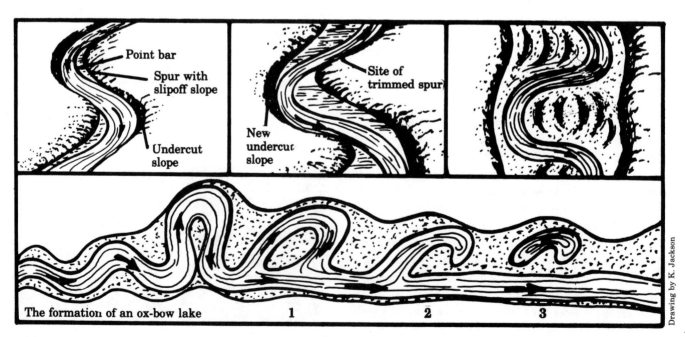

Figure 3. Floodplain Features

and course) of a river. Headward erosion serves to smooth out the rough spots that remain.

Curves in a river are formed much as waterfalls are formed: as the water follows the path of least resistance, its path twists and turns as it is diverted by resistant substrata. Rivers constantly change and do not continue indefinitely in their courses once they are formed. Water is continuously seeking to decrease the energy required to move from the source of the river to the mouth. Understanding this fact is essential to understanding erosion.

Moving water erodes the outside of river bends and deposits much of the eroded matter on the inside of the turn, thereby forming a sand or gravel bar. Jagged turns thus become sweeping bends. The result in more mature streams is a meander, or the formation of a series of horseshoe-shaped and geometrically predictable loops in the river (see Figure 3). A series of such undulating loops markedly widens the valley floor. Often, as time passes, the current erodes the neck of a loop, creating an island in midstream and eliminating a curve in the river.

As we have observed, headward erosion works upstream to smooth out the waterfalls and rapids. Lateral erosion works to make more room for increased volume, and downward erosion deepens the bed and levels obstructions and irregularities. When a river is young (in the geological sense), it cuts downward and is diverted into sharp turns by differing resistance from underlying rock layers. As a stream matures, it carves a valley, sinking even deeper relative to sea level and leaving behind, in many instances, a succession of terraces marking previous valley floors.

In the theoretically mature stream, the bottom is smooth and undisturbed by obstructing boulders, rapids, or falls. Straight stretches in the river give way to serpentine meanders, and the river has a low gradient from the source to the sea. Of course, there are no perfect examples of a mature stream, although rivers such as the Ohio and the Mississippi tend to approach the mature end of the spectrum. In contrast, a stream exhibiting a high gradient and frequent rapids and sharp turns is described as a young stream in the evolutional sense of the word (stream maturity having more to do with the evolutional development of a stream than with actual age; see Figure 4).

All streams carry a load that consists of all the particles, large and small, that are a result of the multiple forms of erosion we have discussed. The load, then, is solid matter transported by the current. Rocky streams at high altitudes carry the smallest loads. Their banks and bottoms are more resistant to erosion, and their tributary drainages are usually small. Scarcity of load is evident in

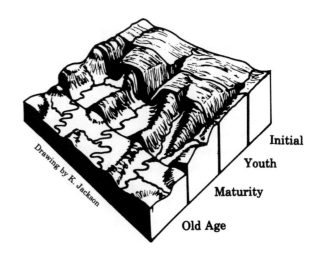

Figure 4. Stream Dissection Cycle: Evolution of a Landscape

the clarity of the water. Rivers such as the Mississippi and Ohio carry enormous loads collected from numerous tributaries as well as from their own banks and bottoms. Water in these and in similarly large rivers is almost always dark and murky with sediment. Since it takes a lot of energy to move a load, many rivers transport conspicuous (readily visible) loads only during rainy periods when they are high, fast, and powerful. When the high waters abate, there is insufficient energy to continue to transport the large load that then, for the most part, settles as silt or alluvium on the bottom of the stream.

Understanding stream dynamics gives any boater an added advantage in working successfully with the river. Knowledge of stream evolution and morphology tells a paddler where to find the strongest current and deepest channel, where rapids and falls are most likely to occur, and what to expect from a given river if the discharge increases or decreases. But more, understanding the river's evolution and continuing development contributes immeasurably to the paddler's aesthetic experience and allows for a communion and harmony with the river that otherwise might be superficial.

Components of Stream Flow

Being able to recognize potential river hazards depends on a practical knowledge of river hydrology—why the water flows the way it does. Since river channels vary greatly in depth and width and the composition of streambeds and their gradients also enter into the river's character, the major components of stream flow bear explanation.

Discharge is the volume of water moving past a given point of the river at any one time. The river current, or velocity, is commonly expressed as the speed of water movement in feet per second (fps), and stage is the river's height in feet based on an arbitrary measurement gauge. These terms are interrelated; higher water levels mean increased volume and velocity.

Another factor in assessing stream difficulty is gradient, which is expressed in feet per mile. As gradient increases, so does velocity. The streams profiled in this book have gradients that range from about 1 foot per mile to an astounding 200 feet per mile. The gradient in any stream or section of a stream changes with the landforms, the geology of the basin. If a river flows over rock or soil with varying resistance to erosion, ledges, water-

falls, and rapids sometimes form and dramatically affect the river's gradient.

Velocity is also affected by the width and depth of the streams. Rapids form where streams are shallow and swift. Large obstructions in shallow streams of high velocity cause severe rapids. Within a given channel, there are likely to be rapids with different levels of difficulty. The current on straight sections of river is usually fastest in the middle. The depth of water in river bends is determined by flow rates and soil types. Water tends to cut away the land and form deep holes on the outsides of bends where the current is the swiftest.

Paddler Information

Rating the River

For years concerned paddlers have sought to rate rivers objectively, and central among their tools has been the International Scale of River Difficulty. While certainly useful, the International Scale (provided in part V of the Safety Code of the American Whitewater Affiliation found later in this chapter) lacks precision and invites subjective, judgmental error. A more objective yardstick is the River Rating Chart, which allows boaters to assign points to a stream based on various aspects of river difficulty (see Table 2). While more complex, it does succeed in describing a river more or less as it really is. Gone is the common confusion of a single rapid's being described as Class II by the veteran while the novice perceives a roaring Class IV. Also eliminated is the double standard by which a river is rated Class III for open canoes but only Class II for decked boats. Additionally, this system helps eliminate regional classification discrepancies. Points are awarded as prescribed for conditions observed on the day the river is to be run. The total number of points describes the general level of difficulty.

Once the basic difficulty rating is calculated for a river, however, how is it to be matched against the skill level of a prospective paddler? The American Whitewater Affiliation relates the River Rating Chart back to the International Scale of River Difficulty and to traditional paddler classifications (see Table 1).

Making the foregoing comparisons helps, but only to the extent that the individual paddler understands the definitions of "Practiced Beginner," "Intermediate," "Experienced," and so on. Most paddlers find these traditional titles ambiguous and hard to differentiate. Many paddlers probably classify themselves according to self-image. When this occurs, we are back to where we started.

Rating the Paddler

Correctly observing the need for increased objectivity in rating paddlers as well as in rating rivers, several paddling clubs have developed self-evaluation systems where paddlers are awarded points that correspond to the point scale of the River Rating Chart (Table 2). Thus an individual can determine a point total through self-evaluation and compare his or her skill, in quantified terms, to any river rated through use of the chart. The individual paddler, for instance, may compile 18 points through self-evaluation and note that this rating compares favorably with a river difficulty rating of 17 points and unfavorably with a difficulty rating of 23 points. It should be emphasized here, however, that river ratings via the river difficulty chart pertain to a river only on a given day and at a specific water level.

Table 1. A Comparison of Ratings

International Scale	Approximate Difficulty	River Ratings (from Table 2)	Approximate Paddler Skill Required
I	Easy	0-7	Practiced Beginner
II	Requires Care	8-14	Intermediate
III	Difficult	15-21	Experienced
IV	Very Difficult	22-28	Highly Skilled (Several years with organized group)
V	Exceedingly Difficult	29-35	Team of Experts
VI	Utmost Difficulty- Near Limit of Navigability	36-42	Team of Experts with every precaution

Table 2. River Rating Chart*

Points	Obstacles, Rocks, and Trees	Waves	Turbulence	Bends	Length (feet)	Gradient (ft/mile)	Resting or Rescue Spots	Water Velocity (mph)	Width and Depth	Temp (°F)	Accessibility
0	None	Few inches high, avoidable	None	Few, very gradual	<100	<5, regular slope	Almost anywhere	<3	Narrow (≤75 ft) and shallow (≤3 ft)	>65	Road along river
1	Few; passage almost straight through	Low (up to 1 ft), regular, avoidable	Minor eddies	Many, gradual	100–700	5–15, regular slope		3–6	Wide (>75 ft) and shallow (≤3 ft)	55–65	<1 hour travel by foot or water
2	Courses easily recognizable	Low to med. (up to 3 ft), regular, avoidable	Medium eddies	Few, sharp, blind; scouting necessary	701–5,000	16–40, ledges or steep drops		7–10	Narrow (≤75 ft) and deep (>3 ft)	45–54	1 hour to 1 day travel by foot or water
3	Maneuvering course not easily recognizable	Med. to large (up to 5 ft), mostly regular, avoidable	Strong eddies and cross-currents		>5,000	>40, steep drops, small falls	A good one below every danger spot	>10 or flood	Wide (>75ft) and deep (>3 ft)	<45	>1 day travel by foot or water
4	Intricate maneuvering; course hard to recognize	Large, irregular, avoidable; or med. to large, unavoidable	Very strong eddies, strong cross-currents								
5	Course tortuous, frequent scouting needed	Large, irregular, avoidable; or med. to large, unavoidable	Large-scale eddies and cross-currents, some up and down								
6	Very tortuous; always scout from shore	Very large (>5 ft), irregular, unavoidable; special equipment required					Almost none				

Source: Prepared by Guidebook Committee—AWA (from "American White Water," Winter 1957).

*To rate a river, match the characteristics of the river with descriptions in *each* column. Add the points from each column for a total river rating.

Some paddler self-evaluation systems seem to emphasize strength and individual fitness at the expense of river skills, perhaps encouraging fit but inexperienced individuals onto rivers too difficult for them. To shift the focus toward river skills, author Bob Sehlinger has redefined the rating system, creating a more complex, exhaustive, and objective paddler self-evaluation. Heavy emphasis is placed on paddling skills, with descriptions adopted from several different evaluation formats, including a nonnumerical system proposed by Dick Schwind ("Rating System for Boating Difficulty," *American Whitewater Journal*, vol. 20, num. 3, May/June 1975).

The paddler rating system that follows will provide a numerical point summary. The paddler can then use this information to gauge whether a river of a given ranking is within his or her capabilities.

Paddler Rating System

Instructions: All items, except the first, carry points that are added to obtain an overall rating. All items except "Rolling Ability" apply to both open and decked boats. Rate open and decked boat skills separately.

1. Prerequisite Skills. Before paddling on moving current, the paddler should:

a. Have some swimming ability
b. Be able to paddle instinctively on nonmoving water (on lakes). (This presumes knowledge of basic strokes.)
c. Be able to guide and control the canoe from either side without changing paddling sides
d. Be able to guide and control the canoe (or kayak) while paddling backward
e. Be able to move the canoe (or kayak) laterally
f. Understand the limitations of the boat
g. Be practiced in "wet exit" if in a decked boat

2. Equipment. Award points on the suitability of your equipment to whitewater. Whether you own, borrow, or rent the equipment makes no difference. Award points for either Open Canoe or Decked Boat, not both.

Open Canoe

0 Points: Any canoe used for tandem with seats mounted too low to safely place the paddler's feet under while kneeling; any canoe used for solo that offers no mid-area braced kneeling position
1 Point: Canoe with moderate rocker and full depth; should be at least 14 feet long for tandem and at least 13 feet for solo and have bow and stern painters

2 Points: Whitewater canoe with strong rocker design, full bow, full depth amidships, no keel; meets or exceeds minimum length requirements as described under "1 Point"; made of hand-laid fiberglass, Kevlar, Marlex, or ABS Royalex; has bow and stern painters. Or a canoe as described under "1 Point" but with extra flotation.
3 Points: A whitewater canoe as described under "2 Points" but with extra flotation

Decked Boat (K1 or 2, C1 or 2)

0 Points: Any decked boat lacking full flotation, spray skirt, or foot braces
1 Point: Any fully equipped, decked boat with a wooden frame
2 Points: Decked boat with full flotation, spray skirt, and foot braces; has grab loops; made of hand-laid fiberglass, Marlex, or Kevlar
3 Points: Decked boat with foam wall reinforcement and split flotation; Neoprene spray skirt; has knee braces, foot braces, and grab loops; made of hand-laid fiberglass or Kevlar only

3. Experience. Compute the following to determine preliminary points, then convert the preliminary points to final points according to the conversion table. This is the only evaluation item where it is possible to accrue more than 3 points.

Number of days spent paddling each year:
Class I rivers   x 1 =____
Class II rivers   x 2 =____
Class III rivers   x 3 =____
Class IV rivers   x 4 =____
Class V–VI rivers   x 5 =____
Preliminary subtotal   =____
Number of years of
paddling experience   x____
Total preliminary points   ____

Conversion Table

Preliminary Points	Final Points
0–20	0
21–60	1
61–100	2
101–200	3
201–300	4
301–up	5

4. Swimming

0   Points: Cannot swim

1   Point: Weak swimmer

2   Points: Average swimmer

3   Points: Strong swimmer (competition level or skin diver)

5. Stamina

0   Points: Cannot run a mile in 10 minutes or less

1   Point: Can run a mile in 7 to 10 minutes

2   Points: Can run a mile in less than 7 minutes

6. Upper Body Strength

0   Points: Cannot do 15 push-ups

1   Point: Can do 15 to 25 push-ups

2   Points: Can do more than 25 push-ups

7. Boat Control

0   Points: Can keep boat fairly straight

1   Point: Can maneuver in moving water; can avoid big obstacles

2   Points: Can maneuver in heavy water; knows how to work with the current

3   Points: Finesse in boat placement in all types of water; uses current to maximum advantage

8. Aggressiveness

0   Points: Does not play or work river at all

1   Point: Timid; plays a little on familiar streams

2   Points: Plays a lot; works most rivers hard

3   Points: Plays in heavy water with grace and confidence

9. Eddy Turns

0   Points: Has difficulty making eddy turns from moderate current

1   Point: Can made eddy turns in either direction from moderate current; can enter moderate current from eddy

2   Points: Can catch medium eddies in either direction from heavy current; can enter very swift current from eddy

3   Points: Can catch small eddies in heavy current

10. Ferrying

0   Points: Cannot ferry

1   Point: Can ferry upstream and downstream in moderate current

2   Points: Can ferry upstream in heavy current; can ferry downstream in moderate current

3   Points: Can ferry upstream and downstream in heavy current

11. Water Reading

0   Points: Often in error

1   Point: Can plan route in short rapid with several well-spaced obstacles

2   Points: Can confidently run lead through continuous Class 2; can predict the effects of waves and holes on boat

3   Points: Can confidently run lead in continuous Class 3; has knowledge to predict and handle the effects of reversals, side currents, and turning drops

12. Judgment

0   Points: Often in error

1   Point: Has average ability to analyze difficulty of rapids

2   Points: Has good ability to analyze difficulty of rapids and make independent judgments as to which should not be run

3   Points: Has the ability to assist fellow paddlers in evaluating the difficulty of rapids; can explain subtleties to paddlers with less experience

13. Bracing

0   Points: Has difficulty bracing in Class 2 water

1   Point: Can correctly execute bracing strokes in Class 2 water

2   Points: Can correctly brace in intermittent whitewater with medium waves and vertical drops of 3 feet or less

3   Points: Can brace effectively in continuous whitewater with large waves and large vertical drops (4 feet and up)

14. Rescue Ability

0   Points: Self-rescue in flatwater

1   Point: Self-rescue in mild whitewater

2   Points: Self-rescue in Class 3; can assist others in mild whitewater

3   Points: Can assist others in heavy whitewater

15. Rolling Ability

0   Points: Can only roll in pool

1   Point: Can roll 3 out of 4 times in moving current

2 Points: Can roll 3 out of 4 times in Class 2 white-
    water

3 Points: Can roll 4 out of 5 times in Class 3 and 4
    whitewater

Add your points from items 2 through 15. To see what types of rivers might be appropriate for your skill level, compare your skill level rating to the river difficulty rating in Table 2. While these systems provide a better way to choose what rivers are appropriate for you than the International Scale of River Difficulty alone, there is no guarantee of a smooth trip.

Hazards and Safety

Hazardous situations likely to be encountered on the river must be identified and understood for safe paddling. The American Whitewater Affiliation's safety code is perhaps the most useful overall safety guideline available. (The much-discussed International Scale of River Difficulty is included in Part V of the code.)

Safety Code of the American Whitewater Affiliation

This code has been prepared using the best available information and has been reviewed by a broad cross section of whitewater experts. The code, however, is only a collection of guidelines. Attempts to minimize risks should be flexible—not constrained by a rigid set of rules. Varying conditions and group goals may combine with unpredictable circumstances to require alternate procedures.

I. Personal Preparedness and Responsibility

1. Be a competent swimmer, with the ability to handle yourself underwater.
2. Wear a life jacket. A snugly fitting vest-type life preserver offers back and shoulder protection as well as the flotation needed to swim safely in whitewater.
3. Wear a solid, correctly fitted helmet when upsets are likely. This is essential in kayaks or covered canoes and recommended for open canoeists using thigh straps and rafters running steep drops.
4. Do not boat out of control. Your skills should be sufficient to stop or reach shore before reaching danger. Do not enter a rapid unless you are reasonably sure that you can run it safely or swim it without injury.
5. Whitewater rivers contain many hazards that are not always easily recognized. The following are the most frequent killers:

A. High water. The river's speed and power increase tremendously as the flow increases, raising the difficulty of most rapids. Rescue becomes progressively harder as the water rises, adding to the danger. Floating debris and strainers make even an easy rapid quite hazardous. It is often misleading to judge the river level at the put-in, since a small rise in a wide, shallow place will be multiplied many times where the river narrows. Use reliable gauge information whenever possible, and be aware that sun on snowpack, hard rain, and upstream dam releases may greatly increase the flow.

B. Cold. Cold drains your strength and robs you of the ability to make sound decisions on matters affecting your survival. Cold water immersion, because of the initial shock and the rapid heat loss which follows, is especially dangerous. Dress appropriately for bad weather or sudden immersion in the water. When the water temperature is less than 50°F, a wet suit or dry suit is essential for protection if you swim. Next best is wool or pile clothing under a waterproof shell. In this case, you should also carry waterproof matches and a change of clothing in a waterproof bag. If, after prolonged exposure, a person experiences uncontrollable shaking, loss of coordination, or difficulty speaking, he or she is hypothermic and needs your assistance.

C. Strainers. Brush, fallen trees, bridge pilings, undercut rocks, or anything else which allows river current to sweep through can pin boats and boaters against the obstacle. Water pressure on anything trapped this way can be overwhelming. Rescue is often extremely difficult. Pinning may occur in fast current, with little or no whitewater to warn of the danger.

D. Dams, weirs, ledges, reversals, holes, and hydraulics. When water drops over an obstacle, it curls back on itself, forming a strong upstream current which may be capable of holding a boat or a swimmer. Some holes make for excellent sport; others are proven killers. Paddlers who cannot recognize the differences should avoid all but the smallest holes. Hydraulics around man-made dams must be treated with utmost respect regardless of their height or the level of the river. Despite their seemingly benign appearance, they can create an almost escape-proof trap. The swimmer's only exit from the "drowning machine" is to dive below the surface where the downstream current is flowing beneath the reversal.

E. Broaching. When a boat is pushed sideways against a rock by strong current, it may collapse and wrap. This is especially dangerous to kayak and decked canoe paddlers; these boats will collapse and the combination of indestructible hulls and tight outfitting may create a deadly trap. Even without entrapment, releasing pinned boats can be extremely time-consuming and dangerous. To avoid pinning, throw your weight downstream toward the rock. This allows the current to slide harmlessly underneath the hull.

6. Boating alone is discouraged. The minimum party is three people or two craft.

7. Have a frank knowledge of your boating ability, and don't attempt rivers or rapids that lie beyond your ability.

A. Develop the paddling skills and teamwork required to match the river you plan to boat. Most good paddlers develop skills gradually, and attempts to advance too quickly will compromise your safety and enjoyment.

B. Be in good physical and mental condition, consistent with the difficulties which may be expected. Make adjustments for loss of skills due to age, health, or fitness. Any health limitation must be explained to your fellow paddlers prior to starting the trip.

8. Be practiced in self-rescue, including escape from an overturned craft. The Eskimo roll is strongly recommended for decked boaters who run rapids of Class IV or greater, or who paddle in cold environmental conditions.

9. Be trained in rescue skills, CPR, and first aid with special emphasis on recognizing and treating hypothermia. It may save your friend's life.

10. Carry equipment needed for unexpected emergencies, including footwear that will protect your feet when walking out, a throw rope, a knife, a whistle, and waterproof matches. If you wear eyeglasses, tie them on and carry a spare pair on long trips. Bring cloth repair tape on short runs, and a full repair kit on isolated rivers. Do not wear bulky jackets, ponchos, heavy boots, or anything else which could reduce your ability to survive a swim.

11. Despite the mutually supportive group structure described in this code, individual paddlers are ulti-mately responsible for their own safety, and must assume sole responsibility for the following decisions:

A. The decision to participate on any trip. This includes an evaluation of the expected difficulty of the rapids under the conditions existing at the time of the put-in.

B. The selection of appropriate equipment, including a boat design suited to their skills and the appropriate rescue and survival gear.

C. The decision to scout any rapid, and to run or portage according to their best judgment. Other members of the group may offer advice, but paddlers should resist pressure from anyone to paddle beyond their skills. It is also their responsibility to decide whether to pass up any walk-out or take-out opportunity.

D. All trip participants should constantly evaluate their own and their group's safety, voicing their concerns when appropriate and following what they believe to be the best course of action. Paddlers are encouraged to speak with anyone whose action on the water is dangerous, whether they are a part of your group or not.

II. Boat and Equipment Preparedness

1. Test new and different equipment under familiar conditions before relying on it for difficult runs. This is especially true when adopting a new boat design or outfitting system. Low-volume craft may present additional hazards to inexperienced or poorly conditioned paddlers.

2. Be sure your boat and gear are in good repair before starting a trip. The more isolated and difficult a run, the more rigorous this inspection should be.

3. Install flotation bags in noninflatable craft, securely fixed in each end, designed to displace as much water as possible. Inflatable boats should have multiple air chambers and be test inflated before launching.

4. Have strong, properly sized paddles or oars for controlling your craft. Carry sufficient spares for the length and difficulty of the trip.

5. Outfit your boat safely. The ability to exit your boat quickly is an essential component of safety in rapids. It is your responsibility to see that there is absolutely nothing to cause entrapment when coming free of an upset craft. This includes:

A. Spray covers that won't release reliably or that release prematurely.

B. Boat outfitting too tight to allow a fast exit, especially in low-volume kayaks or decked canoes. This includes low-hung thwarts in canoes lacking adequate clearance for your feet and kayak footbraces that fail or allow your feet to become wedged under them.

C. Inadequately supported decks which collapse on a paddler's legs when a decked boat is pinned by water pressure. Inadequate clearance with the deck because of your size or build.

D. Loose ropes which cause entanglement. Beware of any length of loose line attached to a white-water boat. All items must be tied tightly and excess line eliminated; painters, throw lines, and safety rope systems must be completely and effectively stored. Do not knot the end of a rope, as it can get caught in cracks between rocks.

6. Provide ropes that permit you to hold on to your craft so that it may be rescued. The following methods are recommended:

A. Kayaks and covered canoes should have grab loops of ¼"+ rope or equivalent webbing sized to admit a normal-sized hand. Stern painters are permissible if properly secured.

B. Open canoes should have securely anchored bow and stern painters consisting of 8–10 feet of ¼" line. These must be secured in such a way that they are readily accessible, but cannot come loose accidentally. Grab loops are accept-able, but are more difficult to reach after an upset.

C. Many rafts and dories have taut perimeter lines threaded through the loops provided. Footholds should be designed so that a paddler's feet can-not be forced through them, causing entrap-ment. Flip lines should be carefully and reliably stowed.

7. Know your craft's carrying capacity and how added loads affect boat handling in whitewater. Most rafts have a minimum crew size which can be added to on day trips or in easy rapids. Carrying more than two paddlers in an open canoe when running rapids is not recommended.

8. Car top racks must be strong and attach positively to the vehicle. Lash your boat to each crossbar, then tie the ends of the boat directly to the bumpers for added security. This arrangement should survive all but the most violent vehicle accident.

III. Group Preparedness and Responsibility

1. Organization. A river trip should be regarded as a common adventure by all participants, except on instructional or commercially guided trips as defined below. Participants share the responsibility for the conduct of the trip, and each participant is individually responsible for judging his or her own capabilities and for his or her own safety as the trip progresses. Participants are encouraged (but are not obligated) to offer advice and guidance for the independent consideration and judgment of others.

2. River Conditions. The group should have a reason-able knowledge of the difficulty of the run. Partici-pants should evaluate this information and adjust their plans accordingly. If the run is exploratory or no one is familiar with the river, maps and guide-books, if available, should be examined. The group should secure accurate flow information; the more difficult the run, the more important this will be. Be aware of possible changes in river level and how this will affect the difficulty of the run. If the trip involves tidal stretches, secure appropriate information on tides.

3. Group equipment should be suited to the difficulty of the river. The group should always have a throw line available, and one line per boat is recom-mended on difficult runs. The list may include: carabiners, prussick loops, first aid kit, flashlight, folding saw, fire starter, guidebooks, maps, food, extra clothing, and any other rescue or survival items suggested by conditions. Each item is not required on every run, and this list is not meant to be a substitute for good judgment.

4. Keep the group compact, but maintain sufficient spacing to avoid collisions. If the group is large, consider dividing into smaller groups or using the "buddy system" as an additional safeguard. Space yourselves closely enough to permit good commu-nication, but not so close as to interfere with one another in rapids.

A. The lead paddler sets the pace. When in front, do not get in over your head. Never run drops when you cannot see a clear route to the bot-tom or, for advanced paddlers, a sure route to the next eddy. When in doubt, stop and scout.

B. Keep track of all group members. Each boat keeps the one behind it in sight, stopping if necessary. Know how many people are in your group and take head counts regularly. No one should paddle ahead or walk out without first informing the group. Weak paddlers should stay at the center of a group, and not allow themselves to lag behind. If the group is large and contains a wide range of abilities, a designated "sweep boat" should bring up the rear.

C. Courtesy. On heavily used rivers, do not cut in front of a boater running a drop. Always look upstream before leaving eddies to run or play. Never enter a crowded drop or eddy when no room for you exists. Passing other groups in a rapid may be hazardous: it's often safer to wait upstream until the group has passed.

5. Float plan. If the trip is into a wilderness area or for an extended period, plans should be filed with a responsible person who will contact the authorities if you are overdue. It may be wise to establish checkpoints along the way where civilization could be contacted if necessary. Knowing the location of possible help and preplanning escape routes can speed rescue.

6. Drugs. The use of alcohol or mind-altering drugs before or during river trips is not recommended. It dulls reflexes, reduces decision-making ability, and may interfere with important survival reflexes.

7. Instructional or Commercially Guided Trips. In contrast to the common adventure trip format, in these trip formats, a boating instructor or commercial guide assumes some of the responsibilities normally exercised by the group as a whole, as appropriate under the circumstances. These formats recognize that instructional or commercially guided trips may involve participants who lack significant experience in whitewater. However, as a participant acquires experience in whitewater, he or she takes on increasing responsibility for his or her own safety, in accordance with what he or she knows or should know as a result of that increased experience. Also, as in all trip formats, every participant must realize and assume the risks associated with the serious hazards of whitewater rivers. It is advisable for instructors and commercial guides to acquire trip or personal liability insurance.

A. An "instructional trip" is characterized by a clear teacher/pupil relationship, where the primary purpose of the trip is to teach boating skills, and sometimes is conducted for a fee.

B. A "commercially guided trip" is characterized by a licensed, professional guide conducting trips for a fee.

IV. Guidelines for River Rescue

1. Recover from an upset with an Eskimo roll whenever possible. Evacuate your boat immediately if there is imminent danger of being trapped against rocks, brush, or any other kind of strainer.

2. If you swim, hold on to your boat. It has much flotation and is easy for rescuers to spot. Get to the upstream end so that you cannot be crushed between a rock and your boat by the force of the current. Persons with good balance may be able to climb on top of a swamped kayak or flipped raft and paddle to shore.

3. Release your craft if this will improve your chances, especially if the water is cold or dangerous rapids lie ahead. Actively attempt self-rescue whenever possible by swimming for safety. Be prepared to assist others who may come to your aid.

A. When swimming in shallow or obstructed rapids, lie on your back with feet held high and pointed downstream. Do not attempt to stand in fast-moving water; if your foot wedges on the bottom, fast water will push you under and keep you there. Get to slow or very shallow water before attempting to stand or walk. Look ahead! Avoid possible pinning situations—including undercut rocks, strainers, downed trees, holes, and other dangers—by swimming away from them.

B. If the rapids are deep and powerful, roll over onto your stomach and swim aggressively for shore. Watch for eddies and slackwater and use them to get out of the current. Strong swimmers can effect a powerful upstream ferry and get to shore fast. If the shores are obstructed with strainers or undercut rocks, however, it is safer to "ride the rapid out" until a less hazardous escape can be found.

4. If others spill and swim, go after the boaters first. Rescue boats and equipment only if this can be done safely. While participants are encouraged (but not obligated) to assist one another to the best of their ability, they should do so only if they can, in their judgment, do so safely. The first duty of a rescuer is to not compound the problem by becoming another victim.

5. The use of rescue lines requires training; uninformed use may cause injury. Never tie yourself into either end of a line without a quick-release system. Have a knife handy to deal with unexpected entanglement. Learn to place set lines

effectively, throw accurately, belay effectively, and properly handle a rope thrown to you.

6. When reviving a drowning victim, be aware that cold water may greatly extend survival time underwater. Victims of hypothermia may have depressed vital signs, so they look and feel dead. Don't give up; continue CPR for as long as possible without compromising safety.

V. International Scale of River Difficulty

This is the American version of a rating system used to compare river difficulty throughout the world. This system is not exact; rivers do not always fit easily into one category, and regional or individual interpretations may cause misunderstandings. It is no substitute for a guidebook or accurate firsthand descriptions of a run.

Paddlers attempting difficult runs in an unfamiliar area should act cautiously until they get a feel for the way the scale is interpreted locally. River difficulty may change each year due to fluctuations in water level, downed trees, geological disturbances, or bad weather. Stay alert for unexpected problems!

As river difficulty increases, the danger to swimming paddlers becomes more severe. As rapids become longer and more continuous, the challenge increases. There is a difference between running an occasional Class IV rapids and dealing with an entire river of this category. Allow an extra margin of safety between skills and river ratings when the water is cold or if the river itself is remote and inaccessible.

The Six Difficulty Classes

Class I: Easy. Fast-moving water with riffles and small waves. Few obstructions, all obvious and easily missed with little training. Risk to swimmers is slight; self-rescue is easy.

Class II: Novice. Straightforward rapids with wide, clear channels that are evident without scouting. Occasional maneuvering may be required, but rocks and medium-sized waves are easily missed by trained paddlers. Swimmers are seldom injured and group assistance, while helpful, is seldom needed.

Class III: Intermediate. Rapids with moderate, irregular waves which may be difficult to avoid and which can swamp an open canoe. Complex maneuvers in fast current and good boat control in tight passages or around ledges are often required; large waves or strainers may be present but are easily avoided. Strong eddies

and powerful current effects can be found, particularly on large-volume rivers. Scouting is advisable for inexperienced parties. Injuries while swimming are rare; self-rescue is usually easy but group assistance may be required to avoid long swims.

Class IV: Advanced. Intense, powerful but predictable rapids requiring precise boat handling in turbulent water. Depending on the character of the river, it may feature large, unavoidable waves and holes or constricted passages demanding fast maneuvers under pressure. A fast, reliable eddy turn may be needed to navigate dangerous hazards. Scouting is necessary the first time down. Risk of injury to swimmers is moderate to high, and water conditions may make self-rescue difficult. Group assistance for rescue is often essential but requires practiced skills. A strong eskimo roll is highly recommended.

Class V: Expert. Extremely long, obstructed, or very violent rapids which expose a paddler to above-average endangerment. Drops may contain large, unavoidable waves and holes or steep, congested chutes with complex, demanding routes. Rapids may continue for long distances between pools, demanding a high level of fitness. What eddies exist may be small, turbulent, or difficult to reach. At the high end of the scale, several of these factors may be combined. Scouting is mandatory, but often difficult. Swims are dangerous, and rescue is difficult, even for experts. A very reliable eskimo roll, proper equipment, extensive experience, and practiced rescue skills are essential for survival.

Class VI: Extreme. One grade more difficult than Class V. These runs often exemplify the extremes of difficulty, unpredictability, and danger. The consequences of errors are very severe and rescue may be impossible. For teams of experts only, at favorable water levels, after close personal inspection, and taking all precautions. This class does not represent drops thought to be unrunnable, but may include rapids that are only occasionally run.

Standards Adopted 1959; Revised 1989

Injuries and Evacuations

Even allowing for careful preparation and attention to the rules of river safety, it remains a fact that people and boats are somewhat more fragile than rivers and rocks. Accidents occur on paddling trips, and all boaters should understand that accidents can happen to them. Although virtually any disaster is possible on a river, including drowning, there are specific traumas and illnesses that occur more frequently than others. These include the following:

1. Hypothermia
2. Dislocated shoulder (especially common in decked boating)
3. Sprained or broken ankles (usually sustained while scouting or getting into or out of the boat)
4. Head injuries (sustained in falls on shore or during capsize)
5. Hypersensitivity to insect bite (anaphylactic shock)
6. Heat trauma (sunburn, heat stroke, heat prostration, dehydration, etc.)
7. Food poisoning (often resulting from sun spoilage of lunch foods on a hot day)
8. Badly strained muscles (particularly of the lower back, upper arm, and trapezius)
9. Hand and wrist injuries
10. Lacerations

Many paddlers are well prepared to handle the first aid requirements when one of the above injuries occurs on the river, but they are ill prepared to handle continued care and evacuation.

You and your paddling partners should have up-to-date CPR and first aid training and should improve your rescue skills by taking the courses in river rescue offered by many river outfitters. In addition, study works about river rescue such as *The American Canoe Association's River Safety Anthology*, edited by Charlie Walbridge and Jody Tinsley; *River Rescue*, by Les Bechtel; *The American Canoe Association's 1992–1995 River Safety Report*, edited by Charlie Walbridge; and *The American Canoe Association's River Safety Flashcards*. These can help prepare you for continued care and evacuation of the injured or ill.

Be prepared for such contingencies. Carry topographic maps and know where you are in relation to roads. If an emergency occurs, don't panic. If possible, send two people out to find help, carrying written instructions about the nature of the injury or illness and the specific location of the victim or a rendezvous point if the remainder of the party is beginning an evacuation. Because helicopter rescues are available only near military bases or high-use areas and because helicopters need more room to land and hover than Appalachian river valleys typically allow, don't expect a dramatic helicopter rescue. If you have the manpower and know-how, you may decide to carry out the victim, being sure to keep him or her safe, calm, and warm during the evacuation. Otherwise, once help is sent for, psychologically prepare yourself for a long wait.

Hypothermia

Although this guide is by no means a first aid manual, hypothermia, the lowering of the body's core temperature, is so common and so deadly that it deserves special attention here. Hypothermia can occur in a matter of minutes in water just a few degrees above freezing, but even 50°F water is unbearably cold. To make things worse, panic can set in when the paddler is faced with a long swim through rapids. Heat loss occurs much more quickly than believed. When the body's temperature drops appreciably below the normal 98.6°F, sluggishness sets in, breathing is difficult, coordination is lost to even the most athletic person, pupils dilate, speech becomes slurred, and thinking becomes irrational. Cold water robs the victim of the ability and desire to save him- or herself. Finally unconsciousness sets in, and then, death. A drop in body temperature to 96°F makes swimming and pulling yourself to safety almost impossible, and tragically, the harder you struggle, the more heat your body loses. Body temperatures below 90°F lead to unconsciousness, and a further drop to about 77°F usually results in death. (But this same lowering of the body temperature slows metabolism and delays brain death in cases of drowning; therefore, rescue efforts have a higher chance of success.)

Paddlers subjected to spray and wetting from waves splashing into an open boat are in almost as much danger of hypothermia as a paddler completely immersed after a swim. The combination of cold air and water drains the body of precious heat at an alarming rate, although it is the wetness that causes the major losses, since water conducts heat away from the body 20 times faster than air. Clothes lose their insulating properties quickly when immersed, and skin temperatures will rapidly drop to within a few degrees of the water temperature. The body, hard-pressed to conserve heat, will then reduce blood circulation to the extremities. This reduction in blood flowing to arms and legs makes movement and heavy work next to impossible. Muscular activity increases heat loss because blood forced to the extremities is quickly cooled by the cold water. It's a vicious, deadly cycle.

The best safeguards against cold-weather hazards are recognizing the symptoms of hypothermia, preventing exposure to cold by wearing proper clothing (wool or synthetic fabrics, waterproof outerwear, wet suits, or dry suits), understanding and respecting cold weather and water, and knowing how to treat hypothermia when it is detected. Actually, cold weather deaths may be attributed to a number of factors: physical exhaustion, inadequate food intake, dehydration, and psychological elements such as fear, panic, and despair. Factors such as body fat, the metabolic rate of an individual, and skin thickness are variables in a particular person's reaction and endurance when immersed in cold water.

Exercise may warm a mildly hypothermic person, and shivering is involuntary exercise. But the key to bringing victims out of serious hypothermia is heating their bodies from an external source. In a field situation, strip off all wet clothes and get the victim into a sleeping bag with another person. Skin-to-skin transfer of body heat is by far the best method of getting the body's temperature up. By all means, don't let the victim go to sleep, and give him or her warm liquids. Build a campfire if possible. Mouth-to-mouth resuscitation or CPR may be necessary in extreme cases when breathing and pulse have stopped, but remember that a person in the grips of hypothermia has a significantly reduced metabolic rate, so check carefully before administering this treatment.

Paddlers' Rights and Responsibilities

While it is essential to have knowledge of first aid and rescue techniques, it is also very important to know your legal rights and responsibilities while on the river. A paddler's legal right to run a river is based on the concept of navigability. This situation is somewhat unfortunate, since navigability as a legal concept has proven both obscure and somewhat confused over the years. The common law test of navigability specifies that only those streams affected by the ebb and flow of the sea tides are navigable. Obviously, if this were the only criterion, none of the streams in the Appalachians would be navigable. Fortunately, most states expressly repudiate the common law test and favor instead the so-called civil law test— thus a stream is considered navigable if it is capable of being navigated in the ordinary sense of that term, which relates essentially to commerce and transportation. But even if a stream is not navigable from a legal perspective according to the civil law test, it may still be navigable in fact, meaning that its navigability does not depend on any legislative act but is based rather on the objective capability of the stream to support boating. Thus, a creek swollen by high waters may become navigable for a time.

If a stream is navigable according to the civil law test, ownership of the streambed is public. In this case, the public possesses all navigation rights as well as incidental rights to fish, swim, and wade. Property rights to those who own land along a navigable stream extend only to the ordinary low water mark. If the water later recedes or islands form in the bed of the stream, the property remains that of the state.

On the other hand, if a stream is only navigable sometimes (as in the case of a seasonal stream), the title of the land under the water belongs to the property owners over whose land the stream passes. However, the ownership is subject to a public easement for such navigation as the condition of the stream will permit.

Regardless of the question of navigability, the right of landowners to prohibit trespassing on their land along streams (if they so desire) is guaranteed. Therefore, access to rivers must be secured at highway rights-of-way or on publicly owned lands if permission to cross privately owned land cannot be secured. Legally, paddlers are trespassing when they camp, portage, or even stop for a lunch break if they disembark from their boats onto the land. If approached by a landowner while trespassing, by all means be cordial and explain your reason for being on the property. Never knowingly camp on private land without permission. If you do encounter a perturbed landowner, be respectful and keep tempers under control.

Landowners, in granting access to a river, are extending a privilege that should be appreciated and respected. Do not betray a landowner's trust if you are extended the privilege of putting in, taking out, or camping. Do not litter or drive on grass or planted fields. Leave gates the way you find them (typically, closed). In some cases, property owners may resent outsiders arriving to float through what the landowner may consider private domain. Indeed, it is not unusual for landowners firmly to believe that they own the river that passes through their land.

Landowners certainly have the right to keep you off their land, and the law will side with them unless they inflict harm on you; in that case, they may be both civilly and criminally liable. If you threaten a landowner verbally and physically move with apparent will to do harm, the landowner has all the rights of self-defense and self-protection in accordance with the perceived danger that you impose. Likewise, if the landowner points a firearm at you, fires warning shots, assaults, injures, or wounds you or a boater in your group, you are certainly in the right to protect yourself.

Although the chance of such a meeting may be rare, paddlers nonetheless should know their rights, and the rights of the landowners. Without question, confrontations between belligerent paddlers and cantankerous landowners are to be avoided. On the other hand, good manners, appreciation, and consideration go a long way when approaching a landowner for permission to camp or launch. The property owner may be interested in paddling and flattered that the paddler is excited about the countryside and so may be quite friendly and approachable. Cultivate and value this friendship and avoid giving landowners cause to deny paddlers access to the river at some time in the future.

Courtesy and respect should be extended to the river environment as well as to landowners. The streams listed in this guide flow through national parks and forests, state-owned forests and wildlife management areas, and privately owned lands that in some cases are superior in quality and aesthetics to lands under public ownership. It is the paddling community's responsibility to uphold the integrity of these lands and their rivers by using these waterways in an ecologically sound way. Litter, fire scars, pollution from human excrement, and the cutting of live trees are unsightly and affect the land in a way that threatens to ruin the outdoor experience for everyone.

Paddlers should pack out everything they pack in: all paper litter and such nonbiodegradable items as cartons, foil, plastic jugs, and cans. Help keep our waterways clean for those who follow. If you are canoe camping, leave your campsite in better shape than you found it. If you must build a fire, build it at an established site, and when you leave, dismantle rock fireplaces, thoroughly drown all flames and hot coals, and scatter the ashes. Never cut live trees for firewood (in addition to destroying a part of the environment, they don't burn well). Dump all dishwater and bathwater in the woods away from watercourses, and emulate the cat—bury all excrement. Let's all show these rivers the respect they deserve.

How to Use This Guide

This series of guidebooks on the whitewater of the Appalachian Mountains is divided into two volumes. *Appalachian Whitewater: The Southern Mountains* covers the Appalachian rivers and streams of Alabama, Georgia, Kentucky, Maryland, North Carolina, South Carolina, Tennessee, Virginia, and West Virginia. *Appalachian Whitewater: The Northern Mountains* covers Maine, Vermont, New Hampshire, Connecticut, Massachusetts, New York, Pennsylvania, Delaware, Maryland, and West Virginia. The emphasis in each volume is on the classic whitewater streams, though a number of lesser-known but no less spectacular streams are also included. No attempt is made to review a river from source to mouth. Rather, only the better whitewater sections of each stream are detailed.

For each stream in this guide you will find a stream description and at least one stream data list and map. For our purposes, we are defining a stream as flowing water; this may be a river, a creek, or a branch or fork of a river.

Stream Descriptions

Stream descriptions are intended to give you a feel for the streams and their surroundings and are presented in general, nontechnical terms.

Stream Data

Each stream data list provides technical and quantitative information, as well as some additional descriptive information. For added emphasis, certain facts will occasionally be covered in both the stream description and the data list. Each list begins with the specific stream section to which the data apply and the counties in which the stream is located. Fuller explanations of many of the categories on the data lists are as follows:

Difficulty. The level of difficulty of a stream is given according to the International Scale of River Difficulty, provided in the previous chapter. Such ratings are relative and pertain to the stream described under more or less ideal water levels and weather conditions. For streams with two International Scale ratings, the first represents the average level of difficulty of the entire run, and the second (expressed parenthetically) represents the level of difficulty of the most difficult section or rapids on the run. Paddlers are cautioned that changes in water levels or weather conditions can alter the stated average difficulty rating appreciably. We strongly recommend that paddlers also assess the difficulty of a stream on a given day by using the River Difficulty Rating Chart (Table 2 in the previous chapter).

Gradient. Gradient is expressed in feet per miles and refers to the steepness of the streambed over a certain distance. It is important to remember that gradient, or drop, as paddlers refer to it, is an average figure and does not tell the paddler when or how the drop occurs. A stream that has a listed gradient of 25 feet per mile may drop gradually in one- or two-inch increments (like a long, rocky slide) for the course of a mile, or it may drop only slightly over the first nine-tenths of a mile and then suddenly drop 24 feet at one waterfall. As a general rule, gradient can be used as a rough indicator of level of difficulty for a given stream: the greater the gradient, the more difficult the stream. In practice, gradient is almost always considered in conjunction with other information.

Average Width. Rivers tend to start small and enlarge as they go toward their confluence with another river. The average width is an approximate measure. Pools form in some places, and in other places the channel may constrict, accelerating the current. It should be remembered that wide rivers create special problems for rescuers.

Velocity. Velocity represents the speed of the current, on the average, in nonflood conditions and can vary incredibly from section to section on a given stream, depending on the stream's width, volume, and gradient at any point along its length. Velocity is a partial indicator of how much reaction time you might have on a certain river. Paddlers should remember that a high-velocity stream does not allow them much time for decision and action.

Rivers are described here as slack, slow, moderate, and fast. Slack rivers have current velocities of less than a half mile per hour; slow rivers have velocities over a half mile per hour but less than two miles per hour. Moderate velocities range between two and four miles per hour, and fast rivers are those that exceed four miles per hour.

Rescue Index. Many of the streams in this book run through wild areas. A sudden serious illness or injury could become an urgent problem if you can't get medical attention quickly. To give you an idea of how far you may be from help, a brief description is given of what might be expected. Accessible means that you might need up to an hour to secure assistance, but evacuation is not difficult. Accessible but difficult means that it might take up to three hours to get help, and evacuation may be difficult. Remote indicates it might take three to six hours to get help, and extremely remote means that you might be six hours from help and would need expert assistance to get a victim out.

Hazards. Hazards are dangers to navigation. Because of the nature of rivers and ongoing human activity, many existing hazards may change, and new ones might appear. Low-hanging trees, which can be a nuisance, may become deadfalls, blowdowns, and strainers. Human intervention creates hazards such as dams, low bridges, powerboat traffic, and fences (an especially dangerous strainer). Some watersheds have soils that cannot retain much water, and the streams in that watershed may have a flash flood potential. Additionally, geologically young rivers, usually whitewater rivers, may have undercut rocks, keeper hydraulics, difficult rapids, and a scarcity of eddies.

Scouting. This guidebook attempts to list specific spots on rivers where scouting is required, that is, recommended for the continuation of life and good health. Because hazards may change quickly, this guidebook also strongly recommends that you scout anytime you cannot see what is ahead (on whitewater or flatwater and even on familiar rivers). That small, turning drop that you have run a thousand times may have a big log wedged across it today.

Portages. Dams should be portaged. Additionally, portages are recommended for certain rapids and other dangers. The fact, however, that a portage is not specified in this guidebook at a certain spot or rapid does not necessarily mean that you should not portage. It is the mark of good paddlers to be able to make safe and independent decisions about their own abilities for a given river or rapid.

Scenery. Taste is relative, and our preference is that you form your own conclusions about the beauty of these streams. Knowing, however, that it takes a long time to run all of the Appalachians' major drainages, we include a comparative scenery rating based on our own perceptions. The ratings run from unattractive, through uninspiring, through gradations of pretty and beautiful, to spectacular. To give you some examples, here are our ratings of some popular canoeing streams:

> Little Miami River (Ohio): Pretty in spots to pretty
> Whitewater River (Indiana): Pretty in spots to pretty
> Nantahala River (North Carolina): Pretty to beautiful in spots
> Current River (Missouri): Beautiful in spots to beautiful
> Elkhorn River (Kentucky): Beautiful in spots to beautiful
> New River (West Virginia): Beautiful in spots to beautiful
> Red River (Kentucky): Exceptionally beautiful to spectacular
> Chattooga III, IV (Georgia): Exceptionally beautiful to spectacular

Highlights. This category includes special scenery, wildlife, whitewater, local culture and industry, history, and unusual geology.

Gauge. Where possible, we give the most direct number to find information about current water levels. If there are other phone numbers to call, we list them under Additional Information. You may also want to check the World Wide Web (see appendixes).

Runnable Water Level (Minimum). The lowest water level at which a given stream is navigable is referred to as the minimum runnable water level. Where possible, water levels are expressed in terms of volume as cubic feet per second (cfs). The use of cfs is doubly informative in that knowledge of volume at a gauge on one stream is often a prime indicator of the water levels of ungauged runnable streams in the same watershed, or for other sections of the gauged stream, either up- or downstream.

Runnable Water Level (Maximum). In this book, "runnable" does not mean the same thing as "possible."

The maximum runnable water level refers to the highest water level at which the stream can be run with reasonable safety. This level may vary for open and decked boats. With the exception of the few streams that can be run only during times of extremely high water, this categorically excludes rivers in flood.

Sources of Additional Information. Various sources of additional information on water conditions are listed. Professional outfitters can provide both technical and descriptive information and relate the two to paddling. Tennessee Valley Authority (TVA) and the various hydraulics branches of the respective district Corps of Engineers offices can provide flow data in cfs but will not be able to interpret the data for you in terms of paddling. Other sources listed (forest rangers, police departments, etc.) will normally provide only descriptive information,

for example, "The creek's up pretty good today," or, "The river doesn't have enough water in it for boating."

Maps

The maps in this guide are not intended to replace topographic quadrangles for terrain features. Rather, they are intended to illustrate the general configuration of the stream, its access points, and surrounding shuttle roads. Some of the maps are congested to the point that access letters may not be exactly where they should be. A county map to the area may help in finding the put-in and take-out points. Keep in mind that you may have to scout the area before launching. Letters on the map correspond to letters found in the text. A brief explanation of the different symbols can be found below.

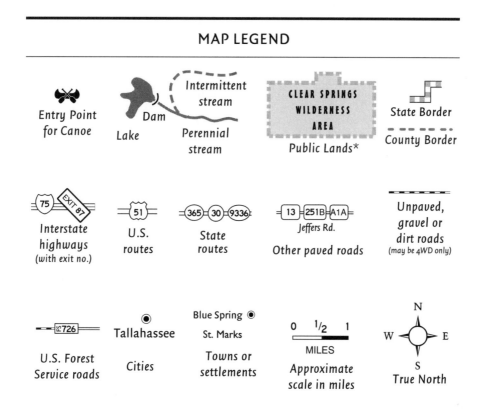

MAP LEGEND

Entry Point for Canoe

Lake   Dam   Perennial stream   Intermittent stream

CLEAR SPRINGS WILDERNESS AREA
Public Lands*

State Border

County Border

75   EXIT 87
Interstate highways (with exit no.)

51
U.S. routes

365 30 9336
State routes

13 251B A1A
Jeffers Rd.
Other paved roads

Unpaved, gravel or dirt roads
(may be 4WD only)

726
U.S. Forest Service roads

Tallahassee
Cities

Blue Spring
St. Marks
Towns or settlements

0   1/2   1
MILES
Approximate scale in miles

N
W   E
S
True North

MAINE

Dead River

The Dead River is about 60 miles north and west of Skowhegan. Take Route 201 north from Interstate Route 95, and head toward Quebec Province. Forty-five miles north of Skowhegan is a town called West Forks. It lies at the confluence of the Kennebec and Dead Rivers: hence the name, Forks.

Drive the speed limit through town or you will miss Webb's Store on the left. It is situated just a few yards from the riverbank. This is where you should hire your shuttle: the network of logging roads to the put-in is confusing and tough on your vehicle. The shuttle is affordable, and the store is your take-out for the Dead.

The shuttle involves a pleasant, 3-mile ride up Route 201 north, with a left turn down a 12-mile network of logging roads. The drive is beautifully forested, with a number of logging operations along the way. There is a good chance of seeing moose, deer, and even black bear. International Paper Company has begun charging river runners a road use fee of about $6 per person. If you are paddling on a scheduled release date, the road can be busy. It is one-way for the last few miles, and parking and turnarounds are at a premium once you near the Spencer Stream put-in.

Flows on the Dead are regulated by Kennebec Water Power Company from Flagstaff Dam. A release schedule is developed each year for recreational flows; they will eagerly share the information with you, if you contact them. The scheduled high-water releases are usually the third and fourth Mondays of May. These flows are usually 7,000 cfs or more. At these levels the river is serious, continuous Class III–IV with few eddies and lots of debris. The water reaches up into the alder trees lining the bank.

Put in at the mouth of Spencer Stream and paddle upstream on the Dead, or cross the stream and walk up the Dead to Grand Falls. Grand Falls is a 40-foot-high, river-wide horseshoe waterfall—particularly awe-inspiring at high flows. (It doesn't appear to be runnable, in case you are wondering.) This remote, heavily forested region typifies the river run. Once your shuttle leaves, West Forks is your next sign of civilization.

The 15-mile run is continuous, with highlights being Spencer Rips (below the put-in, point A); The Basins, about two and a half miles downstream, with a huge pourover right of center; Apple Tree, which has very large holes for threading; and Elephant Rock Rapid, with a large pourover on river right. Little and Big Poplar Hill Falls come toward the end of the run. Big Poplar has a large hole, about 40 feet from the left shore, which is famous for eating boaters.

Section: Spencer Stream to West Forks
County: Somerset
USGS Quads: Pierce Pond, The Forks
Difficulty: Class III–IV
Gradient: 29 feet per mile (35 feet per mile maximum)
Average Width: 200 feet
Velocity: Slow to very fast
Rescue Index: Difficult to remote
Hazards: Rapids
Scouting: Big Spencer Rips
Portages: None accessible
Scenery: Beautiful—wilderness
Highlights: Scenery, wildlife, whitewater
Gauge: Kennebec Water Power Company, (207) 872-6624
Runnable Water Levels: | Minimum | Maximum
| 1,200 cfs | Not established
Months Runnable: May through September, selected recreational dam release dates
Additional Information: Release schedule—FLOW recording, (800) 557-3569. Shuttle and camping information—Webb's General Store, (207) 663-2214.
Special Notes: Be sure to walk up the Dead from the put-in to see Grand Falls. During spring releases bring black fly repellent! We recommend Avon Skin-So-Soft. (It is not caustic and it works!) Blackflies for the rest of the state are raised here. Just forget running shuttle and hire Webb at Webb's Store in The Forks to take you to the put-in.

Dead River • Maine

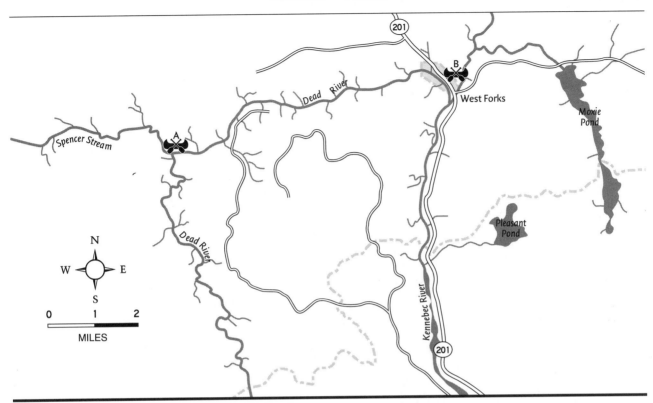

The river can be read easily from your boat at all levels. At high water pay attention to pourovers and large holes. Due to lack of eddies you may want to enter questionable rapids slowly; be prepared to alter your route.

High water provides unlimited surfing and enders. If you aren't totally exhausted and draped over your boat by the take-out, you have not taken full advantage of this river's finest assets. At lower water, rocks are of concern; they channel the river into a variety of routes. Some routes are deeper than others, and there are some surfing opportunities. The final quarter of the run leading up to the last rapid, Poplar Hill Falls, Class III at low flows and Class IV at high flows, is progressively steeper and more difficult. The river is wide, and if you have heard Poplar Hill Falls horror stories, remember the rule that is applied to this section of the river: "When in doubt stay right." The "big stuff"—waves, holes, and pinning rocks— are down the left side of the river where the main flow travels. This "right-hand rule" does not apply to the rest of the river; for instance, large pourovers in The Basins and Elephant Rock Rapid are on the right, and common sense should tell you to go left!

There are a couple of miles of Class II rapids following Poplar Hill Falls. You will begin seeing houses and you will parallel Route 201 to West Forks and the take-out at Webb's Store, point B, on river left.

Paddlers without a roll should wait for the lower flow releases which come later in the summer and over the July Fourth holiday. The summer releases range from 900 to 1,200 cfs. The river slows down and becomes much more manageable. It is basically Class II with a couple of Class III rapids. Rescue is easier and swims not so consequential. The National Open Canoe Whitewater Championships are held on 1,200 cfs flows. It is plenty of water to get down the river, but should not be a very heavy whitewater experience.

Kennebec River Gorge

The Kennebec River Gorge lies 12 miles north of The Forks off Route 201 on the Moxie Road. The 13-mile run begins at the foot of Central Maine Power Company's Harris Station Dam Project on Indian Pond.

The Gorge itself is four miles long and contains continuous, fast and powerful Class IV water. Put in at Harris Station Dam, but be sure that the full charge of water is headed downstream, and be sure that you know how long the release is going to last. Flows vary radically, as this is a peaking power facility. You can find out about the flows by calling Central Maine Power Company prior to your arrival. You can get updated at the gate when you check in, or at the station itself. It is not a lot of fun to run out of water because it is a long way out of this remote gorge. Flows have been known to last for as short as 30 minutes, so know what's going on.

The Gorge has tall, vertical, rock walls with a lot of slate. When the water is turned on at Harris, the river deepens and its speed is sobering. The first several miles are continuous and free of boulders, with waves varying in shape and size depending upon the flows. Eddies occur only along the shoreline, so stopping is difficult and rescues are even more so. The rocks are sharp, so groping your way to shore can be challenging. Although the first couple of miles are basically one continuous rapid, sections of waves and holes have been named for the sake of reference. The initial wave in the Gorge is called Taster; the first rapid of concern, The Sisters, is about a mile downstream of the dam.

The Sisters are a series of large, powerful waves capable of stopping or flipping kayaks and rafts alike. These waves, including Big Mama, are right of center and lie just downstream of an old log sluice on river right which looks like a gravel slide. This is ender territory, so be careful!

Below The Sisters lie Whitewasher and The Alleyway. The Alleyway is the best wave train in the Upper Gorge and is a good surfing and ender rapid.

Below, the river slows into boiling eddies in what is called The Cathedral. The eddies mellow out as you approach Z-Turn Rapid, the site of much surfing and many enders.

After Z-Turn, the river widens and there is a broad horizon line spanning the river. You have arrived at Magic Falls, the most difficult rapid on the river. Scouting is best from river left. Magic Hole is at the top left of the rapid—not a place where you want to spend a lot of time. Just downstream and right of center there is a very nasty pourover hydraulic: Maytag. It's a good one to avoid. The clean run is between Magic and Maytag, moving from right of center to the left, then down the wave train below. If you run through Magic Hole, remember to take a good deep breath first and watch your shoulder!

Section: Harris Station Dam to Crusher Pool
County: Somerset
USGS Quad: The Forks
Difficulty: Class III–IV+
Gradient: 25 feet per mile (60 feet per mile maximum)
Average Width: 125 feet
Velocity: Fast to very fast
Rescue Index: Accessible, but difficult to remote
Hazards: Rapids, lack of eddies, keeper hydraulics, sharp rock shoreline
Scouting: Magic Falls
Portages: None
Scenery: Spectacular—wilderness
Highlights: Scenery, whitewater, geology
Gauge: Central Maine Power Company, (207) 872-6624

Runnable Water Levels:	Minimum	Maximum
	3,000 cfs	What you can handle!

Months Runnable: May through October
Additional Information: FLOW recording, (800) 557-3569
Special Notes: Some landlocked salmon fishing; splendid sidestream hikes, especially into Moxie Stream up to the 90-foot falls.

Kennebec River Gorge • Maine

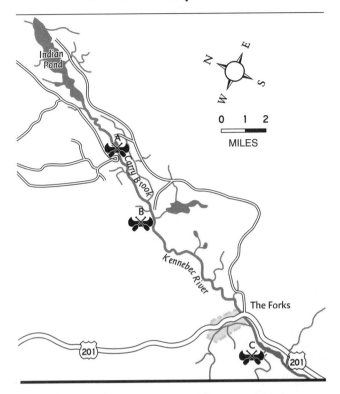

Dead Stream enters a mile below Magic Falls on river right in the form of a waterfall. It also marks the beginning of the last rapid in the Gorge, which ends at Carry Brook, point B.

For paddlers not seeking a continuous and possibly consequential big Class IV experience, this is a better put-in than the dam. The boat carry and walk to the water is less than convenient and may make you wonder if it would have been easier to just swim the gorge with your boat. The remaining nine miles of the Kennebec is a terrific, continuous Class II–III float with some surfing waves and long rapids. The first rapid below Carry Brook of any concern is Black Brook Rapid. It is about a mile long and begins with a large wave train along the right bank. At moderate flows there is a nasty hole called Surprise Hole about 200 yards upstream of the next right bend in the river. It is a little left of center, and avoiding it is a good idea. Two miles upstream of The Forks, Moxie Stream enters on river left. Half a mile up the stream is a 90-foot waterfall, which is well worth the walk.

From here on it's smooth sailing to the Crusher Pool take-out. Crusher Pool is a gravel pit take-out well downstream of the Route 201 bridge in The Forks, on river left.

Bill Zollinger heads into the teeth of Magic Falls during one of the first descents of the Kennebec Gorge. Photo by Jim Michaud.

Kennebec River, East Outlet of Moosehead Lake

The Kennebec River begins at the East Outlet of Moosehead Lake, 12 miles north of Greenville on Route 15 on the west side of the lake.

This continuously flowing stretch of Class II–III river has plenty of surfing waves, holes, and even two pop-up spots, one in each of the two Class III rapids.

About one-quarter mile into the trip, which begins on river right below the Route 15 bridge, is the first Class III rapid. It is called Sluice Rapid, named from the sluicing of logs into the river at this point during the log drives. Scout on the left when the river picks up speed and you see a steep bluff on the right bank downstream. The rapid is not very complex; it is easy to read as you paddle downstream, should you choose not to scout from shore. It is all wavy Class II to the last rapid. The last rapid is called Swimmers Rapid and is the most complex rapid on the river. It can be scouted on river right, and the clean tongue between holes is evident. This is also a good rapid for life jacket swimming, as well as pop-ups in the hole. Below the rapid is Indian Pond. The level of the pond, controlled by Central Maine Power Company, and the flow of the river, controlled by Kennebec Water Power Company, determine whether or not you can get pop-ups in the last rapid.

There is a beach take-out a mile down the pond, on the left side next to a cabin. The take-out road is a private logging road that comes out on Route 15. Don't use your Porsche for the shuttle because the road is not officially maintained and requires a vehicle that can handle bumps and water hazards.

This river is remote, and sightings of herons, osprey, and moose are frequent. It is a reliable summer run, but flows are usually reduced on the weekends.

Section: Moosehead Lake Route 15 bridge to Indian Pond
County: Somerset
USGS Quads: Moosehead Lake, Brassua Lake
Difficulty: Class II–III
Gradient: 12 feet per mile (25 feet per mile maximum)
Average Width: 150 feet
Velocity: Slow to moderate
Rescue Index: Accessible to accessible but difficult
Hazards: Rapids, deadfalls
Scouting: Sluice Rapid, Swimmers Rapid
Portages: None
Scenery: Spectacular wilderness
Highlights: Scenery, wildlife, whitewater
Gauge: Kennebec Water Power Company, (207) 872-6624

Runnable Water Levels:	Minimum	Maximum
	over 400 cfs	Undetermined
	(1,200 cfs	
	average flow)	

Months Runnable: May through October
Additional Information: FLOW recording, (800) 557-3569. Camping and fire permits—Maine Forest Service, (207) 287-2791 or (800) 367-0223, or local Forest Service stations
Special Notes: Good landlocked salmon and brook trout fishing.

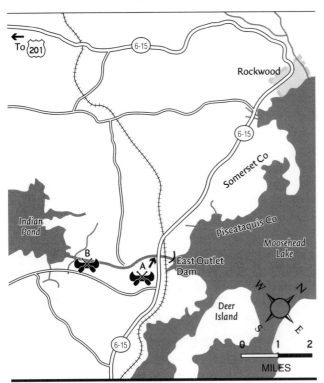

Kennebec River, East Outlet • Maine

Kenduskeag Stream

The Kenduskeag Stream put-in lies six miles northwest of Bangor, upstream of the Route 15 bridge. The take-out is in the city of Bangor, upstream of Route 2. This six-mile run of the Kenduskeag encompasses nearly 100 percent of the stream's whitewater. A downriver race is run each year from the town of Kenduskeag, which includes the 10 miles of flatwater above this section as well.

The rapid at the Route 15 bridge is called Six Mile Falls. It is not six miles long, but it is six miles from downtown Bangor. It is a Class III series of short ledges followed by some waves. There are a number of routes in the rapid leading to the final chute. Steer clear of debris and logs lodged on the inside of the turn on river right. Carry your boat above this rapid to begin your trip. Following Six Mile Falls and the Route 15 bridge is a four-mile stretch of Class I–II rapids. The next bridge is called Bull's Eye bridge and marks the beginning of the most interesting section of the stream. Although this section of the stream is in Bangor, paddlers have a sense of nearby suburbia—but it does not dominate the river experience.

There is a mile of Class II with some small waves between Bull's Eye Bridge and Flour Mill Dam. Eddy left to scout and carry. Take a moment to venture onto the observation deck built on the old mill to look at the drop. The man-made water features include a river-wide hydraulic. Therefore it is advisable to carry unless the water level is low enough and your skill level is up to a Class III–IV challenge. Hydraulics are the concern here, and the water level determines the intensity of this drop.

Paddle under the Interstate Route 95 bridge and enjoy the next several hundred yards of right-flow waves.

It is advisable to take out on river right upstream of the next bridge, Valley Avenue. Scout the ledges at the site of the old Maxfield Mill Tannery. The hydraulics are nasty at most levels. The run down the first drop under the bridge is left in the channel. A look at the next drop will reveal a good route just off the left shore.

The next Class II–III rapid is the site of the Kenduskeag slalom race, held in April. If there is enough water, you will find enders in the surfing waves toward the bottom on the right.

There is a parking lot on river right here. This is the take-out, point B, for the Kenduskeag trip.

Section: Kenduskeag to Bangor
County: Penobscot
USGS Quad: Bangor
Difficulty: Class II–III+
Gradient: 12 feet per mile (30 feet per mile maximum)
Average Width: 100 feet
Velocity: Slow to fast
Rescue Index: Accessible
Hazards: Deadfalls, old dams, rapids, keeper hydraulics
Scouting: Six Mile Falls, Flour Mill, Maxfield Mill
Portage: Flour Mill
Scenery: Uninspiring to beautiful
Highlights: Scenery, whitewater
Gauge: Visual only. If the river looks runnable at the put-in, it is high enough.

Runnable Water Levels:	Minimum	Maximum
	300 cfs natural flow	Below flood stage

Months Runnable: Mid-March to early June
Additional Information: Bangor Ski Rack, (207) 945-6474

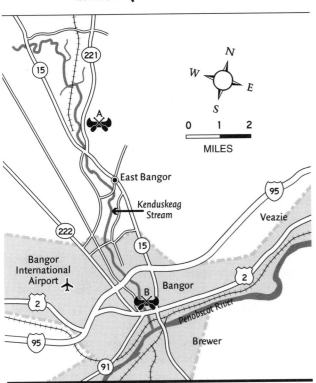

Kenduskeag Stream • Maine

N
W · E
S

0   1   2
MILES

East Bangor

Kenduskeag Stream

Veazie

Bangor International Airport

Bangor

Penobscot River

Brewer

Mattawamkeag River

The Mattawamkeag River is about 60 miles north of Bangor. Take Route 157 south from Interstate Route 95 to Mattawamkeag. The Route 2 bridge over the Mattawamkeag is the take-out, point C. The put-in (A), is about 20 miles up Route 2 to Macwahoc, where you take Route 170 south to Kingman. Put in by the bridge for the 12-mile run. If you want to run only the whitewater section, you should drive seven miles upstream of Mattawamkeag on river left to Mattawamkeag Wilderness Park and put in at the sand beach at Scatterack Rapid (B).

Unlike most natural-flow streams and rivers, the Mattawamkeag's vast, slow drainage extends the runnable season beyond spring into the summer.

The upper stretch is from the Kingman Bridge, point A, to Mattawamkeag Wilderness Park at Scatterack Rapid, point B. This section is mostly flat- or deadwater, with a Class II rapid at the Kingman Bridge put-in and another, Rams Head Falls, about four miles farther downstream. Waterfowl and other wildlife are frequently sighted through this remote stretch down to the park.

The whitewater section begins with a Class II rapid called Scatterack at Mattawamkeag Wilderness Park. There is a sand beach on river left after the rapid.

After some more Class II, the river bends to the right and escalates to Class III, going into a deep, narrow gorge, Slewgundy Heater. You can eddy left and take a look first, or you can make it up as you go along. Don't forget to play on the way down.

The dirt road between Mattawamkeag and the wilderness park is nearby on river left. There is ample access for park visitors to view the river along the whitewater section. In fact, there are observation decks in places. If you are running a rapid and you hear voices above you, don't worry; you are hearing spectators, not God.

At the end of Slewgundy Heater, you enter a series of Class III ledge drops. Leaving the gorge-like rock formation of the Heater behind you, paddle a few hundred yards to the top of Upper Gordon Falls, Class IV–V. Scout or portage river left. The current is pushy, with some sub-

stantial holes; some folks consider the drop unrunnable. However, with enough water there is a choice of routes. Large holes develop in the middle, and if you would rather skirt the meat of the rapids by paddling close to shore, that is a viable strategy. This rapid provides good playing at most water levels.

The last notable rapid, Lower Gordon Falls, Class III, is a few hundred yards downstream of Upper Gordon Falls. There is good surfing at most levels throughout the rapid.

Below Lower Gordon Falls, the river widens, gradient diminishes, and it slowly runs three more miles to the Route 2 take-out bridge in Mattawamkeag (C).

Section: Kingman to Mattawamkeag
County: Penobscot
USGS Quads: Mattawamkeag, Wytopitlock
Difficulty: Class II–V+
Gradient: 10 feet per mile (50 feet per mile maximum)
Average Width: 125 feet
Velocity: Slow to very fast
Rescue Index: Accessible to accessible but difficult
Hazards: Keeper hydraulics, rapids, ledge drops
Scouting: Slewgundy Heater, Upper Gordon Falls
Portages: Upper Gordon Falls
Scenery: Spectacular
Highlights: Scenery, wildlife, whitewater, geology, history
Gauge: Drive up to Mattawamkeag Wilderness Park and look at the rapids. If it looks high enough to run, it is!

Runnable Water Levels:	Minimum	Maximum
	300 cfs natural flow	Undetermined

Months Runnable: May through mid-August
Additional Information: Camping—Mattawamkeag Wilderness Park, Box 104, Mattawamkeag, ME 04459; Bangor Ski Rack, (207) 945-6474
Special Notes: Good fishing for Atlantic salmon, brook trout, and landlocked salmon.

Mattawamkeag River • Maine

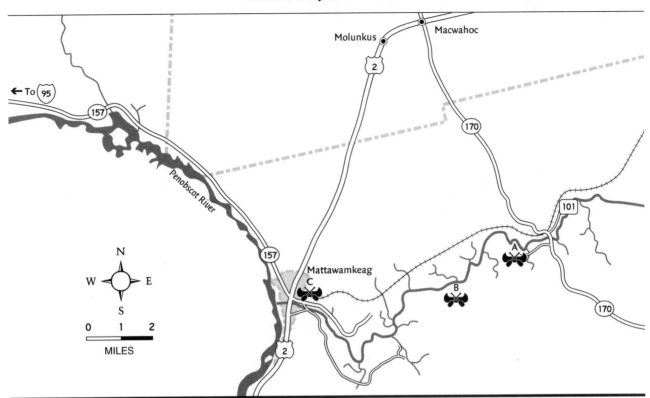

At higher flows, the Mattawamkeag is one of the best playboating rivers in the Northeast. In addition to the hole and wave playing, the challenging rapids and big water make this river a must paddle.

East Branch of the Penobscot River

The East Branch of the Penobscot River lies 100 miles north of Bangor off Interstate Route 95 and 25 miles northwest of Patten on the private road that begins at the end of Routes 11 and 159.

The put-in of this 26-mile trip is below Grand Lake Mattagamon Dam (A). The take-out is below Whetstone Falls off the dirt road out of Stacyville (C). You will need to call Bangor Hydroelectric Company to verify runnable flows. Unless it is a dry summer, the river should have adequate water.

This is a very long trip, and all of the significant Class III–V whitewater lies within the first 12 miles. If you like scenic Class II water, you may run the full 26 miles. However, you can take out below Spencer Rips on river right, point B, where the old logging road parallels the river. You will have to look for your car! It is not a bad idea to have a shuttle driver sit by the river and wait for you. The shuttle is over 50 miles long if you paddle all of the Class II through the maple hardwood section named The Arches. And if you take out at point B below Spencer Rips, you extend your shuttle another 12.5 miles one way. Unless you have a shuttle driver, paddle the entire run to Whetstone Falls or you'll spend more time driving than paddling.

The river is remote, access is very limited, and medical help is a long way away. It is a good idea to be conservative on a river such as this, so if you are looking for Class IV and V drops, run them with safety in mind. Don't create any problems your party cannot solve on its own.

The scenery is splendid. As you venture downstream you will have views of Traveler Mountain and its fellow peaks along the northeast border of Baxter State Park.

You will paddle out of the Mattagamon area leaving hunting and fishing camps behind. Within the first five miles you should see your first waterfowl, as well as moose and deer. The river bends through the Oxbow and then changes character. Stair Falls is an easy Class II–III section of ledges with a multiple choice of routes. Following the Class II rapids below is Haskell Deadwater,

followed by Haskell Rock Pitch, a fairly long rapid with a four-foot drop into a 90-degree left-hand turn. The river definitely changes character here. Take a good look. Scout or portage, depending upon your mood and ability, on river right. About one-quarter mile downstream through Class II rapids is Pond Pitch, a sloping, Class IV ledge about eight feet high with the scout or carry on river left. The manner in which you should run this drop varies with water levels, but it seems to be fairly clean. Stay on river left because Grand Pitch is next and you won't want to miss the eddy. Scout this falls: portaging is advised. Grand Pitch is a two-stage, 18-foot falls in a granite gorge and is Class V+. If you run it, run it on river right. But considering where you are in relation to outside help, discussing the run hypothetically is about as close to it as you should get, even though it appears to be a relatively clean drop. This is a magical place. Sitting in your boat at the bottom of the falls, looking upstream between the granite walls, would convince even the most skeptical that there is a river god. This is also a premier spot for enjoying the snack you brought along.

After another half mile of Class II you will need to pull over on river right above the Hulling Machine, Class V+. Take a close look and don't feel embarrassed about shouldering your boat down the right side. The route in this complex rapid changes with the flow. Higher flows allow a more manageable run down the right, taking advantage of eddies. The Hulling Machine stripped the bark from the logs that passed through it during log drives. Small wonder.

You will paddle through a deep, swirly section into Class II rapids again. It's only a short distance to Bowlin Falls, a Class II rapid. You know that you have run Bowlin Falls when you see Bowlin Camps (hunting and fishing cabins) on river left. After more Class II riffles, you come to Spencer Rips.

If you are doing the long shuttle/short river trip to point B, keep your eyes on the right bank for your shuttle driver or your vehicle.

East Branch of the Penobscot River • Maine

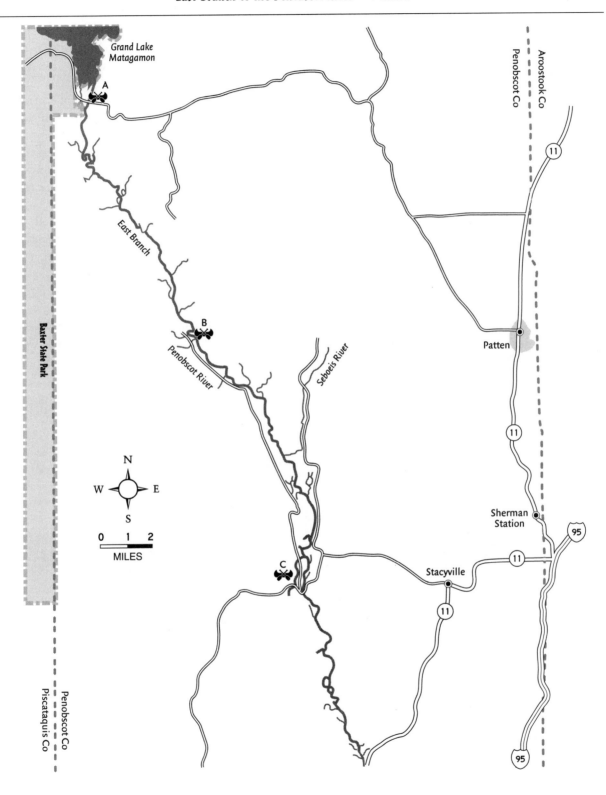

Grand Lake
Matagamon

A

East Branch

Penobscot River

B

Seboeis River

C

Baxter State Park

N
W   E
S

0   1   2
MILES

Penobscot Co
Piscataquis Co

Penobscot Co
Aroostook Co

11

11

Patten

11

Sherman
Station

95

Stacyville

11

11

95

Section: Grand Lake Mattagamon Dam to Whetstone Falls
County: Penobscot
USGS Quads: Traveler Mountain, Shin Pond, Stacyville
Difficulty: Class III–V+
Gradient: 5 feet per mile (65 feet per mile maximum)
Average Width: 75 feet
Velocity: Slow to very fast
Rescue Index: Accessible to remote
Hazards: Deadfalls, keeper hydraulics, rapids, ledge drops, falls
Scouting: Haskell Rock Pitch, Pond Pitch, Grand Pitch, Hulling Machine
Portages: Grand Pitch, Hulling Machine
Scenery: Spectacular, wildlife
Highlights: Scenery, wildlife, whitewater, geology, history
Gauge: Bangor Hydro, (207) 827-2247
Runnable Water Levels: Minimum   Maximum
                        1,000 cfs   Undetermined
Months Runnable: May through September
Additional Information: Camping and fire permits—Maine Forest Service, (207) 287-2791
Special Notes: Take a snack; this is a long day on the river.
   Flows over 1,000 cfs require frequent scouting and portaging on the upper river. There's easy access to Baxter State Park and Mt. Katahdin, Maine's highest peak (hiking, camping, and technical climbing).

If you are continuing to the Whetstone Falls take-out, point C, you will paddle a lot of scenic Class II and some deadwater. The maple hardwood section called The Arches is next. Not long after that, the Soboeis River enters the East Branch on river left.

Now you are on Lunksoos Deadwater. Stop at the Lunksoos campsite and stretch your legs. Take a little walk up the road and you can see Mount Katahdin to the west. Thirteen feet shy of being a mile high, Katahdin is Maine's highest peak and is the northern terminus of the Appalachian Trail.

Continuing downstream, Wassataquoik Stream enters on river right. This stream flows out of Baxter State Park and is one of those springtime-only, steep-creek runs, if you begin far enough upstream.

About a mile downstream is the old Hunt Farm, which, like Pittston Farm on the South Branch and numerous other farms in the north woods, provisioned the log drivers during the log drives.

A couple of miles downstream is the rapid you've been looking for: Whetstone Falls, Class II–III. You can scout from your boat or river right. The usual route is right to left. The take-out, point C, is on the right above the bridge.

Hulling Machine (V+) at dusk on the East Branch of the Penobscot. Photo by Zip Kellog.

South Branch of the Penobscot River

The South Branch of the Penobscot River lies 42 miles northwest of Greenville, which is on Moosehead Lake. From Route 15 north one must follow a network of private logging roads to Pittston Farm, and then to Canada Falls dam, where the three-and-a-half-mile river trip begins. These logging roads are deluxe and don't require a four-wheel-drive. However, if you are following a logging truck, you'll need something to wash the dust down with at the put-in.

This section of river was virtually unnoticed by whitewater boaters until the early 1980s. Combined with an afternoon or next-morning run on the Seboomook stretch of the West Branch, the long drive to this river is well worth your while. Since it is so far from civilization, calling ahead to make sure there is runnable water is highly recommended.

Beginning at Canada Falls Dam, the river has a tendency to lure unsuspecting family canoes off into what later becomes a Class IV–V torrent with numerous ledge drops.

Once the river leaves the camping area at the put-in and bends away from the road, a rule of thumb is to scout and carry on river left.

There are several ledge drops on this section, and depending upon paddlers' abilities and the water levels, they should be either walked or run with safety setup. The first ledge comes at the tail end of an island not much more than a quarter mile into the trip. It is important to recognize this situation because a 10- to 12-foot falls lies immediately at the far end of the island, with only a very small eddy to catch. This is the only exception to the scout-and-portage-left rule. It is recommended that you take the right channel around the island. Go slowly, be sure to get to shore before the falls, and portage on the right. The drop below has been run by paddlers who are accustomed to running waterfalls. Setting up safety is important: keep in mind that medical help is 50 miles away! There is a tendency to smash the left wall at the bottom of the drop.

Except for the ledgy sections, the South Branch is fairly mellow and takes you through some beautifully forested country. At one point the river widens and goes through a marshy area. Stay on river right, because great blue herons, ducks, and other waterfowl are seen here regularly in the tall grasses.

Two and a half miles downstream from the put-in, points A to B, the river turns back toward the road and a small building. Below this point the river resumes its challenging, ledgy nature. If you have found yourself portaging more than you like, take out here, because the last mile to point C is more of the same. The regular

Section: Canada Falls Dam to Pittston Farm
County: Somerset
USGS Quad: Seboomook Lake
Difficulty: Class III–V++
Gradient: 35 feet per mile (70 feet per mile maximum)
Average Width: 75 feet
Velocity: Moderate to very fast
Rescue Index: Accessible to accessible but difficult
Hazards: Deadfalls, keeper hydraulics, rapids, ledge drops, falls
Scouting: Island Falls, others as required
Portages: Island Falls, others as conditions require
Scenery: Spectacular, wilderness
Highlights: Scenery, wildlife, whitewater, geology
Gauge: Great Northern Paper Company flow recording, (207) 723-2328

Runnable Water Levels:	Minimum	Maximum
	Over 87 cfs or 1/4 of 1 gate at the dam.	Undetermined

Months Runnable: May through September, contingent on dam releases
Additional Information: Camping and fire permits—Maine Forest Service, (207) 287-2791, or local Forest Service stations
Special Notes: Productive fly-fishing for pan-sized brook trout.

South Branch of the Penobscot River • Maine

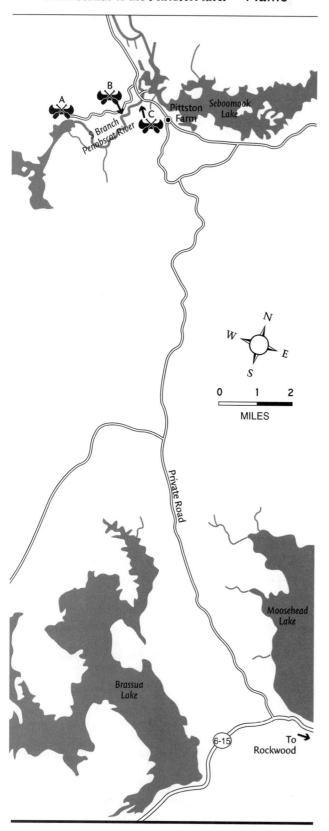

take-out for this run is at the bridge next to the forest ranger's house. This area is called Pittston Farm, named after the nearby farm, which was active during the log drives on the Penobscot.

West Branch of the Penobscot River

The West Branch of the Penobscot River is created by its north and south branches joining at Pittston Farm and filling Seboomook Lake. The West Branch, as a river, begins below Seboomook Dam and is dammed into numerous other impoundments before joining the East Branch in Medway, where it creates the main stem of the Penobscot River.

Ripogenus Gorge and Lower West Branch to Debsconeag

The section of the West Branch beginning below Ripogenus Dam at McKay Power Station and ending at Debsconeag can be reached only by private logging roads. It is 42 miles north and east of Greenville, and about 30 miles north and west of Millinocket. This is by far the most popular section of the Penobscot and its branches. Due to the fact that Great Northern Paper Company generates electricity for its mills from the McKay station around the clock, flows are constant and usually range between 1,800 and 3,600 cfs. This flow regime helps facilitate a prolific landlocked salmon fishery as well as quality whitewater recreation. This section of the West Branch, a virtually undeveloped semi-wilderness area, is used by thousands of people annually for angling, camping, hiking, sight-seeing, and whitewater recreation. A healthy rafting industry has cropped up, and private boating is increasing. By some southern river standards this river is not very crowded at all. This is due, in part, to government intervention and regulation on the river, and to the fact that most of the rapids are big, powerful, and consequential—thereby deterring all but the most competent boaters.

Great Northern's "Golden Road" parallels the river for the entire run, so access is very easy except for the section between Pockwockamus (C) and Debsconeag (D). A good length for a day trip, even with a lot of playing, is from McKay station (A) to Pockwockamus. (If you are not comfortable in Class V water, put in at Big Eddy (B), and avoid the upper section through Ripogenus Gorge and the

Cribwork Rapid.) To find point A, drive over Ripogenus Dam and continue down the road on river left. You will be paralleling a section of Ripogenus Gorge called The Dryway, from which Great Northern has diverted the water from Ripogenus Lake to the McKay Power Station. This water passes through a pentstock, bored through the vertical granite wall on river right, that carries the water through the turbines at a higher velocity than if the power station were at the bottom of the dam itself.

When there is too much water to be held back by Ripogenus Dam with full generation at McKay station, the flood gates are opened. This is usually at spring ice-out in April or May. If this normally dry section is running, depending upon the flow, it is a fast Class III–IV run over a half mile long. A good flow is around 1,100–1,500 cfs. The flow in this section is not predictable. If it is running, you need to reevaluate running the Gorge below the powerhouse or the Cribwork. The Dryway is runnable below this flow range and is well worth your time!

Now, back to the river trip. You know when you have reached the end of The Dryway and the usual power house put-in because the river bed has water in it and it is coming from a big, concrete building that makes a lot of noise. This is McKay station, which is reached by a dirt road leading off of the "Golden Road." This is the point in the gorge where water reenters the riverbed from the lake above. Utilize the parking area on the left, then proceed down the road, through the gates, and to the put-in.

The section of river below the powerhouse falls at the rate of 70 feet per mile. Once in your boat, ferry across the discharge from the power station. Notice that downstream the 100-foot-high granite walls narrow, the riverbed drops, and all you can see are the exploding tops of the waves that lead into Exterminator, a huge hole coming off the right wall and extending across the river. We find that if you approach the hole from the center moving to the left through the diagonal waves above Exterminator, you can eddy left next to it and plan your next move. A good line to take is a high ferry across the

West Branch of the Penobscot River • Maine

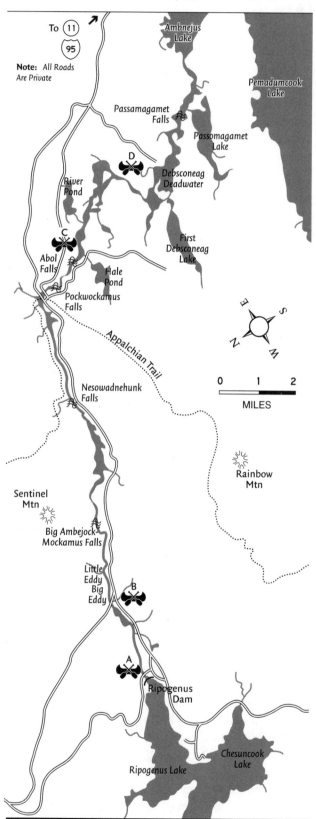

backwash of Exterminator, passing to the right of the collapsing waves in The Staircase and also to the right of a pourover rock named Fist Rock. You can eddy right or left at this point and look for ender waves. Of course, this isn't the only route, and many boaters create their own. Remember to look for playboating opportunities on this river. They are numerous!

A hundred yards or so below is a huge granite island called Big Heater. Passing to the left is easier, but the right channel has more vertical character. It is common to see numerous salmon rising and lots of ducks from here on downstream. Below this island is Little Eddy, which is the first of several nationally renowned salmon fishing holes you will pass through during the day. The fishermen and boaters on the West Branch have worked together to try to save the river from hydro development, so we need to do our part to keep relations strong by giving fishermen a wide berth when passing through these fishing sites.

As you leave Little Eddy pool and enter Little Eddy Rapid below, look downstream. Beyond the long stretch of rapids (including Troublemaker Rapid) is Mount Katahdin, Maine's highest peak, in Baxter State Park. Katahdin is 13 feet shy of being a mile high, and it is the northern terminus of the Appalachian Trail.

Below a steel road bridge the Class V challenge of the Cribwork Rapid awaits. Eddy out on the left in the vicinity of the bridge and scout the Cribwork. If you have strong reservations about running it, carry left. There is no need to be a hero in this rapid. It forgives few sins. If you do run it, the idea is to pass through the chute on the inside of the rapid's left turn. Enter the chute with a good right ferry angle, and move to the right passing alongside the granite island. Run the final chute on the right, then either eddy out or make a hard right in front of the rock wall. From the inside of the turn all the way to the final chute, the river tries to push you left. If you don't get far enough right to make the final chute, you could piton. Or you could go over the jagged boulder pile and check into the Millinocket Hospital. If you are off your line to the right, abort your stunning run right and beat feet for the left side of the river. It is bumpy over there, but it beats the thrashing you'd be taking over the middle of that boulder pile. This rapid has the most pinning potential of any Penobscot rapid.

Below The Crib is Jaw Breaker Rapid. Look for surfing and ender holes. Below here is Big Eddy Rapid and Big Eddy (B), which is the beginning of the intermediate Class III–IV section and the official end of the Gorge section.

From this point the river widens and slows its pace. It alternates between large rapids and long pools or dead-waters. The next significant rapid is Big Ambejackmock-amus Falls. It is a long rapid with enders at the end. Avoid the big hydraulic in the center of the river where the river makes a 90-degree right turn. Scouting and portaging is best on river right.

After a couple of miles of Class II called Horserace Rapid, the river widens into Nesowadnehunk deadwater. At the end of the deadwater is Nesowadnehunk Falls. The falls is a nine-foot-high, inclined ledge drop, usually run on the left and followed by a deep pool.

After a couple of miles of deadwater and more awesome scenery (with Mount Katahdin dominating the skyline) you pass under a bridge and find yourself approaching Abol Falls. The usual route is right of center. Just thread your way through the holes. The end of the rapid is very quick and shallow, so try not to swim it.

The next major rapid is Pockwockamus Falls, a straightforward run. This is a long rapid with waves. Just avoid any holes that look nasty.

Section: Ripogenus Dam (McKay Station) to Debsconeag
County: Piscataquis
USGS Quads: Harrington Lake, Katahdin
Difficulty: Class I–V+
Gradient: 7 feet per mile (70 feet per mile maximum)
Average Width: 200 feet
Velocity: Slow to very fast
Rescue Index: Accessible to accessible but difficult
Hazards: Deadfalls, keeper hydraulics, rapids, ledge drops
Scouting: Ripogenus Gorge, Cribwork, Big Ambejackmocka-mus Falls, Nesowadnehunk Falls, Abol Falls, Big Pock-wockamus Falls
Portages: Cribwork
Scenery: Spectacular to inspiring, wilderness
Highlights: Scenery, wildlife, whitewater, geology, history
Gauge: Great Northern Paper Company, (207) 723-2328
Runnable Water Levels:

	Minimum	Maximum
	1,500 cfs	Undetermined
	(usual flow	
	2,500 cfs)	

Months Runnable: April through October
Additional Information: Camping—Prays' Big Eddy Campground, Millinocket, Maine; Abol Campground, Millinocket, Maine. Camping and fire permits—Maine Forest Service, (207) 287-2791, or local Forest Service stations
Special Notes: Productive fishing for landlocked salmon and some brook trout; easy access to Baxter State Park and Mt. Katahdin, Maine's highest peak (hiking, camping, and technical climbing); frequent sightings of wildlife include bald eagles, osprey, moose, and bear.

Below the next island lies the usual take-out for the trip, point C, on a beach on river left.

Three miles of deadwater beyond this point is Debsconeag Falls. It begins with a Class V drop series at the top, with a Class III run-out. The idea is to steer clear of the terminal hydraulics. Scouting and portaging is done on river left. The take-out, point D, is on river left well below the rapid.

The West Branch of the Penobscot is a nationally significant whitewater-boating and landlocked-salmon fishing river. The majority of the whitewater on the river, and the best of the fishing, lies within the first six miles below Ripogenus Dam and the McKay station. This river was politically removed from the state's protection list, although it ranked the second most valuable in the state. Due to the efforts of the Penobscot Coalition to Save the West Branch, Great Northern Paper Company's application to build the proposed "Big A" dam was withdrawn in 1986. Now, recreation flows, river access, and recreation facilities are provided through conditions of Great Northern Paper's Federal Hydropower Operating License.

Seboomook Section

The Seboomook section of the West Branch lies 49 miles from Greenville and is directly north of Moosehead Lake. From Route 15 north one must follow a network of private logging roads to Seboomook Dam. The logging roads are very dusty, but in good repair; an off-road shuttle vehicle is not necessary. Be careful not to wind up at Pittston Farm. It is at the wrong end of Seboomook Lake. Pass through a Great Northern Paper Company registration check point. Take a right turn shortly after the checkpoint (if you go straight, you will find yourself at Pittston Farm), and you will find Seboomook Dam and the beginning of the two-and-a-half-mile river trip.

Until recently this stretch of river received little attention from whitewater boaters. Combined with a morning or next-day trip on the South Branch at Canada Falls, the long drive to this river is well worth your while. Since it is such a trek from civilization, call ahead to make sure there is adequate water.

Beginning at Seboomook Dam, the river is virtually flat, but moving. Steer clear of salmon fishermen and respect the fact that they may be trying to attract a fish to a fly that lies many yards away from where they are standing.

The first of many river-wide ledges occurs a little less than a mile into the trip. It is the first distinct horizon line that you see, and most certainly will not be the last! The next one-quarter mile drops at the rate of 70 feet per mile. Some of the ledges are short, about one and a half

West Branch of the Penobscot River, Seboomook Section • Maine

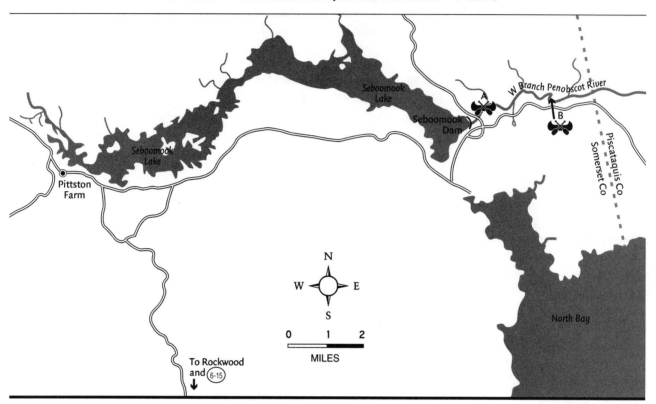

to three feet high, and at times create hydraulics that may be advisable to avoid. There is a clean route for every rapid, and each ledge is followed by a short, flat pool before the next drop. The biggest ledge is about five feet high but is more of a chute. A good rule of thumb is to scout from the right shore. If a portage is necessary, the right shore is best.

Keep safety in mind, especially in the section called Labyrinth. You will recognize this section by the distinct horizon line with treetops below. This series of ledges falls at the rate of 70 feet per mile for about a half mile. If you feel uncomfortable running any of the drops, portage on the right. Take your time on this section and savor every moment. This river is not just a beautiful stretch of spruce- and fir-lined ledge drops; it has some of the best enders and hole and wave surfing available during the summer months.

You will know the Roll Dam take-out (B) by the camping area on river right. Don't bother looking for a dam at the Roll Dam take-out, because there isn't one.

Section: Seboomook Dam to Roll Dam
County: Somerset
USGS Quad: North East Carry
Difficulty: Class III–IV
Gradient: 12 feet per mile (70 feet per mile maximum)
Average Width: 100 feet
Velocity: Slow to moderately fast
Rescue Index: Accessible
Hazards: Deadfalls, keeper hydraulics, rapids, ledge drops
Scouting: Easy
Portages: Scouting and portage trails are usually river right
Scenery: Spectacular—wilderness
Highlights: Scenery, wildlife, whitewater, geology
Gauge: Great Northern Paper Company flow recording, (207) 723-2328
Runnable Water Levels:

	Minimum	Maximum
	over 300 cfs (below 0 on gauge)	Undetermined

Months Runnable: May through September, contingent on dam releases
Additional Information: Camping and fire permits—Maine Forest Service, (207) 287-2791, or local Forest Service stations
Special Notes: Productive fly-fishing for landlocked salmon.

Piscataquis River

The Piscataquis River lies five miles to the west of Monson, down the Blanchard Road. Blanchard is the put-in (A). Carry your boat upstream of Chase Rips, the rapid above the bridge, to begin the 10-mile run. Following this small Class III ledge rapid and its wavy run is a three-mile-long Class II and flatwater stretch which winds its way beneath Russell and Little Russell Mountains. This section of river is mostly wooded and passes by a number of livestock pastures and farmhouses.

The next bridge you come across marks Barrows Falls, a Class III+ rapid channeled through a narrow, slate gorge with walls rising to about 10 feet above the water. Eddy left or right above the bridge to scout. This section is straightforward, with large reactionary waves, some holes, and very few eddies. There is a good recovery pool at the bottom for rescues.

Below Barrows Falls, the river's most significant drop, the Piscataquis descends in consistent Class II fashion with small surfing waves and holes for the next five miles. Pine martins, fishers, deer, and osprey are often seen along the wooded banks of this section.

About two miles from the Upper Abbot take-out on Routes 6 and 15 (B), sporting camps begin to appear on river right.

The Class II rapids continue to the town, where there are houses on both sides of the river. When you see a deteriorated bridge across the river, you know you have reached the take-out. Run the rapid under the bridge next to the abutment. Run to the right of the abutment, but not too far right, because of the pourover-type hole to the right of the channel.

Take out after the bridge on river left. The deteriorated concrete at the take-out rapid on river right is what remains of an old mill dam from the early 1900s.

Section: Blanchard to Route 15 bridge
County: Piscataquis
USGS Quads: Greenville, Kingsbury
Difficulty: Class II–III+
Gradient: 7 feet per mile (20 feet per mile maximum)
Average Width: 75 feet
Velocity: Slow to fast
Rescue Index: Accessible to remote
Hazards: Rapids, deadfalls, blowdowns
Scouting: Barrows Falls, Chase Rips
Portages: None
Scenery: Pleasant to beautiful
Highlights: Scenery, wildlife, geology, whitewater
Gauge: Visual only. If it looks runnable at the put-in, it's runnable.

Runnable Water Levels:	Minimum	Maximum
	200 cfs	Below flood stage

Months Runnable: April through June
Special Notes: Spring ice-out and rains provide the natural flow of the river. With enough rain it may run in summer and fall.

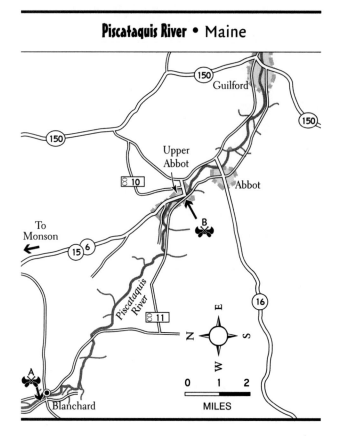

Piscataquis River • Maine

Sheepscot River

The Sheepscot River put-in (A) is seven and a half miles east of Augusta, off Route 126 in North Whitefield. The take-out (B) is 13 miles south off Route 218 in the town of Head Tide. The river is accessible, as Route 218 parallels the river for its length, crossing to river right in Whitefield, about halfway through the trip. This river is great for novice boaters who want to sharpen basic skills.

The Sheepscot is a spring run, so be sure you catch it early in the season. A good rain can bring it up at any time. Mid-June usually marks the end of spring flows.

Put in at the Route 126 bridge in North Whitefield. You won't get your minimum daily requirement of adrenaline on this Class I section, but this is a truly beautiful stream. It is about a five-and-a-half-mile paddle by tree-lined banks and livestock pastures down to the town of Whitefield and the Route 218 bridge.

Below the bridge, take out on either side of the river, and carry the river-wide ledge drops strewn with chunks of concrete from the old Kings Mill dam.

Downstream from Whitefield, the river takes on a more remote atmosphere. It is heavily wooded, and there are fewer signs of development on this section. The current quickens into a mile and a half of Class II rapids. At higher flows there are good surfing waves, and at all levels this is a good stretch for novices to improve their skills. Named The Rapids, this section ends just above Head Tide (B). Take out on river right above the Head Tide Dam.

Sheepscot River • Maine

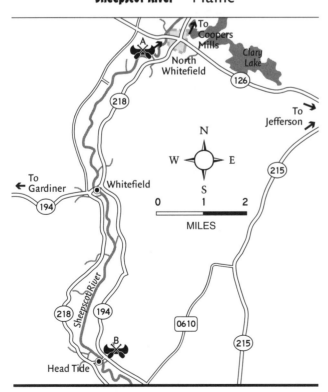

Section: North Whitefield to Head Tide
County: Lincoln
USGS Quads: Vassalboro, Wiscasset
Difficulty: Class I–II+
Gradient: 12 feet per mile (20 feet per mile maximum)
Average Width: 75 feet
Velocity: Slow to moderate
Rescue Index: Accessible
Hazards: Old dams, rapids
Scouting: None
Portages: Kings Mill, left side
Scenery: Pretty to beautiful
Highlights: Scenery, wildlife, history
Gauge: Visual. If there appears to be a runnable flow at the put-in, it is high enough (300 cfs).

Runnable Water Levels:	Minimum	Maximum
	Over 300 cfs	Undetermined

Months Runnable: March through May

Souadabscook Stream

Souadabscook Stream is five miles south of Bangor. Take the Hermon exit, Route 44 west, off Interstate Route 95. This is Goldbrook Road. Take the first left on Emerson Mill Road just beyond the truck stop for 1.8 miles to Manning Mill Road. Go down the road to the bridge over the river. The put-in, point A, for this three-and-three-quarter-mile run is a short walk with your boat upstream of the rapid above the bridge.

This river is a spring mecca for boaters in Maine, and a downriver race is held during April high water. The "Dabscook" has a semi-wilderness atmosphere for the most part but does pass through some backyards and by a cement plant.

Beginning at the Manning Mill put-in, above the bridge rapid, the current is split by an island. If the water is high enough, the river passes through the trees and creates an efficient strainer. This rapid is called Steltzer's Drop, and the easiest route is to the right of the island and left of center in the mainstream. There is a great surfing hole on the right. Below the bridge are some surfing waves. One-quarter mile downstream is more good surfing, and one-half mile downstream from that is a ledge drop at Camp Prentiss that is usually run on the right. Downstream, again, is another ledge at Emerson Mill bridge. The ledge is generally run on the left, and there is good surfing below.

One-quarter mile below the railroad bridge, look for a log cabin on river right. Eddy to the right and scout Hairpin Turn Rapid at the Crawfords' house. The usual route is tight to the left shore over the drop. The more complicated route is to the river right.

The next bridge is Paper Mill Bridge, and it has a potentially significant keeper hydraulic beneath it on the left. Stay to the right and play in the wave train.

After the bridge be sure to take out on river left, point B, because Grand Falls, a recommended portage, is next. This drop is below the third bridge from the put-in. Very few paddlers run Grand Falls because it is a 12-foot, steep ledge drop that has strong bow-pinning potential. There

is a route, although not too terribly terrific, to the right of center in the drop itself. This should only be run at certain flows by qualified, genetically defective boaters. Just below Grand Falls is a deteriorated river-wide dam with a nasty hydraulic and a death slot choked with logs on the left. It does have a runnable slot on the right that feeds you into a rock lying directly below. This dam is a recommended portage also. Both Grand Falls and the dam may be portaged on river left.

There are nice surfing waves below the dam. After a mile of flatwater you will come to a snowmobile bridge and a cement plant on river left. This marks the beginning of a series of three Class II–III ledge drops. These may be run left or left of center.

Section: Manning Mill Bridge to Route 1A in Hampden
County: Penobscot
USGS Quad: Bangor
Difficulty: Class III–V+
Gradient: 30 feet per mile
Average Width: 60 feet
Velocity: Moderate to fast
Rescue Index: Accessible
Hazards: Ledge drops, strainers, waterfall, low head dam, keeper hydraulics
Scouting: Hairpin Turn at Crawfords', Grand Falls, dam below Grand Falls
Portages: Grand Falls, dam below Grand Falls
Scenery: Semi-wilderness to suburban/industrial
Highlights: Whitewater
Gauge: Water running through the trees on the island upstream of the Manning Mill Bridge put-in
Runnable Water Levels: Minimum   Maximum
                       Over 500 cfs   Undetermined
Months Runnable: Mid-March to early June
Additional Information: Bangor Ski Rack, (207) 945-6474
Special Notes: Always be courteous to landowners. Portage, scouting, and access points A and B are privately owned.

Souadabscook Stream • Maine

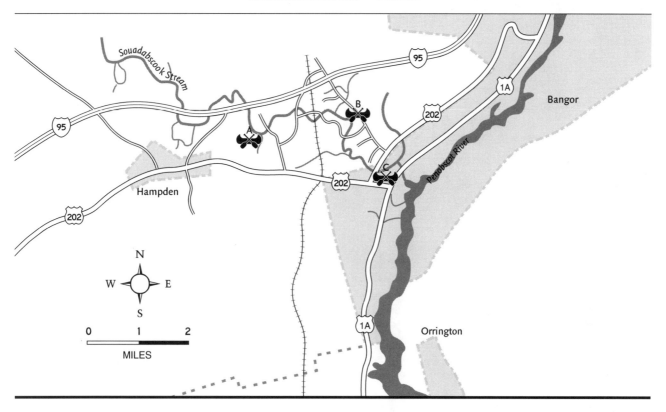

You will find easy Class II from the Route 202 bridge to the river right take-out, point C. This is the old Hampden Water District building on Route IA. Originally, this was an old gristmill. Be careful not to miss the take-out, because there is a terminal hydraulic caused by the low head dam under the Route IA bridge.

NEW HAMPSHIRE

Contoocook River

Freight Train Section

The Contoocook River is a big-water-feeling river, especially through **S**-Turn and Freight Train Rapids. The Contoocook feeds from a large, buffering watershed that makes for a long season. The tea-colored Contoocook is runnable for most of the spring, and in summer and fall, when heavy rains can bring the river up to eight or nine feet. The gauge, whose reading can be found on the Internet, is located two and a half miles southwest of Henniker on Western Avenue, a winding country lane that follows the entire run. Expect some of the finest big-water paddling in the East: rapids blend together at high levels (above 10 feet) and resemble a drop-pool type river at lower flows. The riverbed is a combination of boulders and ledges, with quite a few twists in the channel (and a few places you want to veer away from, especially at high water). Above 10.5 feet, the left side of Freight Train begins to wash into the woods, creating strainers from trees, fences, and an old canal bed.

To reach the usual put-in (A) from Hillsboro, drive northeast on Route 202, 1.7 miles from the intersection with Route 149, and turn right onto Contoocook Falls Road. Follow this road for .9 miles. As it bends to the left and crosses the river, it turns into Western Avenue. Park on either side of the road where shoulder widens and follow a short trail down to the river. The take-out (B) is a half mile upstream from the West Henniker Dam on Western Avenue. The put-in and take-out are both on private land and are being used by permission of the owner. Please be neat and avoid blocking the road. The run starts off in a deep, dark-water pool, with white and yellow pine vying with hardwoods and birch for space along the banks. A Class III section continues around a gradual right bend with plenty of gradient, big waves, and a sticky hole in the center just above a short pool. A left turn follows, with the most shallow rapid of the trip. If the right side looks too low, there probably is not enough water to make the run enjoyable. Class II–III play waves and holes signal a diminishing gradient for the next half mile. At high flows, this calmer stretch is filled with

wave swells of 3 to 4 feet (above 10.5 feet). Roger's Rock follows the next left-hand turn, a huge boulder midstream with an ender spot to its left. It is so named because a local paddler here disproved the theory that it is impossible to ender in a Quest!

S-Turn is the most demanding technical rapid of the run, starting in a right turn. The top third of the half-mile-long rapid contains a series of broken ledges, with the best route starting right-center, then moving left to avoid a few holes on the right below. The second portion swings to the right, with big holes in the center. Next, take a left turn down the steepest gradient of the run, through a section with large boulders, pourovers behind ledges, and very pushy current. Generally, start right and work your way to the left to avoid **S**-Turn Hole, a nearly river-wide ledge extending from the right bank. An island past a large eddy on the right splits the current, with a tight slot to the right that allows easier maneuvering into

Section: Western Avenue to above West Henniker Dam
   (Freight Train)
County: Hillsborough
USGS Quad: Hillsborough 15
Difficulty: Class III, IV (IV+ in high water)
Gradient: 45 feet per mile (60 feet per mile maximum)
Average Width: 75 feet
Velocity: Pushy to sluggish
Rescue Index: Accessible
Hazards: Strainers, water in the trees at high levels
Scouting: Freight Train Rapids
Portages: None
Scenery: Pretty to beautiful in spots
Highlights: Whitewater, scenery
Gauge: Western Avenue gauge

Runnable Water Levels:	Minimum	Maximum
	7.5 feet	12.5 feet

Months Runnable: March through May, heavy periods of rain

continuous Class III+ ledges and boulders. S-Turn is continuous, pounding whitewater at high levels and is much tougher than it looks from the road. Be wary of the island behind S-Turn Hole when running the river in high water, as it will be partially submerged and could strain you into Contoocook tea.

The gauge is just below S-Turn on the right. Here, the river decelerates into a calmer stretch, with pond paddling for the next quarter mile. An alternative take-out point, on river right at the start of a left turn, is a helpful option for those who do not want to be railroaded through Freight Train.

The steam from Freight Train rises above the next right corner, with some Class II leading into a narrow, boulder-crowded, Class IV section. The gradient here is noticeable, and a series of ledges creates some of the biggest waves and stickiest holes in the Granite State. While this section is a technical run at low water, with waves reaching four feet, in high water you will experience waves double that height. A ledge with a bad pourover prohibits a sneak route down the right, and the left bank is the worst place to be on the river, especially during high water. Stay to the center through the biggest stuff, checking your momentum in eddies at the top on the right and farther down on the left. It is possible to surf some of the larger waves here; there is a great surf spot below the last ledge on the left, the Rambowave! A Class III+ section finishes off Freight Train's ride, which ends with a calm stretch, pounded by the lethal West Henniker Dam below. Take out well above the dam, on the right where the river bends to the left.

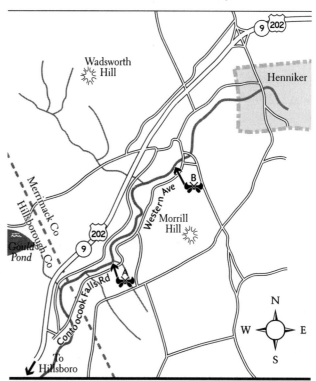

Contoocook River • New Hampshire

Like a sadomasochistic lover, the Contoocook (or "Took," as it is known locally) will either punish or caress you, depending on water level. It is being rafted commercially, and there are ongoing attempts to dam up this section to produce power, possibly flooding out Freight Train forever.

Merrimack River

The Merrimack is the largest river in New Hampshire, with its source in Franklin at the confluence of the Winnipesaukee and Pemigewasset Rivers. A Class B water-quality river until it reaches Manchester, it is stocked with salmon in a successful project that has reintroduced that species in the Granite State. Unfortunately, the water takes a drastic turn for the worst in Manchester, due to sewage flowing into the river. These poor conditions are most evident at very low water in the summer, and when high runoff overwhelms the waste treatment capability of the sewage plants. The top play spot at Arms Park (A) has better water quality than the Route 101 and Railroad Bridge rapids downstream.

The positives of paddling here are a year-round season, guaranteed water levels, easy access, no shuttle, and

Section: Arms Park, Route 101 Bridge, Railroad bridge
County: Hillsborough
USGS Quads: Manchester North
Difficulty: Class II, III
Gradient: 40 feet per mile
Average Width: 225 feet
Velocity: Moderate
Rescue Index: Accessible
Hazards: Industrial debris, questionable water quality
Scouting: None
Portages: None
Scenery: Urban uninspiring
Highlights: Excellent area for training, teaching, and playing
Gauge: Amoskeag Dam
Runnable Water Levels: Minimum   Maximum
                            Always enough   Never too much
                            to paddle
Months Runnable: All, dam-controlled section
Additional Information: The Public Service Company of New
   Hampshire River Flow Information Line has release levels,
   (603) 634-3569

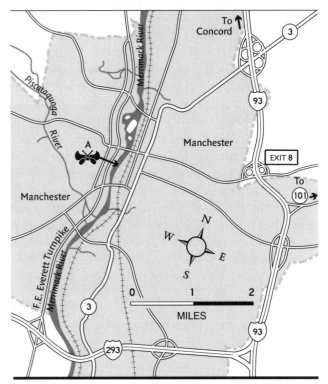

Merrimack River • New Hampshire

three interesting play spots. The drawbacks are the polluted water and the generally bleak industrial landscape. At very high levels (where water floods over Amoskeag Dam) the Class V section can be run, but first be sure you know what you are getting into!

To reach Arms Park, take I-293 North to Exit 5. Turn right onto Granite Street at the end of the ramp, crossing the bridge. Take your first left onto Commercial Street to Arms Park, turning into Arms Park underneath the Notre Dame Bridge.

Rocks have been placed in the riverbed, forming eddies for the gates of a slalom course. This is the location of the Merrimack Riverfest, held in September every year. When the Merrimack is very high, these rocks disappear under the surface and the gates are pulled in, so the racers practice at lower levels. There are also some waves to surf. This area can get very hot in the summer because of its exposure to the sun and all the concrete and asphalt close by.

You can park on either side of the river at the Route 101 bridge play spot (B), although the sewage plant smells worse on the river-right side. There is always something to do here no matter what the level, with an assortment of waves and holes.

From the Route 101 bridge you can see a railroad bridge in the distance downstream. This marks the third play spot (C), although you can't combine them without setting up a shuttle. You may again park on either side of the river. The railroad bridge features a wonderful wave, although it needs substantial water to form.

Mascoma River

The Mascoma is a favorite training run in western New Hampshire, close to the Vermont border, with easy access from Interstates 89 and 91. A five-mile jaunt through wooded ravines and semi-urban areas, the Mascoma is Class II–III with one Class IV drop in high water, Excelsior Rapids, named for a now-defunct mill. The Mascoma enjoys a long season due to the swamps, ponds, and Mascoma Lake upstream, which tend to stretch out available water. There is a higher-level release during the fall reservoir drawdown, usually scheduled around Columbus Day. The run parallels Routes 4 and 4a and begins just downstream from the outlet of Mascoma Lake off Payne Road (A). Route 89 and a railroad also keep you company during the almost four-mile paddle, but their intrusion does not ruin the trip.

The gauge is found just downstream of the put-in (A) at Mascoma Lake along the left bank. A few standing waves lead into continuous Class II–III between the Route 4 bridge and the Route 89 overpass. Watch for fallen trees along this stretch, as the soil is sandy and the banks are steep. The Mascoma follows the interstate for a short stretch, then turns away to the left with more challenging action beyond an old stone bridge. The river is the site of the Mascoma Slalom, the oldest continuously run slalom in the United States. It used to be held at Excelsior Rapids, but due to access problems it has now been moved upstream to a point about a mile below the dam.

A railroad bridge is passed, with the river banking to the right into Excelsior Rapids. Class III at low water, Class IV during medium and high flows, Excelsior Rapids

Section: Mascoma Lake to Route 4, Lebanon
County: Graflon
USGS Quads: Mascoma 15, Hanover
Difficulty: Class II, III (III+ in high water)
Gradient: 40 feet per mile (80 feet per mile maximum)
Average Width: 60 feet
Velocity: Moderate
Rescue Index: Accessible
Hazards: Unrunnable dam below Excelsior Rapids, strainers
Scouting: Excelsior Rapids
Portages: None
Scenery: Fair
Highlights: Whitewater
Gauge: Mascoma Lake dam gauge (A)

Runnable Water Levels:

	Minimum	Maximum
	2.3 feet	Flood stage

Months Runnable: March through May, after heavy rains, fall release

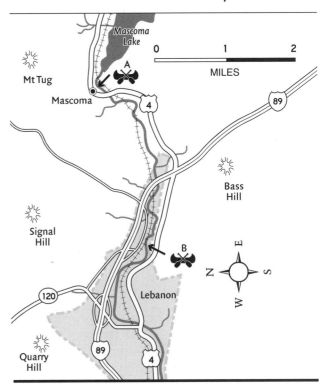

Mascoma River • New Hampshire

are the toughest the Mascoma has to offer. A footpath along the left bank is handy for scouting or for running the section again. Expect heavy going for 100 yards or so through waves, boulders, ledges, and holes, with the route usually starting center and ending up on the left at the bottom to avoid a few boat-munching holes halfway down on the right. The abandoned Excelsior Mill lies on the right bank, and you stroke past the remains of what once must have been a very high dam. The next railroad bridge signals an unrunnable four-foot dam with a bad hydraulic, found in the next right-hand turn. Take out well above this death trap on the left. A short walk upstream along the railroad tracks leads to the top of Excelsior Rapids for another run. To reach the take-out, walk across the railroad bridge to a moving company's parking lot and continue on to the road. Please park next to the road rather than in the company lot; there have been access problems here in the past.

Pemigewasset River

Bristol Gorge

Bristol Gorge is gaining in popularity among northern New England boaters due to its clean water, pleasant scenery, and long season. On the Pemigewasset River, Bristol Gorge boasts a year-round paddling season fed by dam-controlled water immediately above the put-in. The two-and-a-half-mile section is great for a training trip, or just for getting on the river during the summer and fall when everything else in New Hampshire and Vermont has dried up. Negotiations with the power company have resulted in releases on almost every weekend during paddling season. The Merrimack Valley Paddlers hold their annual Pig Roast in Bristol Gorge, with releases guaranteed to be in the 1,500–2,000 range. Mostly Class II whitewater; a couple of ledges at the top add Class III

hole playing and wave surfing, and an ender spot at the take-out is sure to keep accomplished boaters happy for the afternoon. Expect Class IV water throughout at high levels, as large holes and big waves form behind the larger ledge drops.

The put-in is off Route 104 in Bristol, behind a baseball field to the east of town. Take a right onto Ayers Island Road, bearing around a baseball field. Follow this dirt road as it drops steeply down toward the river, with a parking lot on river right just below the dam. The take-out is harder to find. From the put-in, take Route 104 west toward Bristol, making the next left onto Merrimack Street. A hard-left turn brings you onto Central Street; head across an iron single-span bridge to a maintained dirt road on the right (Coolidge Woods Road). The

Section: Bristol Gorge to Coolidge Woods Road
Counties: Grafton, Belknap
USGS Quad: Holderness
Difficulty: Class II, III (IV in high water)
Gradient: 24 feet per mile
Average Width: 120 feet
Velocity: Moderate
Rescue Index: Accessible
Hazards: None
Scouting: None
Portages: None
Highlights: Whitewater
Scenery: Pretty in spots
Gauge: Dam-controlled section

Runnable Water Levels:	Minimum	Maximum
	500 cfs	Flood stage

Months Runnable: All, dam-controlled
Additional Information: Release levels are available through Public Service Company of New Hampshire's River Flow Information Line, (603) 634-3569

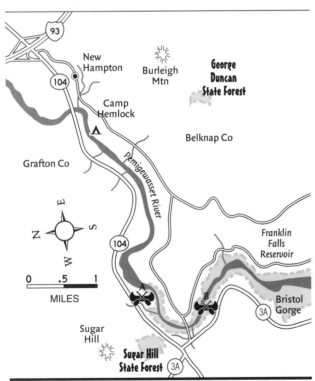

Pemigewasset River • New Hampshire

take-out (B) is alongside a rocky outcrop where a series of ledges and the ender hole are also found.

The play spots on the river depend upon river levels and your craft of choice for their character. At low levels (500 cfs) most of the river is somewhat scratchy, although there is always something to do at the last ledge by the take-out. The hole at the first drop is the "Pig Roast" or rodeo hole. Just below this is the "squirt hole," favored by squirt boaters for its deep water and lack of rocks. The last and most popular play spot is at the take-out, featuring fast surfing waves, with an ender spot appearing at some levels. No matter what the level, the large granite shelf at the take-out provides an excellent picnic and suntanning spot, where swimming, roll practice, and (heaven forbid!) tubing are popular. Below the take-out, the Pemigewasset is flattened out by the Franklin Falls flood control dam, creating a five-mile lake that covers the former town of Hill.

East Branch of the Pemigewasset River

The East Branch of the Pemigewasset River falls from 4,000-foot peaks, along the western end of the Kancamagus Highway in New Hampshire's White Mountains National Forest. Tumbling through sylvan stands of fir, beech, and hardwood between Franconia Brook and Loon Mountain, the East Branch is the home of loon, hawk, porcupine, beaver, and flashing trout. Below Loon Mountain Ski Area, the natural beauty of the proud Pemigewasset is rapidly giving way to the greed of developers and the real-estate-conscious ski business. Instead of dense forest, there is now a view of George and Ethel's living room, and condo-city is becoming the norm beyond the protected boundary of the White Mountains National Forest.

The Pemigewasset is remarkably broad for a White Mountains river, 150 feet wide, cluttered with boulders, and fed by snowmelt and periods of heavy rain. High water frequently moves the large boulders and erodes the gravel bars that comprise the riverbed of the Pemi, resulting in frequent changes to the rapids. Be alert—the rapid you ran last time may not have much in common with what you encounter this trip. The water is so clear that it often looks too scratchy for running at the put-in (B), even though the gauge indicates there is plenty of water. The degree of difficulty of this run rises exponentially with slight increases in water level. From 1.0 to 1.5 feet on the Kancamagus Bridge gauge at the put-in, the run is Class III+–IV. From 1.5 to 2.0 feet, expect Class IV; above 2.0 feet any separation between rapids that existed at lower levels disappears, with Class IV+ exhaustion if you make it to the take-out. Boaters who have survived the East Branch above 3.5 feet say they probably will not paddle it at that level again; it is nonstop, pushy, and extremely dangerous. The minimum run on the East Branch is 0.2 feet, but after bumping down at .5 feet, the lower section (C–D) becomes hazardous because the river is constantly cutting new channels through a long section of gravel bar. The routes become less than obvious, and some channels are even blocked by boulder sieves.

The normal put-in (B) is found off the Kancamagus Highway (Route 112) at the Pemigewasset Wilderness Access Area, three miles east of Loon Mountain. There is now a parking fee for this area and all others in the White Mountains National Forest. The present rates are $5.00 for one week, $20.00 for a year, and $25.00 for a family pass (two cars). The first section of the trip can end at the Loon Mountain Bridge (C), but scout beforehand where you want to pull out to avoid being committed down the right slot below the bridge, a hairy run at any level. The nearly six-mile run ends behind an IGA store in North Lincoln, just past the access ramps for I-93 (D). An alter-

Section: Pemigewasset Wilderness Area to North Woodstock
County: Grafton
USGS Quads: Mt. Osceola, Lincoln
Difficulty: Class IV (V in high water)
Gradient: 69 feet per mile (100 feet per mile maximum)
Average Width: 150 feet
Velocity: Fast and pushy
Rescue Index: Accessible but difficult
Hazards: Abandoned metal culverts, pinning boulders, wide rapids
Scouting: Island Rapids, Loon Mountain Rapids
Portages: Unrunnable dam
Highlights: Whitewater, scenery, history
Scenery: Spectacular to uninspiring
Gauge: Pemigewasset Wilderness bridge (B)

Runnable Water Levels:	Minimum	Maximum
(B–C)	0.2 feet	3.5 feet
(C–D)	0.5 feet	

Months Runnable: March, April, May, after periods of heavy rain
Additional Information: Pemigewasset Ranger Station, (603) 744-9165
Special Notes: Camping within White Mountains National Forest at Big Rock and Passaconaway

East Branch of the Pemigewasset River • New Hampshire

nate put-in (A) lies three miles up a hiking trail from the Pemigewasset Wilderness Area, just below the confluence with Franconia Brook. It is worth walking once—it's a Class IV run with larger boulders and steeper gradient than the section between the Wilderness Area and Loon Mountain Bridge.

Subcompact-sized boulders cramp the slots at the beginning of the run from the Wilderness Area, with larger boulders creating micro-eddies and turbulence near the banks. The Pemi is 35 yards wide here, with Class III+ rapids for the first quarter mile. A right turn and a Class IV chute follow, with the Hancock Branch entering on the left. A maze of Class IV leads past a cluster of birch along the right bank into two powerful chutes that end with a two-foot ledge drop. The second drop demands quick negotiating in high water, with a few boulders to dodge at the bottom of the chute. The Island Rapids are next, following another Class III+ stretch of boulder dodging. The river heads to the right around a large gravel-bar island, with heavy current, plenty of gradient, and a series of boulder-choked, two-feet drops. The small holes found here at lower levels disappear with larger flows, replaced by pourovers formed behind even some of the larger boulders. The second Island Rapid leads into a life-threatening situation on the right below, where old railroad culverts

have been discarded along the bank and lie directly in the main flow of the current. Three mammoth boulders in a V formation block the right side, with two back-to-back holes that must be punched on the left. Directly behind the boulders lie the culverts, the first with its open end facing directly upstream, a real jaws-of-death situation. Avoid being stuffed down this dead-end route at all costs.

Loon Mountain Bridge is visible a quarter mile downstream along with the ski area along the left bank. Loon Mountain Rapids, the toughest of the run, begin immediately with a myriad of routes through a steep, heavily constricted riverbed. A possible take-out lies above the bridge on river right or left. Recent bridge reconstruction has dumped large quantities of sharp-edged rocks into the rapid. It is now frequently portaged, since a mistake is likely to be extremely painful. A bridge pillar splits the channel, with the easier route down the left side. The lower section of the run begins at the bridge, with a tight, big-water slot on the right that requires a dozen moves within a 50-yard stretch, and a four-foot drop into a short pool at the end. The left side is not as steep or constricted, but it is longer—still a demanding Class IV+ negotiation. Loon Mountain Rapids demands your respect; it is easy to find yourself broached and wondering why you ever got into whitewater boating in the first place.

Mist shrouds the put-in on the East Branch of the Pemigewasset. The level here is 1.8 feet. Photo by Roger Belson.

The current converges in a tight spot beside the remains of a dam, with huge boulders cramping the slot. The Pemi enters a long stretch of gravel bar called Decision Rapids, a section of riverbed broken at least four times with channels that have been altered by recent flooding. The chutes lead from the left to the right: if in doubt about which chute to take, scout it. Go by the remnants of another mill dam on the right, then calmer Class III takes over. Float past newly sprouting condominiums on the right, joining older eyesores to the left. A few steeper pitches are mixed in for the next half mile, requiring quick decisions and a lightning-quick roll. An abandoned dump on the right is just upstream of an unrunnable five-foot log dam. A series of ledges leads into a large pool just above the dam on the left, where you can portage over a rock ledge or sneak the dam down a rock slide on the left bank. Below the dam, a series of surfing holes are found. The river narrows below around several islands, with big waves and boiling eddies. The Class IV ride is not quite over yet, as another mile of boulder-dodging weaves through some large holes, pourovers, and ledges past a railroad and two highway bridges. The take-out is on the right, past a midstream sand bar at a clearing in the brush above the confluence of the smaller, main branch of the Pemigewasset. There is now a USGS gauge in Lincoln. A good rule of thumb if the Lincoln is reading 3.5 feet or less is to subtract 2 feet to obtain the reading of the paddler's gauge painted on the Pemigewasset Wilderness Bridge.

If there is high water in the Whites, the Swift River, a four-minute drive east over the Kancamagus Highway, offers a more reasonable challenge than the punishing East Branch of the Pemigewasset.

Smith River

The Smith River is the type of whitewater run western boaters expect in New England; tight, twisting, and technical, the Smith boasts continuous Class IV rapids above 1.0 feet on the Cass Mill Bridge gauge. The Smith careens through beautifully forested western New Hampshire hills, contained by a series of slanting ledges that extend from the banks well into the riverbed. This is a very pushy river in high water; the eddies boil and numerous midstream boulders constrict the current and make for last-minute decisions. The Smith requires considerable rainfall to be runnable, as its watershed is limited. Generally, 0.5 feet is the lowest the Smith should be run; 2.5 feet is an estimate of the maximum level. Many local boaters have caught the Smith higher than three feet, but it is up to you to decide if you should be on this river at those levels. At high water, rescue is difficult because of the steep-sided banks, the continuous nature of the rapids, and the tremendously fast water velocity. Open boaters should strongly consider running another river when the Smith is over two feet, not because of ability, but because most of the Smith will end up in your boat.

The top put-in (A) is on Hill Center Road just off Route 104, two miles northeast of Elmwood. The alternative put-in (B) eliminates some flatwater warm-up and Class II–III rapids. It can be found on Smith River Road, which parallels the run, 1.25 miles east of the top put-in. Smith River Road is also the site for the take-out, which lies under a set of high-voltage power lines below the intersection of Cass Mill Road.

From the top put-in (A), a half mile of flatwater and three-quarters of a mile of Class II–III lead into a 30-yard-long pool, just above two miles of continuous Class IV. Make sure you practice a few rolls in the pool, even if it is cold; you won't have much time between the drops below to be looking for trout. For the next quarter mile to the Smith River Road bridge, the river winds to the right down a series of two-foot ledge drops. A strongly possessive pourover guards the top right; otherwise it is pick-and-choose through this stretch. Put-in (B) can be made

at the top of this stretch, but you will go from the frying pan into the fire, as the Smith does not let up until the take-out. A large eddy lies beneath the bridge, where most groups gather to exchange ominous looks or great river stories.

The next 1.6 miles to the Cass Mill Road Bridge features ultra-continuous Class IV negotiating, and it is through this section that water levels are the most critical. Above two feet it is nonstop, very physically demanding, with irregular waves, staircase-type drops, holes, pourovers, and very few eddies. A series of three ledges begins the action below the Smith Road bridge, then everything blends together into kayaker's heaven, with more white than crystal-clear blue water under paddle. The right bank sports a series of jutting ledges that create

Section: Hill Center Road to Old Route 104, Bristol
Counties: Grafton, Merrimack
USGS Quads: Cardigan, Holderness
Difficulty: Class IV (IV+ in high water)
Gradient: 90 feet per mile
Average Width: 40 feet
Velocity: Pushy
Rescue Index: Accessible but difficult
Hazards: Continuous whitewater
Scouting: Ray's Rapid (just above Cass Mill Bridge)
Portages: None
Highlights: Whitewater, scenery
Scenery: Beautiful to spectacular in spots—classic New England
Gauge: Cass Mill Bridge gauge

Runnable Water Levels:	Minimum	Maximum
	0.5 feet	2.5 feet

Months Runnable: March, April
Special Notes: The nature of the river changes dramatically with variations in cfs

Smith River • New Hampshire

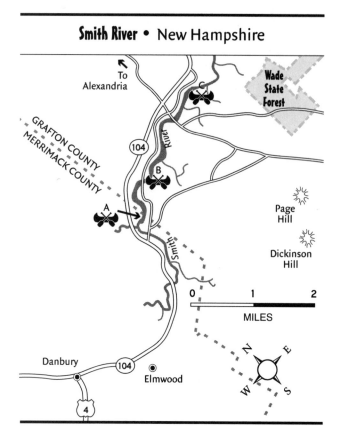

some nasty turbulence, while boulders add their own special ingredients to the witch's brew along the left bank.

The pace lets up a bit as the Smith pools above an island upstream of the Cass Mill Bridge. Here, Ray's (or Island) Rapid is found, with the hero route to the right, the chicken route to the left around the island. Ray's Rapid is the toughest on the Smith, a combination of three drops, the first and third about three feet, the second a two-foot drop. It is only 60 yards long, and the general idea is to stay to the right. A large boulder on the right marks the top of the right-side route, which angles to the right, after the boulder, into the first drop, which has a strong hole at the bottom that must be punched to the right. Stay away from a jumble of glacial erratics, river center, then stay right down the second and third ledges. Ray's Rapid is runnable over 0.5 feet; below that, even plastic boaters grimace.

There is another half mile of continuous Class III+ to the take-out, with a Class IV ledge combination a quarter mile down on the left bank. Double Trouble sports a two- and three-foot ledge with backender possibilities in-the second drop. The take-out is on the left, under a set of high-voltage power lines. If you started before noontime, there's plenty of light left to run the Smith again, to try to remember what flashed by you so fast the first time.

Bob Potter in Ray's Rapid on the Smith River at 3+ feet. Photo by Jim Jackson.

Swift River

The Swift is one of those runs that keeps repeating itself in the back of your mind during the winter months when you try to keep track of how much snow fell and just how soon spring will come to the higher elevations of the White Mountains. The Swift has a long season for an eastern snowmelt river, usually paddleable for at least a month. Recently, it has become popular with rafters. The commercial aspect is new to the Swift, and the Saco District rangers are keeping an eye on its impact on the pristine Swift, with its crystal-clear waters and heavily forested banks. The Swift River is a gem in the rough: in order to keep it that way, when you boat the Swift you should take the time to fill out the rangers' questionnaire, as your input helps decide the future use of the river.

The Swift is a boat-crunching, boater-punching river. Medium-sized by eastern standards, it packs a wallop with serious gradient (up to 100 feet per mile through the Swift Gorge and Staircase sections), plenty of big water phenomena, pinning possibilities, and keeper hydraulics. The Swift constantly provokes you into action and reaction through two hard-core Class IV sections and lesser degrees of Class IV mixed throughout the 5.2-mile section. Swift Gorge and the Staircase can quickly turn into Class V at high flows. At lower levels, you can expect to leave plastic on a lot of rocks; from 1.5 feet on up, the river is no longer scratchy, with most of the drops rating Class III. The swift begins to get pushy at 2.5 feet, resembling a roller coaster with few places to jump off. Most of the smaller rocks will be underwater at 3.0 feet, and when the level nears 4.0 feet, boaters will be faced with running continuous Class IV, interspersed with Class IV–V drops. The Swift has been run at over 6.0 feet by expert boaters familiar with the river. When the Swift is up, the water is always cold, so dress for the occasion.

The suggested put-in (A) is at the Lower Falls access area along the Kancamagus Highway (Route 112). An upper section between the Rocky Gorge access area to the west and the Lower Falls can be run, solid Class III with a few Class IV ledges thrown in. This section is harder to hit when the river is up: it is too scratchy here when the Lower Falls to Darby Field Sign section is at medium levels (1.5 feet). The Lower Falls have been run by a number of true river crazies, but don't feel like a chicken if you put in immediately below; there are plenty of high-risk spots left downstream.

Amid the cheers of family tourists and members of local motorcycle gangs, the first drop below Lower Falls hits you right smack in the face with plenty of boulders, big waves, crosscurrents, and steep gradient. The next two and a half miles let up a bit: Continuous Class III past a covered bridge and through birch-lined banks, with the occasional red-tailed hawk circling overhead. There are a

Section: Lower Falls to Darby Field sign
County: Carroll
USGS Quads: Crawford Notch 15, Mt Chocorua 15
Difficulty: Class III, IV (IV+ in high water)
Gradient: 80 feet per mile (100 feet per mile maximum)
Average Width: 40 feet
Velocity: Fast and pushy
Rescue Index: Accessible to accessible but difficult
Hazards: Continuous whitewater, pinning spots, undercut boulders
Scouting: Swift Gorge, the Staircase
Portages: None
Highlights: Scenery, wildlife, whitewater
Scenery: Spectacular—inspiring
Gauge: Gauge rock in Swift Gorge on river left
Runnable Water Levels: Minimum   Maximum
                    0.75 feet (scratchy)3.0
Months Runnable: March, April, May, after periods of heavy rain
Additional Information: Saco District Ranger Station has gauge readings during paddling season, (603) 447-5448
Special Notes: Camping within White Mountains National Forest at Blackberry Crossing and Covered Bridge campgrounds

Swift River • New Hampshire

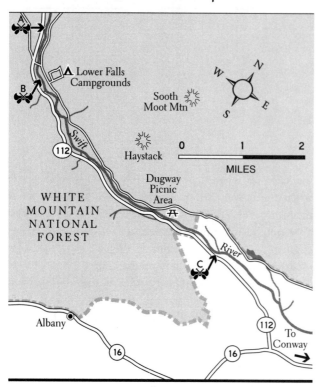

few places to sit in the sun and enjoy a granola bar from your drybag before the first big drop on the Swift, Swift Gorge. A cluster of cottages on the left bank signals the access point (B), where the Kancamagus Highway again comes alongside the river, a convenient departure point if your motor is not running for the Class IV Swift Gorge.

Class III+ rapids lead into the first drop, Initiation, which tumbles through tightly packed boulders down a two-foot drop into a large pool on river left. Initiation lies in a sharp left bend, and the pool should be used to bank-scout the tougher drops within the gorge. At high water the Swift Gorge is a Class V combination of pourovers, poorly padded boulders, strong, pushy current, and few eddies to set up your line in. There are three distinct ledges to conquer. The first is run-out of the left eddy down a diagonal wave into an eddy on the left below, with a ferry across above the second pile of boulders and ledges into an eddy on the right bank. The second row of obstacles involves threading the needle between Turnstile, a large boulder with a bad hole upstream and potholes downstream, and a larger, pillowed boulder that lies six feet to the left and slightly upstream of Turnstile. Immediately below is an almost river-wide pourover known to suck the poggies off submerged paddles. The

safest route here is to the right. A deepwater pool follows where recovery exercises can begin. Even at medium and low levels, the Swift Gorge demands Class IV respect and a scout every time you run it.

The Swift continues its rampage down the mountainside with another mile of boulder-studded Class III+ into the second major drop on the Swift, the Staircase. Considered unrunnable in 1971, this drop is the toughest on the Swift (if you mess it up). A series of three tightly packed ledges fall a total of 15 feet in 50 yards, the last two ledges just over a boat-length apart. A wash of boulders marks the top of this rapid, which lies in a slight left-hand turn. The sneak route is to the left of a boulder island, but this route can be just as trashy if you fail to make a move near the bottom back to the right. The hero route looks harder than it is, a series of eddy hops down the center into eddies on the right. The eddy just above the three ledges is marked by a pyramid-shaped rock—stay to the right here for the set-up out the backside of the eddy down a three-foot ledge, then set up just to the left of an egg-shaped rock for the final ledge. If you err in running the Staircase and find yourself in the center, you stand a chance of playing tag with the spin cycle of a whirlpool washer. You might have your ankles broken by pitoning into one of several shallow ledges, and you certainly risk a lifetime of embarrassing comments from your river buddies.

Although there are no more life-flashing drops, continuous heavy-duty Class III+–IV rapids pound for the next two miles, demanding agility, bracing skills, and a bombproof roll. The racecourse section is first, the site of an annual slalom race; then there are Screaming Left Turn, Big Rock, and Frog Rock. Big Rock contains a deep horseshoe hole behind a four-foot ledge on the right, a great lunch spot (for you and the hole) if you decide to venture in. Frog Rock starts after the second of two right-hand ledge rapids, a mammoth, free standing, undercut boulder that should be avoided to the left. The take-out (C) is on the right, a few minutes downstream from Frog Rock, past a long, shallow rapid. The Darby Field sign can be seen alongside the Kancamagus Highway, a signal that you have earned that frosty waiting for you in the cooler.

The Swift contains many surprises, including some tough minor rapids that can get you into as much trouble as the major drops. The Swift is no place for beginners or for the tame of heart: a beautiful rustic descent among 4,000-foot peaks in New Hampshire's White Mountains National Forest.

The formidable Lower Falls at the put-in for the Swift River. Photo by Roger Belson.

VERMONT

Ottaquechee River

Quechee Gorge on the Ottaquechee River is one of those runs that you have probably peered down into from Route 4, wondering what it would be like to paddle through the isolated, mile-long, 163-foot-deep chasm. An overall Class IV run, the Ottaquechee has one drop that in most cases must be portaged; above and below that Class VI drop the river pounds down a steep 60 feet per mile gradient, with big deflection waves, grabby holes, and a very pushy current. The view from deep within the gorge is spectacular: the arched iron bridge spans the nearly vertical walls; rough, slanting schist and gneiss slabs constrict the river; and the surging whitewater adds to the allure of Quechee Gorge. There are a few drawbacks to the section. The put-in is down a steep, angled ledge: negotiable, but certainly not a Sunday walk in the park. The take-out involves a half-mile hike back up a well-defined state forest path to the bridge—but you are so pumped up after the run that it does not seem all that far a carry. If you have problems in the Gorge and need assistance from the state park rangers, it will cost you a $500 fine, so be sure of your abilities before your boat hits the water. After that, there is no stopping until the takeout.

Quechee Gorge is one of Vermont's main tourist attractions. Formed when the waters from glacial lakes eroded the Green Mountain hills at the end of the last ice age, the gorge was a severe hindrance to east-west travel until 1875. The original bridge was a spidery web of wood supporting an iron railroad bed that brought steam locomotives and trade to Woodstock, six miles to the west. The original bridge was replaced in 1911 with today's steel, arched span; in 1933 the bridge was converted from railroad to horseless carriage use, and became Route 4.

It is difficult to correlate water levels within the gorge, because there is no visual gauge. There is a gauge reading from the USGS, available on the Internet. To measure the flows, you must be aware of what is going on at a hydro project at the top of the section. The power company is required, for esthetic reasons, to allow at least 300 cfs to go over the falls for the tourists. They then use an addi-

tional 500 to 3,000 cfs when they generate power. At 300 cfs the ledge on river right, just below the bridge next to Washermachine (the worst drop on the run), is fully exposed: only a three-foot-wide sluice leads into the terminal Class VI hole on the left. At approximately 1,500 cfs, that ledge is under water, and it is possible to run this drop hard against the right shore—still a Class V move. Scout out this run first from the bridge, which gives you a great overview but tends to flatten out the drops. Then scout out the tougher sections from the banks; it is possible to get down to water level from a path on river right 100 yards downstream of the bridge. From the put-in (A), the top four drops can be scouted. The take-out path leads from the bridge on river left to below the last set of

Section: Quechee Gorge
County: Windsor
USGS Quads: Quechee, Hartland, North Hartland
Difficulty: Class IV
Gradient: 60 feet per mile
Average Width: 30 feet
Velocity: Fast
Rescue Index: Inaccessible
Hazards: Steep-walled cliffs, heavy rapids, mandatory portage
Scouting: All of it
Portages: Washermachine (just below bridge)
Scenery: Spectacular—rugged, steep-walled gorge
Highlights: Whitewater, scenery, history
Gauge: Netam Corporation (hydro project management), (802) 295-1490

Runnable Water Levels:

	Minimum	Maximum
	300 cfs	Undetermined

Months Runnable: April through summer (hydro-generating releases)
Special Notes: Tough put-in, dangerous river when the banks are icy; section is not often run. Level determines if section is runnable (portage route must be above water).

ledges. The put-in is found at the end of a narrow dirt road that begins behind a picnic area on the west, upstream side of the bridge. Depending on ground moisture, it may be possible for vehicles with high clearance to come within 50 yards of the actual put-in. A steep, sloping ledge to the right of the falls leads to the river, with some fast current and turbulence starting immediately. An alternate route involves putting in at the reservoir on the river left side and paddling across to river right, at which point you descend the steep ledge. At higher levels, wave heights exceed four feet and there are a number of holes to stay away from. Lower levels reveal three distinct ledge drops, with defined routes through broken ledges and boulders. The river slams into a jutting

cliff face on the left, with considerable turbulence as well. A pool below, on the right, offers a chance to check your bearings and take in the first view of the bridge from within the gorge. A stretch of continuous Class IV waves and holes—that stop you dead in your tracks—leads beyond the bridge and into Washermachine, the worst drop on the river. Washermachine is generally considered Class VI or unrunnable; it is a slanting, nine-foot drop on the extreme left side that sucks most of the river into a strongly recirculating hole that burrows into the undercut cliff face. At 1,500 cfs, the hole has two lines of interface within the 25-yard backwash. Stay out of this hole at all costs! Instead, portage well above the drop on river right across the exposed ledge. At 1,500 cfs the ledge is

Rugged Vermont beauty
is found deep within
Quechee Gorge of the
Ottaquechee River.
Photo by John Porterfield.

Ottaquechee River • Vermont

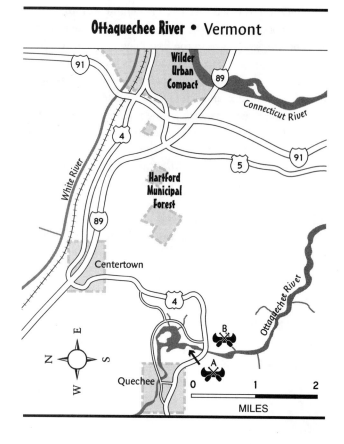

under water, portaging is impossible, and you must either run the 15 feet of drop over 25 yards to the hard right, or skip the run entirely. Run successfully, the Washermachine is Class V; unsuccessfully, it's curtains.

Below Washermachine, Class IV waves pound for the next half mile: continuous at 1,500 cfs, four distinct drops at lower levels. With Washermachine behind you, you can catch those surf waves and play holes you missed before. Two ledges end the descent through the picturesque, narrow gorge, best run to the right. The takeout is along the left bank immediately behind the last ledge.

Quechee Gorge is not a run for everyone. It is a calculated risk adventure for experts, with little room for error or for rescue. If you do not feel up to par, or are unsure of your abilities, skip the run and take some pictures instead.

Wardsboro Brook

Wardsboro Brook is a steep-creek run that tumbles alongside Route 100 for four and a half miles through boulder fields and sharp ledge drops. The run is continuous Class III–IV with a mile of demanding Class IV at the end. Unfortunately, the Wardsboro can only be paddled for a few days each year, unless early spring rains lengthen the runoff from the snow melt. The Wardsboro cuts through steep-sided Green Mountain slopes, through conifers and alongside exposed ledges and countless boulders. It is a demanding run that requires sharp eddy turns and good bracing skills through extended sections of turbulence. It is almost always cold when the Wardsboro is up, so dress appropriately.

The most common put-in is near an iron bridge in North Wardsboro (A). There is a fun but sharp ledge just upstream of the bridge; put in above or below it, depending on your mood. It is possible to put in several miles upstream at another bridge in West Wardsboro, although this III–IV section requires even more water than the rest of the run. Recent ice storms have left numerous trees in the river, so keep an especially sharp eye out for strainers. The first take-out (B) is above the final Class IV section at a Route 100 bridge, 3.5 miles below North Wardsboro. The final take-out (C) is found at the confluence of Wardsboro Brook and the West River, where two bridges at Route 100 are found. The gauge is located on the first Route 100 bridge upstream from the confluence with the West River. It has not yet been fully calibrated, although 2.0 is a high level and 1.5 medium-high.

A warm-up section begins the float from Wardsboro past another green iron bridge 1.2 miles downstream. Below this second bridge, the river steepens and heads to the right, away from the road, with some Class III–IV negotiating. Big waves, sneaky holes, and a few pourovers are found through this constricted section. Be wary of boulder sieves as the river cuts through a gravel bar—the channels change from year to year. The 1975 floods washed the Wardsboro through Route 100, requiring modification of the streambed by heavy equipment. Look for a partially submerged island with the most flow on the left. This drop is particularly tight and can be scouted on the left. Knife Edge Rapids appears around the next right-hand bend, a Class IV plummet between two exposed ledges that angle lengthwise with the current. Knife Edge can be seen from the road, so scout this drop beforehand. Class IV negotiating is continuous through cluttered boulders, steep gradient, and strong crosscurrents. A few holes are found through another heavy section just above the Route 100 bridge (B); watch out for a few holes and a three-foot ledge that gets nastier with increases in water levels. There is not much room to maneuver here, as the Wardsboro is less than 30 feet wide, with undercut ledges along the banks creating as much turbulence as the midstream boulders.

The lower section from the Route 100 bridge (B) to the confluence take-out (C) is a bit more demanding than the

Section: North Wardsboro to West River
County: Windham
USGS Quads: Londonderry 15, Saxtons River 15
Difficulty: Class III, IV (IV)
Gradient: 97 feet per mile
Average Width: 30 feet
Velocity: Fast
Rescue Index: Accessible
Hazards: Strainers, changeable riverbed
Scouting: Entire run, from Route 100
Portages: None
Scenery: Pretty to beautiful—Vermont mountain towns and forest
Highlights: Whitewater, scenery
Gauge: Visual only at Route 100 gauge

Runnable Water Levels:	Minimum	Maximum
	0.7	2.5

Months Runnable: March

upper section. The river here is wider, with more slots and more decisions on the best routes to take. The pace is faster and the slots narrower, bank scouting is at times impractical, and downed trees can add a deadly surprise around the next corner. This is a real adventure run if the water is high, so take along only the paddling buddies you trust. You will recognize the toughest drop of this continuous Class IV section when you see a small island, with the main channel on the left. Follow the narrow channel to the left, filled with boulders, ledges, and holes. A large boulder is next on the left, with a tight squeeze to the right of the boulder through yet another boulder maze. This drop is tricky even at runnable levels below 2.0 feet on the gauge. The take-out lies a short distance below here at two Route 100 bridges, just above the confluence with the West River.

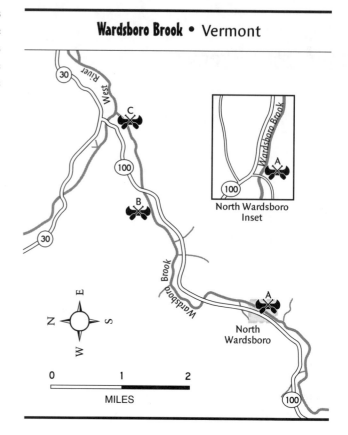

Wardsboro Brook • Vermont

North Wardsboro Inset

North Wardsboro

N E S W

0   1   2
MILES

West River

The West River releases by the New England Army Corps of Engineers are usually scheduled for the last weekend in April and October. Flows during releases range from 1,300 to 2,200 cfs, with Class III negotiating around ledges, boulders, heavy waves, and other boaters. On release weekends in the fall, running the rapids can be less dangerous than running into other boaters thrashing around in the eddies. The river starts off steep and narrow just below the put-in at Ball Mountain Dam, but widens considerably, allowing a good view of the Green Mountain forests and their spectacular fall foliage. A dirt road runs alongside the West, allowing for early exits and easy hiking for that nonboating friend. Scouting is not necessary except for the Dumplings, which look worse than they are. The West is a great run for the budding intermediate to the experienced open-and-closed boater, with several runs possible in one day.

The put-in (A) isn't the easiest but is cheaper than the shuttle provided by enterprising Jamaica State Park rangers in the fall. Vehicle traffic, except for the shuttle, is prohibited from the riverside access road. Take Route 30 north to a right turn onto the access road for the Ball Mountain Dam. Past a maintenance facility, you bear left down a gated road that leads to a gravel parking area next to the spillway of the dam. Carry your boat to the river left side of the dam, where a steep trail leads down to the put-in pool next to the discharge tube. The shuttle leaves from the parking lot at Jamaica State Park and ends at Cobb Brook, from where you can either put in or walk up the access road the remaining one-half mile to the put-in.

The take-out (B) is at Salmon Hole within Jamaica State Park; a cheaper take-out is found just beneath the Jamaica State Park bridge, with parking in a field behind a school.

The first rapid below the dam is a long and continuous wave train, featuring the heaviest water of the run, which frequently swamps tandem open canoes. The end of this rapid features a popular surf wave and sticky side-surf hole; the eddies on both sides of the river are usually full during release weekends. The river widens into a Class III ramble for the next mile, past Cobb Brook on the left, the point where the state park shuttle ends. Two right turns below you will find strong currents and a few pourovers, with a number of great waves for surfing. A left bend with a large pool marks an excellent squirting spot, with a strong eddy line on the right and a cliff face for splattering. Below lie the Dumplings, the most intimidating-looking rapid on the West. For the uninitiated, scouting is best achieved on the left bank. Large, glacial boulders obstruct the current, forcing most of the river to the left. The usual route starts left and heads right into an eddy on the right behind the first doughlike boulder. Stay well away from a poorly padded boulder that obstructs the left channel. There are other interesting variations on this theme, including a slot to the right of the first enormous

Section: Ball Mountain Dam to Jamaica State Park
County: Windham
USGS Quad: Londonderry 15
Difficulty: Class III (IV)
Gradient: 40 feet per mile
Average Width: 60 feet
Velocity: Moderate
Rescue Index: Accessible
Hazards: Overhanging trees
Scouting: Dumplings
Portages: None
Scenery: Beautiful in spots—Green Mountain forest
Highlights: Scenery, play spots, alien river fauna
Gauge: Jamaica State Forest gauge

Runnable Water Levels:	Minimum	Maximum
	1,300 cfs	Flood stage

Months Runnable: During scheduled releases in May through October
Additional Information: Jamaica State Park, (802) 874-4600; Ball Mountain Dam, (802) 874-4881

West River • Vermont

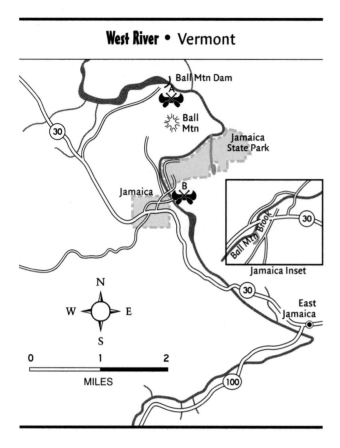

boulder, and a three-foot vertical drop along the right bank. An excellent ender hole lies 100 yards downstream on the right, past a wave train. The eddy below is a real zoo, with strong upstream current and up to 20 boaters jammed together, slam dancing and vying for a shot at an ender or a pirouette. Put that non-paddling friend to work with his camera! More easy negotiating leads around the next right bend into a large hole river center. Surf-a-matic is the best play hole on the river, not as possessive as the surfing hole near the beginning of the run. Surf-a-matic is easily skirted to either side, with easy Class II paddling to the take-out on the left at Salmon Hole, or an eighth of a mile below at the Jamaica State Park bridge.

The West River is more of a social event than a tough day of paddling on the river. Many a frosty meets its end with clubs gathering for a seasonal celebration. There is camping for a fee right at Jamaica State Park, or for free at the Army Corps of Engineers campground alongside the Winhall River. Take Route 30 north to Route 100 north (2.3 miles) and follow another 2.4 miles to a right-hand turn marked by a sign for Winhall Brook Campgrounds. At a fork, stay to the right for just over another mile. In the fall, the Community Church of Jamaica puts on a great supper within walking distance of the state park.

First Branch of the White River

The First Branch of the White River has the steepest gradient in the White watershed and rivals the upper stretches of the Main Branch of the White River for best-scenery awards. The narrow, ledgy stream cuts through prime Vermont farmland, with old Bessie and the goats checking out your descent during early spring runoff. Water levels are critical, and since there is no gauge on the First Branch, eyeballing and correlation to the West Hartford gauge on the White River are necessary. Generally, if there is a reading of 7.6 feet on the West Hartford gauge, the First Branch should be up and running. Scout out the entire run beforehand, as the First Branch is prone to bank washouts and strainers in the streambed.

The put-in for the six-mile paddle is just above the town of Chelsea, next to the Route 110 bridge at the Chelsea Health Center (A). Just above is an unrunnable dam with a deadly keyhole slot that makes running the stretches above unfeasible. The take-out is alongside Route 110 just above an old sawmill dam where the river is close to the road. The river courses among the backyards of downtown Chelsea, through a narrow walled-in section, under another Route 110 bridge, and then south into rolling farmland. Expect Class III for the first half mile, but with a few eddies at high water for catching your breath. The gradient increases through a section of boulders and broken ledges, and a few strainers are found, making for a dangerous maze game. A large tree is marooned on a steep section of ledge another half mile below; again, make sure you scout this run out beforehand! The Class IV part of the trip begins in earnest below, past another Route 110 bridge that spans a brook entering on the right. The river heads away from the road for the next quarter mile through a steep-banked section, into a Z-shaped rapid. Tricky two-foot ledges complicate the first corner; heavy waves and continuous rapids extend for the next half mile past an old bridge pillar, with a few signs of civilization returning. Another brook enters on the right, with a partially submerged island at high water splitting the current just above a hard-left bend. Another series of Class IV ledges follows under one of the many covered bridges along the First Branch and past a sand pit on the left. The take-out is just a tenth of a mile downstream on the right, along a grassy knoll with a dirt road leading down an embankment from Route 110. The sawmill dam is below, a three-foot drop into debris with plenty of opportunities for a bow pin.

While most of the White River watershed is known for its Green Mountain scenery and manageable whitewater, the First Branch offers whitewater enthusiasts a real kick-in-the-pants run at high water levels.

Section: Chelsea Health Center to above Sawmill Dam
County: Orange
USGS Quad: Strafford 15
Difficulty: Class III, IV (IV)
Gradient: 86 feet per mile
Average Width: 25 feet
Velocity: Fast
Rescue Index: Accessible
Hazards: Strainers; steep, constricted drops; dam below take-out
Scouting: Entire run, from Route 110
Portages: None
Scenery: Attractive in spots to pretty—rural Vermont farmland
Highlights: Whitewater, scenery
Gauge: White River West Hartford gauge

Runnable Water Levels:	Minimum	Maximum
	7.6 feet	Undetermined

Months Runnable: March, April, following heavy rains
Additional Information: New England River Forecast Center has the West Hartford gauge reading on the Internet

First Branch of the White River • Vermont

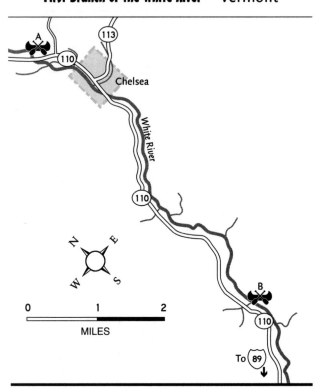

Winhall River

The Winhall River offers one of Vermont's longest continuous whitewater trips with Class III difficulty. Draining Stratton Mountain and its ski area, the Winhall has a short season due to a small watershed. The streambed is obstructed by boulders and ledges, but this river is not nearly as obstructed as nearby Wardsboro Brook. At low levels, the canoeist or covered-craft paddler must negotiate around visible boulders and shelves of bank ledge. At high levels, holes and pourovers must be avoided, and the Winhall has quite a few holes to choose from! One rapid, Londonderry Rapid, must be scouted; the rest of the seven-mile stretch is runnable by open canoes. There is a new gauge on the Route 30 bridge immediately upstream from the intersection of Routes 30 and 100. Unfortunately, at this time there is no information on what levels the markings correspond to.

The put-in is found one mile up a dirt road behind the Grahamville School. The school is one mile west of Bondville on Route 30. The take-out is at the Ball Mountain Dam/Army Corps of Engineers Winhall Brook campgrounds. From the intersection of Routes 30 and 100 in Rawsonville, head north on Route 100. Go two and a half miles to the sign for the Winhall Brook Campgrounds, and turn right. Stay right at the fork: the campgrounds are just over a mile away alongside the Winhall, just above the confluence with the West River.

The first mile from the put-in (A) to the Grahamville School Bridge is an easy Class II–III, and this bridge is another access point for those desiring a shorter trip. The next mile brings more of the same, until the action begins to pick up at the second bridge. The river begins to course through sharper curves and heavier rapids between the second and third (green) highway bridges. A sloping three-foot drop is next, in a left turn within sight of a few homes in Rawsonville, with a clear route down the center. Below another Route 100 bridge, a two-foot ledge drop traverses the stream. An abrupt drop is found on the right, an easier route to the center and the left. A stream enters on the right, with continuous Class II–III to the next bridge, immediately above Londonderry Rapids. An alternative take-out for a shorter trip can be made here, as well as for scouting or portage of Londonderry Rapids below. By far the worst drop on the Winhall, Londonderry Rapids demands Class IV skills through a slot either to the extreme left or right of a vertical four-foot drop. Water levels are critical for this drop, as there has to be sufficient flow to avoid smashing into a broken ledge on either side of the river. The right route is tighter but less technical than the left—which requires negotiation of a sticky hole shortly after the initial drop. If in any doubt, carry around on either side below the first drop. The channel is choked with boulders and ledges and requires more maneuvering than in the section above Londonderry Rapids. Class III returns an eighth of a mile below the drop, with some big waves present at high levels. Take out just above the confluence with the West River, on the right at the Winhall Brook Campground.

Section: Grahamville School Road to Winhall Campgrounds
Counties: Bennington, Windham
USGS Quad: Londonderry 15
Difficulty: Class III (one Class IV drop)
Gradient: 62 feet per mile (100 feet per mile maximum)
Average Width: 25 feet
Velocity: Moderate
Rescue Index: Accessible
Hazards: Strainers, ice shelves
Scouting: Londonderry Rapids
Portages: Londonderry Rapids (optional but recommended)
Scenery: Beautiful in spots—Vermont forest and meadows
Highlights: Whitewater, scenery
Gauge: Rawsonville Route 100 bridge gauge

Runnable Water Levels:	Minimum	Maximum
	NA	NA

Months Runnable: March, April

Winhall River • Vermont

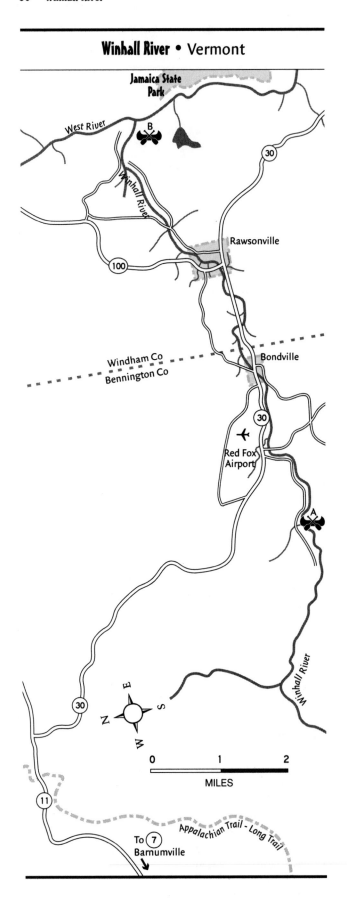

MASSACHUSETTS

Deerfield River

The Deerfield is a fairly extensive watershed that offers natural-flow steep creeking during spring runoff and during the fall hurricane season. It recently has offered extensive dam-released Class II–IV whitewater through the summer months on the Monroe Bridge and Fife Brook sections. Originating in the Green Mountains of Vermont, the Deerfield drains southward into the Connecticut River. The East Branch of the Deerfield drains the slopes of many ski areas along the southern end of Vermont skier's highway, Route 100. While the East Branch is fairly tame, its significant flows join the much steeper West Branch and help it to churn a path through the glacial till of the Berkshires west of Readsboro, Vermont. Below Readsboro, Sherman Reservoir is formed from the impoundment of the first of nine dams to help cool the now-decommissioned Yankee Rowe Nuclear Power Plant, the nation's first commercial nuclear power plant. A mile below, the lower cooling pool is formed by the dam at Monroe Bridge, the put-in for the Monroe Bridge Class II–IV section. Monroe Bridge offers 32 releases between May and October; most on Fridays, Saturdays, and Sundays. When water isn't flowing down the Monroe Bridge section, it travels down a canal and is pumped up the hillside at the Bear Swamp Pumped Storage Project. Evidently, it is economically feasible to pump the water uphill to create more generating head at the Bear Swamp Dam, which returns the Deerfield to its banks for the Class I–III Fife Brook Section, a great beginner's run with over 106 days of releases. The Zoar Gap Rapid (Class III) is the only drop of consequence on that stretch, which is normally concluded at the Route 2 bridge. Slalom gates are strung here, with good squirt lines and splat rocks to keep you entertained. Here you should respect the needs of trout fishermen, as this is a nationally known trout "stream." Excellent dining and entertainment are found in nearby Charlemont; stop in on the way at Zoar Outdoors, a rafting concession and outdoor store along Route 2. The annual Deerfield River festival is held across the street in the large field. Check the FLOW website for exact dates, as flow times and dates may change from year to year.

New England FLOW, a coalition of private and commercial whitewater interests led by Tom Christopher, Bill and Joan Hildreth, and Berkshire AMC chair Norman Sims, are owed huge thanks by the northeastern boating community for negotiating predictable summertime boating flows. A battle of words that started in 1988 and culminated in the landmark 1996 Deerfield River Settlement Agreement has resulted in 32 releases on the Monroe Bridge section and 106 releases on the Fife Brook stretch, and those releases have breathed life back into southern New England summertime boating. American Whitewater, New England FLOW, and the Deerfield River Basin Environmental Enhancement Trust have also been able to set aside 1,800 acres of riverside land, ensuring access along portions of this fettered yet remote watershed.

West Branch of the Deerfield

The Class V–VI West Branch drops over the edge with the help of Prospect Mountain's gradient and several tributaries that bring the levels up surprisingly quickly. Truly a steep-creeking run for experts: big boulders choke down the riverbed, and twisted lines drop over horizon lines into short pools and into the next set of vertical drops. The views from the cockpit resemble the chairlift rides at those upstream Vermont ski areas. This part of the Berkshires looks more like West Virginia than the rest of southern New England.

The put-in for the 3-mile West Branch run is 2.8 miles above the town of Readsboro, Vermont, along Route 100. (From the Monroe Bridge section, head north and turn left in Readsboro). A small bridge and run-down mill marks the spot along a tight gorge. The take-out is in the town of Readsboro at the first bridge on the Monroe Bridge road, just off Route 100. Route 100 keeps you company the entire length of the run; at times the scramble

Section: West Branch of the Deerfield

County: Bennington

USGS Quads: Wilmington (VT); Rowe (MA)

Difficulty: Class V–VI

Gradient: 200+ fpm

Average Width: 30–40 feet

Velocity: Fast, pushy, and centrifugal!

Rescue Index: Accessible but difficult due to stream velocity and boulder congestion. You can leave the river at any point you can catch a riverside eddy.

Hazards: Everything. This is Class V–VI, with the requisite number of pinning situations, ledges, and boulders. Drop above Readsboro has some industrial infrastructure.

Scouting: Everything you can't see

Portages: Everything you don't feel comfortable or capable of running; Tunnel Vision (Class VI)

Scenery: Exceptionally beautiful for roadside boating

Highlights: Rugged Green Mountain topography with quaint New England villages

Gauge: River right gauge rock below High Chair

Runnable Water Levels: Minimum   Maximum
                           1.7   By eye

Months Runnable: March–May after rains and snowmelt; fall hurricane season after heavy rains

Additional Information: Zoar Outdoors, (800) 532-7483; (413) 625-8414 Deerfield River information line

Special Notes: This run is a real hoot! Other creeks, like the Cold River along Route 2, offer somewhat easier thrills, especially if the water levels are high.

West Branch of Deerfield River • Massachusetts

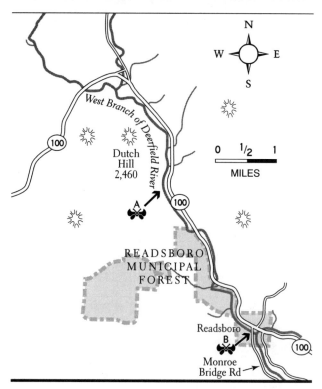

up the bank to the guardrails offers you the best vantage point for scouting.

The action starts right away; play this run a bit conservatively, especially at high flows, when there are few if any eddies to catch. Scout what you can't see, hike what you don't like. The drops are very continuous and congested, snake-lines between boulder scree piled on top of bedrock ledges. The gradient increases steadily, with the difficulty switching back and forth between V and V+ drops. Below the put-in drop and the next mile and half of Class V boogie, you pass under the first Route 100 bridge. Make sure you have control of your boat from here down to the second bridge, which in reality is a giant culvert with the Class VI Tunnel Vision Rapid above. This rapid really screams, and so will you if you don't manage to stay upright—head injuries are a real possibility here. The scout and portage here are along the roadside on river right.

Below Tunnel Vision the road remains on river-left until the take-out. One-third of a mile below Tunnel Vision, a small bridge crossing into a town park comes at a short break in the middle of a long Class IV boulder section. High Chair (Class V) is an old dam site, another third of a mile down from this bridge. High Chair starts off with a seven-foot drop. A 90-degree left-hand turn is required after punching the hole. A short distance later the river cuts back to the right over a sloping ledge with a nasty keeper at the bottom. Paddle hard to punch. Finish this rapid on the right above the next bridge. There is some industrial iron thrown in here for added danger. Low Chair (Class IV+/V) begins immediately below the bridge. Pick up High Chair swimmers very quickly! Low Chair is a steep maze of boulders creating numerous lines, easily scoutable from the bridge. The run ends another third of a mile below in the center of Readsboro, with a multiple ledge drop and boulder garden. The take-out is usually made on river left just below the next bridge.

Monroe Bridge Section, Deerfield River

Nestled in a pocket of Berkshire valley tucked up against the corner of New York State and Vermont, this section of the Deerfield River wasn't even run until the mid 1980s, when dam repairs forced water back down the long-dried-up streambed and past a few of the nine dams

Deerfield River • Massachusetts

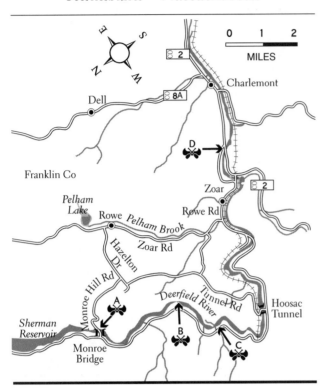

Section: Monroe Bridge

County: Franklin

USGS Quad: Rowe

Difficulty: Class II–IV

Gradient: 60 feet per minute

Average Width: 90–120 feet

Velocity: Moderate to fast at release levels; pushy at levels over 3,000 cfs

Rescue Index: Somewhat inaccessible between put-in and take-out

Hazards: Other boaters, pourovers, rafts

Scouting: Where appropriate; Dragon's Tooth

Portages: None or wherever you don't feel comfortable

Scenery: Exceptional

Highlights: Rural, hilly Berkshire topography with quaint New England villages, decommissioned Yankee Rowe Nuclear Plant, Hoosac Railroad Tunnel

Gauge: New England FLOW, (888) 356-3663

Runnable Water Levels: Minimum   Maximum

                      500 cfs   Unestablished

Months Runnable: Scheduled dam releases May to October

Additional Information: www.kayak.com/kayak/schedule.html; Zoar Outdoors (800) 532-7483

Special Notes: In cooperation with and requested by the Massachusetts State Police, FLOW adds the following phrase to the annual Deerfield River Recreational Whitewater Release Schedule: "As part of a Massachusetts State Police Community Policing initiative, funding has been sought and received to enhance the safety of all persons affected by the Deerfield River use on these release dates. Anticipate local traffic laws being strictly enforced."

that wrestle electricity from its pristine waters. A Class IV gem with scheduled releases and decent flows, it is close to major urban areas—Albany, Boston, Hartford, and New York City. As a direct result of the Deerfield River Settlement Agreement, there are 32 whitewater releases on the Monroe Bridge section between May and October, with most releases falling on the weekends during the summer months, when good whitewater is extremely scarce outside of Maine. The releases are for four hours on Fridays starting at 11 A.M. and on Saturdays for five hours starting at 10 A.M. Sunday releases are four hours long and begin at 10 A.M. Flows vary from 900 to 1,100 cfs. The FLOW web page (http://www.kayak.com/kayak/schedule.html) offers a precise schedule of releases for both the Monroe Bridgesection and the Fife Brook section downstream.

The four-mile Class II–IV Monroe Bridge run starts just below a dam in the village of Monroe Bridge, a quiet New England mill town that now benefits directly from the onslaught of weekend whitewater boater traffic. Unloading is allowed along the roadside at the dam, but continue a short distance up the hill on Monroe Hill Road to a visitor center to park. An alternate put-in is a half mile downstream on river right. Parking for the take-out is at Dunbar Brook Picnic Area; you may drive down to the river to load your boats.

Easy Class II provides a half-mile warm-up to the alternative put-in, where a Class II–III rock garden begins. Watch out for heavy raft and boater traffic; several rafting companies have permits here, and since it's often the only whitewater game in the summer, it gets a bit crowded (a la the West River releases in Vermont).

The river bends to the left through Atom Splitter (named for the Yankee Rowe nuclear plant upstream). Atom Splitter is a Class III+ with a large rock that splits the flow into routes on either side. Finish up by following the main flow back into the center of the river, with a pourover in the tree shadows at bottom left. Shallow ledges predominate the next quarter mile into Boneyard, a Class III drop run left of center at the top and again back to the center at the bottom. A pool leads into Funky Move (Class II+), with the funkiness on the right down a chute over a small ledge. To avoid all forms of funky behavior (except that of your boating buddies), opt for the left side.

Next is Dunbar Brook Rapid, the first technical rapid on the run. Large boulders offer plenty of eddy-hopping and chutes to spice up your playtime. False Tooth is next, named because the next rapid, Dragon's Tooth, has some consequence. False Tooth has a neat setup to the left or right of the dominant boulder at the top, a move to avoid a pourover top left and slot move down the right between two boulders.

Dragon's Tooth is scouted on the left from the tip of a gravel island. It's a Class IV- drop with a big-water feel, and most boaters start left, avoiding the Dragon's Tooth rock and hole on the right, and then work right away from the funny water that dances with the boulder shoreline on the left below. A fairly long rapid, this one has some nice waves, a few holes, and few places you don't want to be.

A pool below offers a brief respite before Labyrinth, another Class IV- rapid. The lower the impounding lake below, the better the rapid, as there are a few holes at the bottom. This one is the most technical rapid on the Monroe Bridge section, with numerous options down through house- and car-sized boulders. In general, start right center, heading back to left center, working your way down a number of boulder slots and boiling eddies. Watch out for a hole half way down (it's half way down when the lake is low!), with the normal line to the right of the hole. Finish up with a few more technical lines down to the lake, and take out on river right. A paved road is found at the top of a talus slope, a one-half-mile walk in the country back to the Dunbar Brook Picnic Area and the cooler in your snazzy shuttle vehicle.

Fife Brook Section

This is a great predictable beginner run that almost always has water, thanks to over 100 releases between May and October. If your group has a few paddlers who aren't quite up to the Monroe Bridge section, take them down the Fife Brook run after you have finished your playtime in the rapids above. Take River Road toward the town of Zoar. Shortly below the Fife Brook Dam, take a very sharp left turn onto a dirt road, which leads down to the river-right put-in. The take-out is on river left just below Zoar Gap next to the bridge. For a longer trip , you can continue onto the Shunpike rest area along Route 2, where the Deerfield leaves the forest and enters the pastoral Mohawk Trail Valley near Charlemont.

Section: Fife Brook
County: Franklin
USGS Quad: Rowe
Difficulty: Class I–II (III)
Gradient: 25 feet per mile
Average Width: 40–50 yards
Velocity: Slow
Rescue Index: Remote
Hazards: Strainers, other boaters
Scouting: Zoar Gap Rapid
Portages: Zoar Gap Rapid for rank beginners
Scenery: Sylvan
Highlights: Rural, hilly Berkshire topography with quaint New England villages, decommissioned Yankee Rowe Nuclear Plant
Gauge: New England FLOW, (888) 356-3663)

Runnable Water Levels:	Minimum:	Maximum:
	Release levels offer 700 cfs, min.	Unestablished

Months Runnable: Most. Predictable releases run April–October
Additional Information: New England FLOW, http://www.kayak.com/kayak/schedule.html, (888) 356-3663); Zoar Outdoors, (800) 532-7483
Special Notes: In cooperation with the Massachusetts Police, FLOW adds the following to the annual Deerfield River Recreational Whitewater Release Schedule: "As part of a Massachusetts State Police Community Policing initiative, funding has been sought and received to enhance the safety of all persons affected by the Deerfield River use on these release dates. Anticipate local traffic laws being strictly enforced." Hoosuc Tunnel, a five mile railroad tunnel with a 1000 foot ventilation shaft is nearby.

Past the put-in the river meanders over four miles down Class I riffles and Class II challenges. Osprey are often visible along this stretch, diving and dining on brook and rainbow trout. The only rapid of consequence, Zoar Gap, is a Class III drop with a ledge and a few boulders and slalom gates to negotiate. Scout this one along the railroad tracks on river left. Below Zoar Gap the pace slows, trees begin to overhang the banks and you will probably spot at least one trout fishermen wading in felt soled shoes to catch those big lunker trout hiding in the deep pools.

Farmington River

Upper Farmington Section

The Upper Farmington section, also known as the New Boston section of the Farmington River, is a pushy Class IV run at high water, five feet and above on the New Boston gauge. At levels below four feet two inches, it is a bottom-scraping run, and your chances of pinning on small boulders are great. You can leave behind plenty of polyethylene and fiberglass at the lower, fall release levels from Otis Reservoir; recent dam renovations have further reduced the cfs output of the tubes. The fall release (usually two weekends in October) may no longer be worthwhile unless you want to watch other people destroy their boats.

The Upper Farmington is not a run to be taken lightly in high water, when the rapids blend together; many of the boulders that were obstacles at lower levels become pourovers above seven feet. Some of the ledges wash out, but other drops turn into snarls of turbulence. The river is pushy, the water is cold, and hypothermia is a real danger if someone in your party swims.

You can scout nearly the entire run from the drive north to the put-in at the Tolland State Forest bridge, three miles above the take-out (B) at the Route 8 bridge in New Boston. Route 8 plays companion with the Upper Farmington for the entire run. Although it may detract from the "wilderness experience" one might expect with a river as scenic and steep as this, it's nice to have easy access for rescuers and for swimmers who—on a cold March afternoon—decide they have had enough of the river.

The best time to run this stretch is when it is flooding in the Berkshires. Above seven feet, the river washes out a bit; trees present obstacles along the banks, a few pourovers are found, and reaction waves are created by the ledgy banks and the gradient. Some rather large holes are found above five feet, when there is enough water to make the rocks obstacles instead of hindrances. The gauge is on the Internet and can be accessed through the New England River Forecast Center or the USGS. It is hard to locate on foot, downstream of the take-out in Berkshire County, a third of a mile below the confluence of the Clam River.

The put-in (A) is usually a dynamic snowbank launch just above the Tolland State Forest iron bridge, with swift current leading into a patch of Class III boulders. There are plenty of eddies with which to warm up your flexibility, needed for the twisting channel of the Upper Farmington. A sharp two-foot ledge lies 100 yards downstream in the midst of the racecourse section, best run to either side in low water. The high-water route here cuts down through the center. The river tumbles continuously through most of the run, the boulders and ledges are too numerous for us to describe each drop. The first "named" rapid, Decoration Rock, appears after another 100-yard section of boulders and surfing waves. It sits a boat-length off the right bank, adorned with Kevlar, fiberglass and aluminum. The standard route is usually to the right of the rock over a small abrupt ledge. Running to the left is possible but tighter, especially at the low levels that characterize the fall releases. At levels above five feet, Decoration Rock is padded, making it a great place for a splat in a squirt boat.

Around a right bend is a ledge for hole surfing. The clear shot past is on river left, down a slanting three-foot shallow ledge. Here the Foster Grants or the Vuarnets come in handy, because the sun flattens out the surface with glare. The river approaches Route 8 again, then turns sharply to the left over another three-foot ledge, easily punchable in the center. Continuous Class III rock gardens lead into the big finale, Corkscrew. A concrete bridge piling and a stone wall mark the entrance of this rapid, and scouting is possible from the right bank. Corkscrew is deceptive, a series of diagonal ledges that converge in the center, with several more hydraulics waiting behind. At five feet it is very pushy: the direct route is down the center, using your bracing skills to stay upright.

The final half mile to the take-out in New Boston is considered Class III, with a few play spots and dynamic

Section: Tolland State Forest bridge to New Boston Route 8 bridge

Counties: Berkshire, Hampden

USGS Quads: Otis, Tolland Center

Difficulty: Class III–IV (IV+ in high water)

Gradient: 75 feet per mile (100 feet per mile maximum)

Average Width: 30 feet

Velocity: Fast

Rescue Index: Accessible

Hazards: Strainers, constricted riverbed, continuous whitewater

Scouting: Corkscrew, remainder of the run from Route B

Portages: None

Scenery: Beautiful in spots—twisting road, forest, and river

Highlights: Whitewater, scenery

Gauge: West Branch Farmington at New Boston

Runnable Water Levels:　　Minimum　　Maximum
　　　　　　　　　　　　　3.7 feet　　Flood stage

Months Runnable: March, April, and October race releases

Additional Information: Boston AMC, (781) 433-7108

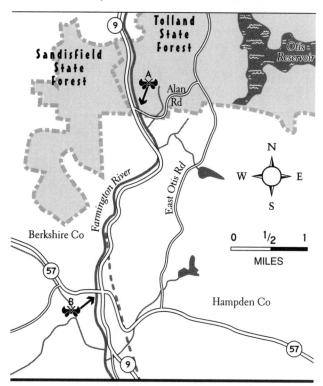

Farmington River • Massachusetts

eddies for squirt boaters. At high water, squirt boaters would feel right at home, but at lower levels even the plastic boaters grimace. During the fall release, for a small fee, you can park in a field rented by the local chapter of the AMC next to the American Legion hall a few hundred yards below the Route 8 bridge. On nonrelease days there are roadside pull-offs slightly farther south along Route 8. To avoid annoying the locals please do not take out at the Route 8 bridge in the center of New Boston. Local merchants like your business, but not the traffic and parking problems that boaters bring to the take-out. Check with the store owner for the best place to park, as the site often changes from year to year.

Hubbard Brook

Its tight chutes have attracted adventurous swimmers and divers since the turn of the century: local boys dared each other into leaps from granite cliffs into the deep cold pools. Folks on an outing from the big cities of Springfield, Pittsfield, and Hartford dangled their toes in the fast-running stream and slid down moss-covered waterfalls, wearing out the seats of their britches.

Nowadays, we bring recycled-milk-bottle boats, a drysuit, and a smile to this southwestern Massachusetts gem, just minutes from the Connecticut border and the closed (Metropolitan District Commission) Barkhamstead watershed. We leave behind little, save a few polyethelene rinds, and gain a new perspective on what "steep" means in this corner of southern New England. Though they initially passed over this run as being too steep, at over 300 feet per mile at the take-out, whitewater enthusiasts looking for a little "pump" now await the National Weather Service forecast alert "There are flood warnings in the Berkshires," which usually coincides with spring runoff, the hurricane season, and strong summertime thunderstorms. If nearby Sandy Brook and the New Boston section of the Farmington are up, so is the Hubbard—but get there quickly!

The put-in is at a bridge and turnout along Route 57 just over seven miles east of the town of New Boston, where the Class III–IV Upper Farmington section is found. The take-out is on Route 20 along the Connecticut border; the shortest route is through Granville State Park to Route 20, turning left and continuing for two and half miles until you cross Hubbard Brook. A parking area is on river left next to the gauging station. A note of caution: the park rangers put up with kayakers in Granville State Park, but the MDC folks are a bit hard-core. Take out well above the Route 20 bridge, as, technically, the MDC owns the land (which is posted) 40 yards above the bridge and all the way downstream into Barkhamstead Reservoir, the drinking water supply for the Hartford area. Good relations here will help us keep access open to this steepwater gem.

The run starts out with an innocuous 60 feet per mile gradient above and within the confines of Granville State Park. A meandering course starts off under the first bridge, where if there's enough water to clean the drop, there's enough water to do the run. Congested volcanic talus and granite boulder gardens dominate the initial two miles, giving way to a few pools and then a ledgy granite good-to-the-last-drop experience. Outside of a few bar-be-cue pits and tent sites, there are few signs of man's incursion here, making your excursion a bonafide wilderness experience. There's also the safety of a river-left trail that keeps you company from the Granville State Park bridge all the way to the take-out. This run is akin to Massachusetts Cold River, the West Branch of the Westfield, and the upper West Branch of the Deerfield.

At the Granville State Park bridge, a channelized drop is found after a sharp left turn. This technical twister drops six feet and is a good test for those unsure whether they want to continue. The next eighth of a mile is a boulder fest, easier than the initial Bridge Rapid, a 20-yard-wide stretch with few eddies and always the possibility of a strainer or two.

A large boulder on river left marks Seven Foot Falls, a clean drop scouted on the right. A short walk up river right makes this one an easy-to-repeat thrill. If you are having problems here, head back to your car via the park road on river right.

Civilization, mild gradient, and calm interludes are left behind as the drops get technical, a Class IV rubble rumble down to Nose Pin. A clean approach and a boof move over a four-foot ledge into a boulder pile here avoids a nosebleed; this is a particularly shallow drop. More Class IV leads into Bump and Grind Slide, a sloping 30-foot-long shallow bottom planer.

Double Drop, a series of abrupt and relatively clean ledges, marks one of the more beautiful stretches on the river. The gradient here is really noticeable as you boof each river-wide ledge into a short pool. Conifers define the edges of this 30-yard-wide stretch to The Big One.

Section: Route 57 bridge to Route 20 Bridge

County: Hampden

USGS Quad: Southwick (MA/CT)

Difficulty: Class IV–V (The Big One, V-; S-Turn, V)

Gradient: 300 feet per mile maximum

Average Width: 60–90 feet

Velocity: Fast and pushy, technical and steep

Rescue Index: Accessible but difficult, depending on snow level

Hazards: Watch for trees, ice dams

Scouting: The Big One

Portages: None

Scenery: Beautiful stretches

Highlights: Whitewater

Gauge: Visual (stick gauge)

Runnable Water Level: Minimum   Maximum
                         3.5   Undetermined

Months Runnable: February–April with heavy rain or snowmelt; hurricane season

Additional Information: A better gauge is to look at the put-in rocks: if there is enough to float under the bridge, there's enough to paddle the Hubbard.

Special Notes: Access river by maintained trail between

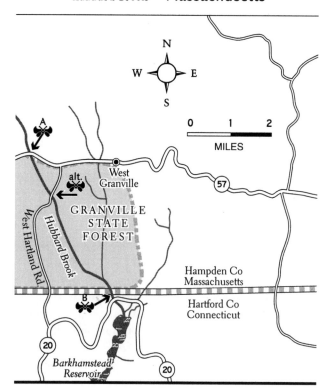

Hubbard Brook • Massachusetts

The Big One, Class V for danger rather than technical difficulty, channelizes the entire stream flow down to a five-foot-wide slot up against a house-sized boulder on river right. If you are not careful, you will run this one unintentionally: grab the eddy on a gravel bar on river left above the lip. The total drop is about 20 feet, the first 8 down a vertical slot onto a shallow, carved riverbed that shoots up roostertails around you. It's an awesome sight as you exit the lip and see nothing but foam and your paddling buddies yards below you. Stay upright unless you plan on joining Ichabod Crane on his moonlit horseback rides through the Berkshires.

The run is not over by any means as the gradient tilts up another notch for the last boulder-filled technical bop to the take-out. Probably the most technical stretch on the run, Outer Limits never lets up—each drop is steeper than the last. You will easily see the 300 feet per mile

gradient here, culminating in S-Turn, Class V for technicality, a screwy set of must-make moves that end in a short pool on river left above a four-foot concrete dam. This dam marks the end of legal boating, with a few more tantalizing technical falls down to the bridge. Take out above the dam to avoid hassling with the drinking water detectives.

The Granville General Store is only a few miles away, a haven for cheddar cheese, maple syrup, and apple aficionados. Reminiscent of the way life used to be in New England, this store is a "must see" for you and those non-paddling friends that want a weekend in the country.

When you need to turn it up a notch and it's flooding time in the Berkshires, yell "Oh, Mother Hubbard!" and get out of the cupboard to get your share of (cheddar) curds and (granite) whey!

Quaboag River

The Quaboag River is a favorite early-season run for New England boaters despite its poor water quality and semi-urban scenery. The Quaboag contains three Class IV rapids at medium levels (5.5 feet on the West Brimfield gauge), with most of the run becoming Class IV at high levels (above 6.0 feet). Scouting the five-and-a-half-mile run is difficult from the shuttle. If you are a newcomer, there are two mandatory scouts at the Mouse Hole and Trestle Rapids, a couple of broken dams to run, and one dam that must be portaged. The Quaboag has a long season due to a system of lakes upstream that buffer the effects of short droughts and heavy rainfall in the late spring and fall. For open boaters, the Quaboag is exciting from 4.4 feet; closed boaters look for levels above 5.5 feet for the best adrenaline pump. At high levels, the river becomes a bit pushy, but there are fewer obstacles to dodge. At medium levels, the rocks grow out of the waves and holes and make the going more technical. At levels lower than 4.2 feet, only the artful dodger will emerge with his hull unscathed.

The put-in (A) is at the Lucy Stone Park in Warren, a half mile north of Warren Center off River Road. The take-out (B) is along Route 67 at one of several roadside turnouts above West Brimfield and the Massachusetts Turnpike.

A chute begins the trip at Lucy Stone Park: a short drop on the left brings you down below the bridge and past another gauge on the left. This gauge correlates roughly with the West Brimfield gauge, which lies below the take-out. The New Hampshire–based Merrimack Valley Paddlers keeps track of this gauge through a network of spotters. Class II continues below the park to the Route 67 bridge in Warren, with a few ledges and larger waves below the first railroad bridge. Mouse Hole Rapids is next, deserving a scout on the right for the uninitiated. Mouse Hole is a broached dam with a bad strainer-sluice-way on the left, where most of the current goes. On the right lies a narrow but runnable slot through two concrete pillars. The slot is three feet wide, with a three-foot

drop into a hole and backwave . . . not the place to be sideways or upside down looking for trout! Below Mouse Hole a wave train leads into another, easier ledgedrop under a secondary road bridge. A railroad bridge (the second of the trip) signals Trestle Rapids, another 75-yard section worthy of scouting. Don't scout from the train trestle; two paddlers attempting to scout the drop were hit and killed by a train. A few routes exist through a series of ledges, boulders, and heavy waves. The chicken route is along the right bank; the hero route involves a short drop on either side of the trestle, moving left into the main current, with plenty of waves, rocks, and a few surprise holes near the bottom of the rapid.

Section: Lucy Stone Park in Warren to Route 67
Counties: Worcester, Hampden
USGS Quad: Warren
Difficulty: Class II–IV (IV in high water)
Gradient: 30 feet per mile (85 feet per mile maximum)
Average Width: 60 feet
Velocity: Moderate
Rescue Index: Accessible
Hazards: Dam strainer at Mouse Hole, unrunnable dam, water quality
Scouting: Mouse Hole Rapids, Trestle Rapids
Portages: Unrunnable dam
Scenery: Poor to uninspiring
Highlights: Whitewater
Gauge: West Brimfield gauge

Runnable Water Levels:	Minimum	Maximum
	3.9 feet	6.5 feet

Months Runnable: February through June, heavy rainfalls
Special Notes: It holds water well. Easy access to Massachusetts Turnpike; it's the only New England river with a permanent outhouse overhanging its banks, so bring your nose clips.

A runnable broken dam follows on the right, with Class II–III waves leading into a rocky rumble to either side of an island. A pool follows with an unrunnable 15-foot dam. The mandatory carry is on the right (quite a grunt), up, around, and down the concrete structure. Class II, then III, rock-dodging leads past another railroad bridge and a small island. Another broken dam, this one a three-footer, follows, runnable on the extreme left of two pillars. At high water, take the time to check out this slot before making the plunge. Angel Field Rapids begins after two more bridges with three- to four-foot waves that present a problem for unwary open boaters. A sewage treatment plant follows, adding more than cfs to the Quaboag. Devil's Gorge begins after the next railroad bridge–island combination, and at high levels the three distinct rapids flow together into a Class IV experience. The take-out is three-quarters of a mile downstream on the right, alongside Route 67.

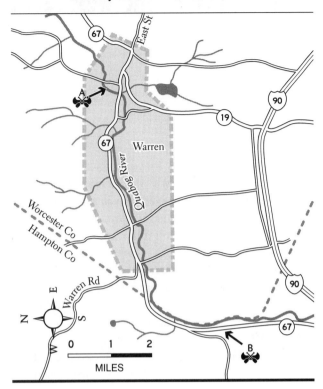

Quaboag River • Massachusetts

West Branch of the Westfield River

The West Branch of the Westfield River flows out of Becket into a deep, steep-walled canyon that winds well away from towns, gas stations, and even roads. The West Branch is a narrow, ledgy river full of surprises. If there is a mishap, only the river and the railroad along its banks offer access for rescuers. The railroad adds a touch of nostalgia to the adventure; the engineers are friendly and will slow down to watch you play among the broken ledges and overhanging trees. The canyon is a haven for wildlife: deer, raccoon, and a variety of feathered predators are on the prowl for a meal. The Mahkeenac Indians fished these waters before settlers expanded west from Boston, and angling for trout is still rewarding today.

The top section, from Becket to Bancroft (A–B), is steeper and more technical than the paddle from Bancroft to Chester (B–C). The first portion offers an average gradient of 80 feet per mile, with sections over 100 feet per mile. The West Branch is a whitewater sleigh ride with a big-water feel in a small streambed, with deflection waves forming off the buttresses of the many railroad bridges that cross the river. The top put-in (A) lies in the town of Becket, off Route 20. Turn right onto High Street, go past a bridge over the narrow West Branch, and over the railroad tracks to a dirt road on the right, which leads down to the river. The take-out for the first section and the put-in for the second (B) lies in Bancroft. Take Route 20, north from Chester, 2.2 miles to Bancroft Road on the right. Three and a half miles later, what's left of Bancroft appears at a bridge next to an abandoned mill. The take-out in Chester (C) is on Route 20 near the Chester Inn. The Boston and Maine Railroad crosses the West Branch of the Westfield 13 times during the trip. Only two roads, one in Bancroft and the other downstream above Chester (to Middlefield), span the river.

The float from Becket begins with Class III+/IV passages through boulders and numerous ledges. After the sixth railroad bridge (about three miles), eddy out on the left onto a flat rock and scout the drop below. The river pours over a five-foot ledge into a pool, with a submerged rock at the bottom of the drop. To avoid "crashing and burning" during the first third of the trip to Chester, head to the right when you take on this ledge. Two ledges below, another fierce drop rattles your ankle bones—a tight, boulder-choked chute that demands plenty of artful dodging. The next danger spot to look for is a log dam, which can be run if you know where. Scout from the left: the high-water route is on the left side; the low-water route is in the center. Have someone downstream line you up so that you hit the water instead of the debris below. Class IV ledges and waves continue the tumble to Bancroft, the first nonrailroad bridge you encounter.

Below Bancroft (B) expect more of the same drop-pool-type rapids as above, with some rather sticky holes mixed in to keep you on your toes. The first half of this section contains the best action, with an island less than a mile below Bancroft creating two technical channels.

Section: Becket to Chester
Counties: Berkshire, Hampshire
USGS Quads: Chester, Becket
Difficulty: Class III–IV (IV+ in high water)
Gradient: 66 feet per mile (100 feet per mile maximum)
Average Width: 40 feet
Velocity: Moderate to fast
Rescue Index: Inaccessible
Hazards: Dams, strainers, steep drops
Scouting: Second ledge drop, log dam
Portages: Log dam [optional]
Scenery: Beautiful to exceptionally beautiful—wilderness, wildlife
Gauge: Huntington gauge (visual only)
Highlights: Scenery, whitewater, wildlife

Runnable Water Levels:	Minimum	Maximum
	3.0 feet	Flood stage

Months Runnable: March, April, after heavy rains

West Branch of the Westfield River • Massachusetts

The cleanest route is down the right side, with a rock garden and then a few tense moments as the river careens off a rock wall on the right, with a pool downstream to collect your bearings.

Narrow canyon walls again constrict the river, with Class III+ ledge-running continuing past another railroad bridge until yet another railroad span approaches on river right. Double Ledge, two tightly packed drops totaling four feet, block the river—runnable at medium flows in the center. If you are on the West Branch at higher flows (five feet five inches and above), scout this drop. The second, larger drop contains a bad hydraulic. The railroad bridge spans the river at the far end of this pool, with easier, less continuous going until just above the Middlefield Road bridge, the second highway bridge of the entire run. A heavier rapid follows for a quarter mile, then it's Class II–III to the take-out at the first bridge in Chester, just off Route 20 near the Chester Inn.

North Branch of the Westfield River

The North Branch of the Westfield, from the Knightville Dam to Huntington, sports the largest riverbed and longest season of the Westfield watershed. Easier than the two sections described on the West Branch of the Westfield, the North Branch flows more gently through farmland, settled areas, and wooded gorge sections. The North Branch grows in volume due to the addition of flows from the Middle Branch and the West Branch during the last half of the run. Dam releases extend the season of the North Branch below Knightville Dam into May. There is a downriver race every April that attracts both novice and world class boaters. This section is an excellent paddle for intermediates and for clubs looking for a training run.

The put-in (A) lies just below Knightville Dam at a birch-lined picnic area. A dam access road is found north of the intersection of Routes 66 and 112, off Route 112. The 5.2-mile run ends in Huntington at a roadside picnic area on Route 20, just below the confluence of the West Branch.

Wide Class III rapids begin in earnest just below the dam, over a runnable, river-wide, two-foot ledge 75 yards below the put-in. They continue for the next mile. A minor gorge follows, cutting through columns of vertical strata with a beautiful deep pool and few signs of civilization. Two shorter rapids follow the pool; the first slides 40 yards down angled ledges into a smaller pool. The second drop is the heaviest of the trip—Class III, with narrow slots to negotiate between an exposed ledge in the center and the steep banks along the sides. A two-foot drop with a backwave can be expected at levels above 4.5 feet. Large waves form below at higher levels; if you are unsure, scout this plunge from either bank.

The Middle Branch of the Westfield enters downstream on the right, adding considerably to the volume of the river. Past the next bridge the gradient picks up, cutting through a Class III boulder patch. These two continuous rock dodges can be seen from Route 112, with roadside Sunday tourists wondering to themselves why anyone would be on the river on a cold, rainy April afternoon.

A Route 112 bridge follows, a possible early take-out site. Class II rapids continue for another mile past a railroad bridge above the confluence of the West Branch and the North Branch, forming the main Westfield River. The take-out is three-quarters of a mile below, at a picnic area on the right, alongside Route 20 in Huntington.

Three other sections of the North Branch of the Westfield River are commonly run. A six-mile stretch for beginners starts at the Berkshire Snow Basin Ski Area on Route 9 and finishes at an iron bridge on Route 9 south of Cummington. From the Cummington access point, heavy whitewater and flatwater stretches combine for 7.2 miles to a bridge at the intersection of Route 143 and Mount Road, just above the Chesterfield Gorge. Use this access point for the third section of Class I, II, and III (Chesterfield Gorge) that ends 9.2 miles later at the Knightville Dam. A dirt road leads from Route 112 into the pond above the dam, approaching from river right.

Section: Knightville Dam to Huntington
County: Hampshire
USGS Quads: Westhampton, Woronoco
Difficulty: Class II–III (III+ in high water)
Gradient: 17 feet per mile (45 feet per mile maximum)
Average Width: 100 feet
Velocity: Moderate
Rescue Index: Accessible
Hazards: Wide riverbed
Scouting: None
Portages: None
Scenery: Pretty in spots to pretty
Highlights: Whitewater, scenery
Gauge: Knightville Dam gauge (visual only)

Runnable Water Levels:	Minimum	Maximum
	4.0 feet	Flood stage

Months Runnable: March–May (affected by dam release)
Special Notes: Longest season of any Westfield watershed section

North Branch of the Westfield River • Massachusetts

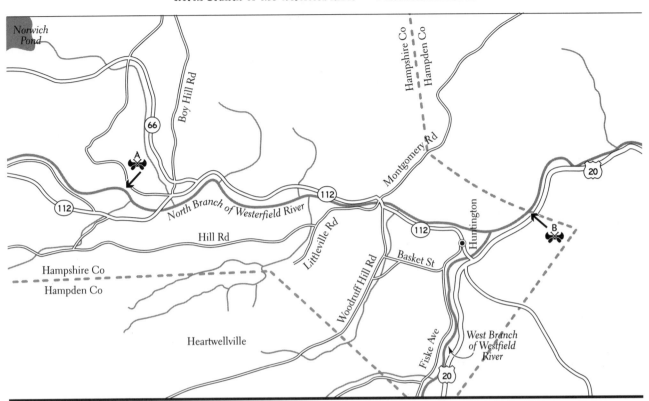

CONNECTICUT

Farmington River

Tariffville Gorge Section

The essence of Tariffville Gorge on the Farmington River is its utility. You can paddle here 12 months of the year; it rarely ices over, and there is a constant supply of dam-fed water from the Hogback Reservoir farther upstream. In the spring, running "the Gorge," as it is known locally, is akin to big-water western boating: a strong, pushy current; bank-full conditions; deflection waves from faulted volcanic canyon walls; big holes; and waves that, at the right levels, resemble those of New England's ultimate play river, the Kennebec River Gorge. At levels above 4.5 feet on the gauge (upstream of the put-in on river right), some holes wash out; others form and develop a taste for roto-molded sandwiches. A swim at high water above the dam is reason for concern, as a terminal hydraulic forms below the partially broached concrete weir.

Most boaters have experienced Tariffville Gorge at medium and low levels; below 2.0 feet, when even the Upper Hole is tamable, aluminum canoes can sometimes escape unscathed.

The put-in (A) can serve as the take-out as well—if you are short a car and would rather run the tougher sections a few times instead of hassling with setting up a shuttle to run another half mile of scratchy Class II above the gorge. The put-in from Route 189 is off Route 187 east toward East Granby. Go over the river and take your first right (Spoonville Road), then an immediate right again onto Tunxis Avenue. Follow to a dead end, passing under a set of high-voltage power lines, where you may want to stop and scout out the dam. At the dead end, a path to the left leads downstream to the beach and the hole section; another path leads upstream to the put-in on river left. You can leave your car here for the take-out, or park it at the dam (B) or under the Route 187 bridge (C). Put in as high as you can walk up the left bank, and then paddle upstream using the rocks and current to your advantage. The gauge is just below an outstanding surfing spot in high water, Cathy's Wave. This wave is often paddled when the levels are too high for playing through the gorge

section immediately below. Past two Class III ledges the river bends to the right, and the gradient becomes noticeable. High overhead, to the left, hikers are often perched 100 feet atop a basalt cliff, energetically waving at you to sacrifice yourself to the river! Here a rough volcanic ledge against the right bank creates a turbulent eddy, with a snaggletooth rock that forces you to make the eddy lower than you would have anticipated. A series of eddies follows. A wave train leads into the Bridge Abutments, which lie to the left and right center. The main route through this section is against the right bank, through standing waves and away from the series of four concrete blocks that acts as a strainer. The abutments are all that is left of a highway bridge, swept away by the 1955 flood, that once connected Granby to Tariffville.

Section: Tariffville Gorge
Counties: Hartford
USGS Quad: Tariffville
Difficulty: Class II–IV
Gradient: 40 feet per mile
Average Width: 50 feet
Velocity: Moderate
Rescue Index: Accessible
Hazards: Bridge abutments; Dam and slalom gate wires at high water
Scouting: Hole section, Dam
Portages: Dam (optional)
Scenery: Beautiful in spots
Highlights: Whitewater, scenery
Gauge: Tunxis Avenue Tariffville gauge

Runnable Water Levels:	Minimum	Maximum
	1.0 feet	Flood stage (except Dam)

Months Runnable: All
Additional Information: Boston AMC River Phone Line, (781) 433-7108
Special Notes: Section runs year-round due to dam release.

Tariffville Gorge, Farmington River.
Photo by John Porterfield.

The Hole section lies an eighth of a mile below, after a section of Class II and quickwater. Starting from the top, there is a series of two-foot ledges on the right that become progressively steeper and gradually encroach on the width of the river by the end of the 75-yard section. A third of the way into this section, the Top Hole offers great surfing and major-league consequences if you roll or swim. The Upper Hole is immediately below, usually very sticky and adept at separating you from your boat. Below lies the Lower Hole, where on a hot Sunday afternoon you can find the local paddlers hand surfing, twirling paddles, squirting, doing rotendos, and juggling beach stones. For a no-heroics run through the Hole section, stay to the left. At a large pool below the Hole section, T-ville Beach offers a great place to relax: bring the wife and kids or party with your friends. The drops below the beach are a constant source of entertainment because of the many tubers (river test probes) and a regional canoe club hung up on whistles and clipboards. Aluminum canoes often meet their end below the pool, wrapped beyond recognition around a section of ledge to the left center below the first two-foot drop. The safest route is down the left side, but there are also tighter routes down

the center and far right over this section of multiple ledge drops. A couple of ledges follow, great squirt spots, then a large pool created by the backwater from the partially broached dam below. The Dam—which has become unstable in recent years and has seen a clean up effort by the local hydro company—can be portaged or scouted from the left bank. The low water route is generally run right center, aiming for the highest mound and into the eddy on the right below. The Dam has been run through the slot as high as six feet, and two river crazies ran over the top of the Dam on the right side at 8.5 feet. One had a clean run, the other broke both ankles: clearly, this is no place to mess around in high water!

Two sections of the Dam were blown out by the same flood that wiped out the bridge farther upstream. One chunk of the remains, Car Rock, creates a nasty pourover (at levels above 2.7 feet) immediately behind the wave train, below the drop through the Dam. Another larger section, Aircraft Carrier, creates its own set of hydraulics above four feet. Avoid the left side of the slot over the Dam. It may look inviting, but it is shallow and there is plenty of rebar and jagged concrete to rip open the bottom of your boat.

A training course with some tricky currents lies down the first channel to the left, below the Dam. Watch for an eddy wall on the right where another channel enters—the remnants of an old stone wall from the days when the dam just upstream was intact. It is not unusual to find U.S. team racers training in this section, often at night with spotlights rigged to car batteries. There is a take-out here, or a quarter mile downstream on the left, just upstream of the Route 187 bridge.

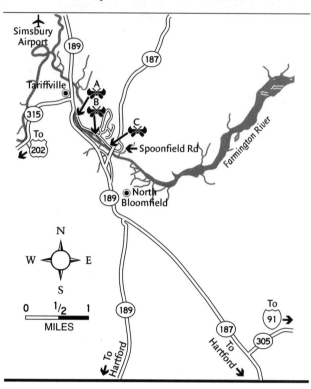

Farmington River • Connecticut

Housatonic River

Bulls Bridge Section

Early spring brings big water to the Nutmeg State at Bulls Bridge, a nearly three-mile section of the Housatonic River south of Kent. From the Staircase to Powerhouse Rapids, "the Bull" kicks up to Class V butt at gauge levels over 7 feet. The top section, the Staircase, has been run above 7.8 feet, with the remaining drops below over 8 feet, but runs at those levels are not generally recommended. It is possible to run this section as low as 1.6 feet when summertime releases from the Falls Village Hydro Station reach the Bulls Bridge section about seven o'clock at night. Be wary, however, of gauge readings: at times all of the water is diverted through a generating canal and is discharged at a power plant just above the gauging station.

The put-in is five miles south of Kent on Route 7 in southwestern Connecticut. Henry Kissinger calls Kent home, upsetting blueberry-picking residents by posting his land, which includes a traditional berry patch. Turn west at the traffic light opposite the Bulls Bridge Inn, and pass through one of Connecticut's few remaining covered bridges. Park where the local authorities have yet to post No Parking signs. The take-out is 2.25 miles south on Route 7 at the second roadside turnout, just below the discharge tubes and gauging station.

It is best to scout the top sections at the put-in, as the geology here is full of potholes and carved kettleholes big enough to swallow your boat. A network of paths leads upstream to the Staircase and downstream to the Funnel. A bridge over Dead Horse Gulch leads to the Funnel. Dead Horse Gulch is an ugly affair that lends considerable volume to the river just above the Funnel, slamming into and over a pile of debris that make a run through its teeth improbable.

There is no warm-up if you decide to run the Staircase, which starts in a pool and plunges 25 feet through eroded kettleholes, boulders, and sharp ledges. Most boaters that run the Staircase start left and work their way right, missing a couple of pourovers at the bottom. Stay in your boat, as the Funnel is just around the corner.

A narrow gorge opens below the covered bridge, with Dead Horse Gulch pumping in plenty of cfs as you work your way right, over to the tongue. The current pushes you left, but you want to be river right, to line up with the wave train that leads into the only tongue down the 10-foot drop. Big-water phenomena follows, with strong eddy lines, shifting waves, holes, swirlies, and occasionally logs. A large eddy below is useful when your paddling buddies decide to have a yard sale.

The Housatonic bends into S-Turn rapids a half mile below the Funnel. This river-wide ledge must be run hard left, as a nearly river-wide pourover lurks below the horizon line, large enough to swallow your shuttle vehicle. Scout from river left on the cliff above the drop: from here both S-Turn and Pencil Sharpener can be seen. The

Section: Bulls Bridge
County: Litchfield
USGS Quads: Kent (CT), Dover Plains (NY)
Difficulty: Class IV (V in high water)
Gradient: 40 feet per mile (100 feet per mile maximum)
Average Width: 100 feet
Velocity: Fast to sluggish in spots
Rescue Index: Accessible to accessible but difficult
Hazards: Difficult drops, strainers, keeper hydraulics
Scouting: All major drops
Portages: None
Scenery: Pretty to beautiful in spots—unusually rugged for Connecticut
Highlights: Whitewater, scenery, local history
Gauge: Gaylordsville gauge

Runnable Water Level:	Minimum	Maximum
	1.7 feet	8.0 feet

Months Runnable: February through April, summer evening releases
Additional Information: Clarke Outdoors in Sharon, (860) 672-6365; Boston AMC River Phone Line, (781) 433-7108 (or 7108); Waterline, (800) 945-3376

Housatonic River • Connecticut

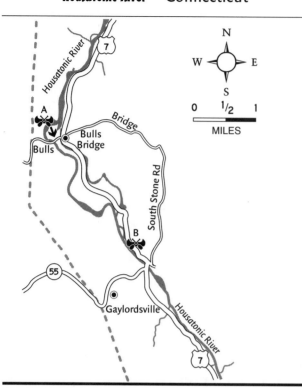

Pencil Sharpener is the downstream point of a series of 40-foot-long wave holes at high water, ledge holes below levels of seven feet. Avoid hitting the V-shaped hole at the bottom right by working your way left above the hole—but not too far left, as a series of pourovers guard the left side of the river.

Powerhouse Rapids comes next, in a hard-right corner one mile below the Ten Mile River confluence on river right. A large hole lies left-center—rotendo city for the unabashed. A less exacting ender spot offers a face-saving alternative as well.

One drop is left between you and that cooler of refreshments at the take-out, just below the Gaylordsville USGS gauge on river left. A sticky boulder-ledge drop lies on river left, with the normal route down the wave train on river right. The take-out is on the left shore at a pebble beach alongside Route 7.

Bulls Bridge, when the water is there, is southern New England's technical equivalent to the Ottawa, albeit a shorter version. After you have run it once at high water, expect your stomach to tighten involuntarily the next time the bull busts loose in south-central Connecticut.

Falls Village Hydro to Swifts Bridge

The Housatonic River from Falls Village to Swifts Bridge offers boaters a chance to hone their whitewater skills on Class II–III whitewater. There is one Class IV high-water pitch just below the covered bridge below West Cornwall, where an annual slalom and downriver race are held. This section of the Housatonic has a long season for southern New England; water releases from the Falls Village Hydro Station add 400 cfs to an otherwise unrunnable natural flow during the late spring and early summer. Typically, there are water releases on Saturdays, and occasionally on Sundays beginning at noontime. Check with Clarke Outdoors, a river outfitter in West Cornwall on Route 7, for water levels.

The Housatonic is wide, the gradient gentle, and the current not nearly as pushy as the Bulls Bridge section farther downstream. "Housatonic" is an Indian name meaning "river beyond the mountains." It cuts through the Berkshires, alongside the Taconic Range to the west in New York State, and through the Litchfield Hills towards Long Island Sound. For interesting glimpses of the river beyond the mountains in days past, read *Boating Trips on New England Rivers*, a chronicle written more than 100 years ago by Henry Parker Fellows.

The Housatonic is steeped in history. A signer of the Declaration of Independence, Roger Sherman, was born downstream along the banks in Milford. Below the West Cornwall put-in, a number of Indian missions thrived in the 1800s until the red man was forced to cash in and move on. A foreign missionary school was founded in Cornwall between 1816 and 1827, with pupils both from surrounding Indian tribes and from as far away as New Zealand attending. Above the Falls Village put-in, there was a gristmill established as early as 1740, with the first bridge to span the Housatonic built alongside it in 1744.

The longest trip is from Falls Village (A) to Swifts Bridge (D), a 13.5-mile trip that begins with a Class III section followed by easier water until the Covered Bridge Rapids in West Cornwall. The put-in is found in the town of Falls Village, across a bridge from the Falls Village Hydro Station. The take-out is in the town of Cornwall Bridge at a training site for local racers. From Route 7 south, turn left onto a local paved road just upstream of the Route 7 concrete highway bridge. Continue past a few farms; the road will change to dirt and then intersect with Swifts Bridge Road. A turnout here serves as the take-out.

The put-in for the shorter, five-mile cruise is off Route 7, in a field one mile north of the West Cornwall covered bridge (B). Take-out (C) is at the Lower Housatonic Mead-

Section: Falls Village Hydro to Swifts Bridge

County: Litchfield

USGS Quads: South Canaan, Sharon, Cornwall, Elleworth

Difficulty: Class II–III (one IV drop in high water)

Gradient: 12 feet per mile

Average Width: 100 feet

Velocity: Sluggish to moderate

Rescue Index: Accessible

Hazards: None

Scouting: Covered Bridge Rapid

Portages: None

Scenery: Pretty to beautiful—colonial Litchfield Hills

Highlights: Scenery, history, whitewater

Gauge: Visual

Runnable Water Levels:

	Minimum	Maximum
	400 cfs	Flood stage

Months Runnable: March through June, dam releases

Additional Information: Clarke Outdoors in Sharon, (860) 672-6365; Boston AMC River Phone Line, (781) 433-7108; Waterline, (800) 945-3376; Gauge Information Fax Line, (800) 945-3375

Special Notes: Camping at Lower Housatonic Meadows State Park and at Macedonia Brook State Park; historical information at Cornwall Historical Society

ows State Park, also on Route 7. Some quickwater and Class II leads into the Class III (IV) Covered Bridge Rapids just below the red covered bridge. Scouting is easiest from the left bank upstream of the bridge. A grabby hole, well practiced in eating canoes at high water, lies against the right bank just under the bridge. A section of three-foot standing waves and a few eddies are interspersed through the quarter-mile section, and a large boulder with a boat magnet in it lurks two-thirds of the way down on the left. The chicken route through the left side takes advantage of a ballroom-sized eddy behind the center bridge pillar, with the best route to the center below.

The river bends sharply to the right around an almost vertical slope, the glacial remnants of the last ice age. The river widens around this bend, notched into the steeply wooded slopes of the Litchfield Hills. A Class III ledge spans the river a few hundred yards downstream; the best route is through a slot, right center. Class II and III paddling continues for the next three miles to the take-out (C)—interesting enough to keep you busy, but not so demanding that the scenery cannot be viewed. There are some quickwater and calmer sections that in the fall reflect the changing hues of the autumn foliage

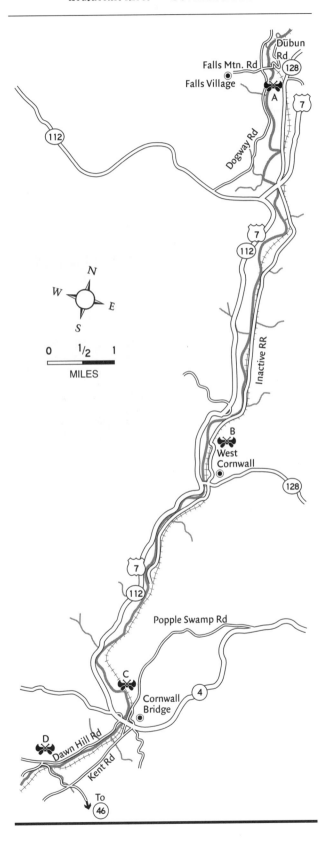

Housatonic River • Connecticut

from the river surface. The water looks clean and smells clean, but industrial pollution farther upstream has contaminated it with PCBs, so do not eat the fish.

The take-out (C) at the Lower Housatonic Meadows follows a section of Class II that includes some house-sized boulders. The river winds away from the road, then back to the right again. You will see smoke from the charcoal grills, smell steaks sizzling, and instantly wish that you had remembered to pack the picnic gear for the trip's end.

You can elect to lengthen your voyage another mile to Swifts Bridge (D), where there is a good section of Class III with three- to four-foot standing waves. At Swifts Bridge, the river bends to the right and then left again over a section of ledge, with some newly placed boulders making the upstream paddle easier here for racer training. Heavy equipment was used to improve this section for year-round training by former Olympians and up-and-coming racers. The take-out is on the right, with minor boulder-climbing to the parking area.

Carved kettleholes frame Bill Adamson's descent of Staircase Rapid on the Bulls Bridge section of the Housatonic River. Photo by Jim Michaud.

Natchaug River

The Natchaug River is a short but intense Class IV drop-pool river in eastern Connecticut, easily reached off Interstate 86. Although the tough section is less than a mile long, the river is worthy of paddling because of its 120-feet-per mile gradient, including a number of runnable waterfall-type drops that challenge the accomplished boater. A nice spot for a picnic, with plenty of play spots, the Natchaug River has clear, clean water and evergreen-covered ledges that keep the senses satisfied. The Natchaug provides drinking water for the Mansfield Reservoir farther downstream and is stocked annually with trout.

The normal take-out is at Diana's Pool (B), a favorite swimming hole and party spot for University of Connecticut students. Parking is quite limited, although when the Natchaug is running at an adequate level you are unlikely to face competition for parking spaces except from other boaters. Local folklore includes tales of a fair maiden, Diana, running from the Indians, plunging herself in desperation over the short falls to be claimed by the river gods in a rocky pool. You may not find Diana's ghost swimming around at the bottom of one of the many holes, but you will see plenty of mermaid-like coeds along the banks. If you want to extend your trip through some progressively easier rapids and quickwater, set up your shuttle farther downstream at the Bassett's Bridge Road bridge (C). Bassett's Bridge Road is found at the intersection of Routes 6 and 203. The extended trip adds two hours and three miles to the top section.

At present there is no gauge on the Natchaug; however, all of the major drops are easily scouted after only a short walk from the take-out (B). The Natchaug is unlike other Connecticut rivers in that its steep-walled gorge section holds water well and does not let it escape into the trees. During non-traditional runoff periods, it takes an inch of rain to bring the Natchaug up to minimum levels. Unfortunately, the Natchaug's watershed does not hold water very long, and the run is usually down again within two days without additional precipitation.

The put-in is one mile north of the take-out off Route 198 (A). Take the next right above Diana's Pool onto England Road, go over the bridge, and park on the left. The river is fairly quiet here, with some quickwater and Class II surfing waves. The river is narrow, about 25 feet wide, and ledges create the turbulence for the next quarter mile. Watch out for strainers along this stretch, as spring rains loosen the sandy eastern Connecticut topsoil and trees topple into the river. Diana's Ledges come into view around a sharp right bend in the river, with an island and large house-sized boulders constricting the channel at the top. You can scout Mousetrap, the top drop, from the island, or beforehand, from the left shore. There are two routes through Mousetrap. The chicken route heads left of a large boulder on the right, over a three-foot sloping ledge into a small hole. The hero route is to the right of the boulder, but stay hard left (against the side of the

Section: England Road to Bassett's Bridge Road
County: Tolland
USGS Quads: Spring Hill, Hampton
Difficulty: Class IV (IV+)
Gradient: 27 feet per mile (120 feet per mile maximum)
Average Width: 25 feet
Velocity: Fast and pushy
Rescue Index: Accessible
Hazards: Strainers, pinning situations
Scouting: Entire top section
Portages: None
Scenery: Pretty in spots
Highlights: Scenery, whitewater, history
Gauge: None

Runnable Water Levels:	Minimum	Maximum
	NA	NA

Months Runnable: March, April, and following heavy rains
Additional Information: Mansfield State Park, (860) 455-9057

rock) to avoid bow-pinning at the bottom of this four-foot vertical drop. Small ledge drops follow for 50 yards into the setup for Cow Sluice, a five-foot sloping falls. There are eddies at either side of this plunge, and the best route is just to the right of the mound in the center of the slot. Converging currents attempt to roll you to the left as you head over the edge (avoid an undercut ledge hole on the bottom left). Diana's Pool follows, and just in time, allowing paddlers a deserved breather and a gander at the scenery.

The ledge section is next, as the Natchaug enters a short, steep-walled gorge. Above the first of the three tricky ledge drops is a fairly sticky hole with high-penalty surfing. Angle perpendicular to the current for the first two ledges, and avoid yet another hole in between. Each drop is about two feet high, and the holes at the bottom of each are sticky.

Eddies are scarce between the second and third ledge, making the setup for this particularly bad drop difficult. The third ledge is heavily angled toward the left bank, with the left side the easiest to punch. In high water, a poorly pillowed rock creates a nasty hole on the left just below the ledge. Michaud's Hole is undercut into the cliff face on the left, so try to stay out of this aquatic adventure. At high levels, it is possible to boof the last ledge on the right over Tombstone Rock.

The intensity of the Natchaug diminishes rapidly below this last drop, with a set of great surfing waves and a benign hole just above the take-out on the left (B). Most boaters elect to carry their boat a quarter mile back up

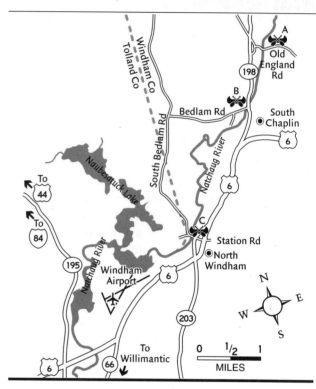

Natchaug River • Connecticut

the left bank to run the tough section again, or you can continue another three miles downstream to (C).

The water is clean, the drops are exciting, and the access easy—just a few factors that make the Natchaug a favorite with Nutmeg State paddlers.

Roaring Brook

Roaring Brook is a scenic three-mile-long, recently discovered Class IV gem about eight miles southeast of Hartford, running through the heart of Cotton Hollow Nature Preserve and containing about a dozen significant rapids. Take-out is easy at a river-left parking lot about 10 yards upstream of where Route 17 crosses Roaring Brook in South Glastonbury, near the intersection of Routes 17 and 16Q. The brook, which de-ices earlier than most of its New England counterparts, runs east to west, starting in East Glastonbury. Topo maps indicate that Roaring Brook has an approximate 100 foot per mile gradient between action's start and the end of Limbo Rapid, sandwiched by brief warm-up and cool-down periods.

There are two put-ins for Roaring Brook, depending on ice conditions on the ponds above the run's first two waterfalls and/or the boater's appetite for waterfalls. The first put-in at Coldbrook Road (off Hopewell Road) gives one some quickwater and pond paddling (don't shorten this stretch by putting in at the Woodland Street bridge, since there's no place to legally park your vehicle there) to a horizon line indicating the start of Roaring Brook's action, a 13-foot, runnable, perpendicular waterfall best scouted from river left. This "waterfall" is actually a runnable dam at the western end of Brainard Pond. Regarding the dam, one might wonder if a paddler designed it; there is an approximately 10-foot-wide notch in the middle of the dam and a pipe sticking out of the water about 15 feet above the dam's lip lining you up for the launching point. A sloping boulder formation on river left allows for multiple runs by making it easy to carry back up to the pond; it also allows for easy portage.

Class III water separates Roaring Brook's two waterfalls, with one significant drop marked by a horizon line above a right-to-left turn in the brook: this drop is best run down the center. Nearly one-third of the way to the end of the brook is a river-left factory alongside a runnable nine-foot perpendicular dam/waterfall. The bottom of this dam is stuffed with dangerous debris, and there's a difficult river-right passage through the debris.

Scouting and/or portaging from river right is strongly recommended. The outflow from the factory's dam is a tricky rapid that ends at the Matson Hill Road bridge, which has two hand-painted gauges on it. The gauges don't match; for unknown reasons, local boaters prefer the river-right gauge. One foot on the river-right gauge is the lowest runnable level for Roaring Brook.

The second put-in is around 50–100 yards below the Matson Hill Road bridge. This marks the steepest section of the brook, where Roaring Brook starts roaring with Poolside Rapid, a loud, tumultuous slide which gets repeatedly scouted even by those who have boated this section often. Poolside's arrival is obvious, with a community pool on the river-right bank (which has a convenient parking lot for use at the second put-in and a tight

Section: Coldbrook Road to Route 17
County: Hartford
USGS Quad: Glastonbury
Difficulty: Class IV
Gradient: 65 feet per mile (150 feet per mile maximum for 0.6 mile)
Average Width: 35 feet
Velocity: Fast
Rescue Index: Nature Preserve Trail from Poolside to take-out
Hazards: Logjam at factory dam, Rodney Rock, Limbo Log; downed trees
Scouting: Horizon lines
Portages: Factory dam
Scenery: Pretty to beautiful
Highlights: Whitewater, scenery, history
Gauge: River right gauge on Matson Hill Road Bridge
Runnable Water Levels: Minimum   Maximum
                            Unestablished   Unestablished
Months Runnable: February to April after rain with snowmelt, after heavy rains
Additional Information: Salmon River correlation

river-right entry caused by stones coming in from river left from a former dam. Whichever bank you scout from, it's important to take account of the Rodney Rock, a submerged table rock extending out from the right shore, creating an apparently hospitable deflection wave that isn't what it appears. Boats with ample rocker and properly positioned occupants have come to screaming halts when hitting this seemingly innocent wave; some ankles haven't been so lucky.

The next named rapid is O'Brien's Corkscrew, marked by a blind horizon line (scout from the river-left rock formation) where the entire brook tumbles over a tight ledge left to right, burrowing into a cliff, immediately thereafter moving right to left into a kettlehole. Any swimmers in Corkscrew are lucky to have a pool below with a sizable river-left eddy, but they need to keep in mind it's a moving pool with nastiness at its end in the form of Double Drop Rapid. At levels below 1.5 feet, the undercut right side of Double Drop's top center boulder comes into play. At levels above 1.5 feet, the left side of that top center boulder contains a hole that has involuntarily surfed numerous capable boaters in a mini-box canyon.

Three Class III–IV rapids separate Double Drop and Limbo: feel free to scout these, as they are not self-evident from boat level, especially the second one, a.k.a. the Slide Limbo Rapid, which is preceded by the river-right stone remnants of a Civil War gunpowder factory. It's Roaring Brook's last rapid and warrants mention because of the large log that led to this rapid's name. The log is suspended from a river-central island all the way to the brook's right bank. At levels above 1.75 feet, a channel opens up left of the island for uncomplicated passage. At lower levels, things get interesting here, and every boater needs to make his/her own decision: "Is there enough air under that log for me and my boat?" If you decide to go for it, you'll have to adhere to your boat's deck, and don't capsize, since it's shallow and rocky. Glastonbury residents request that all would-be lumberjacks leave Limbo Log untouched, since they use it as a bridge.

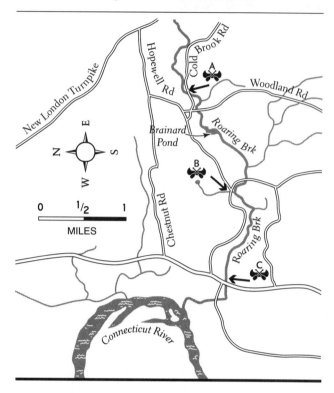

For those who can't easily access Roaring Brook's hand-painted gauge, the best correlate for water levels is the Salmon River, which is on the Internet under the Connecticut River watershed (see appendix). For Roaring Brook to be high enough to boat, the Salmon needs to be running at least 600 cfs. The highest runnable level has not yet been established, but three feet on the gauge is a highly pushy level on this brook, which already has a relative paucity of eddies below Poolside. Paddling on Roaring Brook at lower levels has the advantage of affording the boater an opportunity to see some truly beautiful scenery surprisingly close to a sizable metropolitan area; at high water, one will miss much of the beauty of this nature preserve.

Sandy Brook

Sandy Brook is Connecticut's premier steep-creek run, a boulder-choked technical descent that even with moderate flows has that big-water feel. There are two awesome drops at the start of the whitewater section, the Waterfall and the Block, which turn into Class V religious experiences at high levels. The run has been successfully negotiated at flood levels by a strong team of experts who were intimately familiar with the Sandy—and scared as hell during the run! Sandy Brook is a real punisher in high water: steep, continuous, nonstop dodging, with scarce eddies to boat-scout from. There are usually more boaters starting the run on the Sandy than actually finishing it. Sandy Brook Road runs mostly unobserved alongside the river, so those who would rather drink than get dunked can make an early exit.

The Sandy unfortunately has a short paddling season, runnable usually when there is still snow in the woods. When the weatherman says it's flooding in the Berkshires, Sandy Brook is up, although it won't stay up for long. Because the riverbed drains so quickly, if you're not paddling in a rainstorm you need to be very quick to catch it at a runnable level. The Sandy also comes up in the fall during the hurricane season.

The top put-in (A) off Route 183 is advantageous for a couple of reasons. It gives you a chance to warm up on a Class II meander through the countryside; and it allows access to the top drop, the Waterfall. The Waterfall is a Class IV (V) tumble over a two-stage ledge that really cranks up the adrenaline. Scout from river right, catch the tongue right-center, and aim to the left. At high water, the route is up to you, either down the drop or across the rocks on the bank! Below a small pool, the roller coaster continues with big waves, plenty of rocks and few eddies. A series of ledges drops into the set-up for the Block, the most difficult rapid on the Sandy. Make sure you scout this drop, either from the shuttle to the put-in, or from shore during your run. The Block obstructs the channel from the center of the river, the Sandy's flow splits off a poorly padded rock face, and the

left chute is usually clogged with debris. So plot your route down the sharp, twisting, four-foot drop on the right.

A pool below offers an alternate put-in (B), especially at levels above five feet. Continuous Class IV with four- and five-foot waves follows under two bridges, through nonstop boulder gardens with plenty of holes and gradient. Past the second bridge the river bends sharply left, then sharply right—a perfect Z-turn. Z-turn Rapids include the biggest and meanest hole on the river, commanding most of the left side, with the mandatory sneak route against the right bank. Another large hole on the left follows around the next bend. Stay left and punch this one instead of becoming a Sandy salad, strained through a nasty boulder sieve on the right. Through another left bend, the Sandy twists and drops through a steep boulder patch. The boulders here are huge, with the best route splitting the two largest granite chunks in the

Section: Route 183 bridge to Route 8 bridge
County: Litchfield
USGS Quads: South Sandisfield, Tolland, Winsted
Difficulty: Class IV (V in high water)
Gradient: 80 feet per mile (110 feet per mile maximum)
Average Width: 30 feet
Velocity: Fast and pushy
Rescue Index: Accessible
Hazards: Continuous whitewater, strainers, pinning spots
Scouting: Top two major drops
Portages: None (or all!)
Scenery: Pretty to beautiful in spots—rural Connecticut
Highlights: Whitewater, scenery
Gauge: Sandy Brook Road bridge gauge

Runnable Water Levels:	Minimum	Maximum
	1 foot	undetermined

Months Runnable: February, March, after heavy rains

center of the river. Class IV maneuvering continues under a third bridge as the Sandy's nonstop pace finally diminishes. Watch for blowdowns along the more eroded stretches of riverbank. The take-out is beyond the fourth Sandy Brook Road bridge, past an island on the downstream side of the first Route 8 bridge. If you look upstream of the Route 8 bridge, you will see a flat rock with two horizontal lines on it, both marked "OK." If the river level is at or above the lower of these lines, there is enough water for a run. There is now an improvised gauge replacing the one lost with the reconstruction of the Route 8 bridge. It is a steel yardstick fastened to a strip of wood on the downstream, river-right side of a bridge on Sandy Brook Road, 3.2 miles up from the take-out. It is not yet fully calibrated, although 1 inch is a very scratchy minimum level.

There is camping nearby at both People's State Forest and the American Legion Forest in Riverton. You will find great sandwiches in Riverton at the General Store, and you can consume them while scouting out the Class V drop in the Still River Gorge, two miles east of the Sandy take-out on the road to Riverton. Among nearby rivers likely to be up at the same time as the Sandy, Hubbard Brook is more difficult, while the Upper Farmington along Route 8 in New Boston is somewhat easier.

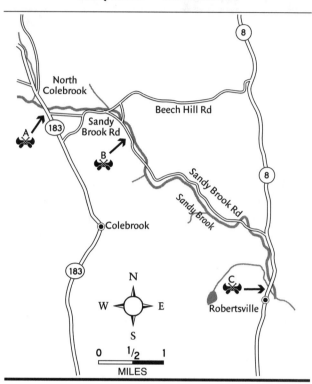

Sandy Brook • Connecticut

NEW YORK

Black River

While the scenery on the Black River in Jefferson County, New York, may be schizophrenic, the big-volume, drop-pool nature of the rapids is consistent throughout the seven-and-a-half-mile paddle. Starting off in downtown Watertown, mill buildings, city bridges, and urban-associated pollution create a bleak backdrop for the first half of the paddle. Once past the city limits, the scenery changes dramatically, as the river enters a narrow, secluded canyon where great blue herons, cedar waxwings, and even a pair of bald eagles have been spotted. All signs of the city are gone: deer are often seen watering along the banks, and barred owls hoot majestically from lofty perches.

The water quality of the Black, long tainted by the first of New York State's paper mills, has improved dramatically in recent years. This has allowed successful stocking of trout and salmon in the river. The Black is now considered a Class B waterway, which means you can safely swim, eat the fish, and drink the water after treating it.

The Black's unusually long season is its best selling point. It runs during the summer from mid-May to mid-October, when most other northeastern streams have dried up for the year. The Black is too high to be run during the normal spring season; a necessary portage around a 30-foot falls is difficult. Fed through a system of water-control dams that provide an average daily flow of 1,200 cfs, average water levels during the summer range from 1,200 to 2,000 cfs, well within the Class IV range for this run. Water levels may fluctuate several times during a trip, but there is usually enough water within a few minutes to continue downstream. The minimum level for the run is 944 cfs (2.6 feet on the Van Deuzee Street bridge gauge); the maximum is 5,500 cfs (5.3 feet). Because of the abundance of water and the difficulty of the rapids, the Black is rafted commercially throughout the summer.

The upper section above Glen Park Falls is anything but straightforward. Ledges jut at weird angles, holes can hold rafts and hard boats indefinitely, and sight lines are obscured, requiring bank-scouting of the major drops. Below Glen Park Falls, undercut limestone cliffs line the lower gorge section, adding real danger to an otherwise classic whitewater run. The rapids in the lower stretch are continuous, with standing waves, holes, eddies, and readable whitewater. The Black is a run for the confident and experienced boater who understands his abilities and limitations.

The put-in (A) is at Adirondack River Outfitters clubhouse on 140 Newell Street in Watertown. Parking is tight at times, so inquire at the raft company as to the best place to leave your vehicle. The take-out (B) is on Fish Island, a public boat access point in Dexter. An alternate take-out can be made at the Brownville Bridge, but the climb is steep, the land is private, and the safety of your vehicle is in question.

Club House Turn lies just below the put-in, a 50-yard Class III warm-up with a big eddy on the right. Burn's Wall is next, another Class III wave train a quarter mile below. The first major rapid is a mile downstream: Hole Brothers features a fun ledge-surfing hole, a forgiving foam-filled workout. Three-quarters of a mile of swiftwater and a mile of uphill paddling lead to the next test, the Class IV+ Knife's Edge.

Knife's Edge Rapid is a nearly river-wide series of three ledges, the last ledge being the actual Knife's Edge. Take out river left and scout. Under your feet are an interesting mix of fossilized shells, trilobytes, and other sea creatures of millenniums past; don't overload your boat with booty! The best route is to run left center, over a three-foot ledge, then ideally off the corner of the Heater, a v-shaped ledge on the left, and avoiding Merry's Hole on the right. Too far left and you are into the Heater (a diagonal hole that burrows into the cliff face), or too far right and you won't be feeling very merry (Merry's Hole is a horseshoe-shaped keeper). At high water (over 4,000 cfs) there is a sneak down the right side. Shaw's Wall is below, an undercut limestone rock face with strong current that urges you to get a little bit closer.

Another Class II pool backs up to the dam at Glen Park Falls, the next big drop on the Black. The Falls are a 30-foot cascade with a plume at the bottom. Carry river right down an obvious trail or scout on river left. A dam at the top right here dewaters the gorge below the falls, with the water returning to the streambed at the Wailing Wall. Glen Park Falls has been run regularly at levels around 4,000 cfs, and up to 5,000 cfs by boaters on the edge. Scout from the left edge of the dam: the main flow drops over three ledges, with the current bouncing off a wall on the right at the bottom into a recirculating eddy on the left. Impressions of the Tidy Bowl Man are seen here on a frequent basis, as it is difficult to exit this eddy without a bit of speed and initiative.

The gorge below is usually dewatered unless you politely ask the damkeeper to turn on the water for you (no kidding). A flow of 4,000 cfs is a great level; flows under 1,100 cfs are a bit too scratchy for fun. The gorge feels like a rain forest paradise due in part to problems with water seeping out of the diversion canal above. Hundreds of waterfalls on river right keep the environment moist, epouring from horizontal faults between light-colored limestone plates in the cliffs.

The sights, sounds, and smells of the city are replaced by an isolated wilderness setting. Three Rocks Rapid is first, scoutable from the portage put-in. Class III–IV turbulence tumbles through two huge boulders that become pourovers above 3,000 cfs. Zig Zag is next, two distinct rapids with big waves and strong eddy lines. A large recirculating eddy (Fossil Eddy) lies on the right above Zag. Zag features Panic Rock, which pillows most of the current off its face. Big waves and a few pourovers lead into a hard-left turn, where The Cruncher is found. Below 2,000 cfs, The Cruncher is a violent, sticky window-shading hole that becomes more possessive as the water level drops. At higher levels, The Cruncher becomes an exploding wave. A huge eddy is found just downstream, a place for picking up the pieces. Hadrian's Wall is next, a 10-foot vertical dam face runnable as "the rocket ride" at levels above 2,000 cfs. Hadrian's Wall must be portaged to the left below that level. The Poopchute, a broached section of dam to the right of Hadrian's Wall, is another story. Conservatively rated a Class V drop, the Poopchute is a violent encounter with underwater forces of the third kind. Boaters have been known to run the Poopchute regularly, surfacing 25 yards downstream in the middle of the next rapid.

Wailing Wall Rapid lies above the Wailing Wall, so named because a raft full of customers once was stuffed into a large undercut in the cliff face—luckily without injury. The river's diverted flow returns below this rapid

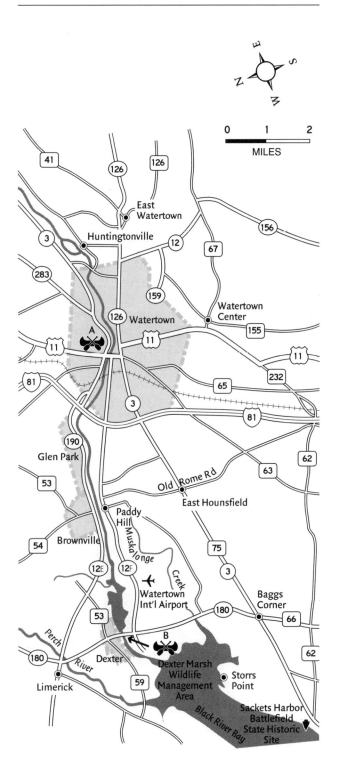

Black River • New York

on river right. With flows through the gorge, this rapid is run on the right over a few ledge drops, then back to the left of a big rock down the third chute. The Wailing Wall is on the right as the river bends to the left. Common sense should keep you out of the main force of the current that slams into the wall.

Tall Rock Gorge, the most beautiful section of the trip, follows another set of standing waves. Cedar trees line the steep banks, birds are evident everywhere, and in the late afternoon an orange light pervades the canyon, creating a peaceful setting. Less demanding Class II rapids, Square Rock and Shave-and-a-Haircut, allow for extended glimpses of the impressive sights within the narrow, forested walls. Brownsville Bridge follows, with a risky take-out; then there's a mile and a half of flatwater (oh, no!) to the Fish Island take-out in Dexter. The island is to the right of a series of dams that span channels on the left side of the river.

The Black is usually a three-and-a-half-hour trip, with plenty of time included to scout the major drops. Undercuts are part of the paddling experience of the limestone-laden Black, so be sure of your line and your roll when on this river.

Section: 140 Newell Street, Watertown, to Fish Island, Dexter
County: Jefferson
USGS Quads: Watertown, Dexter
Difficulty: Class IV (V in high water)
Gradient: 28 feet per mile
Average Width: 140 feet
Velocity: Fast to sluggish
Rescue Index: Accessible to accessible but difficult
Hazards: Undercut rocks, scarcity of eddies, waterfalls
Scouting: Knife's Edge, Lower Gorge section
Portages: Glen Park Falls, Hadrian's Wall/Poopchute
Scenery: Urban, uninspiring to beautiful
Highlights: Whitewater, history, geology, wildlife
Gauge: Van Deuzee Street bridge gauge, waterline gauge code 361158

Runnable Water Levels:	Minimum	Maximum
	2.6 feet	5.3 feet
	(944 cfs)	(5,500 cfs)

Months Runnable: May through late October
Additional Information: Adirondack River Outfitters, (315) 788-1311

Dave Barbour off his line on the Knife's Edge, Black River. Photo by Michael A. Gross.

Boreas River

The Boreas River within the Adirondack Park contains one of the more continuous sections of Class IV whitewater in the Northeast. A narrow river filled with boulders and ledges, the Boreas tumbles into the larger Hudson River at an average gradient of 45 feet per mile, with the more difficult midsection dropping 90 feet per mile. The upper section has several steep pitches, including a runnable eight-foot waterfall. Sections of quietwater allow enjoyment of the wild and narrow valley. The sole intrusion is the railroad paralleling the river from Vanderwacker Brook to the Hudson confluence. Cedar and balsam fir compete for sunlight on the banks, while birds and squirrels live where humans are rare intruders.

The Boreas begins on the south slopes of Mt. Marcy, filling several small ponds in soggy flats that buffer the Boreas by storing snowmelt and heavy rainfall. Boreas water levels are difficult to check. The Hudson River gauge in North Creek records combined flow and may miss localized conditions. A 7.0-foot North Creek reading is considered minimum flowage. The Northwoods Club Road bridge that serves as a take-out after the steeper middle section or a put-in for the lower section has a hand-painted gauge. Parking is available. The bridge is four miles west of 28N, and half of the drive is on gravel that may be impassable in early spring. Levels over one foot are considered runnable. Maximum flows have not been determined, but high water drowns eddies and turns larger boulders into pourovers. Low levels take their toll in boat pins and breakage.

The put-in (A) for the Boreas's upper section is five miles south of Boreas Road, NY Route 2, on NY 28N. An old paved-road section southeast of the bridge leads to a campsite, parking, and river access. Rocks at the bridge show six inches above water when the Northwoods Club Road gauge reads 1.5 feet. The river is too low to run when rocks are showing at the put-in.

A calm stretch from the bridge allows warm-up before a sharp left turn into the first set of rapids. The riverbed becomes crowded with medium-sized rocks and ledges where quick maneuvering through offset corners is required. A chute follows with a vertical drop, setting the tone for more intricate rapids downstream. The two-stage tongue of the eight-foot waterfall follows. Scout or portage on river right. Another hard left leads into a sharp drop before the Boreas splits around an island into a Class II section past the entrance of Vanderwhacker Brook. The Delaware & Hudson Railroad appears high on the West bank. Three miles of calmer water allow relaxation and time to enjoy the wilderness before the storm.

The quiet is broken by a shallow right bend into two and a half miles of continuous Class IV rapids until just before the bridge on Northwoods Club Road. The Boreas compresses to an average 40-foot width, with some sections only a boat-length wide. The 90 foot per mile gradient is obvious, with the current forced into deflection

Section: Route 28 North to Minerva bridge
Counties: Essex, Warren
USGS Quads: Thirteenth Lake, Newcomb
Difficulty: Class IV (V in high water)
Gradient: 45 feet per mile (90 feet per mile maximum)
Average Width: 40 feet
Velocity: Pushy
Rescue Index: Accessible but difficult
Hazards: Tight, constricted riverbed, scarcity of eddies
Scouting: As needed, from railroad tracks
Portages: As needed
Scenery: Beautiful, wilderness
Highlights: Whitewater, scenery
Gauge: Hudson Telemark gauge, waterline gauge code 361431 (North Creek)

Runnable Water Levels:	Minimum	Maximum
	7.0 feet (estimate)	Undetermined

Months Runnable: March, April
Additional Information: Hudson River Telemark gauge, (518) 251-2777 (beep gauge)

Boreas River • New York

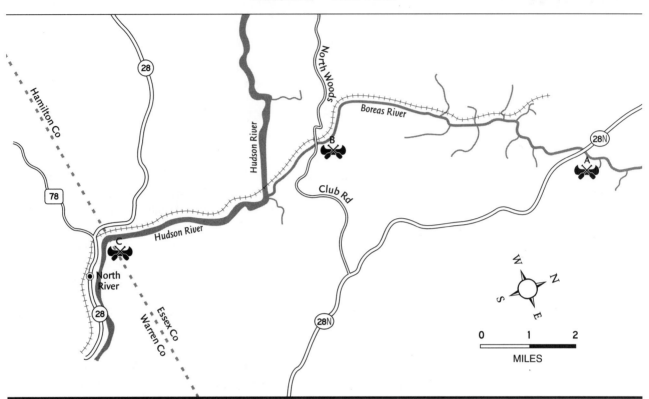

waves careening off bank walls, sticky holes, violent eddy lines, and plummeting chutes with confused cross-currents.

The continuous nature of rapids through the gorge is intense, with scouting available from the railroad when suitable eddies can be found river right. One drop involves two large boulders with a three-foot drop between them. **Z**-Turn Rapids follows, with several boul-der-choked turns requiring technical skills. After **Z**-Turn, difficulty eases to Class III levels down to the Northwoods Club Bridge Road bridge (B) and a potential take-out. Past the bridge, Class III+ rapids continue to the confluence with the lower Hudson River gorge. Read that description for the three-and-a-half-mile paddle to the take-out (C) at either of two Warren County parking areas at North River on NY Route 28.

Fish Creek

Fish Creek is one of New York State's most scenic whitewater runs, slicing through over five miles of sheer slate-walled canyon. Eighteen waterfalls cascade into the canyon, some free-falling over 90 feet. The canyon creates a sense of wilderness isolation, with hawks circling overhead and clean water providing habitat for trout and walleye. But Fish Creek offers its challenges. Several boats are lost on Fish Creek every year. The canyon section is very deep, narrow, and inaccessible. Inexperienced boaters find self-rescue extremely difficult in the continuous Class III–IV gorge riffs.

Much of Fish Creek courses over slate ledges beneath towering slate canyon walls. Below the canyon, its bed is through gravel and changes with flooding. Strainers are common, because tree roots easily wash out of the gravel banks.

Fish Creek is best run in April and May during spring snow runoff, but any moderate rain can bring water levels to runnable depth throughout the year. The cautious will check the painted gauge on the east side of the Route 285 bridge in the village of Taberg. Water levels vary from 1.5 to 4.5 feet for best conditions. Take-out (C) is on the west bank immediately upstream of the NY 285 bridge. The take-out below Taberg (D) adds a mile of riffs and two miles of flatwater to reach parking at a bridge across West Branch on Blossvale Road, a few hundred yards upstream from its junction with Fish Creek.

To put in, drive seven miles north on Coal Hill Road to its T into Yorkland Road. The put-in (A) at the Frederick Palmer Jr. bridge is one-half mile east of the T, with parking west of the bridge. The sedimentary slate forming the Fish Creek Canyon is exposed on river left. The first few miles are Class II+, with many standing waves and adequate eddies. Pock Point Creek enters from river left a half mile into the run. Two and a half miles farther, the river quiets in one-eighth-mile-long Rome Reservoir. Shrouded by steep banks, the small impoundment is created by 20-foot Boyd Dam, with a mandatory portage on river left. Despite numerous No Trespassing signs, emergency exit from the river is out a road on the east bank to Frenchtown Road.

Below the dam, Fish Creek's gradient increases to 54 feet per mile, with Class III+ rapids competing with the fantastic scenery for paddlers' attention. At higher water levels, this section nears Class IV due to the continuous nature of the difficulties. A swim will have potentially severe consequences, as lack of eddies complicates paddler rescue and gear retrieval. Several lives and many boats have been lost on this section at higher water levels.

Major tributaries include Fall Creek and Florence Creek, both entering on river right from the West. Immediately above the Florence Creek junction, a ledge forms the keeper named Hotel California, which is best run on river right. Below, the valley opens and the bottom transitions to gravel. The bridge on Palmer Road (B) offers parking on river left for an early take-out, or you

Section: Point Rock Bridge, Ava, to Taberg
County: Oneida
USGS Quads: Point Rock, Lee Center
Difficulty: Class III (III+ in high water)
Gradient: 54 feet per mile
Average Width: 50 feet
Velocity: Fast
Rescue Index: Inaccessible to remote
Hazards: Strainers, changeable riverbed, scarcity of eddies
Scouting: Lower section, for strainers
Portages: Boyd Dam
Scenery: Spectacular—wilderness canyon
Highlights: Scenery, whitewater, wildlife
Gauge: Taberg bridge gauge, visual

Runnable Water Levels: Minimum   Maximum
                               1.5 feet   4.5 feet

Months Runnable: March through May, after periods of heavy rain
Additional Information: Mountain Sports, (315) 896-4421

can continue two easy but sweeper-choked miles to Taberg.

Alternate trips for flatwater boaters include West Branch from Westdale or Camdem on Route 13 to the Blossvale junction above Fish Creek. Dams at Camden and McConnelsville are both portaged on river left. Another gentle run is from Taberg to a take-out at the Route 49 bridge or Fish Creek Landing on Route 13.

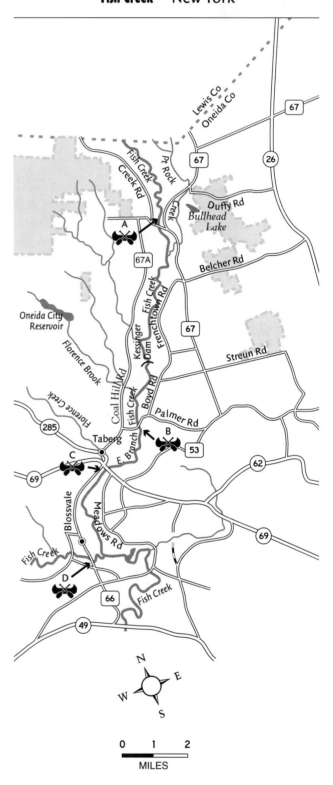

Fish Creek • New York

Hudson River

The Hudson River begins life on the west slopes of Mount Marcy in the central Adirondacks and drains them to the south. It offers the entire spectrum of paddling opportunities before reaching New York Harbor and flowing around the Statue of Liberty.

The Hudson starts as a flatwater paddle from the old MacIntyre Mines upper works on Lake Henderson south past the tailing of the lower works, where the town of Tawhawus disappeared as the mine grew under it. This historic flatwater paddle has access points off Essex County 25, which leads north from Essex County 2 (Boreas Road) just two miles east of its junction with NY Route 28N. The flatwater stream below Sanford Lake ends abruptly at the Route 25 bridge across the Hudson.

From the Route 25 bridge, the Hudson turns to the northwest, dropping 100 feet in a narrow channel over the next two miles for a Class III run that needs scouting for strainers. It calms for the last five miles to take-outs at Harris Lake State Campground, north off NY Route 28N three miles east of Newcomb.

The 12-mile pitch from the NY Route 28N bridge to the junction with Indian River combines moderate whitewater with an enchanting stillwater wilderness. The chute of Long Falls followed by the Class III drop at Ord Falls calms to five miles of enchanting wilderness ending in the Blackwell stillwater, where wildlife seldom views humankind. An old dam ends the stillwater, and the river moves through rapids again to its junction with Indian River. Take-out is possible through the Gooley Club with prior permission obtained from Finch-Pruyn Paper Company in Glens Falls, New York. The paddler may also continue for another 13 miles through the Hudson River Gorge to the Warren County River parking areas at North River on Route 28. Gaining two miles of the Indian River to its put-in is difficult in low water, impossible at high levels.

Indian River Gorge Section

Due to ease of access and controlled dam releases, the Hudson River Gorge is best reached from the Indian River. The scenery is breathtaking. Blue Ledge towers over the river at the Gorge mouth. Heron, osprey, and hawks float above hemlock and cedar, with faulted rock cliffs adding to the isolated vista. At lower water levels, the Indian and Hudson offer technical Class III and IV paddling. At higher levels, difficulties increase to Class V and waves reach 15 feet. The best information is the North Creek gauge, phone (518) 251-2777. Minimum

Section: Indian River to Barton Mines Road (Route 28)
Counties: Hamilton, Essex, Warren
USGS Quads: Utica, Thirteenth Lake, Newcomb
Difficulty: Class III+–IV (IV+ in high water)
Gradient: 36 feet per mile (Hudson); 60 feet per mile (Indian)
Average Width: 200 feet
Velocity: Fast to sluggish
Rescue Index: Inaccessible to remote
Hazards: Undercut rock walls, continuous whitewater, river congestion
Scouting: The Narrows section
Portages: None
Scenery: Beautiful to spectacular, wilderness gorge
Highlights: Whitewater, wildlife, scenery
Gauge: North Creek gauge (Telemark System); waterline gauge code 361431

Runnable Water Levels:	Minimum	Maximum
	3.0 feet	10.0 feet
	(573 cfs)	(17,340 cfs)

Months Runnable: March through May
Additional Information: Hudson River Telemark gauge, (518) 251-2777 (beep gauge)
Special Note: This is a remote wilderness-experience trip requiring appropriate safety precautions.

Hudson River Gorge • New York

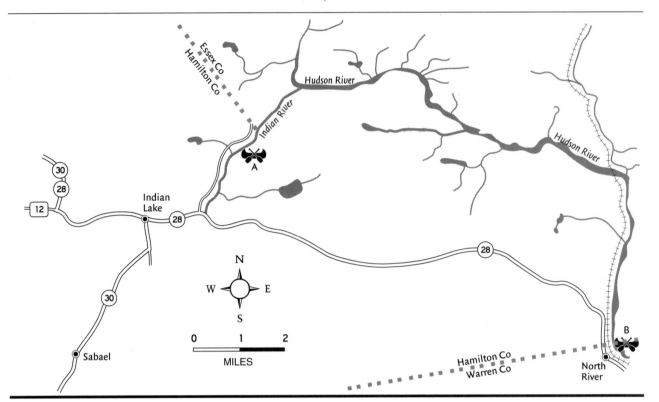

runnable levels are three feet, with 10-foot levels a big-water maximum.

Leave a shuttle at one of the Warren County River Access areas in North River (B). The larger lot east of town offers a better beach. Drive north on NY Route 28 and turn north on Chain Lakes Road one mile east of Indian Lake Village. Continue north along the west bank of Lake Abanakee, past the dam and Class IV–V Otter Slide to a large parking area west of the road. Carry across the road and down a draw to a protected eddy behind an island in Indian River. Dam releases contracted by commercial rafting operators in April, May, June, and fall weekends raise the Indian nearly three feet and the Hudson a half foot. Be considerate of the congregating rafters—they are paying for the ride.

Indian Head Rapids starts the Indian's run, followed by Prying Islands, Gooley Steps, and Photo Hole for a wild, 2.5-mile, Class III ride to a calm confluence with the Hudson. Here the river drops into the 10-mile Hudson Gorge, beginning with Class III Cedar Ledges and Black Hole Rapid. Elephant Rock looms on river left, announcing Duck Pond Flats. A mile of calmer water features Mink Falls and Virgin Falls, entering on river left. A sweeping turn to river right is followed by a sharp left entry into Blue Ledge Rapids. Out-of-boat excursions are best on river left before entering the .75-mile, continuous

Class IV Narrows. Continue on through Osprey Nest Rapid, a .25-mile series of Class III ledges to a rest stop at Carter's Landing on river right across from Split Rock on river left.

OK Slip Brook enters on river right, featuring a 100-foot waterfall a short hike back from the river. It also warns of Big Nasty, the technical, big-water, Class IV Kettle Mountain Rapid. Stay clear of the packed boulders on river left and the boiling center eddy and be prepared for extreme turbulence. Below, a hard-left turn reveals Gun Sight In Notch to the west. Another quarter mile shows Gun Sight Out Notch to the east before a sweeping right turn leads to Harris Rift Rapids. The ledges of Harris Rift Mountain on river right shelter falcon nests, which may be viewed while scouting the rapids from river right. Harris features multiple holes, with a big keeper below a large rock just left of center that is very dangerous when water is pouring over the top.

The pool below Harris Rift Rapids allows regrouping before less intense Little Split Rock, Bobcat Den, and Fox Den Rapids. A railroad trestle announces the river-left entrance of the Boreas River. The run leaves the Hudson Gorge, turns south, and calms for a mile of Class I–II before reaching the two-foot-plus drop at Bus Stop. The ledge is nearly river-wide, with a sneak route on river left saving paddlers from punching through the big hydraulic below the drop. Three miles of moving water below Bus Stop reaches the shuttle sites at North River.

Other Sections of the Hudson River

From North River the Hudson flows southerly, with moving water interspersed with Class II–III rapids, and can be run in short sections between easy shuttle sites. The five-mile drop to a shuttle off NY Route 28N or Route 28 at North Creek includes Perry Eller Rapid, the site of the Hudson River Whitewater Derby slalom races. The seven-mile run from North Creek to Raparius comprises the Derby's down river racecourse and includes Bird Pond Falls and Class III Spruce Rapids before reaching the Warren County Access below the New York Route 8 bridge. The six miles between Raparius and The Glen include a three-foot ledge with a powerful back-roller that is best scouted before running left of center. Race Horse Rapids one-half mile below is the last difficulty before arrival at parking below the Route 28 bridge on river right, south of The Glen. From The Glen, a final two-foot ledge guards six miles of moving water to a shuttle site west of Warrensburg on New York Route 418 where the Schroon River joins the Hudson. The remaining 16 miles offer a sedate trip through river-bottom forests to a take-out at Hadley-Luzerne. NY Routes 1, 4, and 9N all lead to satisfactory take-outs above impassable falls.

Buried up to his gunwales, Jim Michaud successfully runs Otter Slide on the Indian Creek section of the Hudson River. Photo by John Barry.

Moose River

Lower Section

The Lower Moose River lies 10 miles outside of Old Forge, two and a half miles downstream of the Route 28 bridge. The put-in (A) is a quarter of a mile upstream of the Old Iron Bridge, which crosses the river. Once the river leaves the road at Tannery Rapid, the next ready access is the take-out at the Fowlerville Road Bridge (B).

It is a good idea to put in just above the warm-up rapid about one-quarter mile upstream of the Old Iron Bridge so you can loosen up a bit before getting into the thick of things. Iron Bridge Rapid, Class IV, the first rapid you need to be concerned with, is deceptively powerful and has some large holes in the approach just after the bridge. There will be a large rock outcropping from the left shore as the river bends around it slightly to the left. In the main current you will find holes and large breaking waves. The conservative route is to dive into the eddy on the left behind the rock outcropping. From this point you may either continue downstream to Tannery Rapid or go out and surf up a storm.

Tannery Rapid is a river-wide horizon line, the first of many on the Moose. The nature of the river alternates between big Class IV–V drops and long Class II riffles. Eddy left and take a look at this one. It is a long, arduous, pushy, Class IV–V rapid with an array of holes that have an appetite for boats. Enter the rapid through and to the right of the first big hole, which feeds right to left. Pick your way down the right side, through and over a dozen holes. At the bottom there is a large boulder in the center of the river. The correct route is to the right of the boulder, over a drop into a hole. Your speed should carry you through the hole if you don't find a clean spot. The rapid is several hundred yards long; if you have ever run the Gauley in West Virginia, this rapid will feel a lot like Lost Paddle Rapid, but without the negative vibes.

Continue through some Class II to Parson's Pitch, or Rooster Tail Rapid, Class IV. This, too, is a long rapid with a wild ending. Enter tight to the left bank as the river bends left. If you don't hug the left bank closely enough, you stand a chance of getting an unexpected surf in a steep, powerful hydraulic. The river straightens out a bit, and you'll want to get back to the right. There will be a large boulder on the right, downstream; the main flow passes to its left. Here the river drops quickly and constricts, thereby creating a big-water drop with unexpectedly huge waves and holes. If you like playing large holes, you will have to take advantage of the opportunity as you run the rapid, because it is a pain to try to get back up to them.

Following still more Class II is Froth Hole Rapid, Class V. Eddy out on river left to scout. This is one of those rapids where you need not be ashamed to shoulder your boat if you are just not in the right mood. Froth Hole is well known: it is even named on the ancient USGS quadrangles. It is a river-wide ledge six to seven feet high with no easy route and certainly no route that is readily recognized—especially at high water. The approach is a basic Class III, but it seems more difficult due to your concern with the drop below. At lower levels you can run left of the wave train leading up to the drop and run the ledge left of center. However, at higher levels the hole gets ugly and you need to change your strategy. To the right of the straight part of the ledge is a boulder. Just to the left of this boulder is an apparently clean chute that will leave the frothy ugliness on your left. This chute has a rock at the bottom, and while inflatable rafts ride comfortably over it, kayaks have experienced eerie underwater pins. Don't go there if you are in a decked boat.

If the level isn't high enough to sneak down the left side and finesse the drop just to the left of the hole, you need to either walk or consider lining up on that wave train in the approach to the drop, and try to jump the foam pile of the hole. This looks stupid, but it usually works. Pay attention to the box canyon on river left below Froth Hole. Set up safety for anyone running the drop, because there is potential for pinning and nasty

Section: Old Iron Bridge to Fowlerville Road Bridge
County: Lewis
USGS Quad: Utica
Difficulty: Class III–V+
Gradient: 38 feet per mile (maximum 85 feet per mile)
Average Width: 75 feet
Velocity: Slow to very fast and pushy
Rescue Index: Accessible to remote
Hazards: Ledge drops, hydraulics
Scouting: Tannery, Froth Hole, Mixmaster, Elevator Shaft
Portages: Froth Hole, Mixmaster
Scenery: Beautiful
Highlights: Large ledge drops
Gauge: One-quarter mile upstream of Old Iron Bridge

Runnable Water Levels: Minimum Maximum
3 feet 8 inches Unestablished

Months Runnable: April
Additional Information: For gauge information, contact
    Mountain Sports, (315) 896-4421; or Hudson River–Black
    River Regulating District, (315) 788-5440.

swims in these rocks. If Froth Hole is high enough to run the chute left of the hole, then the box canyon rocks may be creating holes. If something goes terribly wrong and you need to get off the river, there is an old road on river left at Froth Hole. It is the Deer Run Camp Road. The next stop is Fowlerville Road.

More Class II, and then you come to the infamous Mixmaster Rapid, Class V. There are more horror stories of good runs gone bad in this rapid than in any other rapid in the state. Pull over on river right to scout, and if you scored over 100 on any subject on your S.A.T. test, you should consider walking this one.

Mixmaster is a river-wide ledge dropping 10 or so feet. But there is a kink to this drop, even though it is basically a one-move run. The approach is about 30 or 40 feet from the right shore. The river bends right, and you will want to move right to set up for the drop. The idea is to scream across the drop from left to right, using the curler at the top to help you surf across to home plate (the eddy at the bottom). The current tries to push you down the center of the drop, and if it wins, you lose. Halfway down the drop is a monstrous hole that is certain to mess you up and drop you into the Mixmaster hole at the bottom of the drop. Water feeds the Mixmaster from all four sides. We have seen one-and-a-half-foot rafts with crews of eight disappear vertically into this hole! The swim is fairly clean, but injuries have occurred, and things tend

to stay in the hole for a long time. Clean run or not, Mixmaster is quality adrenaline at all levels.

There is more Class II between Mixmaster and Elevator Shaft, with one Class III rapid called Wishbone just before Elevator Shaft. Wishbone has some nice surfing holes, so don't pass them up.

Elevator Shaft deserves a Class IV rating even though it seems like a Class III, straight-shot paddle over a six- or seven-foot ledge. A lot of tail stands and backenders occur here, and not just with hard boats! Sixteen-and-a-half-foot rafts have backendered, pivoted, squirted, and flipped in this seemingly benign drop. What's happening here is that the hole at the bottom of the drop is being fed by a huge recirculating eddy on river right. This provides the effect that is so surprising. Scout this rapid on river right from either the rock ledge or your boat. The farther left, the better, but runs are unpredictable.

There is more Class II water, before Fowlerville Bridge. The rapid above it is Class III+, with some very powerful holes. Avoid the meat of these holes at higher levels, because if you have a problem, you may not get all of the pieces picked up before they get washed over the 60-foot drop below the bridge. Take out just above the Fowlerville Bridge on river right. Make sure you and your friends are all safe at the take-out before you head for the beer cooler. Some bizarre things have happened to stragglers in that last rapid above the falls. Needless to say, the anxiety level is upped when the last boater of your party swims under the bridge, gear everywhere, and everyone else is leaning against the van cracking open cold ones. On the Moose, the run isn't over until all the boats are out of the water.

Bottom Section

This section of the Moose is not for the faint of heart, nor is it for paddlers with any questions about their skills in serious Class V water. If you are not prepared to paddle questionable Class V drops of serious consequence, don't put your boat in the water on this section—run either the Lower or Middle Moose sections upstream. The Bottom Moose can be run, but while skilled boaters have not met their demise on the Bottom Moose, the hazards are great, and there are things to look out for. This section is usually run at lower flows. As the Lower Moose gets too low, the Bottom Moose becomes more runnable.

The Bottom Moose is a ledgy river, as is the Lower, with flatwater and minor rapids between the major drops. Every horizon line on this four-mile run is to be scouted, and any drop you don't feel comfortable running should

Section: Fowlerville Bridge to Lyons Falls
County: Lewis
USGS Quads: Port Leyden, Brantingham
Difficulty: Class V+
Gradient: 126 feet per mile (80 feet per mile average)
Average Width: 75 feet (200 yards maximum to 50 feet minimum)
Velocity: Fast and pushy
Rescue Index: Accessible to accessible to difficult
Hazards: Keeper hydraulics, pinning rocks, undercuts, potholes
Scouting: Every horizon line
Portages: Anything you don't feel comfortable running, especially hydrodams
Scenery: Fair
Highlights: Whitewater, geology
Gauge: McKeever gauge, waterline code 361522
Runnable Water Levels:

	Minimum	Maximum
	2.6 feet	5 feet

Months Runnable: May, June, July with rain
Additional Information: Gauge information through Hudson River–Black River Regulating District, (315) 788-5440
Special Notes: Be careful: good boaters have died on this section.

be portaged. Put in at the Fowlerville Bridge. Just downstream is a huge slide, dropping 60 feet in a distance of 40 feet! Scout this one from the left side. Depending on the water levels, there are at least three lines over the falls. The most common line is down the left side following the flow. Beware of the hydraulic. The higher it gets, the worse it becomes. Downstream of the 15-foot ramp to the 40-foot slide is an island with an 8-foot ledge. There are lines through both channels.

Diamond Splitter, also known as F$%k-up Falls, is next. The river gathers around to the right, then drops steeply to the left between parallel ridges of bedrock. Scouting and portaging is best done on a long ridge of granite on the right. Pay close attention to the diagonal hole leading into the final slide down to the Diamond Splitter—aim right and stay right here.

Knife's Edge is the next big drop and should be scouted on the right. There are three parallel ridges of rock. The center ridge splits the current. The normal line is a zig-zag move over the two ledges in the right channel. Look at this one carefully before making the attempt. There is a serious pinning situation on the far right side of this drop that claimed the life of a boater some years ago. There is also a sneak route to the left through a blasted channel created to retrieve that unfortunate boater. To

sneak, follow the flow through the hole in the center ridge of rock and work your way around and back in below the main drop.

Double Falls is next and appears as a horizon line with a road bridge and dam in the distance. This one is best scouted from the right. The hero line follows the flow over the first 8-foot drop on river right. Stay right of center and boof the second ledge. An easier line is also available by running far river left. Boof into the large eddy on river left and work your way down the left side. Stay close to the wall on the left for the second ledge. Too close to the middle and you'll find a sticky hole. After crossing the pool, take out on the left at the bridge and carry around the next dam and falls. Put in at river right below the dam and across from the paper mill. Across the next pool is another horizon line. This line is actually a small dam just above 18-Foot (Agers) Falls. Scout this from the right side. The Falls is run right over the center into the pool below, which pours busily over a Class IV ledge.

Surform is the next, major rapid—the shallow river bottom is like a Surform file. The rapid can be scouted and portaged from left or right. A rock island splits the rapid into two channels, with lines down both sides. Higher water brings more options. Choose a line carefully. A flip here might leave you with a stub for a head.

Powerline Rapid is next, with boulders strewn about at the bottom. A large eddy on the left makes for an easy scout. A fun rapid to eddy-hop, the basic line is to follow the main flow over the weird wave while attempting to negotiate the holes which follow. Pick up swimmers quickly, as Crystal is not too far below.

From a psychological standpoint Crystal is probably the most awesome drop on the run. The scout is on river right. The rapid, a total drop of 35 feet, basically consists of a series of ledges leading into the final 15-footer best run hard left, aiming at the left cliff. Once again there are different lines to choose from, and all of them are relatively complex and consequential.

The final dam/falls, Lyons Falls, is optional. There may or may not be enough water going over the dam, depending on whether or not the powerhouse is generating. Look at this one very carefully before making the attempt. The sneak route (comparatively speaking!) is on the right over the dam and down a separate carved channel where you are shot out of a 12-foot spout. There is take-out parking above this drop on the left and below the drop on the right side of the river. River-right parking belongs to a power company and may not be available in the future.

Releases are scheduled on most weekends in May, the first weekend in June, and all weekends in October.

Moose River • New York

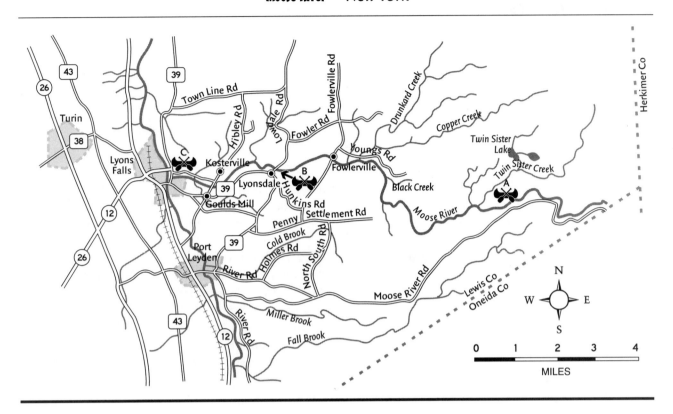

Sacandaga River

The Iroquois name "Sacandaga" means "cedar in water-drowned lands," and for much of this multibranched river's course the name fits. The Sacandaga drains the southern Adirondacks toward the east, where it joins with the Hudson River at Hadley-Luzerne. Its branches include steep creeks, moderate whitewater runs, calm sections, a massive impoundment, and a dam-controlled whitewater run.

Main Branch

The Sacandaga begins in the Jessup River Wild Forest swamp in Hamilton County, west of US Routes 8, 10, and 30 in the southern Adirondacks. The swamp drains easterly into Sacandaga Lake, which connects to Lake Pleas-ant; the town of Speculator lies at the northern end of the lake. From Speculator, the Sacandaga is deep-channeled and calm to its junction with the Kunjamuk. Take out of this placid stream at the Duck Bay picnic area or continue through Class II riffles to the old US Route 30 bridge. The bridge is a mandatory take-out, because less than 200 yards below lies the power station at Christine Falls.

Middle Branch

The Middle Branch of the Sacandaga below Christine Falls to its junction with the East Branch is a technical steep creek with flatwater sections broken by Class IV–VI rapids. The next seven miles must be scouted by paddlers prepared to tote their boats.

The put-in (A) is below the posted powerhouse property half a mile down Old US 30. The action is fast before a long flat. Two miles below the put-in, the flat ends and Old 30 returns to the east bank. Austin Falls is 200 yards below. Get out and scout this drop. Austin Falls is a 200-yard-long ramp dropping 40 feet, with a 3-foot drop in the center and a 4- to 10-foot drop at the end, depending on water levels. Some levels dangerously undercut sharp ledges, and high water forms a massive hole at the end. Scout, think, and carry.

Below Austin Falls the Sacandaga continues moving to the closed Old US 30 bridge (B). This site has parking, and 2.5 miles of Auger Flats lies below. At the end of the flats the river picks up velocity and starts a left turn. Stop. Get out on river right. Scout Auger Falls before making the 500-yard carry around it. Auger Falls can also be scouted from a gravel road east of New US 30 roughly two miles north of the 30 and 8 junction. Auger Falls begins with 4- and 6-foot drops before the main drop. At

Section: Old powerhouse to Old Route 30 (30b) to junction of US Routes 8 and 30
County: Hamilton
USGS Quads: Kunjamuk Creek, Wells
Difficulty: Class V+
Gradient: 250 foot per mile (325 feet per mile maximum)
Average Width: 20 feet
Velocity: Fast and pushy
Rescue Index: Accessible
Hazards: Long steep obstructed slides, deadfalls, undercuts, strainers
Scouting: All of it. Use old road grade on river left. Middle of run on use new road grade of US Routes 8 and 30 on river right.
Portages: Auger Falls (mandatory)
Scenery: Beautiful
Highlights: Whitewater, geology, scenery
Gauge: Visual at old powerhouse dam

Runnable Water Levels:	Minimum	Maximum
	1 to 4 inches of water over the dam (200–300 cfs)	Caution is advised

Months Runnable: April
Special Notes: This river is unforgiving; so bring along a throw bag and a first-aid kit. A peak runoff river.

low water Auger splits into Double Drop and 25-foot Auger Chute on the left. Water deflecting off the left canyon wall rolls over on itself, hence the name. There are continuous drops for another 300 yards, then two miles of Class II and III whitewater before the Sacandaga's junction with East Branch and the take-out (B). Parking at the confluence is best below the bridge on river left.

East Branch

The Sacandaga's East Branch ends in another technical steep creek. It may be paddled as an enjoyable moving-water stream by putting in at picnic areas three to five miles north of the Hamilton/Warren County line along US 8. The mandatory touring boat take-out across the river at Griffin on Extract Creek serves as the whitewater put-in (A). Below this point the East Branch plunges over a ledge and through Griffin Falls, a series of Class IV–V drops, before easing to a continuous Class III at high water levels for the three miles to its junction with Middle Branch (C). An alternate put-in (B) bypasses the severe drops at Griffin Falls. Very high water upgrades the lower riffles to Class IV.

Section: Griffin to the junction of Routes 8 and 30
County: Hamilton
USGS Quads: Wells, Griffin
Difficulty: Class III–IV
Gradient: 65 feet per mile (80 feet per mile maximum)
Average Width: 75 feet
Velocity: Fast to pushy
Rescue Index: Accessible but difficult
Hazards: Keeper hydraulics, difficult rapids
Scouting: The gorge at Griffin
Portages: Middle drop (very steep) in the gorge at Griffin
Scenery: Pretty to beautiful in parts
Highlights: Whitewater, geology
Gauge: Visual only at Griffin gauge (300 feet upstream of highway bridge)
Runnable Water Levels:

	Minimum	Maximum
	1,000 cfs	Caution is
	(2,000 cfs for the	advised
	gorge section)	

Months Runnable: April and May
Special Notes: Flows vary greatly due to the fact that it is a natural-flow river that depends mostly upon melting snow. Camping is available at Sacandaga Public Campsite, at the confluence of the West and Main Branches of the Sacandaga.

Main River to Great Sacandaga Lake

Below the junction of its Middle and East Branches, the Sacandaga runs four miles to Lake Algonquin. The run is fast, with Class III riffles at high water, before slowing as the lake is approached. Access for kayaks is available at the lake's upper end, while open canoes may continue two miles across the lake to access at the lower end. Below Lake Algonquin the Sacandaga continues for another two miles to Sacandaga Campground at the confluence with the West Branch.

From the Sacandaga Campground, where the West Branch joins, the river continues south for three miles through shingle with Class II+ riffles at high water levels. It slows through another three miles to an access point at Hope. Another three miles of increasingly sluggish water reaches the Route 30 bridge, the last take-out option before the muddy-shored impoundment of Great Sacandaga Lake.

West Branch

West Branch runs from its origins in the high valleys above Piseco Lake west of NY Route 8. The sections of the branch below Route 10 boast extreme drops, unrunnable falls, and no access by road or footpath. The

Sacandaga River, East & Middle Branch • New York

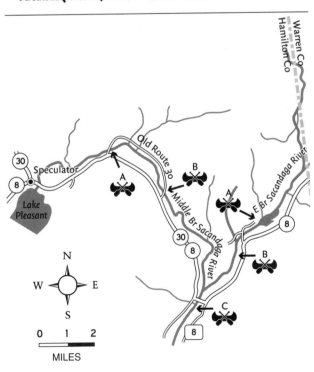

Section: Stewarts Dam near Hadley to Hudson River
County: Saratoga
USGS Quad: Lake Luzerne
Difficulty: Class I–III
Gradient: 15 feet per mile
Average Width: 150 feet
Velocity: Slow
Rescue Index: Accessible
Hazards: None
Scouting: None
Portages: None
Scenery: Pretty
Highlights: Whitewater, scenery
Gauge: Waterline gauge code 361646 (Stewart Bridge), 365722
    (dam release)
Runnable Water Levels:

	Minimum	Maximum
	Dam-controlled, usually minimum flows	Flood stage

Months Runnable: Memorial Day through Labor Day
Additional Information: Sacandaga Outdoor Center may be
    reached at (518) 745-5130.
Special Notes: Water is not usually released on Sundays.

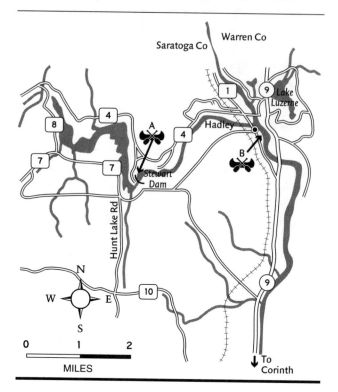

Sacandaga River, Lower Section • New York

Lower West Branch, which runs from Lost Lake Mountain to join the Sacandaga River three miles south of Wells, is accessed by West Valley Road from Wells. West Valley Road, gravelly and deteriorating, dead-ends at Whitehouse, site of an abandoned hotel. Put in under the suspension bridge crossing the creek. The river turns right, through a hole, into continuous Class I and II rapids. Reading and paddling this creek to its confluence with the Sacandaga is a joy.

Lower Section

This three-and-a-half-mile section of the river receives heavy commercial rafting traffic on its easterly course from Stewart Dam on Great Sacandaga Lake to its confluence with the Hudson River in Hadley-Luzerne. Dam releases control the river level to easy Class II–III riffles. Access is by portage across NIMO property north of Stewart Dam off CR 4 or by shuttle south of the dam off Mt. Anthony Road (A). The take-out (B) is in the town of Hadley off Stony Creek Road, which crosses CR 4.

PENNSYLVANIA

Lower Youghiogheny River

Confluence to Ohiopyle

The Yough in Pennsylvania is much milder than its Maryland headwaters; it's suitable for practiced intermediates. The 10-mile run from Confluence (A) to Ohiopyle (B) passes through a beautiful winding gorge. You can put in on river left in Confluence; however, if there is not enough discharge from the dam, put in downstream beyond the mouth of the Casselman or at the Riversport Camp a mile or so downstream. For about two miles below the dam, there are only occasional riffles, with flat water predominating. About a mile below the outskirts of town, the river turns away from the broad valley and heads left into narrow confines. The first of several Class II rapids begins here. These are all easily read and delightful to run. Soon the rapids recede and the river broadens out considerably for three or four miles. If

it is a windy day, this section can be painfully arduous (the wind always blows upstream for some reason). Soon, however, the canyon walls begin to squeeze the river, and rapids re-form for the last three miles of the trip. Aside from the railroad tracks on either side, the river flows through a roadless, peopleless setting. Also, there is a bicycle trail on river left from Confluence to Stewarton except when it crosses the loop below Ohiopyle.

When you see the first signs of Ohiopyle in the distance on the right bank, you should begin to plan your exit from the river; dangerous Ohiopyle Falls is just downstream. Conservative paddlers will want to hang to the left of the island above the Ohiopyle bridge and land on the rocky "beach" just below it. There is a large parking area here. More experienced paddlers will want to run Z-Turn Rapid (Class III-) to the right and take out downstream on the river-right side. In water under two feet, an upset at this point is not serious; all you have to do is stand up and walk to shore. Nonetheless, a take-out in Ohiopyle should always be made with caution and with consideration for the inexperienced members of the group. Do not paddle beyond the abandoned railroad bridge, as this will commit you to running the falls.

Section: Confluence to Ohiopyle
Counties: Somerset, Fayette
USGS Quads: Confluence, Ohiopyle
Difficulty: Class I–II
Gradient: 11 feet per mile
Average Width: 300 feet
Velocity: Slow to fast
Rescue Index: Accessible but difficult
Hazards: Falls just below the take-out
Scouting: None
Portages: None
Scenery: Excellent
Highlights: Challenging rapids
Gauge: Pittsburgh Weather Service (Ohiopyle gauge), (724) 262-5290

Runnable Water Levels:

	Minimum	Maximum
	1.0 feet	8–9 feet

Additional Information: Minimum enjoyable level is 2.0 feet; 4.0 is high and fast; 8–9 feet is the maximum. Ohiopyle State Park, Ohiopyle, PA 15470, (724) 329-8591

Ohiopyle to Stewarton

The seven-mile Ohiopyle (B) to Stewarton (C) run on the Yough was for many years the single most popular whitewater paddling run in the eastern United States (slipping only recently into second place behind the Nantahala River in western North Carolina). With beautiful scenery, dependable year-round flow, and delightful Class III+ rapids, the Yough has it all. Rich in paddling history, the "Lower Yough" was the birthplace of commercial rafting in the eastern United States (1964) and the training ground for some of the nation's best paddlers. Popularity, however, is not without its costs. Many are the summer Saturdays when you could seemingly walk from Ohiopyle to Stewarton by hopping from raft to raft

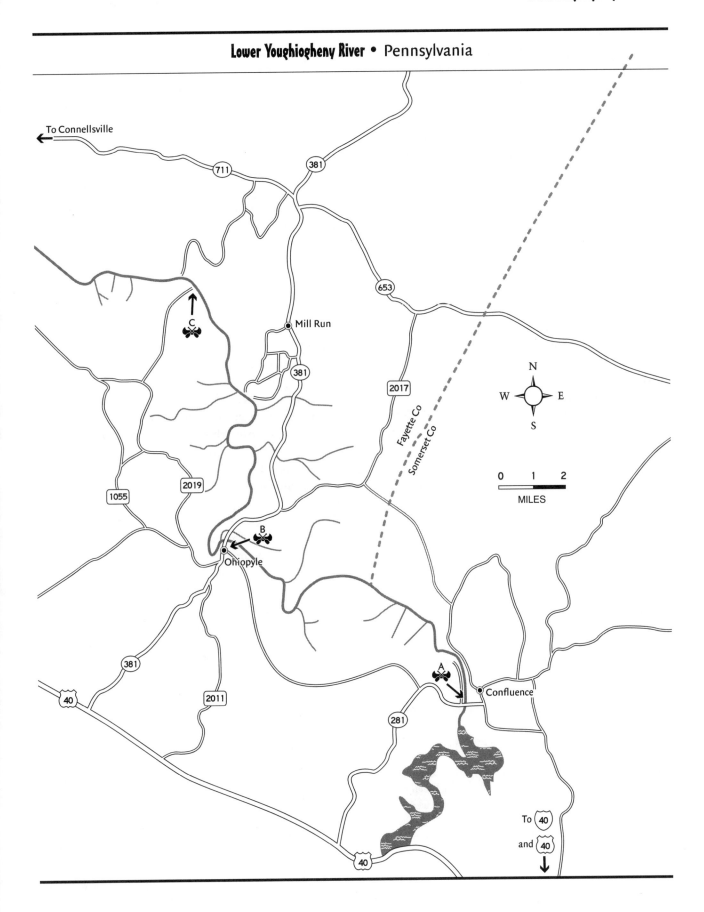

and kayak to canoe in an endless river-choking flotilla of private and commercial craft. Neoprene and ABS were to the Yough what water hyacinths are to the Suwanee. A bike trail brings additional crowds into Ohiopyle, and traffic and parking can reach urban levels on peak days.

Because of the river's popularity and resulting huge crowds, the "Lower Yough" is tightly managed. Consequently, there is a quota system and fee for running the river in season (April through mid-October). While walk-ons are still allowed, those traveling long distances should call in advance for details. Free launches are available for hard boaters after 3 p.m. Another fee covers a bus shuttle from the Brunner Run take-out up a long hill to a huge parking lot where boaters leave their vehicles after running the primary shuttle of six miles.

The first mile of the run, known as the Loop, is the most popular and contains a great deal of action. Paddlers have everything thrown at them but the kitchen sink. For openers, after putting in below Ohiopyle Falls, the paddler must face a series of ledges and then a rock garden known as Entrance Rapids without any warm-up. It is a long, tortuous course with twisted currents. For indiscretions, a huge rock near the top (Sugarloaf) stands in midriver as a sentinel to broach paddlerless boats or even paddled boats. Half of the upsets on the Loop take

Section: Ohiopyle to Stewarton
County: Fayette
USGS Quads: Ohiopyle, Mill Run, Ft. Necessity
Difficulty: Class III+
Gradient: 27 feet per mile (48 feet in the loop)
Average Width: 300 feet
Velocity: Fast
Rescue Index: Accessible but difficult
Hazards: None
Scouting: Dimple, Rivers End, and Railroad Rapids
Portages: None
Scenery: Excellent
Highlights: Ohiopyle Falls, Fallingwater by Frank Lloyd
    Wright, Ferncliff Peninsula
Gauge: Pittsburgh Weather Service (Ohiopyle gauge), (412)
    262-5290

Runnable Water Levels:	Minimum	Maximum
Ohiopyle gauge	1.0 feet	4.5 feet
Confluence gauge	1.5 feet	8–9 feet

Additional Information: The enjoyable levels start at 2.0 on the put-in gauge, 2.5 feet at the Confluence gauge. Ohiopyle State Park, Ohiopyle, PA 15470, (724) 323-8531; National Weather Service, (703) 260-0305 (Washington, DC)

place here. At higher levels (four feet and above), there is a hungry hydraulic on the left side halfway down. Most paddlers stick to the left of center and regroup in an eddy below Entrance to mend boats, bandage bodies, retrieve paddles, and gather courage for the next rapid, Cucumber.

Here a long rock garden precedes an extremely vigorous drop through a narrow passage. Usually you should stick to the far left, carefully avoiding anything resembling a broaching situation, and gradually move to the right, where huge boulders have forced the course of the river. As you are forced right, continue to stay far left. At lower levels, run the main drop of Cucumber about four feet to the right of a large flat rock on the left. At three feet on the put-in gauge, this flat rock gets covered up, but the route remains the same. Going through Cucumber with or without a boat is what it must be like to be flushed down the john.

The next rapid is called Piddly—a Class II surfing hydraulic below the larger channel on the right. This is followed by Camel and Walrus, named for two distinctively shaped offset rocks in midstream. Eddy Turn is next. The sneak is on the left, and the right is a rock jumble chock-full of eddies, with a two-foot ledge lurking half-way down. After this comes Dartmouth Rapid, with its usually punchable hole at the bottom center.

The final Loop rapid is Railroad (Class III–IV)—another infamous boat chewer. Several passages exist over this steep drop. However, you will notice Turtle Rock in the river, with its back on the right and its head on the left. With enough water you can sneak between the neck and the head. However, the classic way of running Railroad is about 10 feet to the left of the turtle's head over a diagonal ledge going from left to right. Do not run underneath the turtle's head or you will enter Charlie's Washing Machine—a vigorous hole that flips most paddlers in a heartbeat. Once below this diagonal ledge, the paddler is faced with a choice. At high water, you can go straight over some padded rocks. At lower water, these rocks offer pinning possibilities, so be prepared to go far right or far left immediately after running the ledge by Turtle Rock.

Generally, paddlers spend a lot of time playing around on the Loop and then go on to Stewarton. For those not up to handling such rough water, a put-in can be made below Railroad Rapids and, with a few judicious carries, the trip can be made to Stewarton in comparative safety. The first two miles below the Loop are open and easily read Class II descents, with only one Class III, which drops rather sharply.

Soon below this Class III rapid, the river narrows and appears to end, but a loud roar coming from the left warns the paddler of a special treat. A paddler who is on this section for the first time may want to scout this—Dimple's Rapids, considered by some to be the most difficult of the Lower Yough. The current is choked down into a bulging filament, smashes directly into Dimple Rock (left bank), and veers off to the right. Immediately below, this Class III–IV rapid continues with a dazzling combination of reefs and boulders, and below these are a long field of haystacks and a river-wide, gaping hydraulic (Swimmers' Rapids), followed by more haystacks; hence, flipping in Dimple's can be the start of a long day for a paddler. Be sure to miss Dimple Rock; it is undercut. Run the channel, which slams into Dimple, as far right as possible. At medium water levels you can sneak this drop by running down a center channel to the right of Dimple Rock.

The feisty hydraulic at Swimmers' Rapids is a popular lunch stop. Rafting groups stop here so their customers can jump off the left bank upstream and float through it. More experienced kayaks, duckys, and canoes jump into it for a vigorous surf. However, surfers have to wait in line and contend with the waves of rafts and swimmers punching the hydraulic.

The next rapid after Swimmers' is Bottle of Wine. The right channel is a vigorous drop into two big waves, and the far left is more gentle. After a long rock garden comes Double Hydraulic, which is just what it says. The first hydraulic is bigger and stickier. Scout from an eddy on the left or from the right bank. Sneak both hydraulics on the right.

Right after Double Hydraulic is River's End (Class III–IV), where the river seems dammed up but instead funnels over a steep drop on the left. Scout this drop from the left. You run it just the opposite of Dimple. Enter tight left next to a big rock near the left bank. As you pass this rock, be ready for a sharp left turn to avoid Snaggletooth Rock just below, which has snagged its share of errant rafts and boats. After a long mellow Class III run-out and pool comes Schoolhouse Rock—so named for the large rock at the bottom that has collected expensive tuitions in the form of broached boats. Be sure to miss this rock right or left.

Below Schoolhouse Rock on river right is Million Dollar Wave—an exquisite surfing spot. Then comes Stairstep—a feisty short ledge series in the center with a sneak on the far left. Then, be sure your life insurance premium is paid, because Killer Falls (Class II) is next on the far right. The last rapid is Brunner Run, or Dragon's Tooth (so named for a distinctive triangular rock upstream). The most conservative route is on the right. The Brunner Run take-out is just below the rapids on river left. In the off-season, you can park cars here and use the access road; during the peak season, however, you'll have to use the shuttle. Check the bulletin board at the put-in for shuttle dates and times.

Swimmer's Rapid on the Lower Yough. Photographer unknown.

Slippery Rock Creek

Slippery Rock Creek has long been a favorite of Pittsburgh and northern Ohio boaters, combining beauty, accessibility, and challenging whitewater. Although the best part of the run is protected within McConnells Mill State Park, all access points are on private land. The landowner relations at the Route 422 bridge at Rose Point (B) are strained at best; use the downstream left side and be sure your car is off the road but not on the grass. There is a private campground on the other side which permits access for its patrons. You can avoid all this hassle by putting in at the Route 19 bridge at Kennedy Mill (A), or by parking at the state park offices on McConnells Mill Road and following a trail to the river. The creek has been run as far upstream as Route 173; this is a flatwater run, quite unspoiled, broken only by an occasional Class I riffle.

The first few miles below Kennedy Mill are not exciting, but the river begins to pick up below Route 422. The rapids are a series of S-shaped boulder gardens, with powerful twisting currents at high levels and tight maneuvers during dry periods. One of these, Airport Rapids, has a vigorous eddy-line pop-up spot. The river is deep, offering lots of opportunities for squirts. The last rapid dies in the

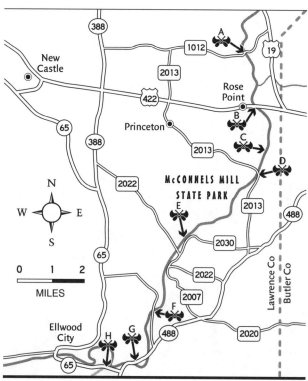

Slippery Rock Creek • Pennsylvania

Section: Kennedy Mill to Connoquenessing Creek
County: Lawrence
USGS Quads: Portersville, Zelienople, Beaver Falls
Difficulty: Class III–IV
Gradient: 23 feet per mile
Average Width: 23 feet
Velocity: Fast
Rescue Index: Accessible
Hazards: Dam at McConnells Mill State Park and three others on the last stretch, just above Connoquenessing Creek
Scouting: None
Portages: All dams
Scenery: Pretty to beautiful
Highlights: McConnells Mill State Park
Gauge: Pittsburgh Weather Service, (412) 262-5290. Listen for the Slippery Rock reading. The river can rise several feet after a good rain!

Runnable Water Levels:	Minimum	Maximum
	0.5 feet	3.0 feet is high water (Class IV); 5.0 is near flood stage (Class V)

Additional Information: Optimum level is 2.0 feet. McConnells Mill State Park, (724) 368-8091. Moraine State Park, RD 2, Portersville, PA 16051, (724) 368-8811. Pittsburgh Council, American Youth Hostels, 6300 Fifth Avenue, Pittsburgh, PA 15232. The latter has an excellent guidebook to western Pennsylvania.

backwash of a low dam at McConnells Mills. Carry on either side; the left appears to be easier. There is road access to this point, and trails parallel the river from here on (C).

Below the dam is a mile of continuous rapids formed by huge sandstone boulders. The river is extremely constricted here. At low water, the maneuvering is tight and many drops are blind. High levels can exhibit extremely violent holes; the river should not be underrated. Below this "mad mile" the river opens up a bit, and Eckert Bridge (Breakneck Bridge) is reached (D). The popular whitewater run ends here, and there is a gauge on the bridge which corresponds well to the Slippery Rock readings.

The river now begins to open up, and the river gets quieter as the walls recede. This is a popular novice-intermediate training run. The rapids, while easier, retain the "S-Turn" character seen upstream; an assortment of large boulders add to the fun and make for good teaching eddies and ferry sites. The stretch between Eckert and Harris Bridge is also a good alternate for weak parties at high water. A gauge at Harris Bridge can also be used to track water levels. The river can be paddled all the way to its mouth at Wurtemburg. This is a flatwater run broken by Class I riffles, and it requires that three dams be portaged. Take out on the far side of Connoquenessing Creek, or continue downstream through the Elwood City Gorge.

Dark Shade Creek, Shade Creek, and Stony Creek

Western Pennsylvania has a number of outstanding runs originating in its high central plateau. This run is unusual in that it connects three streams into a continuously difficult whitewater run. Starting with the steep, boulder-filled drops of Dark Shade Creek through the ledges of Shade Creek to the rolling power of the lower Stony, this run is one of the most interesting in the eastern United States when high water levels permit an attempt. At lower levels both Shade and Stony creeks offer exciting sport in an area not commonly visited by paddlers.

Dark Shade Creek
Section: Cairnbrook to mouth of Clear Shade Creek
County: Somerset
USGS Quads: Central City, Windber
Difficulty: Class IV–V
Gradient: 90 feet per mile
Average Width: 30 feet
Velocity: Fast
Rescue Index: Accessible
Hazards: Difficult rapids
Scouting: Advisable
Portages: None
Scenery: Beautiful
Highlights: Intense rapids!
Gauge: Visual only. Walk down to the mouth along Clear Shade Creek from Route 160. If the last rapid looks runnable, the rest of the stream is OK. You'll need really high water in order to run this!
Runnable Water Levels: See gauge.
Months Runnable: February to March during high runoff or after heavy rains
Additional Information: Edward Gertler, 503 Bonitant Street, Silver Spring, MD 20910. He publishes an excellent Pennsylvania guidebook that covers many small streams in the area.

Dark Shade Creek/Shade Creek

The put-in for Dark Shade is at the Cairnbrook bridge (A). There is about a mile of fast-flowing, riffly water for a warm-up before the bottom falls out. The remainder of the run is a series of the steepest, tightest, blindest drops north of the Upper Youghiogheny. While the water and rocks are discolored by mine acid, the banks are unspoiled, and the overall effect is one of wilderness. First-timers, however, will be too busy to notice the difference. And all too soon, it's over. You can walk about 50 yards from the mouth to Route 160 (C), or continue on down the Shade.

Dark Shade, Shade, & Stony Creek • Pennsylvania

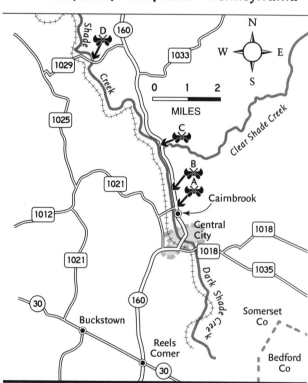

Shade Creek
Section: Junction of Clear Shade and Dark Shade creeks to
    Stony Creek
County: Somerset
USGS Quads: Windber, Hooversville
Difficulty: Class III–IV
Gradient: 60 feet per mile
Average Width: 50 feet
Velocity: Fast
Rescue Index: Accessible
Hazards: None
Scouting: None
Portages: None
Scenery: Attractive to beautiful
Highlights: Excellent rapids
Gauge: Visual only. Check the creek at the take-out.
    Casselman River at Markleton should be over 3.5 feet, and
    the Ferndale gauge should be at least 6.0 feet; call
    Pittsburgh Weather Service, (412) 262-5290.
Runnable Water Levels: See gauge.

Shade Creek paddlers must portage downstream 50 yards along the banks of Clear Shade Creek from the Route 160 bridge. At one time this was a continuous Class III stream; the floods of 1977 changed it into a drop-pool run which approaches Class IV in a number of spots. The harder rapids are formed by rubble piles in combination with ledges. Many island passages are braided, and strainers are not uncommon. As with Dark Shade Creek, the water is unattractive but the banks are beautiful. A late spring run amid the rhododendron and mountain laurel blooms is always quite memorable. There are three bridges on the run: at 4.2 miles (D), at 6.3 miles (E), and at 9.3 miles in Seanor (F), just above the mouth of the Stony. The last rapid, a delightful series of ledges, is a great place to play.

Stony Creek

Shade Creek empties into the Stony below Seanor. This river has more than twice the volume, and in its continuous rapids the contrast is quite exciting. Most drops are formed by sloping sandstone ledges which create marvelous shallow-entry playing holes. At high water

Stony Creek
Section: Seanor (mouth of Shade Creek to LR 55127 southwest
    of Paint)
Counties: Somerset
USGS Quads: Hooversville, Johnstown
Gradient: 35 feet per mile
Difficulty: Class III–IV
Average Width: 120 feet
Velocity: Fast
Rescue Index: Accessible but difficult
Hazards: Dam near end of run; pipeline crossing 100 yards
    below dam
Scouting: None
Portages: Dam must be carried. Pipeline carry is recom-
    mended, especially in high water.
Scenery: Pretty in spots
Highlights: Whitewater
Gauge: Visual only, located at the Hollsopple bridge (two
    miles upstream of the put-in off Route 403)

Runnable Water Levels:	Minimum	Maximum
Hollsopple gauge	1.5 feet	3.0 feet
Markleton gauge	3.5 feet	
Ferndale gauge	4.0 feet	

Additional Information: Watch out for giant holes at 4.0 feet or more on the Hollsopple gauge. For Markleton and Ferndale gauges, call Pittsburgh Weather Service, (412) 262-5290; Pittsburgh Council, American Youth Hostels, 6300 Fifth Avenue, Pittsburgh, PA 15232. The latter publishes a guidebook to western Pennsylvania.

(over three and a half feet) the river is extremely wide and powerful, with huge stoppers to be found in every rapid. Low levels can be pickier but offer better playing opportunities. Difficulty is comparable to the Lower Youghiogheny. Three-quarters of the way downstream, a steep rapid empties into a pool behind a dam. This should be carried. A short distance below, a pipeline crosses, creating a nasty hydraulic. Portaging is recommended, but you can sneak it on the far left. There are easy riffles to the take-out (G), a bridge just upstream of the mouth of Paint Creek. This take-out is sometimes tricky to find; if you get lost, continue under the Route 219 bridge to where numbered highways reach the river. The river can be run all the way into Johnstown, but it is not very attractive or challenging.

Dark Shade, Shade, & Stony Creek • Pennsylvania

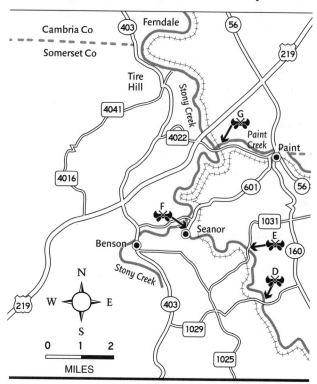

Pine Creek

Pine Creek is a beautiful, unspoiled stream which drains the wild plateau country of north-central Pennsylvania. The upper reaches in the Grand Canyon of Pennsylvania are near-wilderness; the lower stretch, paralleled by a road, is still attractive and rural. Both have easy access and camping facilities for the canoeist.

The Grand Canyon run starts at the Big Meadows access area in Ansonia (A), where Route 6 crosses Little Pine Creek. There is a gauge on this bridge which allows a final check of water levels. The river quickly leaves the valley behind and enters the canyon, paralleled by a private dirt road on river right. The run is quite mild, with one exception: Owassee Rapid, a Class II–III drop, which occurs on a left bend at the base of the first real cliffs seen in the canyon. The waves at higher levels can easily swamp an open boat; the sneak route is on the extreme left and should be scouted.

Below here the canyon becomes an uncomplicated float, with easy riffles alternating with fast-moving pools. The high green hills and the sparkling water create a memorable scene. There is road access at Tiadaghton nine miles downstream on the left; primitive camping can be found just upstream of this point; well water, sanitary facilities, and fireplaces are provided. Camping is not permitted in state park land or on posted private lands but is permitted on state forest and game lands. Check the Pine Creek topographic map before you make camp. Since the railroad runs along the left bank throughout the canyon, the river is popular with fishermen. Wherever possible, pass behind them or across the river from where they are fishing.

There is a boater access area at Blackwell (B) where Route 414 crosses the river. While more developed, the lower run is still quite attractive. Here deep green pools are linked by Class I–II drops. Except for big waves at high levels, there are no difficulties, leaving paddlers free to drift or fish. There is another access area at Slate Run (D) and a camping area (Black Walnut Bottom) two miles downstream. Access to the camping area is by foot or boat

only. The closeness of the road permits other unofficial access, but much of the land along the stream is private.

As you move down the stream, the rapids become more widely spaced. Slate Run to Cammal (E) is a run

Section: Ansonia to Blackwell
County: Tioga
USGS Quads: Tiadaghton, Cedar Run
Difficulty: Class I
Gradient: 16 feet per mile
Average Width: 150 feet
Velocity: Moderate
Rescue Index: Remote
Hazards: Owassee Rapid, Class II–III
Scouting: Owassee Rapid
Portages: None, except that novices may want to carry Owassee on the left
Scenery: Exceptionally beautiful
Highlights: Leonard Harrison State Park; Grand Canyon of Pennsylvania; West Rim Trail
Gauge: National Weather Service in State College, PA, (814) 234-9861

Runnable Water Levels:	Minimum	Maximum
Cedar Run gauge	2 feet	Undetermined
Rt. 6 bridge gauge	1 feet	Undetermined

Additional Information: A reading of 2.5 feet on the Cedar Run gauge gives solid Class II rapids at Owassee. With a 2 feet or more reading on the Route 6 gauge, swamping becomes a problem for open canoes in a few rapids. You can call Waterline at (800) 297-4243, gauge #421537.
Tioga State Forest, Box 94, Wellsboro, PA 16901, (570) 724-2868. Tiadaghton State Forest Bureau of Forestry,423 East Central Avenue, South Williamsport, PA 17701, (570) 327-3450. The latter has a folder, "Canoeing Pine Creek" and a topographic map of the West Rim Trail that shows river access points and camping areas. For guided raft trips or canoe, kayak, raft, or ducky rentals, contact Pine Creek Outfitters, RD 4 Box 130B, Wellsboro, PA 16901, (717)

popular with the Penn State Outing Club. We have ended the run at Waterville, but a trip could be made down the widening valley all the way to the Susquehanna, and thence downstream to Harrisburg and the Chesapeake Bay. The lower river has water throughout the summer except during a drought; however, you may have to drag your canoe across a few gravel bars.

Section: Blackwell to Waterville
Counties: Tioga, Lycoming
USGS Quads: Cedar Run, Cammal, Slate Run, Jersey Mills
    Tiadahton
Difficulty: Class I
Gradient: 9 feet per mile
Average Width: 200 feet
Velocity: Slow to moderate
Rescue Index: Accessible
Hazards: Large waves at high water
Scouting: None
Portages: None, but there may be drag on gravel bars at low
    water
Scenery: Pretty
Highlights: Scenery
Gauge: Williamsport Weather Service, (570) 368-8744

Runnable Water Levels:	Minimum	Maximum
Slate Run gauge	1.75	NA

Additional Information: The minimum enjoyable level is 2.5.
    Tioga and Tiadaghton State Forests (addresses above);
    State College Weather Service, (814) 234-7861

Cedar Run Gauge Conversion

Level (feet)	Flow (cfs)
2.0	376
2.2	532
2.4	708
2.6	891
2.8	1,090
3.0	1,319
3.2	1,562
3.4	1,817
3.6	2,086
3.8	2,378
4.0	2,699
4.5	3,595
5.0	4,613
5.5	5,757
6.0	7,054
6.5	8,496
7.0	10,070
7.5	11,780
8.0	13,620

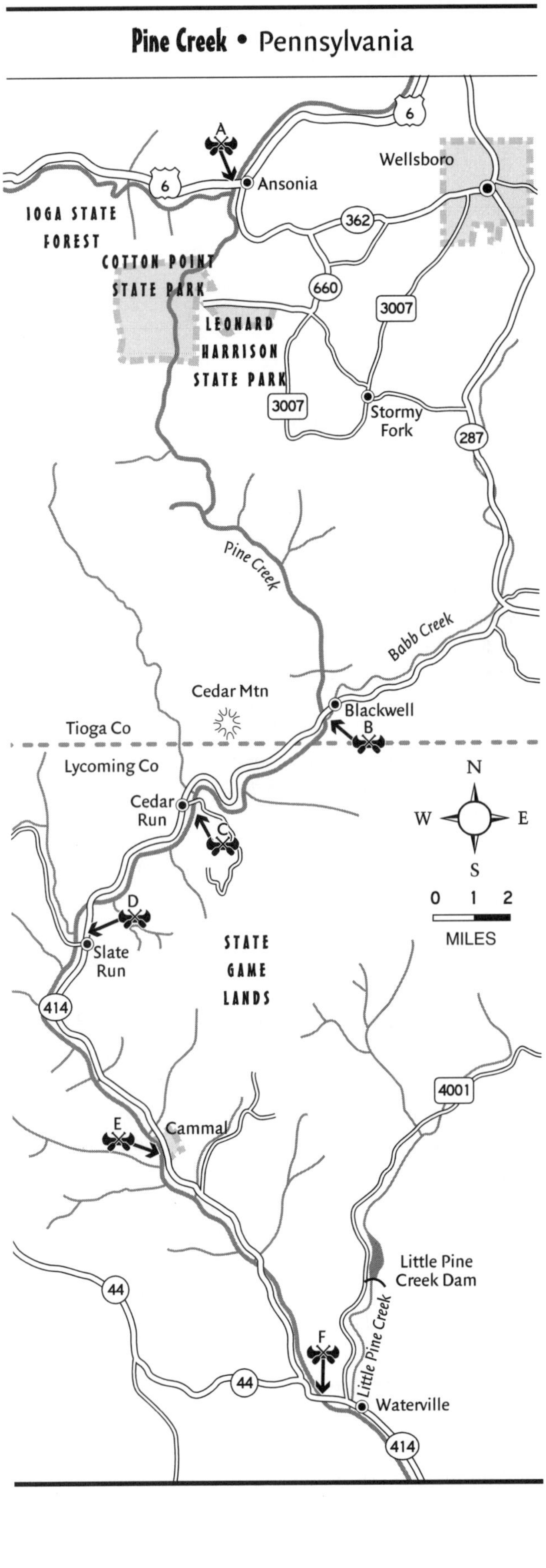

Pine Creek • Pennsylvania

A

6

Wellsboro

6   Ansonia

TIOGA STATE FOREST

COTTON POINT STATE PARK

362

660

3007

LEONARD HARRISON STATE PARK

3007   Stormy Fork

287

Pine Creek

Babb Creek

Cedar Mtn

Blackwell
B

Tioga Co

Lycoming Co

Cedar Run

C

N
W — E
S

0 1 2
MILES

D

Slate Run

414

STATE GAME LANDS

4001

E   Cammal

44

Little Pine Creek Dam

F

Little Pine Creek

44   Waterville

414

Loyalsock Creek

The Loyalsock Creek drains the Endless Mountains of Sullivan County, an area famous for outstanding hunting, fishing, and hiking throughout the year. The river is outstandingly beautiful, with unspoiled banks and crystal-clear water making the exciting rapids even more enjoyable. On the downside, this is a cold-weather river. It lies in mountains which are as far north as the Massachusetts line, and the river when runnable is composed mostly of snowmelt. Once the snow has gone, it takes a lot of rain to bring the water back up. The river is also extremely popular among trout fishermen, requiring paddlers to take special care on the way downriver. It would be foolish and perhaps even dangerous to attempt to run this stretch on the opening weekend of trout season. Dress warm and be on your best behavior when you canoe the 'Sock!

The Lopez (A) to Route 220 (B) stretch is quite small and rocky and can only be done in times of high water. Put in at the Route 487 bridge at Lopez. The run starts easily and builds gradually to Class III, passing through hilly, unspoiled forest country. The rapids are continuous, but quite manageable in open canoes. Below Route 220, the river continues in much the same fashion until a long pool and steep banks announce the presence of a greater challenge. The Haystacks, named for the huge boulders deposited here ages ago, is rated Class IV+ to V depending on the water level. While runnable by experts in decked canoes or kayaks, most river runners carry along the right bank, following a faint but passable trail.

Below the Haystacks the river increases in difficulty, alternating between easy and hard rapids. Four miles below the highway, Sportsmans Park Bridge spans the creek. At lower water levels most people begin their trip here. The river bounces merrily down to the highway, then discreetly curves away under a high bluff. This curve marks the start of the "S-Bend," a long and heavy rapid which approaches a Class IV rating at moderate to high water levels. Experienced kayakers will have no trouble, but open canoes should scout on the right shore and sneak the upper drop on the inside of the turn.

Section: Lopez to Route 220 bridge
County: Sullivan
USGS Quad: Laporte
Difficulty: Class II–III
Gradient: 30 feet per mile
Average Width: 65 feet
Velocity: Fast
Rescue Index: Accessible
Hazards: None
Scouting: None
Portages: None
Scenery: Beautiful and unspoiled
Highlights: Endless mountain scenery
Gauge: Worlds End State Park, (570) 924-3287

Runnable Water Levels:	Minimum	Maximum
Rt. 87 bridge gauge	4.5 feet	NA

Additional Information: Waterline Service, (800) 297-4243, gauge #4421448. World's End State Park in season, (570) 924-3287

The Loyalsock now returns to the road and enters World's End State Park, and it is here along Route 154, within World's End State Park, that the greatest fishing pressure occurs. The river is now at its most beguiling. Exciting rapids with challenging routes and good playing opportunities alternate with sparkling pools. The low bridge within the park has been replaced and raised substantially, making this run more enjoyable in high water. But beware of the Ice Canyons, sheer walls of ice up to six feet high which remain for a few weeks after winter releases her grip. These can make rescue and even stopping almost impossible. Just above the Route 87 bridge in the park, the river runs along high shale cliffs overtopped by sparkling waterfalls. This is one of the prettiest places in the state. Below the bridge, the river pools before dropping through a narrow slot in a low dam. This is the site of the annual kayak slalom races put on by the Penn

State Outing Club of State College, PA. Take out at the park, at the covered bridge a few miles downstream. There are campsites and cabins available for those who wish to stay overnight.

The lower river is considerably easier and can be run all the way to the Susquehanna River below Montoursville. The last 20 miles are flat and relatively unattractive, so most people prefer to take out at Loyalsockville. The upper part, from Forksville to Hillsgrove (10 miles), has the best continuous whitewater. The first part, between the covered bridge at Forksville and the junction with the Little Loyalsock Creek a half mile downstream, is the most difficult, and inexperienced parties should put in one mile below, where the river first comes close to the road. Three miles below Forksville is a low dam which should be approached with caution; at low water, there is a chute on the right. Most rapids are open and straightforward but at high levels can generate large waves which can swamp an open canoe. If you're unfamiliar with the river, stay to the inside of any turns.

Below Hillsgrove the rapids become more spaced out, but the river is still delightful. In high water, you can cover considerable ground in a single day. Sneaking through tight island passages in the warm sun of late spring and drifting through sparkling pools is certainly central Pennsylvania paddling at its best. Route 87 parallels the river closely below Hillsgrove, offering innumer-

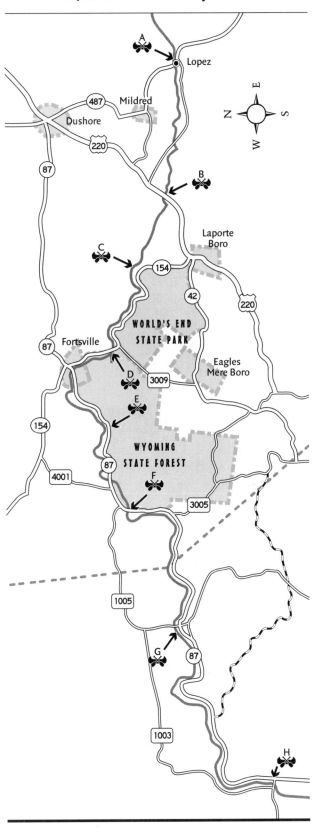

Loyalsock Creek • Pennsylvania

Section: Route 220 bridge to Forksville
County: Sullivan
USGS Quads: Laporte, Eagles Mere
Difficulty: Class III (Class IV at high water)
Gradient: 40 feet per mile (one mile at 50 feet per mile)
Average Width: 80 feet
Velocity: Fast
Rescue Index: Accessible
Hazards: Haystacks falls, park dam
Scouting: Haystacks, S-Bend, park dam
Portages: Optional at Haystacks, park dam
Scenery: Beautiful and unspoiled
Highlights: World's End State Park
Gauge: World's End State Park, (717) 924-3287

Runnable Water Levels:	Minimum	Maximum
Rt. 87 bridge gauge	4.0 feet	6.0 feet

Additional Information: Waterline Service, (800) 297-4243, gauge #4421448. World's End State Park in season, (717) 924-3287. This stretch has been run by experts at levels up to 7.0 feet.

able access points. The river is wide enough that fishermen can be passed by keeping to the opposite side of the creek and drifting quietly. This stretch is often canoeable well into June, when the warm weather makes the occasional need to drag your boat through the shallows pleasant. Beware the late-afternoon upstream wind, which makes solo canoeing almost impossible in the flat stretches. Take out at the Route 973 bridge or at any other suitable spot.

Loyalsock Creek at Loyalsockville, PA

Level (feet)	Flow (cfs)
3.5	211
4.0	429
4.5	742
5.0	1,179
5.5	1,760
6.0	2,491
6.5	3,392
7.0	4,372
7.5	5,485
8.0	6,638
9.0	9,200
10.0	11,960
11.0	15,340
12.0	19,200
13.0	23,660
14.0	28,740

Section: Forksville to Loyalsockville
Counties: Sullivan, Lycoming
USGS Quads: Eagles Mere, Barbours, Huntersville, Loyalsockville
Difficulty: Class I–II
Gradient: 15 feet per mile
Average Width: 150 feet
Velocity: Moderate
Rescue Index: Accessible
Hazards: Low dam 3 miles below Forksville
Scouting: None at moderate levels
Portages: None
Scenery: Pleasant; considerable private land
Highlights: Nothing outstanding
Gauge: World's End State Park, (570) 924-3287

Runnable Water Levels:	Minimum	Maximum
Rt. 87 bridge gauge	3.5 feet	NA

Additional Information: Waterline Service, (800) 297-4243, gauge #4421448. World's End State Park in season, (570) 924-3287

Lehigh River

The Lehigh River is one of the most popular runs in eastern Pennsylvania. Passing through an unspoiled forest setting in the Pocono Mountains, it contains two fine intermediate sections with easier water both upstream and downstream. The normal spring paddling season from March to May is supplemented by special recreational water releases from the Francis Walter Dam in the late spring and early fall. Because the Lehigh is close to the New York and Philadelphia metropolitan areas, it really gets crowded when the weather is warm. In addition to canoe and kayak enthusiasts, four outfitters run trips on the river. The Lehigh Gorge State Park, running from White Haven to Jim Thorpe, is a major center of outdoor activity. There's hiking and biking in addition to paddling, as well as good fishing on sections I and II.

The Francis Walter Dam is operated by the U.S. Army Corps of Engineers for flood control and water supply. Because the dam was poorly designed, storing water for recreational releases quickly floods a road running across its upstream face. The dam is often operated capriciously, with little regard for downstream recreation. It's not unusual for the river to run all week during the summer only to "dry up" on the weekend. Contact the Lehigh Gorge State Park, (717) 427-1861, on Friday for projected river flows over the weekend. The National Weather Service in Mt. Holly, New Jersey, (609) 261-6612, gives current flows at White Haven, at the start of Section II, and Lehighton, below Section IV. You can also call the Waterline Service at (800) 297-4243 (gauge #421395 for White Haven, #421714 for Lehighton).

Below the Francis Walter Dam the Lehigh runs over boulders and gravel bars, creating a delightful mixture of Class I–II rapids. This part of the river is not commonly run; it is closed to commercial raft trips; and is very popular with fishermen. To put in, you must carry your boat a quarter mile down a steep dirt road on the right side of the dam. Take care not to disturb the fishermen at the base of the dam, as this is where most of them hang out. The upper part of the run is quite wild, running between low forested hills. The only feature of note is a river-wide stopper which is not difficult but might cause trouble for beginners. It is an ideal run for those who are not quite ready for the "gorge sections" below, but please stay away on the opening day of trout season!

The float through White Haven is unattractive but short. Access has been developed under the Route 80 bridge. To get there, exit I-80 and follow 940 through White Haven. You will make a sharp right turn into town and head downhill. Just after you cross the railroad tracks, turn right into a shopping center and drive across the parking lot. There is a dirt road on the far side which

Section: Francis Walter Dam to White Haven, Section I
County: Luzerne
USGS Quads: White Haven, Hickory Run, Pleasant View
    Summit
Difficulty: Class II
Gradient: 23 feet per mile
Average Width: 150 feet
Velocity: Fast
Rescue Index: Accessible but difficult
Hazards: River-wide stopper halfway down
Scouting: None
Portages: None
Scenery: Attractive and unspoiled
Highlights: F. Walter Dam
Gauge: Lehigh Gorge State Park, (717) 427-1861 (manned
    8 A.M. to 3 P.M.)
Runnable Water Levels: Minimum   Maximum
                                500 cfs   2,500 cfs
Additional Information: A reading of 750 cfs is the minimum
    fun level, and 1,500 cfs is the optimum.
    Lehigh Gorge State Park, RD 2, Box 56, Weatherly, PA
    18255, (717) 427-5000; Whitewater Challengers, Star Rt.
    GA-1, White Haven, PA 18661, (717) 443-8345; Pocono
    Whitewater, Rt. 903, Jim Thorpe, PA 18229, (717) 325-3656

Lehigh River • Pennsylvania

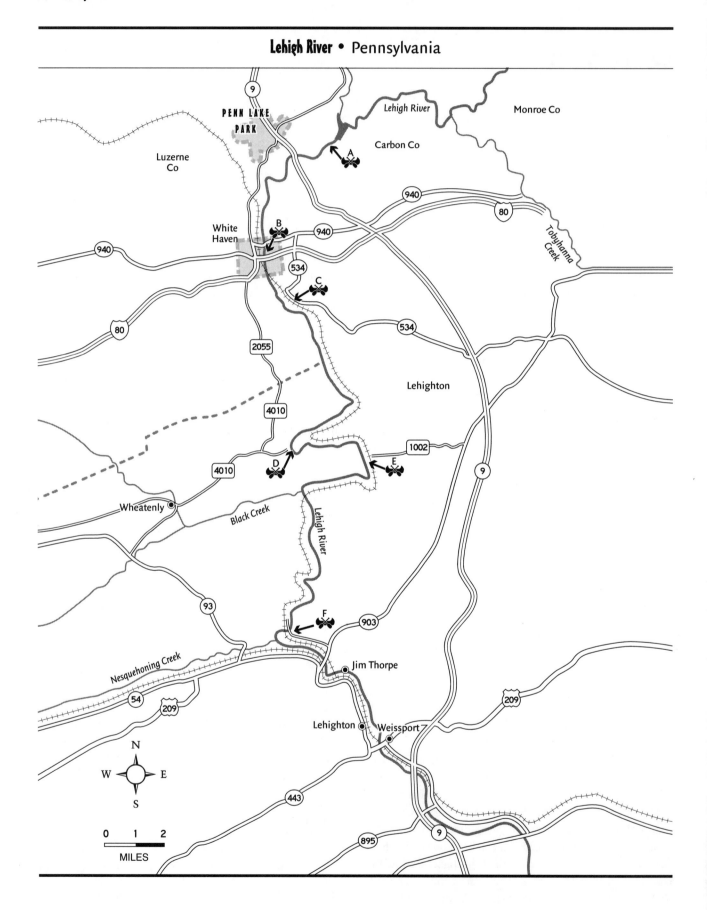

Section: White Haven to Rockport, Section II

Counties: Luzerne, Carbon (PA)

USGS Quads: White Haven, Christmans, Weatherly, Hickory Run

Difficulty: Class II–III at low to moderate levels

Gradient: 26 feet per mile

Average Width: 160 feet

Velocity: Fast, but with pools

Rescue Index: Accessible but difficult

Hazards: None

Scouting: None

Portages: None

Scenery: Beautiful and unspoiled, except around White Haven

Highlights: Old locks and canal remains

Gauge: Lehigh Gorge State Park, (570) 427-1861 (manned 8 A.M. to 3 P.M.)

Runnable Water Levels:

	Minimum	Maximum
	500 cfs	10,000 cfs

Months Runnable: March to June and on special water release dates

Additional Information: A reading of 750 cfs is minimum fun level, and 1,000–2,000 cfs offers a moderate run. The river is run regularly at high levels (5,000–10,000 cfs) by experienced Class IV boaters.

Lehigh Gorge State Park, RD 2, Box 56, Weatherly, PA 18255, (570) 427-5000; Whitewater Challengers, Star Rt. GA-1, White Haven, PA 18661, (570) 443-8345; Pocono Whitewater, Rt. 903, Jim Thorpe, PA 18229, (717) 325-3656

Section: Rockport to Glen Onoko, Section III

County: Carbon

USGS Quads: Christmans, Lehighton

Difficulty: Class II–III at low to moderate flows

Gradient: 24 feet per mile

Average Width: 180 feet

Velocity: Fast, but with pools

Rescue Index: Accessible but difficult

Hazards: None

Scouting: None

Portages: None

Scenery: Outstanding

Highlights: The deepening gorge

Gauge: Lehigh Gorge State Park, (570) 427-1861 (manned 8 A.M. to 3 P.M.)

Runnable Water Levels

	Minimum	Maximum
	600 cfs	10,000 cfs

Additional Information: A reading of 750 cfs is minimum fun level, and 1,000–2,000 cfs offers a moderate run. The river is run regularly at high levels (5,000–10,000 cfs) by experienced Class IV boaters. Release level from the dam will be augmented by tributary flows after heavy rains.

Lehigh Gorge State Park, RD 2, Box 56, Weatherly, PA 18255, (570) 427-5000; Whitewater Challengers, Star Rt. GA-1, White Haven, PA 18661, (570) 443-8345; Pocono Whitewater, Rt. 903, Jim Thorpe, PA 18229, (570) 325-3656

follows the old railroad bed that paralleled the Lehigh on river right. About a half mile downstream, a steep trail leads to the river. There is plenty of parking, and several good eating spots nearby for after the run.

Section II, the Upper Gorge from White Haven to Rockport, is one of the finest trips in the state. Interesting rapids and lazy pools alternate as the gorge deepens and the forests rise up along the side. It is also a good place to find derelict canoes, left by those foolish enough to attempt the run without extra flotation and sound whitewater skills. The stretch between White Haven and Tannery is popular among fishermen. It would pay to avoid this run early in trout season.

The run starts off quickly and with interest. There are nice surfing waves just above Tannery bridge which serve as a warm-up. A mile below the bridge is Triple Drop, marked by a large island which divides the current. Go left and you'll encounter a ledge with a hole called Volkswagen Bus Stopper. This can be rather stout at high

water levels. Lunch Rock, a Class II gravel bar with a rock shelf on the right, is hard to miss. On popular weekends hundreds of rafters and kayakers will be found relaxing on the warm rocks on river left. Below here, No Way and Staircase, both long Class III rapids with complex low water routes, lie waiting to separate the unwary paddler from his boat. There is an interesting drop below the mouth of Mud Run, which enters on river left. This is the home of the Beaver Hole, a popular play spot which has worn down the nose of many a kayaker trying for an ender. Wilhoyt's Rock, another Class III, lies just downstream. Named after a well-known canoeist of the 1950s who left a boat here, this rock is most dangerous at low water levels, as its undercut upstream face pins rafts and canoes. At levels of over 1,000 cfs it is underwater and heavily pillowed, making it easy to avoid. Rockport, the intermediate access point for the gorge, lies just downstream. The take-out lies partway down a rapid, so you'll have to work hard to catch the eddy on river right.

Rockport was, at one time, a way station on a canal which ran from Jim Thorpe to White Haven. Twenty

Section: Glen Onoko to Bowmanstown, Section IV

County: Carbon

USGS Quad: Lehighton

Difficulty: Class I–II

Gradient: 9 feet per mile

Average Width: 250 feet

Velocity: Moderate

Rescue Index: Accessible but difficult

Hazards: None

Scouting: None

Portages: None

Scenery: Attractive to beautiful; water may be murky

Highlights: Deep gorge; easy water

Gauge: Lehigh Gorge State Park, (570) 427-1861 (manned 8 A.M. to 3 P.M.)

Runnable Water Levels:

	Minimum	Maximum
	100 cfs	2,000 cfs

Additional Information: The river is not run much at high levels; 2,000 cfs is a reasonable cutoff for novices. Lehigh Gorge State Park, RD 2, Box 56, Weatherly, PA 18255, (570) 427-5000; Whitewater Challengers, Star Rt. GA-1, White Haven, PA 18661, (570) 443-8345; Pocono Whitewater, Rt. 903, Jim Thorpe, PA 18229, (570) 325-3656

Lehigh River

White Haven, PA At the put-in of Section II		Lehighton, PA 3 mi below take-out of Section III
Level (feet)	Flow (cfs)	Level (feet)
3.8	@ 500	2.5
4.2	@ 750	2.8
4.4	@ 1,000	3.2
4.9	@ 1,500	3.7
5.2	@ 2,000	4.1
5.5	@ 2,500	4.5
5.8	@ 3,000	4.8
6.0	@ 3,500	5.1
6.3	@ 4,000	5.4
6.7	@ 5,000	5.8
7.1	@ 6,000	6.2
7.4	@ 7,000	6.6
7.8	@ 8,000	7.0
8.1	@ 9,000	7.4
8.4	@10,000	7.8
8.9	@12,000	8.5
9.5	@14,000	9.3
	@16,000	10.0
	@18,000	10.8
	@20,000	11.5

Because of natural inflow from side streams, if there is 1,000 cfs at Lehighton, Section III is runnable regardless of the dam release.

locks allowed the coal barges from the mines upstream to make the 26-mile trip in nine hours, about the time that well-conditioned boaters require to do the run. The canal ran profitably for 27 years, until a great flood swallowed up the waterworks. It was later replaced by Asa Packer's Lehigh Valley Railroad, and only remnants remain. In the early 1970s Rockport was the site of an access controversy when angry fishermen leased the river-right railbed from the defunct Jersey Central Railroad, set up barricades, and ran paddlers off the river with guns. The impasse was broken when they ran off a scout leader who was a trustee of the railroad. He promptly modified the lease, and access was restored until the land was purchased by the state for the Lehigh Gorge State Park. Today the rails on river right are gone, replaced by a bike path that runs from White Haven to Jim Thorpe.

Section III of the Lehigh, beginning at Rockport (in the heart of the gorge), is the most spectacular part of the run. Also, because of accumulating mine acid drainage, this section is of less interest to fishermen. There are a number of uncomplicated Class III rapids below here as the river inscribes a wide bend from Rockport to Penn Haven, which is marked by a high stone wall on river right and a railroad bridge crossing just below. Here, at the mouth of

Black Creek, was a mining town only accessible by railway or canal. The river eases up below here, alternating pools and long Class I riffles, until Bear Creek enters on the left. Pipeline, the heaviest rapid on the river, begins at the end of a long pool, running hard up against high cliffs at river right, which rise almost 500 feet. This is the Lehigh at its most scenic. Below are two long, rock-filled rapids which can get very turbulent at high water. Open canoes will need a big bail bucket and helpful rescuers when the river is running at 1,500 cfs or more. Snaggletooth, also known as Tower Rapid, is an exciting run with numerous interesting chutes. (It is a long, unpleasant swim!) Below here the river makes a sharp right turn at Hole in the Wall, a place where an attempt to build a railroad tunnel failed due to constant cave-ins. The Glen Onoko take-out, recently built by the Bureau of State Parks, is just below here. This can easily be reached from Route 903 in Jim Thorpe. Cross the bridge over the Lehigh, turn left at the sign to Jim Thorpe River Adventures, then turn left again at the sign for the access road. Tiny Glen Onoko Creek is nearby, and a hike up a trail that follows this gem of a stream is very worthwhile.

Most people will want to end their trip at Glen Onoko, but the river downstream is quite enjoyable. There is one easy Class III rapid just downstream, and the rest of the river to Jim Thorpe is mostly Class I riffles. The quaint town of Jim Thorpe has become a tourist attraction: the Asa Packard Mansion, a scenic railroad, and many small shops draw people to the area. Not surprisingly, parking is a problem and you must pay to use the lot near the old railway station where paddlers used to take out.

The next five miles to Bowmanstown is a very scenic Class I float. Long popular as a training run, it is used by the rafting outfitters to provide "summer float trips" for fresh-air-starved New Yorkers at levels as low as 100 cfs. The gorge is surprisingly deep and wild here, making this trip enjoyable for novices and experts alike. Except for a nasty Class II cribwork partway down the run which is hell on inflatables, there are no difficulties. Take out below the Bowmanstown bridge on river right. Parking is a problem here and much of the land is private, so mind your manners.

Nescopeck Creek

Tiny Nescopeck Creek is a longtime favorite of paddlers in the Philadelphia area. Although not difficult, its rapids are lively and interesting even at low flows. The scenery is outstanding, with large flakes of rock, mountain laurel, and high cliffs vying for the paddler's attention. It is a popular early-season "icebreaker" and a later-season training run among area canoe clubs. Philadelphia Canoe Club runs an annual training camp on a property at the end of the run.

There is a little-used Class I run from Honey Hole Road to the Route 93 bridge, but the lower run is so enjoyable that few paddlers use it. Most paddlers put in on the river-left bank upstream of the bridge, where there is ample parking space. Although there is a gauge on the river downstream on river left, many paddlers "eyeball it" at the Route 93 bridge. What you see is what you get, and if you scrape your canoe here, you'll do the same thing throughout the run.

While none of the rapids are exceptionally demanding, a few are memorable. Slide Rapid begins a few hundred yards past the second bridge; it is a long drop ending with a delicious slide into a roller. At higher levels there is excellent surfing here. This rapid and the one below it get heavy and continuous at high water and narrow and picky at marginal flows; most of the other runs are easier. About a quarter mile past Halfway Bridge (the third bridge encountered on the run) there is a three-foot-high ledge drop with a huge flake of rock over 20 feet high downstream. This drop should be looked over by open boaters at high levels using the road which parallels the creek on river right.

The next significant drop is above a private campground on river left. It is long enough to swamp an open boat which strays into the waves at high water, but at lower water it's just tight and picky. Slalom Rapid is next; it is a series of interesting drops against a sheer right-hand bank. The Philadelphia Canoe Club holds its annual training camp here. The river pools before dropping into Eagle Rock Hole, a delightful mild playing hydraulic named for a huge overhanging flake on the left that looks like an eagle's profile. Below here lie a few minor riffles, then flatwater. It is a good time to enjoy the mountain laurel, which blooms in late April or early May. If there's water in the creek at this time, the run will be truly memorable.

The usual take-out is at the fourth bridge on the run, at river left. It is on private land, but the farmer who owns the field likes boaters (indeed, the whole area is extremely friendly). Don't do anything to change this situation. There is good road access downstream for quite some distance. The run down to Black Creek is easier and extremely pretty. Thickly forested slopes are broken by cliffs while the river provides a mixture of Class I–II

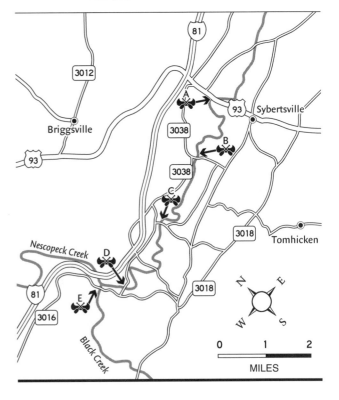

Nescopeck Creek • New York

150

Section: Route 93 bridge to last bridge above I-80

County: Luzerne

USGS Quads: Seibertsville, Nurenburg, Berwick

Difficulty: Class II

Gradient: 27 feet per mile

Average Width: 50 feet

Velocity: Fast

Rescue Index: Accessible

Hazards: None

Scouting: None for qualified boaters

Portages: None

Scenery: Pretty to beautiful

Highlights: River-running

Gauge: Visual only. The gauge is at the first bridge below the put-in, 100 yards downstream on river left

Runnable Water Levels:

	Minimum	Maximum
	6 inches	3 feet

Additional Information: A reading of 1 foot is enjoyable; 2.5 feet is a transition level from rock-dodging to missing waves and holes; 3 feet offers continuous Class III; 4 feet is flood stage, with the river high and fast. Philadelphia Canoe Club, 4900 Ridge Avenue, Philadelphia, PA 19128

drops separated by long pools. It is possible to continue your run downstream to the mouth of the river, an eight-mile trip over increasingly flat water. Except for I-80, which parallels the river in some places, the scenery is quite good.

Tohickon Creek

Tohickon Creek is a small, fast runoff stream with its headwaters in Lake Nockamixon, an artificial lake built for broadwater recreation. Once a close-kept secret among Pennsylvania boaters, its fame has spread with the event of the spring and fall releases and the running of several challenging races in Bucks County Park. These releases draw hundreds of paddlers each year, and the resulting traffic bottlenecks and parking problems bring out the worst in boaters. If you plan to use the river at this time, please follow directions and be prepared for crowded conditions.

The upper section of Tohickon Creek begins at the dam but is most easily accessible below Route 611 north of Doylestown. The run consists of Class I–II riffles with easier going in between. Long sections are paralleled by a road, making access easy. There are two dams on the run that demand special care. The first comes shortly below Route 611, just below the junction of the Little Tohickon Creek. The portage is on Tohickon Valley Country Club land; no problems have been reported yet, but mind your manners as you carry! The second dam is Meyers Dam in Stover Park. Carry on the right or avoid entirely by leaving your vehicle at the upper parking lot a short distance upstream. Both dams have been run by plastic kayaks at low to moderate flows, but this is not recommended. At high levels, dangerous hydraulics form, and the pools above the drops are fast-moving.

Below the park bridge is the classic Tohickon Creek run. It inscribes a huge loop, beginning with a gentle warm-up under the bridge, then picks up slowly through small waves. There are plenty of good side-eddies on which to continue the warm-up. The first major drop is "No Fish or Swim Ledge," named for some graffiti on a cliff on river right. The hole there is a vigorous playing hole at low to moderate levels and downright intimidating at high flows. There is a chute at center and a smaller hole at river left. The river then dances gracefully beneath the High Rocks climbing area in a delightful series of chutes and waves before gathering up above a sprightly

four-foot drop best run in the center. At high levels there is a huge stopper on river right. The next spot of note is a river-wide drop of about three feet. There is a center passage, but the left chute is the most fun.

Below this ledge the gradient picks up noticeably. There are four distinct drops, each of which merits scouting by those not familiar with the river. The first ledge is a simple drop with a passage broken out on the right. Enjoy the play waves at the bottom before proceeding to the second ledge, where the runout of a sharp drop is split by a midstream boulder. At the end of the pool below lies the Race Course, a long rapid studded with waves and holes. This drop can easily swamp a canoe, but there is a "sneak" chute on the far right which is not obvious from

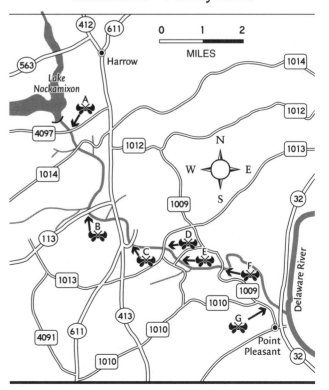

Tohickon Creek • Pennsylvania

Section: South Park Road (LR 09152) to Ralph Stover State
    Park
County: Bucks
USGS Quads: Bedminster
Difficulty: Class I–II
Gradient: 9 feet per mile
Average Width: 75 feet
Velocity: Fast
Rescue Index: Accessible
Hazards: Dam at golf course; dam at Ralph Stover Park
Scouting: None
Portages: Dams
Scenery: Pretty
Highlights: Ralph Stover State Park
Gauge: Visual only, at the Stover Park bridge. (Another gauge,
    at the Route 32 bridge in Point Pleasant, reads 1 foot
    lower than the park gauge at most levels.)

Runnable Water Levels: Minimum 0.0 feet — Maximum 3.0 feet

Additional Information: A reading of 1.0 is a good running level,
    and 2.5 feet is moderate. Beware the dam approaches at
    high water! Ralph Stover State Park, (215) 297-5090

upstream. The third ledge is the most challenging of all, requiring a paddler to thread a careful path between four offset holes. The holes are very playable at moderate flows and incredibly nasty in high water. The river appears to calm down a bit here, but stay alert! After a short pool comes a drop which—if you are not careful—sends you toward a ship's-prow rock. Play it safe by sneaking down the left.

The take-out, especially on release weekends, demands special attention. Most people take out at a small park just upstream of the Route 32 bridge in Point Pleasant. Parking here is limited. The town sees a lot of tubing activity on the Delaware, and the streets are heavily posted against parking. During release weekends, a parking concession is operated at Point Pleasant Canoe and Tube (215-297-8823) by local firefighters. As this is vital to continued use of the river, it pays to patronize these folks. For off-season runs there are spaces at the take-out and at several bars and restaurants. If no spot can be found, the next possibility is Bulls Island, a state park seven miles downstream on the Jersey side just off Route 29. Think about that when you get the urge to do something that might irritate the locals.

Getting water levels for the Tohickon has traditionally been difficult. The river is very flashy, rising and

Section: Ralph Stover State Park to Point Pleasant
County: Bucks
USGS Quad: Lumberville
Difficulty: Class III–IV
Gradient: 40 feet per mile
Average Width: 75 feet
Velocity: Fast
Rescue Index: Accessible
Hazards: None for experienced paddlers at normal flows
Scouting: Major drops for first-timers
Portages: None
Scenery: Beautiful
Highlights: Ralph Stover State Park, High Rocks Climbing
    Area, Bucks County Park
Gauge: Visual only, at the Stover Park bridge. (The Point
    Pleasant gauge on Route 32 reads one foot lower than the
    park bridge.)

Runnable Water Levels: Minimum 0.0 feet — Maximum 3.5 feet

Additional Information: A reading of 1.0 is the minimum exciting level; 2.5 is moderate, with all major drops Class IV; a reading of 3.5 is high flow, with big waves and holes in a hot current; rescue is difficult in some places. Flood stage is 5.0, with huge holes and waves and few eddies; for expert boaters only! The river has been run at levels up to 8.0, but this is emphatically NOT recommended. It needs 2 inches of rain within 24 hours to run.
Ralph Stover State Park, (215) 297-5090 (8 A.M. to 4 P.M.)

falling quickly after hard rains. It takes about two inches of rain to bring the creek up when the ground is dry, and then it can rise from below zero inches to over seven feet in less than eight hours! The paddler's gauge on the bridge at Ralph Stover State Park must be read on-site. The fall release is 1.75 feet; 2.5 feet is moderate; anything over 3.5 feet is high. The river is often run over 4 feet, which is very fast and pushy. Anything beyond that is best left to local boaters who know the river extremely well.

For years local paddlers relied on a network of friends who live near the river for an "eyeball" assessment. Now there's a better way. Recently the Pipersville Gauge, upstream of the park, has been added to the Flow Phone of the National Weather Service in Mt. Holly (609-261-6612). A level of 3.2 feet (750 cfs) equals the normal fall release level of 1.75 feet at the park; 4.6 feet (1800 cfs) equals about 3.25 feet, a medium-high level. Keep in mind that the Tohickon will fall quickly too! After reaching 7 feet, it will drop back to 4 feet in the first 12 hours after the rain lets up, then 1 foot every 12 hours thereafter until it reaches 1 foot. For up-to-the-minute information, call the Waterline Service, (800) 297-4243, gauge #421714. This gauge is also available on the Internet.

Gauge Conversion Table

Reading for Tohickon from Pipersville, PA

USGS Gauge	State Park Gauge	Flow (cfs)
2.0	0.6	153
2.2	0.8	215
2.4	1.0	291
2.6	1.2	385
2.8	1.4	492
3.0	1.6	615
3.2	1.8	740
3.4	2.0	860
3.6	2.2	985
3.8	2.4	1,130
4.0	2.6	1,289
4.2	2.8	1,460
4.4	3.0	1,643
4.6	3.2	1,837
4.8	3.4	2,045
5.0	3.6	2,266
5.5	4.1	2,858
6.0	4.6	3,515
6.5	5.1	4,262
7.0	5.6	5,104
7.5	6.1	6,034
8.0	6.6	7,053
8.5	7.1	8,166
9.0	7.6	9,376
9.5	8.1	10,680
10.0	8.6	12,090

Typical rapid on the Tohickon.
Photo by Ron Knipling.

Delaware River

The Delaware River marks the boundary between Pennsylvania, New York, and New Jersey. From the junction of the East and West Branches just below Hancock, New York, to tidewater downstream of Trenton, New Jersey, the river flows free. Major highways seldom follow it for any distance, and except for Easton, Pennsylvania, and Trenton, New Jersey, at its terminus, there are no major cities to pollute its waters. It has been a popular canoe route for generations, and many people (including your author) got their first taste of river paddling here.

The Delaware is the major water supply for New York City and Philadelphia; the former gets its supply from reservoirs in the Catskills, while the latter draws its from the Torresdale Intake near tidewater. During the droughts of the 1960s, New York refused to release water from its reservoirs. The entire upper river went almost dry, and the salt line crept upstream toward Philadelphia's water intake. Pennsylvania sued New York, and a Supreme Court decision laid the groundwork for the Delaware River Basin Commission, which has the power to control all dams within the watershed to assure a reasonable flow in the river during low-flow periods. Thus there is always enough water in the river to float a canoe, even in periods of extreme drought.

The river's location close to metropolitan New York has brought about considerable recreational use. There are many large liveries which put thousands of canoes on the water each weekend, most of them piloted by inexperienced hands. With the arrival of these hordes, the patience of some residents has begun to wear thin. At one time you could camp almost anywhere, especially on privately owned islands or railroad property. Increased use and complaints from landowners has brought this practice to an end. The river from Narrowsburg to Port Jervis is now the Upper Delaware National River. Except for in established campgrounds, legal camping is hard to find. National Park Service Rangers patrol the river and force trespassers to move their camps or be fined. Contact the NPS for a list of private campgrounds.

The "middle river" lies within the Delaware Water Gap National Recreation Area and runs from Matamoras, Pennsylvania, to Belvidere, New Jersey. This is the best, stretch for canoe camping; there are a number of primitive campsites available, and the river, although quite attractive, is much less heavily used. The river below Easton is even less popular, except for a few short stretches used for tubing. Protected by railroad tracks and canals, the bank remains relatively undeveloped, and water quality is surprisingly good. There are a number of widely spaced riffles and several major drops. The latter draw considerable day use from local whitewater paddlers for training.

The Upper Delaware stretch begins just upstream of Hancock, New York. You can start your trip on PA Route

Section: Hancock to Narrowsburg

Counties: Delaware, Sullivan (NY); Pike (PA)

USGS Quads: Hancock, Lake Como, Long Eddy, Calicoon, Damascus, Narrowsburg

Difficulty: Class I–II

Gradient: 4 feet per mile

Average Width: 250 feet

Velocity: Slow to moderate

Rescue Index: Accessible

Hazards: None for competent river paddlers

Scouting: Skinner's Palls

Portages: None

Scenery: Attractive to beautiful

Highlights: Pleasant, unspoiled scenery, camping

Gauge: National Park Service, (914) 252-7100; phone rings 5 times before answering

Runnable Water Levels:	Minimum	Maximum
Barryville gauge	2.9 feet	5+ feet

Additional Information: National Park Service, P.O. Box C, River Road, Narrowsburg, NY 12764, (717) 685-4871 (manned number)

Delaware River (A) • Pennsylvania

191 on the West Branch or NY Route 97 on the East Branch, depending on the water levels left by reservoir operations upstream. The Hancock area can get pretty crowded during the summer. The upper river flows between high, green hills and flat, grassy banks. The area is surprisingly remote, and very attractive. Paddling in midsummer is definitely a communal experience; canoe and tube traffic is very heavy. But in late fall and early spring the river is all but deserted, offering solitude to the hardy boater. Off-season paddlers should be aware of the dangers of capsizing on such a wide, cold river and protect themselves accordingly.

Access to the river is plentiful; places have been set aside for canoeists and fishermen by dozens of state agencies. Unfortunately, the Pennsylvania Fish Commission requires that nonpowered boats be registered in Pennsylvania or the user's home state in order to use their access points. Waterways patrolmen will ticket you if your paperwork is incorrect. Parking is often difficult, so be careful where you park and be prepared to move to another access point if your preferred point is jammed. Once again, respect the property rights of the people who live along the river and don't cross posted land except in an emergency. For a complete list of access points and camping areas, call the National Park Service at (570) 588-2451.

Section: Narrowsburg to Port Jervis
Counties: Sullivan, Orange (NY); Pike (PA)
USGS Quads: Narrowsburg, Eldred, Shohola, Pond Eddy, Port Jervis North, Port Jervis South
Gradient: 5 feet per mile
Difficulty: Class I–II
Average Width: 300 feet
Velocity: Slow to moderate
Rescue Index: Accessible
Hazards: Mongaup and Shohola rapids
Scouting: None
Portages: None
Scenery: Pretty to beautiful
Highlights: Roebling Bridge (at Lackawaxen), camping
Gauge: National Park Service, (914) 252-7100; phone rings 5 times before answering

Runnable Water Levels:	Minimum	Maximum
Barryville gauge	2.9 feet	5+ feet

Additional Information: Delaware Water Gap NRA, River Road, Bushkill, PA 18324-9999, (570) 588-2451

Most of the rapids on the Upper Delaware are straight shots over gravel bars, and thus eminently suited for inexperienced paddlers. At high levels they may have large waves or wash out entirely; at low water you may have to get out and drag your canoe for a short ways. One rapid is not so easy. Skinner's Falls is located about five miles upstream of Narrowsburg and is the most hyped-up drop on the river. It is not particularly difficult: a straightforward Class II+ rapid which at high water has good surfing waves and interesting hydraulics. But things get lively when the livery clientele gets there. You can witness innumerable capsizings, quantities of non-lifejacketed human debris, multiboat pileups on Killer Rock, unattended equipment floating downstream, and throngs of enthusiastic spectators taking it all in. A competent whitewater paddler will have no trouble; a skilled lake paddler should put on a life jacket and scout. Novices should consider carrying. If you want to witness this unique spectacle, the Park Service has an access point nearby.

Below Narrowsburg the river continues to be attractive, with fine scenery and mild rapids. There are Class II rapids at the mouth of the Shohola River, just upstream of Barryville, and at the mouth of the Mongaup River a few miles upstream of Port Jervis. Both are popular training rapids for kayakers but deserve respect by open-boat paddlers, especially at high water. The deepest pool on the river, 113 feet deep, is just downstream of Narrowsburg. Fishing here in the heat of the summer is said to be excellent. The suspension bridge at Minisink Ford, built by John Roebling, used to carry the Delaware and Hudson Canal over the Lackawaxen. It was here that he perfected the designs he would later use to construct the Brooklyn Bridge.

At Port Jervis the river takes a hard turn to the west just below the mouth of the Neversink River. The pools on this section are longer, and the rapids shorter. The Delaware Water Gap National Recreation Area begins about four miles below Matamoras. It has its origins over a fight to dam this stretch with a huge structure at Tocks Island. The preservationists won out after a decade-long fight, but not until much of the land had been condemned and purchased by the Corps of Engineers. The banks are now returning to their original unspoiled state, and this makes for an unusually attractive canoe trip. This is also the best stretch of the river for canoe camping; there are a number of primitive sites available on a first-come, first-served basis. Contact the Park Service for a complete map showing all campsites. Running the entire section makes for a delightful multiday trip. The Middle River ends at the Delaware Water Gap near Stroudsburg, Pennsylvania.

Delaware River (B) • Pennsylvania

Section: Port Jervis, NY, to Belvidere, NJ

Counties: Pike, Monroe (PA); Sussex, Warren (NJ)

USGS Quads: Port Jervis South, Milford, Culvers Gap, Lake
    Maskenzoha, Flatbrookville, Bushkill, Portland, Belvidere

Difficulty: Class I

Gradient: 4 feet per mile

Average Width: 300 feet

Velocity: Slow

Rescue Index: Accessible

Hazards: None

Scouting: None

Portages: None

Scenery: Pretty to beautiful

Highlights: Delaware Water Gap, camping

Gauge: National Park Service, (570) 588-6637

Runnable Water Levels:	Minimum	Maximum
Port Jervis	2.3 feet	Flood stage

Additional Information: The river should present no hazards
    except in flood. Delaware Water Gap National Recreation
    Area, Bushkill, PA 18324, (570) 588-6637

The Water Gap is magnificent, but it is crossed and paralleled by numerous highways. The close proximity of the Appalachian Trail means that good opportunities for hiking exist on both sides of the river. Below here the river enters a short canyon, home of the treacherous Class II+ Foul Rift rapid. Downstream there are several power plants, large factories, and a large number of houses along the banks. This is the least attractive stretch of the Delaware. It is generally flatwater, with occasional riffles and a few good drops to provide interest. The scenery improves below Easton and is surprisingly attractive as the river passes through Bucks County on the way to Trenton. Shielded by the Delaware Canal on the Pennsylvania side (now protected by Roosevelt State Park) and the Raritan Canal on the New Jersey side, the banks have remained undeveloped. Tubing is popular, especially on the stretch just north of Point Pleasant. You will not be alone if you run past here on a summer weekend, but the rest of the river is surprisingly quiet and peaceful.

There are several places which demand special attention. Foul Rift is located just below Belvidere, New Jersey, and is a strong Class II drop over jagged limestone ledges. The rapid is over a mile long and offers continuous action. It is a bad place to swim at low water, and the home of huge waves during the spring runoff. Scout from the Jersey side if in doubt and proceed cautiously.

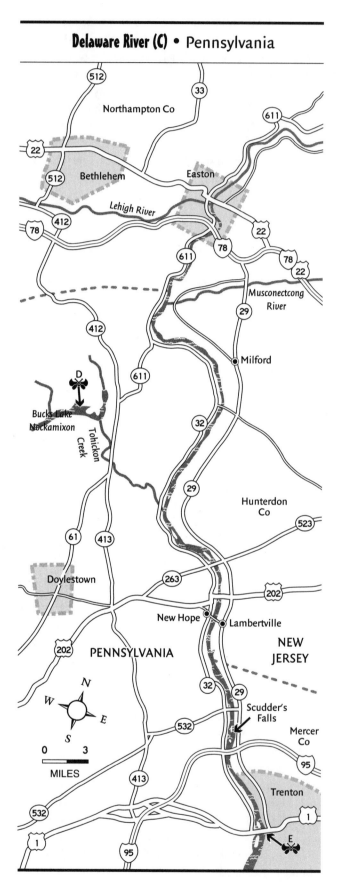

Delaware River (C) • Pennsylvania

Section: Belvidere, NJ, to Trenton, NJ

Counties: Warren, Hunterdon, Mercer (NJ); Northampton, Bucks (PA)

USGS Quads: Belvidere, Bangor, Easton, Riegelsville, Frenchtown, Lumberville, Stockton, Lambertville, Pennington, Trenton West

Difficulty: Class I; major drops are Class II–III depending on water level

Gradient: 4 feet per mile

Average Width: 500 feet

Velocity: Slow, except at major drops

Rescue Index: Accessible

Hazards: Major drops for untrained paddlers

Scouting: Major drops for untrained paddlers

Portages: Major drops for untrained paddlers

Scenery: Uninspiring to pretty

Highlights: City of Easton; major drops at Foul Rift, Lumberville, Lambertville, and Scudder's Falls

Gauge: New Jersey Weather Service, (609) 261-6612

Runnable Water Levels:	Minimum	Maximum
Trenton gauge	8.1	Flood stage

Additional Information: Beware of flood water, especially at major rapids! Delaware River Basin Commission, P.O. Box 7360, Trenton, NJ 08628; they publish an excellent map of the entire river, available for $5.00; their information line, staffed between 6:30 A.M. and 2:30 P.M., is (609) 261-6600

Lumberville Wing Dam is located below Point Pleasant near Bulls Island State Park. The two half-dams at the shores were originally built to divert water into the Delaware and Raritan Canal, which begins here. The "wings" concentrate the flow of water at the center of the river. It is not difficult when run in the center, but do not blunder over the sides at high water, when dangerous hydraulics form to catch the unwary. Also remember that the river is quite wide, and off-season swims by unprotected paddlers are potentially deadly.

Wells Falls, also known as Lambertville Rapids, lies just downstream of New Hope, a popular tourist and shopping destination. It has wing dam structures on the

sides also, but the drop is considerably harder, reaching Class III at high water. Scout from the wings before running; to miss the worst of the drop, lift over the wing on the Jersey side and run the rest of the drop. If the wings are underwater, the entire rapid may be too heavy for an open canoeist, and dangerous hydraulics will form along the sides. This spot is a popular hangout for local kayakers, and there is good squirting and surfing to be had here. There is also a mellow beginner's surfing hole on the right side of the river just below the wing dam at summer levels. At high water it is a big "flush" with few playing opportunities.

To reach the Lambertville Rapid, turn onto the main street in Lambertville from New Jersey Route 29, then turn left into the parking lot of the Station Restaurant. Drive all the way through the parking lot bearing left, pick up a dirt road by the hotel, then take the right fork at the natural gas distributor. The put-in is here, just upstream of the sewer plant.

The river flows placidly past Washington's Crossing, where the rebel forces ferried across the ice-choked river on their way to the Battle of Trenton. A state park commemorating the event provides access on both sides of the river. Scudder's Falls, the last significant drop on the river, lies several miles downstream just above the I-95 bridge. The main channel is a Class I+ riffle, but there is an interesting side chute along the Jersey Shore to the left of a scrubby island. This channel contains great surfing waves at the right water levels. Local boaters come here when the levels at Lambertville Rapid are too high for good sport. The play wave is easily reached from Route 29; there's a side road and a bridge over the canal just upstream of the I-95 on-ramps. If the weather and water conditions are right, you'll have to share the wave with teenaged surfers on boards.

If you are driving to the Delaware from a distance and want to figure out whether to head for Lambertville or Scudder's Falls, call the National Weather Service in Mt. Holly at (609) 261-6612. Scudder's Falls is best when the river flows at 4.5–7.0 feet at Rigelsville or 9.5–11 feet at Trenton. If it gets too low, go to Lambertville; if it is too high, both places will be washed out.

Muddy Creek

Located north of Baltimore and just a few miles into Pennsylvania, Muddy Creek is a paddler's delight that flows through a small but spectacular cliff-lined gorge. There are two paradoxes, however, that characterize this wonderful stream. First, the name "Muddy Creek" is a misnomer; the water is usually crystal clear. Second, it is hard to believe that such a beautiful natural stream is not too distant from the controversial nuclear power plant at Three Mile Island on the Susquehanna River.

This Class II trip (with one Class III) of about six miles is especially suited for intermediates or shepherded novices when the put-in gauge is one foot or less. At higher levels the trip is somewhat more difficult. Several Class III rapids become heavier water, and hydraulics become more dangerous on the one Class III rapids as the river rises. The journey begins just above or below a seven-foot dam (depending on your nerve and water levels), and then continues into a striking little gorge which is highlighted by Class III Snap Falls. In the gorge there is one portage around a nasty boat-busting rock pile. Finally, the Muddy mellows out through several Class II rapids amid spectacular scenery just before reaching the Susquehanna River.

The best put-in is where Route 74 crosses Muddy Creek. After careful scouting, experienced boaters can run the dam in the center (six inches or so on the gauge). At moderate levels there's no menacing hydraulic at the bottom; indeed, in summer swimmers jump from carefully selected places on the dam into the pool below. The gauge for the river (courtesy of the Conewago Canoe Club) is on the river-left side of the old Route 74 bridge's center abutment just below the six-foot dam.

While passing under the bridge, look for fish in the deep, clear pools. They might be suckers instead of trout, but it's still nice to see them. A Class I–II riffle is located just below the bridge.

After a half mile of relatively calm water, the river splits. Take either channel if there is sufficient water. The paddler will notice that the bank here is covered by

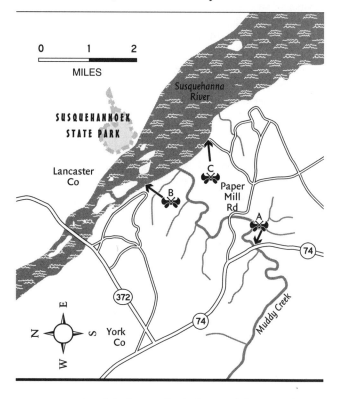

Muddy Creek • Pennsylvania

sycamores, river birches, and maples, and there is a beautiful tributary on river right.

One and a half miles from the put-in lies the bridge at Paper Mill Road, which used to be a put-in. If you put in here and plan to park on river left just downstream of the bridge, please get permission from the landowner first. Inconsiderate folks have trashed his field, and he may not take kindly to strangers leaving vehicles without his blessing. Better yet, park on the upstream river-right side of the bridge and launch your boats on the downstream river-right side.

During the next half mile of paddling you encounter some Class I rapids, enter the gorge, and approach the first good rapids of the trip—a Class II double ledge at moder-

Section: Castle Fin to Susquehanna River

County: York

USGS Quad: Holtwood

Difficulty: Class II (with one Class III section) up to 1.5 feet on put-in gauge; Class II–III at 2-4 feet on put-in gauge

Gradient: 15 feet per mile

Average Width: 20–40 feet

Velocity: Moderate to fast

Rescue Index: Accessible with difficulty

Hazards: One mile below Snap Falls is Muddy Creek Falls— a real boat buster with serious pinning possibilities, carry right. Trees occasionally in river. Snap Falls has bad hydraulics at right/center at high levels.

Scouting: Snap Falls on river right

Portages: Muddy Creek Falls—portage 100 to 150 feet on right

Scenery: Beautiful gorge for most of the trip

Highlights: Beautiful gorge for most of the trip; hemlocks and rhododendrons

Gauge: Visual only.

Runnable Water Levels	Minimum	Maximum
	0 feet	3-4 feet

ate levels. The first ledge is one foot, and the second is two feet. Don't be in a hurry to pass by these ledges because they can have challenging surfing possibilities, particularly below the second ledge with a foot of water on the put-in gauge. Experienced boaters can find some very interesting action here. About a half mile later, after a couple more one-foot drops, you arrive at the best rapids of the trip—Snap Falls. When you hear a roar and see a horizon line, get over to river right and scout at all levels.

The river splits into right and left channels at Snap Falls. The right is a straight drop, while the left is a rocky washboard. Paddlers should run the right side at moderate levels (Class III) because the left is too shallow. However, at higher levels (roughly one and a half to two feet on the put-in gauge) the hydraulics on the right side become quite nasty and the left side (still Class III) becomes padded enough to run. At really high levels (such as three feet on the gauge), the hydraulics on the right and center (now that there is enough water) have keeper characteristics and must be avoided at all costs. Throw ropes should be set below Snap Falls if needed.

This respectable four-foot drop can be deceptively placid to first-timers. At low and medium levels it should be run very tight right on the fast-moving tongue next to the right bank. After hitting the tongue, paddlers should be immediately prepared for a strong brace because the

curler at the bottom of this drop has a strong tendency to flip boaters right or left. Left-handed paddlers should be ready for a very firm low brace and right-handers should be ready for a "rock brace." An appealing alternative is a notch roughly 10 feet out from the right bank. However, there may not be sufficient water for the stern to pass over the edge of the drop without hanging up. If this happens, the paddler stops cold, the boat wobbles violently with a hung-up stern, and a flip often results.

During the next mile (which includes a couple of riffles), the paddler plunges deeper into the gorgeous gorge and can enjoy the large metamorphic rock formations (primarily schist), hemlocks, and rhododendron gracing its sides. At the end of the mile, look for the river necking down to the left between some large rocks. Pull over to the right bank, and once your boat is well beached, go over and study this steep, nasty drop, which is called Muddy Creek Falls. The rocks in this cauldron are large and sharp, and because of their location (the right side is undercut), they can create boat-busting and pinning situations. As the river gets higher, Muddy Creek Falls gets worse. We emphatically recommend that this drop be portaged. In fact, we haven't given it a class rating because we do not want to tempt foolhardy paddlers into running it. The cheap thrill of attempting Muddy Creek Falls is not worth a broken boat or body and becoming a burden to fellow paddlers. Although the 100- to 150-foot portage on river right is bumpy and over large rocks, large groups can form a "boat brigade" whereby boats are slid from one group of hands to another across this rocky spot.

The portage at Muddy Creek Falls is clearly worth the effort because the beauty of the river continues to unfold. The ranks of rocks, rhododendron, and hemlocks pass by unbroken, and folks can revel in the scenery. Just below the portage lies a Class II tight right turn with an eddy on river left just above the turn for those with good boat control. A couple of minutes below the right turn is a tight Class II left turn. During one trip we had to duck under a tree that had fallen across the river here, so be alert. Less than half mile below, a good two-foot drop is best run on the left at moderate levels. Just below the drop you'll see a 25-foot rock face on river left with spectacular little waterfalls cut into it. This provides a real photo opportunity and a super shower possibility in the summer! Plan to stop and enjoy this scenic wonder.

Shortly past the waterfalls lies the last rapid of significance—a strong Class II. Spanning most of the river from the left is a rock forming a two-foot drop and a vigorous surfing hole for the brave of heart and helmeted of head. The story is told of one poor experienced paddler who was surfing in the clutches of this hole. He tried all manner of maneuvers to get out and was getting thoroughly trashed. Finally, out of his kayak and beginning to panic, he put his feet down and touched bottom. He then simply walked out—red-faced but wiser.

Below this last rapid the gorge ends and the river widens and deepens. During the last mile to the Susquehanna, houses appear on the banks and civilization returns. Once you reach the mouth of the Muddy, you have about a mile to paddle upstream or downstream on the Susquehanna, depending on where you set your shuttle. In general, you should choose the downstream take-out at Coal Cabin Beach. If there is no wind or no heavy current on the Susquehanna, and you have a permit from the Pennsylvania Department of Natural Resources, pick the slightly shorter upstream take-out at Boeckel Landing.

If you park at Boeckel Landing without a Pennsylvania boat permit, your car will be ticketed or towed.

In addition to the geologic and plant splendors on the river, there is also wildlife. Not only do kingfishers dart here and there, escorting paddlers down the river, but other birds such as red-tailed hawks abound. On an early spring trip, one author was fortunate enough to come upon three of these hawks, which had (apparently) come together to sort out their territories.

Another nice aspect of this river is that it holds its water well. It is normally very reliable in the winter and spring and surprisingly so in the summer. The only disadvantage is that there is no telephone gauge that correlates to the river. The only sure gauge is the one painted on the old bridge at the put-in.

MARYLAND

Youghiogheny River

The Youghiogheny River in western Maryland's Garrett County is the premier whitewater experience among Maryland rivers. The pristine scenery (including the exquisitely beautiful Swallow Falls State Park), the miles of continuous whitewater, the unique play spots, the accessibility to large metropolitan areas (Pittsburgh, Baltimore, and Washington, D.C.), and the dam-released flows all combine to make this river a classic expert whitewater run.

The Youghiogheny, affectionately known as the "Yough" (pronounced "yock"), originates on Backbone Mountain, Maryland's highest. Runoff gathers in Silver Lake, West Virginia, from which the Youghiogheny flows into Maryland. The serious whitewater begins at Swallow Falls State Park north of Oakland. There are two standard runs. The Top Yough is a short, exciting stretch from Swallow Falls State Park (A) to the power plant at Hoyes Run Road (B, two and a half miles) or to Sang Run Bridge (C, six miles). The better-known Upper Yough is a run from Sang Run Bridge to Friendsville (D, nine and a half miles). The Top Yough is described below; a description of the Upper Yough follows that.

Top Youghiogheny River

The Top Yough begins with about two miles of premium whitewater, followed by roughly half a mile of flatwater to the power plant at Hoyes Run and nearly three and a half more miles of flatwater to Sang Run Bridge. Adding the 9.5 miles to Friendsville, a combined run on the Top and Upper Yough would be over 15 miles long. Over five miles of this, however, is the flatwater from Hoyes Run on the Top Yough to Warm Up Riffle on the Upper Yough. The Top Yough can be run to Hoyes Run in anything from one and a half hours to more than three hours, depending on the group involved. Add one more hour of flatwater paddling to reach Sang Run.

The six-mile trip to Sang Run has a total gradient of 280 feet, most of which occurs at Swallow Falls and the

drops immediately below. The gauge for the Top Yough is located on the downstream east right bridge piling at Sang Run. This gauge can be correlated to the Pittsburgh Weather Service phone gauge reading for Friendsville, (412) 644-2890, which is between 1.2 and 1.3 feet higher than the Sang Run gauge. If the phone reading for Friendsville is 3.4, the reading on the bridge at Sang Run should be approximately 2.15. By subtracting 1.25 feet from the phone gauge reading, you can determine with reasonable accuracy the level at Sang Run without leaving home.

In addition to these gauges, local paddlers and raft guides can often give you a very accurate reading by looking at another gauge on the bridge over the river in Friendsville. The minimum runnable level for the Top Yough is 1.5 feet on the gauge at Sang Run. You'll wind up walking if you catch it any lower. Normal runs are in the 1.7- to approximately 2.5-foot range. Above 2.5 feet, extra caution would be in order. Of course, as with any river of this type, the maximum level will be significantly higher for a skilled paddler who is intimately familiar with the river, or for anyone else with paid-up premiums on his life insurance policy.

The take-out that eliminates most of the flatwater is located at the power plant near Hoyes Run (B). Take Route 42 south from Friendsville to Route 219. Bear right on Old Route 219 (also known as Deep Creek Drive) just past this junction; very shortly thereafter take a sharp right down Sang Run Road. After less than a mile, turn left onto Hoyes Run Road. The power plant and its road are not open to the public. Take out instead at the fishing access at Hoyes Run about 0.5 mile below the dam outflow on river right. Seen from the road, it's a small pullover on the Sang Run side of a small creek. A short (100 yards) trail leads to the river.

The put-in for the Top Yough is located at Swallow Falls State Park. This can be reached from Route 219 by taking Mayhew Inn Road west to Sang Run Road. Take a left on Sang Run Road and a right on Swallow Falls Road, follow-

Richard Hopley running Swallow Falls on the Top Yough. Photo by Pete Martin.

ing the sign to the park. Using the map in this book, you can also reach the park from the power plant take-out.

Swallow Falls is the initial rapid on the Top Yough. This spectacular spot needs no description. You can see

it all from excellent vantage spots in the park. The vast majority of boaters who carefully examine the 18-foot

Section: Swallow Falls to Sang Run
County: Garrett
USGS Quads: Sang Run, Oakland
Difficulty: Class II–V with two miles of steady Class IV–V
Gradient: 45 feet per mile; two miles at 100 feet per mile
Average Width: 30–50 feet
Velocity: Fast
Rescue Index: Remote
Hazards: Swallow Falls (100 yards below Swallow Falls Road bridge) and the first ledge just below it (Swallowtail Falls); Class V Suckhole rapids 1.5 miles below this; many Class IV rapids in the first two miles
Scouting: Suckhole; boat-scouting of other rapids recommended when possible
Portages: Swallow Falls and possibly the first ledge just below it (Swallowtail Falls); perhaps Suckhole rapids
Scenery: Beautiful in many places
Highlights: Beautiful wilderness gorge
Gauge: National Weather Service (Friendsville phone gauge), (703) 260-0305 or (412) 262-5290

Runnable Water Levels:	Minimum	Maximum
Sang Run gauge	1.5 feet	2.5 feet
Friendsville phone reading	2.8 feet	3.7 feet

Additional Information: Precision Rafting in Friendsville, (301) 746-5290; Deep Creek Lake State Park, (301) 387-4110

Top Youghiogheny River • Maryland

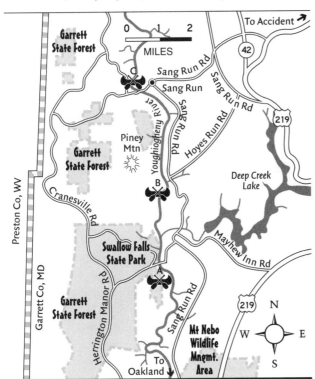

Scott Gravatt in Suckhole on the Top Yough. Photo by Kim Buttleman.

Swallow Falls will elect to put in on river left just below this drop to enjoy the tamer pleasures of the steep creek whitewater that follows. A few hundred yards below is 7-foot-high Swallowtail Falls, which is normally run on the right. It develops a nasty hydraulic at some levels and should be scouted. Carry on the left if needed. Just downstream to the left look up at 70-foot Muddy Falls, Maryland's highest waterfall.

Good, technical whitewater continues from the falls almost without a letup for the first mile or so. Easily the most notorious rapid on this section is Suckhole (Class V) located about 45 minutes (or one and a half miles) into the trip. This rapid can be recognized by the high boulder at midriver with a nasty-looking sieve of timber and trash in the pulsating gap between it and another boulder to its right. An exciting (and true) tale is told of the hapless paddler who went for a swim above Suckhole only to find himself trapped under the debris in this nasty little spot. The story has a happy ending, but it would be a hair-raising swim under the Suckhole rocks and strainers.

To avoid this ugly mess, scout Suckhole from river left and then come down midstream over a series of holes, rocks, and waves that try to push you to the left. Work right against this tendency as you approach the high boulder. You'll find a rock on the left bank just before you reach the high boulder in midstream, a small hole just to the right of this rock, and a good eddy just beyond the rock. You may want to stop in this eddy, but don't drive so close to the rock on the left that you drop

in the hole next to it and get disoriented. At lower levels, there's also an eddy on the right of the river not far above the aforementioned trashy sieve. On the other hand, you could continue without stopping in either eddy, going left of the high boulder in midstream and staying in the center of the chute. Continuing on this route, you descend over steep boulder-studded ledges with holes and waves, including a sizable hole at the bottom (Suckhole). These waves and holes (especially the bottom one) should be punched hard. A sharp rock divides the channel just above the bottom hydraulic. If you go to the right of this rock, you won't have to punch the large bottom hole. The rapid can be carried easily via an old railroad bed on the right.

If you make it smoothly through Suckhole, it's unlikely that you'll have problems with the remaining whitewater. Take out on river right just below the power plant or if you want to make the flatwater trip continue on and take out at the boater's take-out on river right above Sang Run Bridge.

Most of the Top Yough rapids can be scouted from the boat. Suckhole is the exception. Those unfamiliar with the approach to Suckhole would be wise to step out and take a good look. Rescue ropes can be set up at various spots where foul-ups might occur. Keep in mind that the nearest hospital emergency room is in Cumberland, more than an hour away by road from the take-out. If you want to carry, there's an old railroad bed on the right.

Upper Youghiogheny River • Maryland

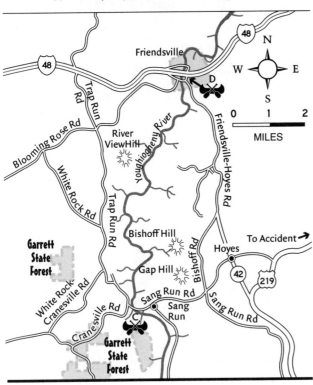

Upper Youghiogheny River

The Upper Yough is the ultimate whitewater run for expert paddlers in Maryland. It is one of the premier streams in the entire eastern United States. Longer and tougher than the Top Yough, it should be attempted only by expert boaters accompanied by someone who knows the river.

The total gradient on the Upper Yough for the entire 9.5-mile run from Sang Run to Friendsville is about 500 feet. From Gap Falls to Friendsville, the gradient is roughly 65 feet per mile, but for the section between Bastard and Heinzerling rapids the gradient is in excess of 100 feet per mile.

A normal run from Sang Run Bridge (C) to Friendsville (D) can take anywhere from three to six hours, depending on the skill levels and the group involved. Local boaters blast down at a much faster pace. If you are dependent on flows released at the power plant (see next paragraph), it would be risky to loiter excessively. Most releases are now three hours, and as long as you catch the beginning of a release and maintain a moderate pace, you will not run out of water.

The Upper Yough is runnable on natural flows throughout the spring and at other times with adequate local rainfall. However, thanks to efforts by local rafting

Section: Sang Run Bridge to Friendsville
County: Garrett
USGS Quads: Sang Run, Friendsville
Difficulty: Class II–V with 4.5 miles mostly steady Class IV–V
Gradient: 53 feet per mile; three miles at 100 feet per mile
Average Width: 30–50 feet
Velocity: Fast
Rescue Index: Remote
Hazards: Class V rapids (National Falls, Heinzerling, Meat Cleaver, Lost and Found); many Class IV rapids. Two dangerous undercuts: Toilet Bowl at second drop on right of Charlie's Choice, Tombstone Rock to left of main channel of Lost and Found
Scouting: Previously mentioned Class V rapids; boat-scouting of others is recommended when possible.
Portages: Paddlers thinking of many portages should not run this river
Scenery: Beautiful in many places
Highlights: Wilderness gorge
Gauge: National Weather Service (Friendsville phone gauge), (703) 260-0305 or (412) 262-5290

Runnable Water Levels:	Minimum	Maximum
Sang Run gauge	1.5 feet	2.5 feet
Friendsville phone reading	2.8 feet	3.7 feet

Months Runnable: Winter/spring after rain or snow melt; summer/fall on weekdays when water is released into Hoyes Run hydroelectric station
Additional Information: Friendsville Gauge: Penn Elec, (814) 533-8911; Precision Rafting, (301) 746-5290; Mountain Surf, (301) 746-5389

companies and the American Whitewater Affiliation, there are now three-hour releases, generally from 10 A.M. to 1 P.M., every Monday and Friday as well as some Saturdays between April 15 and October 15 (provided Deep Creek Lake is not drawn down too far). At moderate natural flow, it takes the release 1.5 to 2 hours to reach the Sang Run put-in from Deep Creek Lake. So if a three-hour release begins at 10 A.M., it will reach Sang Run just before noon. Water starts to fall just after 2 P.M. To get the latest information, contact Mountain Surf in Friendsville at (301) 746-5389 or call Penn Elec at (814) 533-8911. Releases are usually 600 cfs (see gauge chart at chapter's end). The power plant releasing the water was sold, and this could change everything from the phone number to release schedules.

The gauge for the Upper Yough is located on the downstream east (right) bridge piling at Sang Run. (See gauge information for Top Youghiogheny.) Normal run-

Kia Jacobson running Heinzerling on the Upper Yough.
Photo by Mayo Gravatt.

nable levels range from a minimum of 1.5 feet to some-
where around 2.5 feet on this gauge. From 2.5 feet on up,
the steeper sections get noticeably more heavy-duty. Do
not confuse this gauge with the telephone gauge for
Friendsville, which is between 1.2 and 1.3 feet higher than
the Sang Run gauge. There is also a river gauge on the
upstream left abutment on the bridge in Friendsville that
reads 0.1 feet higher than Sang Run. As in the case of
the Top Yough, the maximum runnable level is an individual matter of expertise, bravado, and life insurance.

The Upper Yough does not have the stupendous individual Class V falls and drops that characterize the Upper
Gauley or the Big Sandy in West Virginia. Instead it has a
more narrowly channeled and continuous technical character. Consequently, it is usually accorded an overall
Class IV to V rating. Unfortunately, there have been
numerous accidents—damaged boats, broken paddles,
bruises, and cuts are common. Even broken noses and legs
are not unheard of. Exercise good judgment regarding your
boating skills and those of the other boaters in your party.

No one should paddle the Upper Yough without being
aware of one big problem: politics. Political struggles
have continued in the 1990s over the number and reliability of releases to be made from Deep Creek Lake.
Because this waterway furnishes recreational opportunities to whitewater paddlers, anglers, and lake users as
well as providing power to the citizens of Pittsburgh,
there is no easy answer. The American Whitewater Affiliation continues its struggle and negotiations with Mary-

land authorities to improve the number and reliability of
summer releases from Deep Creek Lake. If you want to
help in this effort, send $20 to join the American White-
water Affiliation, P.O. Box 85, Phoenicia, NY 12464.

The political situation and the pattern of private land
ownership used to make it tough to access the Upper
Yough. Thanks to the National Lands Trust, which purchased the put-in in 1985 and transferred it to the state of
Maryland, things have changed dramatically in the past
few years. The state of Maryland now has a very good
put-in on river right in a field just upstream of the Sang
Run Bridge. Please put in here because it is the only legal
access for the public in this area.

The best take-out is on river left just below the
Friendsville bridge at John Mason's Mountain Surf whitewater shop. Don't change clothes in the open in Friendsville—it angers the town residents. Please thank the
Mountain Surf whitewater shop for providing this important public service. Also, if you take a shower and change
there, please leave a dollar or two for use of his amenities.

If you are doing your own shuttle (see the map), take
Route 42 south from Friendsville to Bishoff Road and go
right on Bishoff Road to its intersection with Sang Run
Road. Turn right on Sang Run Road to reach the put-in.

The political mess is the bad news. The good news is
that miles of challenging whitewater amid a pristine
mountain setting await you. The river is clear, the shoreline is timbered and covered with rhododendrons, and the
rapids are superb. The whitewater ranges up to Class V

Don Ellis running National
Falls on the Upper Yough.
Photo by Mayo Gravatt.

with at least 13 or more spots that have been affec-
tionate names, such as Meat Cleaver or Eddy of Death.

A word of caution: this book alone won't get you down
the Upper Yough. The descriptions provided here can
only give you a rough impression of what to expect. If
you have doubts about your ability to handle difficult,
steep, or technical whitewater, you should go elsewhere
or at least take your first trip with someone who knows
the river well.

If there is one rapid that requires a special warning it
would probably be Meat Cleaver. A blind drop that cannot be scouted entirely from a boat, it contains some
weird currents with the possibility of a broach on sharp
rocks in midstream. More paddlers screw up here than
anywhere else. Meat Cleaver is worth a few doses of
adrenaline, but you will hit lots of good stuff before you
get there. The rapids described below are generally Class
IV (unless otherwise noted) when the Sang Run gauge is
two feet. They are a shade easier at lower levels and
tougher at higher levels.

About two to three miles down from the Sang Run
Bridge you encounter Warm Up Riffle, a Class II rapid
named because it's a good place to goof off and warm
up or picnic while getting your trip together. Not far
downstream from Warm Up Riffle is Gap Falls, a sizable
slide rapid with waves and holes on the way down. Enter
from river left; just before hitting the bigger waves in the
middle, angle right and work right to miss the hole at the
bottom. As you become more familiar with Gap Falls, at

lower levels you may want to try for the Eddy of Death
next to the left bank about three-quarters of the way
down the drop. It derives its colorful name from the
undercut rock guarding its downstream end.

Once you're past Gap Falls, things mellow out for less
than a mile (III+) before an intense three- to four-mile section begins. Bastard is first. Located on river left, it
requires a tight right turn to miss a big hole and pop
lightly into a big eddy on the right, behind the boulder
that forms the right side of the main drop. The rest of the
rapid can be boat-scouted.

Bastard is followed by Charlie's Choice, which can be
run in numerous ways. The normal route is on the left—
a tight, blind, double drop. On the right are two tight
moves between rocks at the top of two drops, both of
which have a pillowed boulder at the bottom. The first
one can be quite abrasive at low levels, but the second
one has more of a pillow. In the next rapid, don't get too
far right on the second drop because of a dangerous
undercut called Toilet Bowl.

Just after Charlie's Choice is Triple Drop (Class III–V).
There is a tricky hole-ledge combination (Snaggle Tooth)
that can be run down the right, entering from the eddy
upstream on the right or a very small eddy at the very top
of the rapid on the left. There are three boulders on the
right as you go downstream; for an uneventful descent,
you should stay close to these boulders as you go down.
There is a good eddy on river right at the end of Snaggle
Tooth before the second phase of Triple Drop, which is

nothing more than some Class II ledges. The third part of Triple Drop contains National Falls. The easiest way to run this from the eddy below Snaggle Tooth is to work your way to the far left over the intervening Class II+ ledges. Then, from the eddy just above the main drop on river left, turn left as you ride the curler down. The other route from the right over Class V National Falls is not for the faint of heart. Crank hard if you go this route, and expect to be trashed by the hole at the bottom if you miss your boof.

Beyond Triple Drop lies Tommy's Hole. Located on the left, this hole is tightly packed between an upstream and a downstream boulder. Some small boats with no edges have trouble getting out. A good sneak route exists to the right near the middle of the river, but you should work your way back quickly to river left just below Tommy's Hole.

After a steep sequence just below Tommy's Hole (called Little Niagara) the paddler confronts Zinger, a diagonal wave-hole combination. Enter from the top eddy on river left. There are two routes. You can stay far left as you exit the eddy, heading about two o'clock (cocking your bow 60 degrees to the right of downstream) and go straight, punching the diagonal curler-hole. To take the other route, first go right toward the large boulder that forms the right side of the drop, then surf the diagonal curler from right to left as you pass the large boulder to your right. Sanctuary can be sought in a good-sized eddy next to the left bank below the large boulder. The exit from this eddy is obvious (to the right if you opt not to catch the eddy). Zinger is not a notorious troublemaker as Upper Yough rapids go, but it has given some paddlers problems. You can sneak Zinger on the far right.

After Zinger and Trap Run Falls (a punchable hydraulic with a rock in its center), and some Class III–type stuff, look for the right-side entrance to Heinzerling, a Class IV–V rapid. If you miss this hard-to-find approach, you will be forced to take a much tougher route down the center and left. To catch the best approach (called Rifle Barrel), cross a shallow rocky area on the right to reach a shady pool upstream and to the right of the initial drop of Heinzerling. The first phase of Heinzerling can be boat-scouted from the bottom of this pool, and it is truly a classic whitewater spot. From the eddy at the top it looks much steeper and more complex than it really is. First you drop several feet over the first ledge and catch an eddy to the right or left to look over the bottom drop. From either eddy you head directly downstream toward the big pillowed boulder visible at the bottom. Ride the pillow on the boulder, bracing right and sliding off it to the left. If you ride high enough on the pillow, you will

avoid the nastier parts of the holes just to the left of the big boulder. Going to the right of the boulder may be bumpy. Just below Heinzerling is an interesting little jumble called Boulder Dance.

Meat Cleaver (a genuine Class V) follows Heinzerling. Paddlers used to start from river right, going over a small drop and turning left behind some big boulders. Because of a recent flood, the best way to enter Meat Cleaver now is over a three-foot ledge on the left of the main channel entering the rapid. You can then see the final drop with two shark-teeth rocks more or less in the center of the drop. Thread your way between (or to one side of) these sharp rocks (the route between the two rocks is preferable). If you eddy out on the left above the shark teeth, your trip will become more exciting because it is more difficult to thread the proper course without broaching. Broaching on the Meat Cleaver rocks is not recommended.

After a few Class III rapids beyond Meat Cleaver, the paddler encounters Powerful Popper, a Class III–IV rapid marked by three midstream boulders. A pop-up-and-squirt stop is in order here. Be sure to work hard enough right to avoid the Death Slot to the left of the big boulder forming the left side of the main drop.

The next major rapid follows quickly and is one of the more technical drops on the river: Lost and Found (Class V). Some choice surfing holes are immediately upstream, so enjoy them while you can. Lost and Found consists of a maze of congested offset rocks. As with almost everything on the Upper Yough, it can be run in different ways. The various possibilities can be boat-scouted to some degree from an eddy just above the rapid. The cautious boater on an initial run may want to look it over from the island on the right side of the main drop. A sneak route is available from the eddy around on far river right; this involves dropping off a four-foot ledge into the pool below all the messy stuff. There are several routes through the hard stuff if you elect to try that. If enough water is available, the easiest route is to squeeze between the round rock on the upper right at the beginning of the rapid and the adjacent rocky island. This approach offers a reasonably straight shot downstream. With this approach you will be less likely to get lost when slaloming right and left around the rocks in midstream. You also will not go so far right as to get tangled up in "F—Up Falls" at the bottom. Also lookout for Tombstone Rock lurking by the left side of the main channel—it is dangerously undercut.

If you have made it this far without incident, you'll probably have few problems with the remaining Class IVs: Cheeseburger Falls, Wright's Hole, and Double Pencil Sharpener. Except for Cheeseburger Falls (a blind drop on river right), these can all be scouted from the boat. Try to run the main drop at Cheeseburger at least one boat-length out from the right bank to avoid a submerged rock at the bottom of the ledge that forms Cheeseburger Falls. This submerged rock has broken several paddles. You can sweep into the eddy on river right just past this hole. Sticky Wright's Hole can be punched at the usual summer-release water levels by driving hard through the left side of the hole. The hole can also be sneaked on far river left or circumvented on river right by surfing down some diagonal waves. Double Pencil Sharpener is just below Wright's Hole and can be boat-scouted from an eddy on river right. After these rapids, three to four miles of less distinguished small stuff and flatwater remain until Main Street in Friendsville.

There is one final item of interest about this spectacular river. Starting in 1981, there has been an annual downriver race on the Upper Yough in August by expert paddlers who know the river intimately. The race continues to draw boaters who are on the cutting edge of paddling. National Falls is one of the best places to view the race. Contact Precision Rafting in Friendsville for details. (Roger Zbel, owner of this raft company, has won the race 17 out of 18 times as of 1998.)

Friendsville USGS Gauge

Procedure to get Sang Run Gauge reading from natural flow plus Penn Elec release from Deep Creek Lake.

1. From the table below, determine the cfs of the early-morning Friendsville natural-flow gauge reading.
2. Add 600 cfs (from the Penn Elec release) to this amount.
3. Determine the revised Friendsville gauge level.
4. Subtract 1.25 feet from this revised Friendsville level to get the Sang Run gauge level.

Note: When comparing natural flows, Friendsville is generally 1.3 feet higher than Sang Run at lower flows and 1.2 feet higher at medium and higher flows. At two feet on the Sang Run gauge, the Friendsville gauge is usually 3.25 feet.

Level (feet)	Flow (cfs)
2.0	45
2.1	60
2.2	77
2.3	100
2.4	130
2.5	168
2.6	211
2.7	261
2.8	317
2.9	380
3.0	449
3.1	526
3.2	610
3.3	713
3.4	826
3.5	952
3.6	1,077
3.7	1,211
3.8	1,355
3.9	1,509
4.0	1,673
4.1	1,847
4.2	2,032
4.3	2,213

Chart from Youghiogheny River Recreational Capacity Study by A. Graefe, et al., December 1989, courtesy USGS.

Savage River

The Savage is a little brawling river that certainly lives up to its name. Here you have four miles of jam-packed continuous whitewater for the advanced paddler. At very low levels (below 2.4 feet on the recorded gauge), strong intermediate paddlers can try the last two miles of this section to see if they're ready for the tougher upper half. However, be warned: there are very few eddies on the relentless downhill scramble to the North Branch of the Potomac. Also, because of the cold, dam-released water averaging 46 degrees Fahrenheit, wet suits should always be used—even in summer months, at this elevation of 1,300 feet. One important safety feature is that the Savage River Road closely follows the river. It provides first-timers with the chance to see what they are up against and a take-out is relatively easy if problems develop. However, some of the major rapids can't be seen from the road, so these will need to be scouted from the river. At moderate levels (800–900 cfs or three feet on the recorded gauge) the river is a continuous heavy Class III with a couple of Class IV rapids thrown in for added excitement. This is the level described below. However, at higher levels, the run gets much tougher because of the relentless 75-foot-per-mile gradient.

The best action and scenery are found within the first two miles of the trip. Here the clear, clean river drops through a small, pretty gorge, and the riverbanks are festooned with rhododendrons, maples, mountain ashes, tulip poplars, and hemlocks. During the second two miles the rapids calm down to an easier, steady, Class III dull roar, and the scenery beyond the riverbanks slowly gets worse as one nears the take-out. Trash is increasingly scattered near the riverbank on the right, and big excavations scar the land beyond the riverbank on the left.

Nevertheless, this river is a gem of whitewater brilliance. The easiest put-in is just over four miles up Savage River Road (A). It is on river right from a very short dirt-road spur about 100 yards upstream of a white concrete bridge. Or you can put in on river left half a mile farther upstream from a dirt road that leaves the camping area just downstream from the same bridge. The description that follows covers the trip from the put-in by the white concrete bridge.

Incidentally, the Savage River Dam is worth a peek if you have the time and don't mind listening to the noisy pumping station. Only three-quarters of a mile upstream from the white concrete bridge near the put-in, this earth-and-rockfill dam is over 1,000 feet wide and nearly 200 feet tall. Its capacity is 6.5 billion gallons of water. Fishermen enjoy the lake formed by the dam and can often be seen casting from the dam's rocky face. Bass, crappie, and brown and rainbow trout can be caught here. Fish are also stocked downstream in the spring for the fishing season. Even if you don't want to fish, Savage Lake is a very scenic flatwater paddle.

About 20 to 30 yards downstream from the put-in is a good 25-yard Class III rapids over two ledge-like drops. This will wake you up immediately—even if the cold, dam-released water does not. You may want to peek at this rapid before running it. A river gauging station used to be found right below this rapid, on the left about 30 yards upstream from the white concrete bridge. Unfortunately, this gauge was washed away by high water in recent years. As a result, you should rely on the recorded message at (703) 260-0305—with one exception. On whitewater race days you should check with race officials or call the Savage Dam to determine the timing and level of cfs released.

Next to the old gauge site and immediately before passing under the bridge, the paddler will encounter a two-foot ledge. A half mile of continuous Class III waves and boulder-garden action follows, until the paddler reaches a pool 100 yards or so long—the only sizable pool encountered before the paddler is disgorged at the take-out on the North Branch of the Potomac. This pool is formed by the five-foot Piedmont Dam.

The dam can be run in two ways. First there is a two-yard notch (exciting) in the dam a few yards from the left bank, or a challenging jumble of rocks on the extreme

John Lugbill at the 1989
World Championships
on the Savage.
Photo by Ed Grove.

Paul Possinger in the middle of
Island Rapid on the Savage.
Photo by Ron Knipling.

right (runnable only by experienced boaters with great care and attentive scouting). At low levels (500 cfs or 2.4 feet on the recorded gauge) there won't be enough water in the notch. At 1,000 cfs a nasty hydraulic develops below the notch on the left side of the river. Nervous boaters can carry on the left. Just below the dam (where the whitewater slalom course is usually set up for regional and national competition) continuous Class III waves and boulder-garden action continue for another good half-mile, then the river flows toward the road, which has a nice, white stone face on its other side. As the

Savage turns right and away from the road, get ready for the first drop of Triple Drop, also known as Crisscross.

At moderate levels this rapid is a low Class IV consisting of three drops. Scout from the left. The first can be run next to a rock on the right side; the second has a nice tongue in the center; the last drop, which can develop a strong hole, is best run on the right. It should be mentioned that trees often fall across this small river. On one trip a tree blocked the third drop, and one boater (who had fallen out of his boat upstream) briefly suffered a body pin on the trunk of this tree.

Section: Below the Savage River Dam to confluence with the
  North Branch of the Potomac

County: Garrett

USGS Quads: Westernport, Barton, Bittinger

Difficulty: Class III–IV up to 800 cfs (up to 3 feet on gauge);
  Class IV from 800 to 1,200 cfs (from 3.0 to 3.5 feet on
  gauge); Class IV–V above 1,200 cfs

Gradient: 75 feet per mile

Average Width: 20–40 feet

Velocity: Fast

Rescue Index: Accessible

Hazards: Trees down in river, large holes at high levels, few
  eddies

Scouting: Advisable for Class III–IV Triple Drop, Class IV
  Memorial Rock, and Class III–IV Island Rapid

Portages: None

Scenery: Pretty to beautiful at the put-in, slowly changes to
  fair at the take-out

Highlights: Beautiful small gorge for most of the trip; dam-
  release river

Gauge: Savage Dam, (301) 359-0361

Runnable Water Levels: Minimum   Maximum
                            2.0 feet (300 cfs)   3.8 feet (1,500 cfs)

Months Runnable: Generally a dam release for races and in winter and spring after hard rains and snowmelt

Additional Information: Corps of Engineers recording, (410) 962-
  7687

Savage River • Maryland

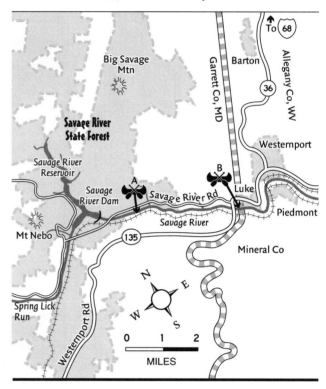

Following Triple Drop, the paddler reaches the tough-est single drop on the river, fittingly called Memorial Rock. At moderate levels this low Class IV can be recognized by a large, pointed boulder sticking out of the water about 10 feet off the left bank. Generally, one should run just to the right of the rock angled left to avoid a sub-merged rock and a mean hole covering the river on the right. Be ready to punch a few holes just below. If there is enough water, you can sneak on the extreme left on the other side of Memorial Rock. No wonder things are so busy during this stretch: the gradient is 100 feet per mile!

Below Memorial Rock, go left of an island to run the best part of Class III–IV Island Rapids. At higher levels you may want to scout this turbulent passage from the left. There are a couple of good holes to avoid or punch as the river closely follows the road again. Then, two miles into the trip, you'll reach a white clapboard church. Just before the church at lower levels, a super surfing hydrau-lic extends over three-quarters of the river from the left and has a nice small recovery pool. This used to be the take-out for those only wanting to run the tougher upper

part of the Savage and the put-in for more nervous souls who did not want to challenge the upper section. How-ever, if you want to use the church (or another spot downstream 100 yards) for access, get permission first.

For the last two miles the Savage continues at a calmer pace. The main items to note on this lower sec-tion include a two-foot diagonal ledge just upstream of a bridge a mile below the church, followed about three-quarters of a mile later by a pool where paddlers can regain composure before the final quarter mile to the North Branch. At press time, the last mile of the Savage had many strainers. Therefore, you may want to consider taking out at the bridge one mile above the take-out. Once you reach the North Branch, you can either take out river left on the Savage or you can paddle 100 yards upstream for a river left take-out on the North Branch.

The Savage is not a river for the inexperienced or unwary. Kayakers should have a bombproof roll under rocky conditions, and open boaters should have full flota-tion, helmets, and wet suits—even in summer months. Swims are generally long and cold despite the small size of this river. Boat recovery is difficult because of the ceaseless nature of the rapids.

As mentioned earlier, this description reflects 800 cfs or 3.6 feet on the recorded gauge. When the level goes from 800 to 1,200 cfs, the river becomes much pushier. Although the rocks are covered and padded, the hydraulics are grabbier and the waves much more powerful. It gets more difficult to catch the few eddies available along the shore because by this time the river is running through the rhododendrons on the banks. Consider this a solid Class IV run. At 1,200 cfs and higher the river becomes very nasty, with very dangerous hydraulics, and should be considered a Class IV–V trip for expert boaters only.

Unfortunately, running this river is dependent on getting releases from the Savage River Dam through the cooperation of the Upper Potomac River Commission. These releases are scheduled sporadically in the spring and summer, particularly if races are scheduled, but sometimes heavy rains will allow the damkeepers to release unspecified amounts in an unscheduled manner.

On the other hand, exciting things have happened to the Savage. The 1989 International Canoe Federation World Championships in Slalom and Whitewater (for decked boats) was held here in June 1989. This was the first time world championships were held in the United States. Our team won several medals—including Jon Lugbill, who won the gold medal, and Davey Hearn, who won a silver medal, both in C-1 slalom.

Savage River Water Level Conversion (Correlation) Table

Savage River Gauge (in cylinder gauging station building located 0.7 miles below Savage River Dam)

Height (feet)	Flow (cfs)
0.6	43
0.8	57
1.0	79
1.2	112
1.4	151
1.6	190
1.8	236
2.0	298
2.2	383
2.4	480
2.6	587
2.8	704
3.0	834
3.2	974
3.4	1,126
3.6	1,290
3.8	1,480
4.0	1,685
4.2	1,905
4.4	1,140
4.6	2,390
4.8	2,656
5.0	2,938
5.2	3,236
5.4	3,550
5.6	3,805
5.8	3,067
6.0	4,337
6.2	4,615
6.4	4,900
6.6	5,143
6.8	5,389

Source: The above data was obtained from the Maryland District Office of the USGS.

North Branch of the Potomac

Steyer to Shallmar

The run from Steyer to Shallmar is the classic section of the North Branch of the Potomac River and is for advanced to expert paddlers only. Be warned that the length and continuous nature of this trip give it an expedition-like quality. Here the North Branch drops at a giddy gradient of over 50 feet per mile, quite a drop for a reasonably sized river. There are no midway take-outs, and the only solace is a set of railroad tracks next to the river, which can be used for emergency walkouts (with or without boats). For the first third of the trip, the tracks are on your left; for the remainder, they are on the right.

Do not venture on this river unless you are very competent and in good physical and mental shape. The whole run is long and strenuous, and a full day should be allowed to complete it by those running this section for the first time. Even highly experienced boaters who know the river well should allow six hours of daylight on the river. Except for the very beginning and the very end you will be working continuously. Throughout most of the trip quiet stretches of water are not more than 50 yards long. Each decked-boater should have a strong roll; each open-boater should be capable of self-rescue in continuous Class III rapids. Naturally, helmets and flotation are mandatory for all boats. Rescue is very difficult, particularly at upper levels, and you're on your own because of the relentless nature of this run. There have been quite a few hairy experiences for intermediate paddlers who have found this river too much to handle. Advanced and expert paddlers have also had real trouble when the river was too high.

To avoid an excessive case of white knuckles or a long walk on a railroad track, pay careful attention to the gauge at Kitzmiller. A reasonable absolute minimum is 4.7 feet. An extra foot of water on this gauge (say, moving from five to six feet) can change this from a demanding Class III–IV trip to an extremely difficult Class IV–V run. A level of five and a half feet on the Kitzmiller gauge would be very taxing for highly experienced open-boaters with full flotation. Expert decked-boaters should think of

six and a half feet as an upper limit, primarily because of the countless hydraulics and the relentless gradient. Clearly, when the water get higher, the hydraulics get grabbier, with many becoming absolute keepers at levels over seven feet.

Besides checking the Kitzmiller gauge at the take-out, paddlers should also check Stony River where it crosses Route 50 to determine the volume of water from this river. The Stony joins the North Branch a third of the way into the trip and nearly doubles the volume of the North Branch.

About a half mile downstream from the put-in at Steyer (A), look for a Steyer river gauge on the left. It should be between 2.9 (very scrapy) and 4.2 feet. Unless you are really into rocks, however, this gauge probably should be a good three feet. If the gauge is underwater, perhaps you shouldn't be here at all.

After a mile or two of placid Class I–II rock garden rapids (quite scrapy if the river is low), the drops become more abrupt and interesting. The first island below Steyer should be run to the right and has a good drop into a hole. The flood of 1985 rerouted the river at the second island, bypassing Corkscrew, an aptly named Class III–IV rapid, which can only be run at 5.5 feet or above, and only if the paddler is aware of its location. Corkscrew is basically a four-foot horseshoe ledge (prongs downstream) and is best entered left of center, headed toward the right. At lower levels, most of the water is channeled to the right of this second island, providing an exciting alternative to Corkscrew. Here a fairly steep drop climaxes in a large but punchable hydraulic. If you have any real problems to this point, strongly consider the three-mile carry back to the put-in. A seemingly interminable walk with a boat is vastly preferable to a seemingly interminable flush down the river without it.

From here to its junction with the Stony, the narrow and rocky North Branch continues falling away at a steep and respectful pace. If you haven't noticed by now, this is probably the ledgiest river you have ever paddled. Surf

Dave Lautenburg on
Rattlesnake Rapid.
Photo by Bob Maxey.

away if you wish, but make sure you save enough energy to complete this long, demanding run. A half mile before the North Branch joins the Stony, look out for a steep rapid that features two powerful offset diagonal holes.

When the Stony joins the North Branch four miles below Steyer, not only does the water volume nearly double but the color generally changes for the better, too. The brown foamy North Branch, usually muddy from strip mines, is diluted by the clearer waters of the Stony. Unfortunately, both rivers are sterile and polluted with mine acids. Once the Stony merges with the North Branch, the river becomes more powerful and pushier. About a half mile below the confluence of these rivers you will pass under a railroad bridge. Get ready, because just below this bridge lies the biggest action of this trip—three large ledges located fairly close together.

The first and perhaps most difficult ledge is Rattlesnake Ledge, a Class IV at moderate levels. It has been given a very salty name by old-time paddlers—"MF" is their abbreviation for this name. Get out and scout this rapid on the left. It is a large, complex sloping ledge of roughly six feet. Enter left of center and move farther left to skirt an impressive roostertail, then punch or miss (to the left) a deceptively nasty hole at the very bottom. Many a paddler has concentrated his attention on the roostertail and breathed a sigh of relief when safely past it, only to be nailed by the hole, whose viciousness can escape a casual glance. This hole is called "Lady Kenmore" by local paddlers.

Fortunately, at moderate levels you'll find a nice pool in which to pick up the pieces. Set throw ropes and rescue boats just below this large ledge and Lady Kenmore on river left. At about 4.8 feet on the Kitzmiller gauge a passage opens on the right that is probably the best slot for open boaters.

Although your attention will be focused totally on the river at this point, do look out for timber rattlesnakes here and elsewhere along the banks, particularly on warm, sunny days. A paddler who was once walking on the bank by this ledge thought the timer in his camera was buzzing, but it turned out to be a three-and-a-half-foot rattlesnake lying in front of him sounding its own built-in buzzer.

Not too far downstream is the second big ledge, the steepest of the three and perhaps the most fun. At reasonable levels, this sharply sloping six-foot ledge is a Class IV rapids. It is a straightforward drop best run with good speed down the center of the ledge into a generally forgiving mass of foam and water.

The third ledge (Class IV) of over five feet also appears very shortly. It should generally be run on the right—a sloping and jagged complex drop with some scraping. At low levels this last ledge has been run on the far left with a turn to the right.

First-timers should scout all three ledges, and even experienced paddlers who know the river should look them over—particularly at higher levels such as five and a half feet on the Kitzmiller gauge. Above six and a half

Section: Gormania, WV (Steyer), to Kitzmiller, MD (Shallmar)
Counties: Garrett (MD), Mineral (WV), Grant (WV)
USGS Quads: Gorman, Kitzmiller, Mount Storm
Difficulty: Class III–IV (Kitzmiller 4.7–5.2 feet); Class IV
    (Kitzmiller 5.2–5.5 feet); Class IV–V (Kitzmiller 5.5–6.5
    feet)
Gradient: 55 feet per mile
Average Width: 30–70 feet
Velocity: Fast
Rescue Index: Remote
Hazards: Occasional trees in river, three large ledges, old
    bridge pier and Maytag rapids near the end of the trip, con-
    tinual hydraulics, heavy water at high levels
Scouting: Corkscrew rapid above confluence with the Stony
    (Class III–IV), three big ledges (Class III–IV) at moderate
    levels, Maytag rapids (Class IV)
Portages: None
Scenery: Pretty or beautiful in spots
Highlights: Heavy continuous whitewater through reasonably
    scenic gorge
Gauge: National Weather Service for Kitzmiller gauge, (703)
    260-0305

Runnable Water Levels:	Minimum	Maximum
Kitzmiller	4.7 feet	6.5 feet
Steyer	2.9 feet	4.2 feet

Additional Information: The Steyer gauge is a half mile down-
    stream from Steyer put-in; Potomac State Forest, (301)
    334-2038

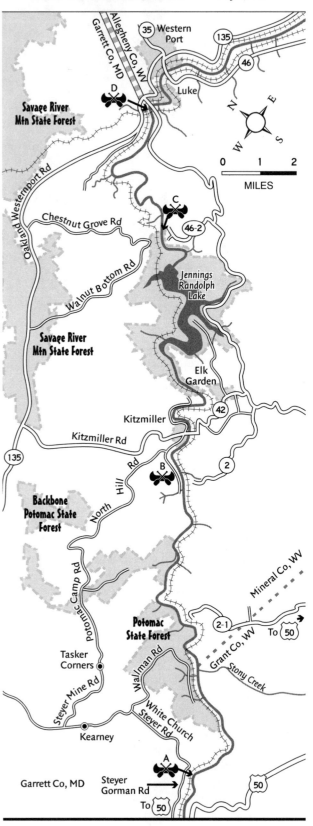

feet on this gauge some of the holes below these three ledges become absolute keepers.

Following these drops the river broadens, and for a short distance the rapids become straightforward wave trains. Then the river narrows and again takes on a serious nature with a seemingly endless series of Class III ledges, boulder gardens, and crosscurrents at moderate levels. Surfing freaks can go bonkers again. Constant maneuvering becomes the order of the day. At higher levels—say, five and a half feet on Kitzmiller gauge—this turns into Class IV stuff. At six feet and above, one rockets along through big waves while avoiding some keeper holes.

Roughly three-quarters of the way through the run, be alert for two dangers: first, a toppled concrete bridge pier, which should be run far left; second, an innocent-looking rapid that contains several powerful holes and a series of sizable offset waves, appropriately called Maytag. More paddlers seem to swim here than anyplace else, perhaps due to fatigue and the fact that Maytag resembles an approach to several other, much easier upstream rapids. There are two ways to know when Maytag is imminent. First, it is located on the third left turn as the river winds close to the railroad tracks on the right. Second, look for a tall, sheer rock cliff on the left reminiscent of the wall above High Falls on the Cheat River in West Virginia. This cliff has a man-made stone wall in the center that distinguishes it from other cliffs on this trip. Maytag is the next rapid downstream from this cliff. It begins as a gentle left bend that looks easy but soon becomes a monster. Approaching six feet on the gauge, this rapid has several large holes in the first half of a long train of big waves. Paddling on the extreme left is generally the way to miss the worst of the holes, but you will still have to keep your balance through some powerful offset waves. Maytag is Class IV at five feet on the gauge and tougher at higher levels. Scout it.

After you have paddled about 11 miles and are panting from maneuvering and playing (if you still have any energy), look for the take-out at the old mining town of Shallmar on the left (B). Abram Creek joins the North Branch on river right just opposite the take-out. By taking out at Shallmar you can avoid two miles of less interesting rapids (dredged channel) and scenery (strip mines) before you get to the Route 42 bridge in Kitzmiller. At five feet and below on the Kitzmiller gauge, parts of the last two miles become almost too shallow and picky to paddle.

Except for the water quality and railroad tracks, this is a very scenic trip when you can get your head out of the rapidly unfolding rapids and look around. There are pretty cliffs, hemlocks, rhododendrons, and forested canyon walls to make you forget your increasingly aching muscles.

For more experienced paddlers who are really in shape, a tougher trip can be had by putting in on the Stony River (with its gradient of 75 feet per mile) at Route 50. This makes the trip two miles and perhaps two hours longer and considerably more demanding. The Stony is somewhat more difficult than the North Branch and consists of many sharp, blind drops throughout its boulder-choked descent. Downed trees are also a particular risk on this narrow stream. Several years ago an experienced paddler was trapped and killed underneath a log hidden just below water level. Paddlers who brave the Stony (a solid Class IV river at even moderate levels) will usually welcome the relatively open and larger nature of the North Branch.

The main negative aspect of this trip is that the North Branch is not up very often. The prime times are during winter and spring two to four days after a hard rain. But keep the faith: it has been run on Labor Day after a humongous rain a couple of days earlier.

The shuttle is straightforward, if somewhat long. From Shallmar drive downstream to Route 38, turn right, and cross the Potomac into West Virginia. Climb to the top of a high plateau. Enjoy the outstanding views before turning right onto WV 42 at Elk Garden, then right again onto US 50. This road crosses over the Stony River and makes a steep run down the mountain into Gormania. Cross the Potomac back into Maryland, take the first right, and follow the river downstream. Stop at a rough parking lot on the right, next to the tracks, where the road heads away from the river.

Barnum to Bloomington

The six-mile section of the North Branch of the Potomac River from Barnum (C) to Bloomington (D) is a solid intermediate run. It is basically composed of long, strong Class II+ wave action and rock gardens interspersed with long pools. At 1,000 cfs, a few of these wave trains approach Class III. To break this delightful monotony, however, a short but strong Class III double ledge appears midway through the trip. It should be scouted the first time. For those who like to play, surfing spots galore during the first third of the trip provide many opportunities.

This section of the North Branch is much gentler than the smaller Savage River, which joins the North Branch at the Bloomington take-out. It is also easier than the tougher big-brother section of the North Branch from Steyer to Shallmar, which ends about 10 miles upstream from the Barnum put-in. However, the steady gradient and general feeling of going downhill often remind one of these other two sections.

The trip is very scenic. The North Branch flows through a beautiful gorge broken only by the occasional appearance of railroad tracks and, near the end, large industrial buildings and logging trucks. The hardwood forest generally extends right down to the river—maples, sycamores, and sometimes oaks are found near the banks, and evergreens such as hemlocks are also seen here and there. The clear waters used to be sterile from earlier mining operations, but since the dam was built, water quality has improved. Now fish and other life appear in the river.

Just below the Barnum bridge abutments you will encounter a 50-yard Class II rapid with a two-foot ledge, followed shortly by a 100-yard-long Class II rapid and a railroad bridge. This bridge is followed by a pool, 100 yards of good Class II–III standing waves, another pool, and then another spot of standing waves. The relaxing monotony of the run continues with yet another pool and

Top of the World Rapid on the North Branch of the Potomac.
Photo by Ron Knipling.

Section: Barnum (WV) to Bloomington (MD)
Counties: Garret
USGS Quads: Kitzmiller, Westernport
Difficulty: Class II–III with two solid Class III rapids
Gradient: 35 feet per mile
Average Width: 40–70 feet
Velocity: Fast
Rescue Index: Remote
Hazards: None
Scouting: Class III Double Ledge
Portages: None
Scenery: Beautiful at start, pretty in spots at end
Highlights: Beautiful gorge, dam-release trip
Gauge: U.S. Army Corps of Engineers (Randolph Jennings
    Dam on Bloomington Lake), (410) 962-7687

Runnable Water Levels:	Minimum	Maximum
	300 cfs	1,250 cfs
	(600 is good)	(max release)

Months Runnable: Several dam releases each year
Additional Information: Bloomington Dam, (304) 355-2346

still another 100 yards of Class II–III standing waves. However, here there is a difference. At the end of these last waves two major surfing ledges appear with several minor surfing spots adjacent or downstream. At 1,000 cfs, one of these ledges brings to mind Swimmer's Ledge on the Lower Youghiogheny in Pennsylvania except that the run-out here is not nearly as clean if one flips. At higher levels these two ledges can create stopper hydraulics.

A couple of minutes and another set of standing waves later, take note of the rock face and pretty evergreen on the left. This pool is called Blue Hole. Ahead, when the river splits, take the larger right channel (if there is sufficient water) and you'll find yourself dropping down a Class II rapid with a cobble bar on the left and a smooth concrete rock face on the right supporting the railroad tracks above. Two nice surfing spots are encountered at the end of this rapid. At 1,000 cfs, the second of these is a particularly enjoyable kayak-sized hole in the middle of the river. A kind but firm teacher, it does not discriminate against open boats. The cobble bar here also makes a nice lunch stop.

Past the cobble bar the long sections of standing waves and pools alternate again. One of these Class II standing wave fields is about 300 yards long. After a few more rock gardens and pools the river splits once again, at an island, and you should take the much larger main channel to the right. About a quarter mile later, when the first island, ends and another small river channel on the left creates a second island, continue on the right, but be alert because the one strong Class III rapid of the trip is approaching.

After three wave patches, the river bends left into a horizon line and a major-sounding rapid. Quickly catch the last-chance eddy on the left. Get out on the island and scout this rapid, which consists of two ledges about 25 yards apart. The first ledge should be run center or left of center because at 1,000 cfs the hole formed by the ledge gets nasty toward the right. This will also set you up to run the second, larger ledge center or left of center. At 600 cfs good tongues mark the routes over these two ledges, but at 1,000 cfs the routes are less obvious. The second island ends shortly after the rapids.

This spicy change of pace is followed by a couple of long rock gardens and a long pool. At the end of this pool, look for a railroad trestle on the left and the point where the river necks down on the right. You have reached Top of the World Rapid, with its Class III twisty waves on the right at 1,000 cfs and a vigorous, punchable hole at the end.

After another pool the river necks down slightly on the left and you're faced with a second helping of standing waves not quite as dynamic as those just upstream. However, there is a vigorous surfing hole and two good surfing waves at the end of this rapid. Next, there is a long pool and another island. If there's enough water, go right. Pools and long Class I–II rapids alternate until you reach a railroad bridge a half mile from the take-out. The bridge is followed by another Class I–II rapid, a long pool, and then the river splits. Go left this time. About five minutes later you will approach a high concrete-and-stone-block railroad bridge. The concrete is located on the upstream face of the bridge and the stone block on the downstream face.

The best take-out is above this bridge on river left. To reach it from WV 46, go west on Route 135 for a long block and take the first left turn. Then take the next left turn that goes down a rutted road to a county park with plenty of parking. When you are on the river, it is hard to see the take-out because of the foliage, so walk down to the ruin so you can recognize where the take-out trail starts before heading to the put-in.

It's a shame that sufficient water on this delightful section is now solely generated by dam releases. As of this writing, water is released several weekends a year from early spring until fall. Remember, this water comes from the bottom of a big dam and therefore is very cold. Decked-boaters in particular should pay attention if the day is brisk and cloudy.

As described above, this section of the North Branch at 1,000 cfs makes for a very pleasant trip. At 600 cfs the river is somewhat gentler and pickier. All rapids except one are no more than straightforward Class IIs, and even the double-ledge exception softens to an easier Class III. Conversely, at 1,250 cfs the river is clearly pushier. At high levels, some of the wave trains develop more of a Class III character.

To reach the put-in at the remains of the Barnum bridge, proceed for about five and a half miles, making several careful right turns, on WV 46, a Class III dirt road (Class IV when it's raining). Look for a right turn by three churches, which will take you about two and a half miles down to the river. Here you will find an elaborate parking area with a changing room. There is a nominal fee to park during scheduled release days. After putting in, don't hurry downstream. There are two small surfing spots about 50 yards upstream on the left for the wide awake and adventurous to warm up on.

Normally the U.S. Army Corps of Engineers conserves lake water, releasing it gradually to serve the needs of downstream communities and industries. These 400 cfs flows are less than boaters prefer. A series of recreational releases are scheduled for April and May, and there are periodic "flushes" to improve downstream water quality. These 800–900 cfs "events" put the river at a very enjoyable level. Scheduled releases are publicized through club newsletters and Web sites. For daily flows, call the U.S. Army Corps of Engineers in Baltimore, (410) 962-7687. For more information call the Bloomington Dam, (304) 355-2346. You can also get this information from the National Weather Service in Washington, D.C., (703) 260-0305.

Sideling Hill Creek

This section of Sideling Hill Creek is a Class I–II pure delight for good novice paddlers. However, the scenery and frequency of mild whitewater action on this 13-mile trip are also sufficient to attract more experienced boaters. The rapids are gravel bars and broken ledges that can be rather spicy when they occur on tight turns. Reasonable boat control and a solid brace are important in these situations. Most of the trip wanders near the base of 1,600-foot-high Sideling Hill, which has 200- to 400-foot-high cliffs and sharp slopes made of crumbling shale, a soft sedimentary rock. Because of the poor shale soil with nutrients leached away by quickly draining precipitation, only the toughest trees grow here—pines and eastern red cedar. Sharp-eyed paddlers can spot columbine as well as prickly pear cactus along the way. In early May red columbine flowers give a bright touch while the yellow prickly pear flowers add their own bit of dazzle in late June.

The first half of the trip passes primarily through woods and a gorge that are partially included in the Sideling Hill Wildlife Management Area. In the latter half, the river skirts abandoned farms and traverses the Boy Scouts of America's Lillie-Aaron Straus Wilderness Area. The main hazard of note is a deteriorating low-water bridge about a mile below Zeigler Road near the take-out by Lock 56 at Pearre. Other hazards include the occasional log in the river and sometimes anglers, particularly during spring.

The put-in for this trip is located at the Old US 40 bridge (A), just downstream or south of the new I-68 interstate. On the downstream side of the bridge you can find the canoeing gauge. Shortly below the put-in you'll wander through a pretty gorge of woods and scenic shale cliffs. Roughly a mile into the trip, after a bend to the right and a nice Class I–II rapids, a pretty waterfall appears on the left. The only real sign of civilization in this gorge is a telephone line two miles or so after the put-in. The cliffs and Class I–II rapids on this winding stream continue with a pleasing frequency until one reaches a Class II ledge just as the river turns sharply left, roughly four miles into the trip. This ledge should be run on the left. Here in the gorge, the gradient is a bit steeper—up to 25 feet per mile at one point. Following the ledge, cliffs and Class I–II rapids continue for another mile or so. After five miles the gorge ends and you'll soon reach Norris Road, a rough, ford-type take-out not recommended except in emergencies.

Just below Norris Road the creek splits around a couple of islands, and more nicely spaced Class I–II rapids continue for a mile or so. You will see farmland on the right and Sideling Hill above on the left, followed by a pretty rock wall on the left. Over a mile later, past three bends and Stottlemeyer Road on the right, is another Class II rapid. At that point you will paddle almost due east—straight toward Sideling Hill—for about a mile. After a right turn below a high bluff is another Class II rapid, followed by high cliffs on a second right turn.

Below the cliffs you cross Zeigler Road. You can take out here if you are pooped and want to avoid a portage downstream. Immediately following Zeigler Road is an easy Class II weir. If you haven't yet seen the Randy Carter gauge upstream, there is enough water for the trip if the weir is runnable. About a mile below Zeigler Road lies the previously mentioned disintegrating low-water bridge that must be approached with care and carried on the left. Roughly a quarter mile below the low-water bridge is the 110-foot arch of a picturesque C & O Canal Aqueduct built in 1848. Just past the aqueduct, Sideling Hill Creek enters the Potomac. The take-out is about a half mile downstream opposite Lock 56 of the C & O Canal at Pearre.

Because much of the Sideling Hill Creek area is remote, this is a good opportunity to spot wildlife. Deer are often seen, as well as beaver, muskrats, raccoons (early morning), and squirrels. Bird life includes wild turkeys, turkey vultures, hawks, and an occasional bald eagle.

Incidentally, if you prefer a big winding river to a little winding stream, you should consider the serpentine, 25-

Icicles on the bank of Sideling Hill Creek. Photo by Ed Grove.

mile section of the Potomac from Paw Paw to Pearre (Class A-l, see note bottom of next page), particularly for low-key paddlers who like weekend canoe camping.

There are periodic "hiker-biker" stops provided along the C & O Canal pathway with such colorful names as Sorrel Ridge, Stickpile Hill, Devils Alley, and Indigo Neck. Sorrel Ridge is near the C & O Canal's scenic Paw Paw tunnel and is very popular among canoeists. These

Section: Old US 40 to Potomac River (Pearre, MD)
County: Allegany
USGS Quad: Bellegrove
Difficulty: Class I–II
Gradient: 16 feet per mile; one mile in gorge 25 feet per mile
Average Width: 15–30 feet
Velocity: Moderate
Rescue Index: Remote
Hazards: Deteriorating low-water bridge one mile below Zeigler Road, occasional logs in stream
Scouting: Approach the low-water bridge carefully
Portages: Low-water bridge one mile below Zeigler Road
Scenery: Beautiful for most of the trip
Highlights: Bluffs and cliffs, Sideling Hill, 1848 C & O Canal Aqueduct
Gauge: Visual only at put-in gauge
Runnable Water Levels: Minimum   Maximum
                           Weir runnable Flood stage
                           below Zeigler Rd.
                           0 feet on put-in
                           gauge
Additional Information: 3.2 feet on Saxton gauge (Raystown Branch of Juniata River) is a very rough correlation to zero on put-in gauge

Sideling Hill Creek • Maryland

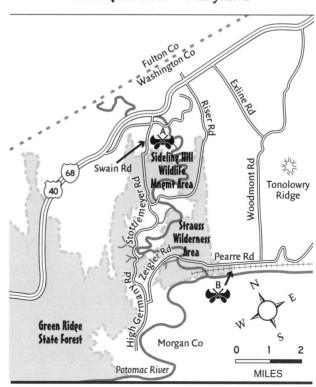

stops provide campsites, outdoor restrooms, and potable water as the Potomac snakes its way between Paw Paw and Pearre. There is also a 14-mile canoeable stretch above this section of Sideling Hill Creek, which is almost as pretty, but the rapids only reach Class I in difficulty.

Finally, when you run this creek the first time, try to go with someone who has run it before. You will need some intelligent help to guess the water level before arriving at the put-in. Although Sideling Hill Creek is up several times during the year, there are no gauges that reasonably correlate to those on the river. Also, the shuttle roads on the western side of the creek are not marked and one can easily make a wrong turn. The shuttle roads on the eastern side of the creek are much easier to follow but are longer and require the substantial effort of crossing Sideling Hill.

Note: Class A is a flatwater classification. Class A denotes standing or slow-flowing water, Class B denotes current between 2.5 and 4.5 miles per hour, and Class C denotes current that exceeds 4.5 miles per hour.

Antietam Creek

Because of the numerous bridges crossing Antietam Creek from Oak Ridge Road (A) in Funkstown to Harpers Ferry Road in Antietam (E), this is a roll-your-own Class I–II novice trip that depends on how many of the 23 miles between these two towns you wish to paddle. The Class I's are numerous riffles formed by gravel bars and small ledges. The Class II's are primarily the remains of old mill dams, thoughtfully spaced over much of this section. The only hazard is located in the Devil's Backbone Park area: a six-foot dam. Also, you should scout the rapids at each bridge and dam; high water will occasionally carry trees into the entrances of rapids around the bridges, making them hazardous. Paddlers should watch for trees in the river (strainers) below some rapids when the water is high.

On this 23-mile stretch, farmhouses, bridges, old mills, and stone walls complement rather than detract from the rural setting. There are scenic lunch stops galore. The remains of dams used to provide water power for the mills have formed good Class II rapids at Poffenburger Road, Wagaman Road, and Roxbury Road during the first third of the trip. There is also a triple ledge two and a half miles downstream from Wagaman Road.

After this ledge and about 10 miles below Funkstown, paddlers must portage the six-foot dam at Devil's Backbone Park just upstream of Route 68. The Antietam

Antietam Creek • Maryland

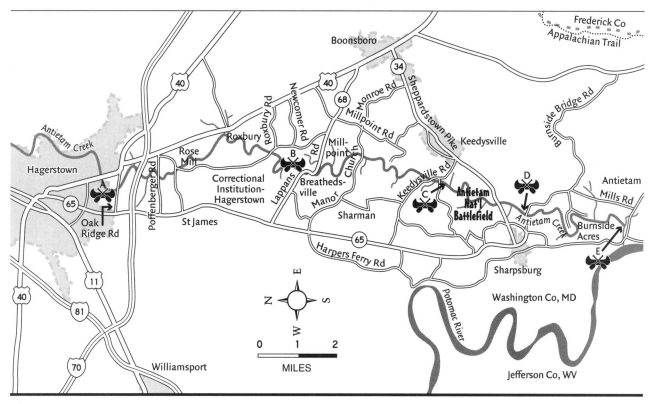

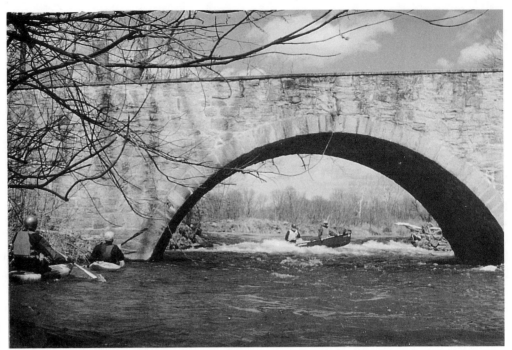

Stone bridge across Antietam
Creek. Photo by Ed Pilchard.

Section: Oak Ridge Road to Harpers Ferry Road
County: Washington
USGS Quads: Funkstown, Keedysville
Difficulty: Class I–II
Gradient: Seven feet per mile
Average Width: 50–100 feet
Velocity: Moderate
Rescue Index: Accessible
Hazards: Six-foot dam at Devils Backbone, three-foot dam one
    mile downstream
Scouting: Recommended for the three-foot dam and at rapids
    formed by bridges/dams, look for trees in chutes
Portages: Six-foot dam at Devils Backbone
Scenery: Pretty to beautiful in spots
Highlights: Picturesque bridges, old mills and farms, Antietam
    Battlefield, wildlife
Gauge: National Weather Service (Antietam Creek gauge),
    (703) 260-0305, or visual at Burnside Bridge

Runnable Water Levels:	Minimum	Maximum
Burnside Bridge	3.2 feet (upper)	5.0 feet (upper)
	2.7 feet (lower)	6.5 feet (lower)
Antietam Creek	about 3.0 feet (upper)	5.0 feet (upper)
	2.5 feet (lower)	6.5 feet (lower)

Additional Information: Antietam Creek Canoe livery, (301) 582-
    1469; Antietam National Battlefield, (301) 432-5124;
    C & O Canal National Historical Park, (301) 739-4200

Creek Canoe livery is just below the Route 68 bridge (B) on the right. A mile below the six-foot dam is a broken three-foot dam that is breached on the sides; the right side can be run with care.

The next five and a half miles from the Route 68 put-in to Keedysville Road (C) are easily paddled and isolated, giving you the opportunity to watch for ducks, beavers, and your favorite songbird. The minimum level for the 10-mile upper stretch above Route 68 is 3.2 on the Burnside Bridge gauge (D) farther downstream.

The last seven and a half miles below Keedysville Road (Hicks Bridge) are quite interesting. To begin with, a beautiful waterfall appears on the right about one mile below Hicks Bridge, and then you enter that stretch of the river wandering through Antietam National Battlefield. Roughly two miles below Hicks Bridge you will reach Route 34 and a nice Class II ledge formed by the remains of an old mill dam. For those who don't have a lot of time or for winter paddlers, the remaining five miles or so downstream from Route 34 make for a scenic short trip.

A mile below Route 34 is Burnside Bridge, where paddlers can admire Antietam Battlefield and its striking markers some more. Also, there is a surfing wave formed by a two-foot, V-shaped dam that is easily run. The Burnside Bridge gauge is located just above the dam on river left below the bridge and should read at least 2.7 feet for the 13-mile lower section below Route 68. Before running the upper or lower sections of this creek, check this gauge, even though the Antietam Creek gauge often gives a slightly lower correlation.

Only four miles remain to the take-out. The main Class II+ rapid on this final stretch is the rock garden slalom just above the Harpers Ferry Road take-out on river right after going under the bridge.

Sharp-eyed folks can spot a surprising amount of domesticated animal and other wildlife on this trip. In addition to catlle grazing in the pastures along the river-banks, there are great blue herons, ducks, woodpeckers, kingfishers, quail, deer, rabbits, beavers, and signs of river otters. One other interesting feature of this creek is that it continues to flow after other rivers ice up. If you crave some winter paddling when ice has your favorite river in its frosty grip, consider checking out Antietam Creek.

The best access points on public land with reasonable parking are Oak Ridge Road in Funkstown, Route 68, Burnside Bridge Road, and Harpers Ferry Road in Antie-tam. All other access points are privately owned and per-mission should be obtained before using them. You can paddle this scenic run at levels lower than the suggested minimums, but you may have to occasionally get out of your boat to get over shallow areas.

Shenandoah and Potomac Rivers

Bull Falls and the Staircase

One of the true classic Class II–III trips for accomplished intermediates and shepherded novices who want to sharpen their paddling skills is Bull Falls and the Staircase. If you are willing to pay the admission price of two to three miles of flatwater, the remaining three and a half miles of whitewater make the trip worthwhile. The flatwater does have a positive side: it's a lazy start for rafters, boaters, and experienced tubers as well as a perfect chance to sharpen novices on whitewater strokes they'll soon need.

Almost halfway through the trip, Bull Falls (Class III) starts off the more serious whitewater with a bang. Below Bull Falls are fairly continuous Class I and Class II rapids through the Staircase until an emergency-only take-out at Harpers Ferry is reached. Below this point there is still Whitehorse Rapids (Class II–III) before the final take-out at Sandy Hook.

The trip from Millville to Sandy Hook is very scenic. The low hills where the Shenandoah and Potomac Rivers merge are very pretty, and there is the charming and historic town of Harpers Ferry to explore after the trip. Also, this is a dependable trip because the rivers hold their water for virtually the entire year. The only dangerous time is when the river is too high on occasion in winter and spring and rarely during other times of the year.

For the put-in on Bloomery Road (A), launch underneath the power lines by the transformer station on the outskirts of Millville, or, to avoid some of the flatwater, put in farther downstream. The last good put-in is River and Trail Outfitters, a quarter mile below the transformer station. However, you should get permission from the Outfitters and join an organized club trip if possible. Finally, be careful about leaving shuttle cars at isolated spots on Bloomery Road; thieves have broken into unattended cars on numerous occasions. Having a gracious camper or outfitter keep an eye on your shuttle cars would probably be very wise.

Wherever you put in along this stretch, notice the many camping spots on river left. Also, silver maples, sycamores, cottonwoods, box elders, and occasional

ashes line the riverbanks. The Route 340 shuttle road is lined with royal paulownia trees that are breathtaking in midspring when they are covered with large, light purple flowers. From the put-in to Bull Falls two to three miles downstream, the river is popular for fishing in canoes, johnboats, and other watercraft. Smallmouth bass, bluegill, channel catfish, and the omnipresent carp are the primary fish that swim these waters. Also, be alert for bird life: great blue herons, turkey vultures, ducks, geese, and swallows are most common, and you may even see an occasional majestic pileated woodpecker.

Just below the power-line put-in the paddler has the choice of running a Class I channel between two islands in the center of the river or continuing down the left to Class I riffles at the end of the second island. About a half mile downstream, you will pass the Millville gauge on the left, followed by the put-ins for various outfitters on the left and summer homes on the right. The river is about 100 yards wide here.

Over two miles from the power-line put-in, some small islands appear on the right, and you will be heading straight toward a hill roughly 200 feet high. Approaching this hill several minutes later, you'll see rocks across the right and center of the river, with a long Class II rock garden on the left. Notice the nice stone wall supporting the railroad track and the interesting rock formations on the left when passing through this rapid. There are also one or two mild surfing spots near the bottom of this slalom.

Then, in the pool below this rapids, look for an exposed broad, flat ledge blocking most of the river. Stop on this 50-foot-long section of the rock ledge between the current flowing through a narrow notch on the right and diagonally from right to left over a more powerful drop to the left. Congratulations! After three miles of warm-up you have arrived at Bull Falls. Novices can now start quivering. At low and medium levels the long, low ledge here is a perfect place to beach boats, rafts, and tubes before scouting, eating lunch, or watching the continuous parade of boats and bodies go over the fall.

Bull Falls and The Staircase • MD and WV

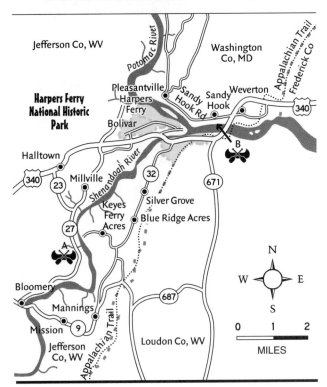

Section: Millville, WV, to Sandy Hook, MD

Counties: Washington (MD), Jefferson (WV)

USGS Quads: Charles Town, Harpers Ferry

Difficulty: Class II–III at moderate levels, Class III–IV at high
levels

Gradient: 10 feet per mile, 3.5 miles at 15–20 feet per mile

Average Width: 250–1,000 feet

Velocity: Moderate to fast

Rescue Index: Accessible

Hazards: Occasional trees in river

Scouting: Bull Falls (Class III)

Portage: None

Scenery: Pretty to beautiful in spots

Highlights: Scenic confluence of Shenandoah and Potomac
Rivers, historic town of Harpers Ferry, wildlife and birds

Gauge: National Weather Service (Millville gauge), (703) 260-
0305

Runnable Water Levels: Minimum   Maximum

Millville Gauge   1.8 feet   5.5 feet

Additional Information: Harpers Ferry National Historic Park,
(304) 535-6298; River and Trail Outfitters, (301) 695-5177

The most classic route here is the three- to four-foot Class III drop immediately to the left of the large, low scouting ledge. The paddler should start this run reasonably close to the scouting ledge to prevent being carried too far left by the current. On reaching the drop, there is a barely exposed rock (low water) or a roostertail (higher water) about five feet from the scouting ledge. Turn hard right 90 degrees and run this drop on the tongue just to the left of this rock/roostertail. The reason for running this drop tight right is simple: the farther left one goes, the greater chance of hitting a submerged rock in the channel.

After running this drop, keep your boat parallel with the current because at lower levels a hydraulic about 25 feet below can flip those who drop into it sideways. Incidentally, this hydraulic is a great teacher for those who want to explore the world of sideways hole-surfing. It is gentle enough not to be a keeper but tough enough to bounce boaters around a bit; sometimes considerable effort is required to exit. If you plan on sitting in it sideways, have flotation in your boat and wear a helmet—the ledge is shallow. Also, have a rescue boater nearby to pick up the pieces in the pool below. As the Millville gauge reaches three feet, this holewashes out and isn't as grabby.

Getting back to Bull Falls, the classic drop described above is actually the third runnable slot from the left

bank. To run the other two, either scout them from below after running Bull Falls the classic way or look them over from the railroad tracks on the left after beaching your boat upstream. The drop closest to the railroad tracks is basically two drops (Class II–III) that can be run center. The second drop from the left (low Class III) can also be run, but scout it first to avoid a nasty rock near the bottom.

The fourth slot (on the right of the scouting rock) is a Class II–III rapid with a one-foot ledge on the top into a narrow slot below that drops two to three feet. Novice paddlers and tubers too nervous about the classic drop just to the left of the scouting rock can run this one if they have some boat control. Incidentally, this slot also has a small surfing spot near the end at moderate levels.

The adventurous can explore other drops farther to the right on this river-wide ledge. The first of these is a straight drop that used to have a tree lodged in the normal runout. The next drop is a narrow slot with a nasty rock to dodge immediately below entry. There are perhaps four other possibilities farther to the right that are unrunnable at low water but may be possibilities at high water—particularly a rocky slalom on the extreme right.

The great thing about Bull Falls is that the easy carry over the scouting rock allows paddlers many opportunities to run this rapids. They can either take alternate

Bull Falls on the
Shenandoah River.
Photo by Ron Knipling.

routes or try again if they don't run it right the first time. However, at really high levels, this river-wide ledge is covered, and parts of Bull Falls take on Class IV characteristics.

After a hopefully invigorating stop at Bull Falls, one reaches a 50-yard pool before hitting 50 yards of Class I–II standing waves. These are followed by another 50-yard pool and a Class II ledgy drop best taken on the far right at lower levels. A nice long pool follows and then the river splits in several places. Going from right to left, the first three splits are straightforward Class I–II drops over covered cobbles with some riffles below. The last alternative on the extreme left, a small Class I–II slalom, gives one the feeling of running a creek.

From the long pool located below the splits you can clearly see the first Route 340 bridge. You are now about to begin the well-known Staircase—named so because it is a stairstep-like series of ledges that continue for a good mile. At lower levels this mile is generally Class II; at high levels it starts taking on Class IV characteristics because of its length, strength, complexity, and the big holes that develop.

The Route 340 bridge marks four and a half miles from the transformer station put-in and is about halfway down the Staircase. At low levels the upper half of the Staircase tests one's water-reading ability because it is very picky. Perhaps the best route at lower levels is to start on the left and then work toward the center. Just above the center abutment of the bridge is a one-and-a-half-foot ledge

that can be run to the right or left of the abutment. The ledge also offers surfing opportunities.

After getting a breather by the center bridge abutment, paddlers can continue their Staircase descent. Just below the abutment to the right is another nice one-and-a-half-foot ledge followed by 100–200 yards of little ledges. Then there is a spicy Class II–III double drop in the center over two one-and-a-half-foot ledges called Hesitation Ledge by local paddlers. Another 100 yards of small ledges follow, and you'll find yourself in a series of nicer Class II ledges and surfing spots until you reach a 10-foot-high wall with a 10-foot circular hole in it on river left. These are the ruins of an old cotton mill. Just below this wall is the Harpers Ferry beach.

Having come five miles below the transformer put-in, you can no longer take out at the massive parking lot on the left in scenic Harpers Ferry. Instead, continue downstream and within a half mile you will reach the confluence of the Potomac and the Shenandoah. Greeting you at this confluence are the abutment remains of an old bridge on the Shenandoah, a working railroad bridge over the Potomac, a striking hill 1,200 feet above the river, and a railroad tunnel. Once past the confluence, look back upstream at the pretty village of Harpers Ferry nestled in the trees.

The last mile begins with an easy set of Class I waves with a good surfing spot on the left. A few minutes later you will encounter a pleasant 50-yard run of Class I–II waves. Shortly below these waves the river flows between two large rocks on the left with some impressive waves below. This is Whitehorse Rapid. At the top left are a couple of surfing possibilities at reasonable levels, and below are about 50 yards of vigorous Class II–III waves, which become Class III at higher levels. There are also two routes to the right of Whitehorse that you should look at before running.

Just below Whitehorse, pick up any errant boats and boaters and begin looking for a wall on the left. The second Route 340 bridge looms just below. After several minutes, you'll notice a sandy beach and a three- to four-foot sandy hill instead of a wall. This is the first possible take-out at Sandy Hook (B), but if you go a couple of minutes farther downstream and remain about 100 yards or so upstream of the bridge, you will find another beach. This spot is the preferred take-out because the walk takes you over more gradual terrain. This 125-yard portage first goes over the C & O Canal towpath (which is also the Appalachian Trail here), then continues down across a new, rustic-style bridge over a muddy stream (the old canal), and finally over the railroad tracks to Sandy Hook Road. Be very careful when crossing the tracks here; freight trains pass frequently at a good clip.

Patoma Wayside is on river right just above the Route 340 bridge, but you can't leave cars here. On the other hand, a nice little cascade from a nearby stream provides welcome wet relief on hot days. Unlike the former take-out at the Harpers Ferry parking lot, it is hard to find a place to park cars at Sandy Hook. You basically have a few sloping places next to the railroad track or in people's driveways on the other side of Sandy Hook Road, but parking in driveways is not recommended unless you get permission. So leave as few cars as possible and watch your valuables; there have been some thefts here, too. Perhaps the best way of dealing with the shuttle for this trip is by convincing a couple of shuttle bunnies to do the chore. While you meander down the river, they can visit

scenic Harpers Ferry and pick you up later in the day.

Harpers Ferry is rich in history. The first settler, a trader named Peter Stephens, arrived in 1733 and set up a primitive ferry service at the junction of the Potomac and Shenandoah Rivers. Robert Harper, a miller and the man for whom the town is named, settled here in 1747 and built a mill. The original ferry and mill are long gone. In the 1790s George Washington was instrumental in establishing a national armory here. By 1801, the armory was producing weapons; arms produced at Harpers Ferry were used by Lewis and Clark on their famous westward expedition of 1804–1806. The arrival of the C & O Canal and the B & O Railroad in the 1830s generated prosperity, and by the 1850s Harpers Ferry had 3,000 residents.

In 1859, however, John Brown's raid on the eve of the Civil War thrust the town into national prominence and set the stage for its eventual decline. When the Civil War began in 1861, the armory and arsenal buildings were burned to prevent them from falling into Confederate hands. Because of the town's geographic location and railway system, both the Union and Confederate forces occupied the town intermittently throughout the war. Discouraged by war damage and fewer jobs, many people left. The finishing blow to the town was dealt by a series of devastating floods in the late 1800s.

Harpers Ferry has since been restored by the National Park Service and today is a delightful place to visit. Besides restored streets, shops, houses, and public buildings, there are other points of interest. On the Shenandoah side above the town is Jefferson Rock. Here, in 1783, Thomas Jefferson was so taken with the view he thought it was "worth a voyage across the Atlantic." Not far from this rock is the grave of Robert Harper and a very interesting cemetery. On the left side of the Potomac River across from Harpers Ferry is the Appalachian Trail and the C & O Canal towpath for day hikers and backpackers.

Gunpowder Falls

Gunpowder Falls is a pleasant Class II–III trip at moderate levels for good intermediate boaters. A 3.3-mile run from Route 1 (A) to Route 40 (B), it passes through a pretty but shallow wooded gorge and has only one drawback: it's too short. One can put in at Lower Loch Raven Dam upstream, but this would mean an additional seven-mile scenic paddle over flatwater with only occasional riffles.

The falls line of Gunpowder Falls begins just below Route 1. You can warm up by running the Class II rapids at the put-in and doing some elementary surfing at the bottom of this rapids. About a quarter mile below is Pot's Rock, a nice long Class II–III rapids entered by way of a rock garden 50–100 yards long. Then, move right with a quick cut back to the left just before dropping over a two-foot ledge. Adding spice to Pot's Rock is a fun surfing spot

Section: Route 1 to Route 40

County: Baltimore

USGS Quad: White Marsh

Difficulty: Class II–III at moderate levels, Class III–IV at high levels

Gradient: 20 feet per mile; a half mile at 40 feet per mile

Average Width: 50–100 feet

Velocity: Moderate to fast

Rescue Index: Accessible but difficult

Hazards: Occasional tree in river

Scouting: Long rapid just below Route 7 is Class III (moderate level) or Class IV (high level)

Portages: None

Scenery: Pretty in most spots

Highlights: Nice wooded gorge

Gauge: Visual only

Runnable Water Levels:

	Minimum	Maximum
	Class II rapid at put-in, cleanly runnable	5 feet of water over put-in rapid

located just below the ledge. Decked boaters can get enders here at one and a half to two feet on the Route 1 gauge. Shortly below Pot's Rock is a Class II rock garden.

The next rapids of significance occurs as the paddler reaches the I-95 bridge. Here a 100-yard Class II rock garden (Class III in high water) appears just above the bridge and continues well beyond. The rock garden ends and a pool is reached just as you pass under the nearby Route 7 bridge. You'll also hear an impressive roar at this point, which is your signal to get to river right and scout because you have a long, strong, Class III rock garden of over 100 yards to run. There are surfing spots toward the end of the rapid. At higher levels it gets tougher because of its length, strength, and complexity.

One can take out at the Route 7 bridge, the most convenient take-out, but this makes the trip only a couple of miles long. Also, the long, Class III rock garden and a couple of other nice rapids will be missed.

Below Route 7 there are two good drops. The first is a relatively short Class II rock garden known as Finger Rock. The second is a Class II–III drop with a ledge on the left and (with enough water) a tight S turn on the right. First-timers should scout from river right. The second rapid also has reasonable surfing opportunities here and there.

The Route 40 bridge take-out follows. Take out on river left, and you'll encounter the only problem with this otherwise pleasant trip: no legal parking near the bridge. The nearest place is one-quarter to one-half mile southwest of the bridge, so have a shuttle driver meet you or be willing to hike.

Unfortunately, things have changed at the Gunpowder Falls put-in. The new Route 1 bridge is much higher than the old bridge, so the portage to the river is more difficult. Also, parking is in a state of flux. Finally, the gauge for this trip disappeared along with the old Route 1 bridge. Consequently, paddlers must use their best judgment concerning water levels. If the Class II rapid at the put-in is cleanly runnable, there should be enough water.

Ed Grove on Gunpowder Falls.
Photographer unknown.

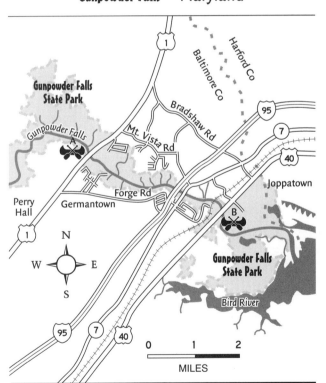

Gunpowder Falls • Maryland

The Gunpowder is basically a winter or spring trip following a recent rain when the Loch Raven reservoir is full of water. This will usually produce runnable levels for a week. There is reasonable bird life along the river, such as herons and turkey vultures, and the scenic gorge is restful. It's too bad this delightful trip isn't longer.

WEST VIRGINIA

Gauley River

Upper Gauley

The Upper Gauley is one of the eastern Appalachians finest runs. It's big, tough, dangerous, and intoxicating. The river flows through a magnificent, steep-walled gorge with few easy access points. At 2,800 cfs the rapids are complex and intense. There are eight major rapids in the Class IV+ to V category on the stretch from Summersville Dam to the Bucklick take-out, with innumerable "minor" Class III–IV drops. But although the whitewater is challenging, the fast water is separated by long pools. These provide a welcome break in the action, allow for rescue, and provide time to appreciate the cliffs and forests of this remote, unspoiled canyon, now managed as a national river by the National Park Service.

A few intrepid explorers rafted and canoed the Gauley during the 1960s, before the Summersville Dam was built. In 1968, with the dam in place, the river was attempted by a group of world-class paddlers in kayaks and C-1s. Running on a 1,500 cfs release, they ran the entire 26-mile stretch in a single day. In the early 1970s only a few dozen people went down each weekend. The river became a qualifying cruise for the title of expert boater. Paddlers gradually became more skilled and better equipped, and now thousands run the Gauley each year. The river is home to many commercial raft outfitters and is considered one of the best commercial trips in the world. All this leads to big crowds during fall release weekends.

The Upper Gauley, for the purposes of this guidebook, consists of the stretch from Summersville Dam (A) to Appalachian Wildwater's take-out at Bucklick (D). Despite its growing popularity, the Gauley is still an intense and dangerous river. The Upper Gauley has many undercuts and sieves that must be avoided, making it impractical for most first-timers to pick their way down. Don't attempt this run without the skill, confidence, and endurance that makes the Cheat Canyon or New River Gorge seem easy. If you still have doubts, try the Lower Gauley first. Then make your first run with experienced paddlers who know the upper section well and are willing to serve as guides. Even with their help, a number of rapids deserve scouting.

Here's a description of the primary rapids of the Upper Gauley at the normal fall release levels of 2,400–2,800 cfs:

After a Class III warm-up rapid, you'll encounter Initiation (Class IV), the first major drop. After a long lead-in the river drops over a high, sloping ledge into a medium-sized stopper. It looks like you could run it anywhere and the smooth wave at the brink of the drop looks tempting to skilled surfers. But a hidden boulder sieve on the right has been responsible for two fatalities and dozens of narrow escapes in the past 20 years. Run to the left of center, then keep working left to avoid the stopper if desired. Don't even think about surfing the top wave; it will throw you into the sieve if you lose control. The right side of the bottom hole is surprisingly sticky at low levels (1,200 cfs). There are several fine Class III drops below here with great wave trains. Rafters should watch out for Bud's Boner (Class IV), which is formed when the river squeezes to the right and plunges over two drops. There are potential pinning rocks in both drops for rafts. Rafters should go left after the first drop and run the second drop with a strong right-hand angle to avoid a sticky hole on bottom left.

After a long pool, a high sandstone wall looms ahead, signaling your arrival above Insignificant (Class V). This rapid was named because the 1968 party reported "no significant rapids above Pillow Rock." Later parties, running at higher flows, encountered unexpected difficulties. Insignificant is one of the most difficult on the river at fall release levels. At the top, a huge pourover in the center and another slightly downstream on the left quicly separates wandering paddlers from their boats. Then the flow sweeps up against a huge sloping rock on the right and into a wave train. A nasty ledge lies on the left side of the river just upstream of this rock. First-timers and marginal paddlers can easily scout this rapid on the far right.

John Deardorff getting up close and personal with Pillow Rock on the Upper Gauley. Photo by Ed Grove.

There are several possible routes. Hard-boaters usually start at the center of the rapid, drop down just to the left of the top two pourovers, and cut quickly to the right to avoid the nasty ledge on the left downstream. Rafters typically cross the river just upstream of the center pourover, then run down on the right. There's an excellent sneak route on the far right that avoids the big holes in the upper part of the rapid. A vigorous wave train at the bottom is fun to play if traffic permits.

After two lesser rapids, Iron Curtain (Class III+) awaits. The rapid is named for the iron oxide stains on a sandstone cliff on river right. The water is channeled toward the left side and you'll find big holes on the right and center. The left chute has a fast wave train and a superstrong left-hand eddy. Rafts should avoid the undercut Sperm Whale Rock, lurking downstream. You can now see the overlook at Carnifex Ferry State Park on the top of the ridge on river right. Pillow Rock Rapid lies just downstream.

Pillow Rock Rapid (Class V) is an impressive 25-foot drop, creating over 50 yards of big waves, large holes, and impressive turbulence. The entrance at the top is rocky, offering many possibilities. Halfway down you'll encounter a series of nasty holes and very confused, aerated water. The hole on the far right side is extremely deep. At the bottom the water piles up against a huge rock wall, creating the impressive pillow that gives the drop its name. Then it roars around and over Volkswagen Rock.

There's a lot happening in here, and it's a good idea to scout on the right or the left side. On fall release weekends large crowds gather to watch the show.

There are two reasonable routes down Pillow Rock and a third that's nothing but trouble. The best hard-boat route is down the center. Enter just right of a boulder at the top center, then hug the left sides of two successive rocks downstream. Now work right, grazing the left side of the big hole near bottom right. Cut in behind this hole to catch the right-hand eddy above Volkswagen Rock, then take a second to decide how much of the downstream craziness you want before peeling out. If you miss this eddy, brace into the pillow at the bottom and ride the current around the rock. The left side of Volkswagen Rock has a very powerful ender spot on the left.

Most rafts prefer the right channel, cutting left to follow a distinct wave train that terminates in the big hole on the far right. Large rafts punch the left side of the hole to slow down so they don't get pushed up on the pillow. From there they move across the river and slide past Volkswagen Rock on the left.

Unless you like big-time craziness, avoid the left-side "hero route" on Pillow Rock. It lines you up for the top hole, then carries you directly into the pillow. Most boaters flip here, and usually it's all right to hang in your boat upside down and wait for things to calm down. But the river could deposit you in the Room of Doom, a terminal, box-shaped eddy to the left of the pillow. Many

Upper Gauley • West Virginia

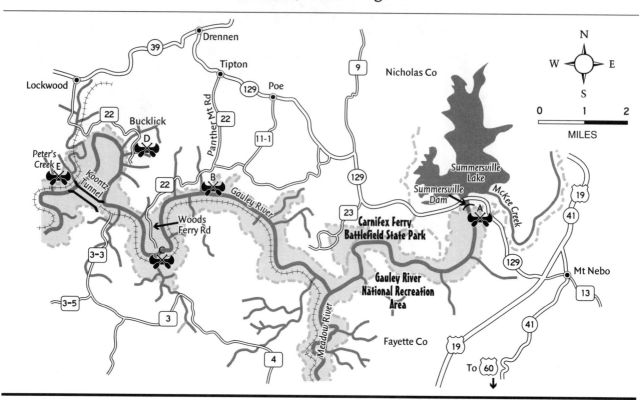

Section: Summersville Dam to Bucklick

Counties: Nicholas, Fayette

USGS Quads: Summersville Dam, Anstead

Difficulty: Class IV–V, with one Class V–VI

Gradient: 28 feet per mile

Average Width: 75–100 feet

Velocity: Fast

Rescue Index: Remote

Hazards: Undercut rocks, long Class V–VI rapids, high water

Scouting: Insignificant, Pillow Rock, the second drop and Tumblehome in Lost Paddle, Iron Ring, Sweet's Falls, Woods Ferry

Portages: Perhaps Iron Ring (especially below 1,500 cfs)

Scenery: Beautiful

Highlights: Unique expert whitewater river, spectacular gorge and rock formations

Gauge: Summersville Dam (dam release and Meadow River), (304) 872-5809

Runnable Water Levels:	Minimum	Maximum
Belva gauge	2.4 feet (800 cfs)	4.5 feet (5,000 cfs)

Additional Information: National Park Service, (304) 465-0508

hapless boaters have spent anxious moments in here wondering why their buddies told them to run it on the left. A few had to be pulled out from above with ropes! If you are in over your head, the steep trail to the overlook at Carnifex Ferry departs at the top of the rapid on river right.

There are several milder drops before the Meadow River comes in on the left. As with most of "easier" Gauley rapids, you must stay alert for undercut rocks and large holes. Rafters should beware of the last Class II–III rapid above the Meadow, known as Flipper's Folly. Marked by an island at the top of the drop, the right side funnels through Toothpaste Slot, which is too narrow for all but the smallest rafts to negotiate. The left channel has some pinning rocks on the left side at the bottom, so start left of center and work right for a clean run.

Lost Paddle (Class V) is the longest rapid on the river. Also called Mile-Long Shoals, it's full of waves, ledges, undercuts, and holes. It's difficult to scout and a murderous carry along the railroad bed on the left. It consists of four distinct drops, with the second and the fourth being the most difficult. Always check the flow of the Meadow River when running the Upper Gauley; anything more than a minimal inflow (200–300 cfs), when added to the

Liz Garland running Sweet's
Falls on the Upper Gauley.
Photo by Mayo Gravatt.

fall release, makes Lost Paddle pushy and rescues become difficult.

The first drop is pretty straightforward; a 200-yard boulder garden with a strong hole at the bottom left. Enter to the left of a pyramid-shaped rock at the top and work left, split two holes, and catch the eddy at the bottom. A second eddy is about 50 yards below on river right, just above the second drop.

The second drop is the steepest, shallowest, and most turbulent part of Lost Paddle. Easily boat-scouted from the eddies above, the top of the drop consists of a large, curling wave extending from the left shore to the center of the river. The wave hides a steep ledge; the best route is just to the right of this crest, no more than two boat-lengths from the left shore. This takes you past the hole into the waves below. There is also a tight, rocky sneak route on the far right that should be scouted from shore first. The rock in the center of the wave train at the bottom (Decision Rock or Six Pack Rock) can be run on either side; this rock and the ones on the left shore are undercut, so swimmers should stay in the center and float with the current.

The third drop is an easy chute with a big hole at the bottom right. Run down the left, easily avoiding a hole on the top left. Quickly pick up swimmers and gear in the calm but swift water below. Watch out for commercial rafts in the right eddy.

The fourth drop is also called Tumblehome and must be run with care. The chutes over the ledge at the top left are badly undercut and were the site of a fatality in the 1970s. A large rock sits in the center of the river above this rapid. Rafts like to run to the right of this rock, punching or skirting a hole, then cutting to the left to catch the next good chute over a rocky ledge. Hard-boaters with good skills can set up in an eddy on the upstream left, then aim for a very narrow chute at right center. They could also ferry behind the big rock, go one chute over, and pick up the raft line. Below here the routes converge; head for the center chute at the bottom of the rapid. There's a great ender spot on the left side of the chute. The next chute over to the right (the mail slot) is very narrow and potentially dangerous.

Some easy, but deceptively dangerous rapids lie below. Conestoga Rapid is easy Class III unless you take the blind chute at river center. The dangerous hole at the bottom, backed up by a rock, is called Darrow's Doucher and is very strong. Take the left chute, then work quickly to the right to avoid some pinning rocks. Table Rock Rapid (also called Shipwreck Rock) is another Class III, but the rock itself is undercut and extends across two-thirds of the river. Most of the river goes under it, creating a deadly trap; this has been the site of two deaths and several narrow escapes. The normal route starts on the left of a rocky island, runs through some large waves, then works through several hundred yards of small waves to the far right side of Table Rock. At the top, be sure to swing to the left to avoid Razor Rock, hiding behind the top wave. Below Razor Rock there's plenty of time to

Two-person raft on the big
tongue entering Iron Ring
on the Upper Gauley.
Photo by Ed Grove.

paddle (or swim) to the right. If you're looking for a safer approach, the top of this rapid can also be run on the right.

Not far below Table Rock, the river bends right and the current is compressed along the right shore by a point of rocks. This is Iron Ring (Class V–VI), named for an iron ring set in the rocks on the left (stolen in 1988). It was used during an attempt to create a log-floating passage here in the early 1900s. Dynamite blasts created an irregular midchannel boulder. The river sharply constricts on the right and drops down a six-foot-high slide into a hole a boat length above the obstructing boulder (Woodstock Rock). The current welling up out of the hole mostly slips down the right side. Some splashes over the now-smooth, man-made block, and about a fourth flushes under and around the left side of Woodstock Rock in a channel between it and its mother stone. The channel is crooked, turbulent, and powerful enough force to fold an errant paddler and boat together. Carry on the left or scout carefully and run from left to right. The proper line is very clean but leaves little margin for error. You start from the left, skirting the right side of two hydraulics to line up for the main rapid. Then you work carefully from left to right (bow angled right) on a large tongue to slip between the Woodstock Rock obstruction on the left and Backender Hole on the right. Don't relax too soon at the bottom because a lot of current slams into rocks on the bottom right. Throw ropes can be set on the left below

the holes. At lower water levels, a very bad hole forms. Most paddlers walk it below 1,500 cfs.

The next mile is easy except for a word of caution about Fingernail Rock Rapid (Class III), three-quarters of a mile below Iron Ring. The rock on the far left is badly undercut. Run right. About eight miles into the trip you reach Sweet's Falls (Class V). Here the Welsh sandstone, shale, and thin strata of Sewell coal rise straight up from the right side of the river. The river jogs right, then left, and drops over a cliff of this sandstone as a heavy, steep, 10-foot falls. It was named for John Sweet, who ran it on the initial Gauley trip in 1968.

The left side of the falls is a technical boulder garden—a Class IV sneak. To run the falls proper, take out on the right well above the entrance for a difficult scout, or run carefully behind someone who knows this drop well. The entrance is three to five feet to the right of an easy hole followed by a small wave train continuing to the lip of the drop just downstream. A large eddy is on the left. The main route to run the falls is very narrow. If you follow the wave train to the lip of the falls, you'll be too far right; here the drop is steepest with a terrible hole below. Running from the calm of the eddy will put you too far left with Snaggletooth Rock and another bad hole as a consequence. The safest line is a tongue or tube just below the seam or small depression where the wave train current and eddy current join. Run the seam. Some paddlers angle right with a strong left brace, others angle left.

Talk to someone who has run this drop to determine your route. After the big plunge, recover quickly to avoid being swept into the rocks below. Rafters should move right to avoid being blown into Postage Due Rock or the nasty Box Canyon on the left. Catch swimmers quickly because the main current blasts diagonally left.

The river calms down for several miles after Sweet's Falls. There are several excellent play spots about a mile below Sweet's Falls. A large pool with a giant, right-side eddy marks the beginning of Class VI River Runners' Mason Branch Road and the steep trail up Panther Creek. The section from Mason Branch to Bucklick is sometimes called the Middle Gauley, a Class II–III run with a number of delightful play spots. At Guide's Revenge the river rushes left toward a large, diagonal hole. It's easy to miss, but if you have some dry passengers aboard it's a good place to get them wet.

Woods Ferry Rapid, sometimes called Little Insignificant, is the hardest drop on the Middle Gauley. This very deceptive Class IV drop starts as a rather inoffensive boulder garden, then picks up speed. A large hole extends out from river left, forcing hard-boaters to swing out to the center to avoid it. But just downstream a big flat rock called Julie's Juicer forces most of the water to the left! Paddlers must make the move or suffer the consequences of dropping into Julie's Juicer hole just left of the rock. Large rafts often punch the hole to be sure they can make it through the slot. Hard-boaters can also get past the Juicer by running the entire rapid down the far right. A short distance below here is the Woods Ferry take-out on the right.

Ender Waves rapid is just below the Woods Ferry pool. It's a snappy Class III wave train with some dynamic surfing opportunities. Then the river alternates between easy rapids and long pools for several miles. Suddenly, the river narrows up against giant boulders and rushes into a large hole at the bottom. This is Back Ender (Class IV). The hole is strongest at flows in the 1,200 cfs range and starts to wash out around 3,000 cfs. Most boaters start by running this drop down the center, cutting to the right to miss the hole. Appalachian Wildwater's Bucklick take-out is just downstream on the right. This is a popular boundary between the upper and lower run.

A word about water levels. Although most people run the river during fall releases, there are many opportunities to run the river at other times. Hard-boaters report good runs with 500 cfs or less! The big rapids are steep and technical, but lack the push of the higher levels. At the other extreme, the run is paddled regularly at 4,000–6,000 cfs. At these levels, the big drops become huge and pushy, making them suitable for experts only.

Lower Gauley

The Lower Gauley from Bucklick (D) to Swiss (E) is the best advanced-level, big-water run in the East. It may be more beautiful than the upper stretch, and the rapids are more open and considerably easier. There are five rapids of Class IV or greater difficulty and many easier drops with excellent play spots. At release levels the biggest waves and the biggest holes on the river are found on this section. It's good fun from 1,000 to 8,000 cfs. At low water it's a good run for intermediates; mostly Class III–III+. At high water levels experts will encounter long wave trains, massive holes, and scores of giant surfing waves.

Here's a description of the rapids at release levels of 2,400–2,800 cfs:

Koontz Flume (Class IV+) has a tricky entrance and big waves. The huge rock on river right is undercut and a few careless paddlers have washed underneath it. There's a large hole on the top left center; most paddlers skirt it to the right, then work quickly left to catch the main tongue. This maneuver can be tricky because a wave at the right edge of the hole kicks the other way. Alternatively, hard-boaters can catch a large but deceptive right-hand eddy and ferry out into the flume. This leads to the main drop, a smooth ride into a big wave train. Whatever you do, don't run the vertical drop on the far right side of the flume; it takes you under Koontz Rock! For the more cautious, the rapid can be scouted and run on the left. There's also a sporty, hole-studded run down the center. Five Boat Hole, at the base, is a bit sticky, but is still a fine play spot. Watch out for oncoming rafts!

Canyon Doors (Class III), ornamented with high sandstone cliffs on the right, may be the most beautiful spot on the river. Run far right, then work left toward the bottom for a good surfing hole. Immediately downstream is Junkyard (Class III)—usually run on the left. There is a safe route on the far right that ends with a good ender spot.

After four minor rapids, the Peters Creek trestle (an alternate put-in), and 3.5 miles of paddling, you come to the Mash brothers, Upper and Lower. Upper Mash (Class III+) is a complex and torturous bump-and-grind over and through a steep, shallow boulder garden. It is perhaps best entered in the center to the left or right of a large rock. In low water, avoid a pinning rock below the two-to three-foot ledge on the left of this rock by staying to the left. After picking your way down the technical center channel, eddy right or left at the bottom. These eddies are your last chance to scout Lower Mash—a big wave train (Class IV) with a big breaking wave that's hard to

Lower Gauley • West Virginia

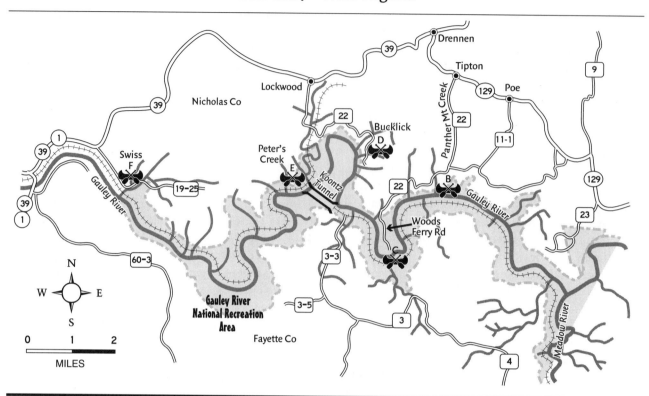

Section: Bucklick to Swiss

Counties: Nicholas, Fayette

USGS Quad: Ansted

Difficulty: Class III–V

Gradient: 26 feet per mile

Average Width: 100 feet

Velocity: Fast

Rescue Index: Remote to remote but accessible

Hazards: Long rapids, high water, undercut rocks, strainers

Scouting: Koontz Flume, Lower Mash, Gateway to Heaven, Riverwide Stopper, Pure Screaming Hell

Portages: None

Scenery: Beautiful

Highlights: Classic trip through pristine gorge, cliffs at Canyon Doors

Gauge: Summersville Dam (dam release and Meadow River), (304) 872-5809

Runnable Water Levels:	Minimum	Maximum
Belva gauge	2 feet (700 cfs)	9 feet (10,000 cfs)

Additional Information: National Park Service, (304) 465-0508

avoid. The most conservative route starts left of center and ends right, in the eddy below the ledge. Beware of an undercut boulder sieve at the bottom left, well below the ledge. At high water levels, run right of center and watch out for big reaction waves crashing in from the left. Rescue flipped boaters quickly because the river continues to flow fast and rocky for several hundred yards downstream.

After being "Mashed," the paddler reaches Diagonal Ledges (Class III), which has some good surfing holes. A chute between two rocks forms an ender slot just to the right of the first drop. Even open-boaters can get enders here, but swimmers will not escape without assistance. Below here, Maui Wave (a.k.a. Hawaii Five-O Wave) forms at the bottom left at high water. It's a great surfing wave that easily surfs (and flips) rafts at high water.

Gateway to Heaven is a long, Class IV rapid where the river necks down and gets squeezed between two large rocks that form the gate. Begin the run by threading your way through the boulder garden at center, then cut left to avoid a nasty ledge/hole that blocks the right side of the river. After passing this boat-eating monster, work right and catch the wave train headed for the Gate. Take the right side of the chute and angle your bow right for the best run. If you stray to the left, the water slams you against the left-hand "gatepost." The entire rapid can be snuck on the left, finishing to the left of the gates; this is the best high-water route and avoids the huge hole that forms in the gates. At high flows do not run through the Gateway, but stay on the far left.

After Gateway to Heaven are three Class III rapids. The first is Rocky Top; run it on the right and look out for a hidden hole right of center near the bottom that gets larger as the river gets higher. To miss it, work left in the lower part of the rapids. You'll find a good ender spot, Chicken Ender, below Rocky Top on the left. Picture Rock is next—a real sneaky rapid upstream of a large, midriver rock. The current goes over a sloping ledge from right to left and can push you farther left than you want to go. Just as you go over the bottom of the drop, water coming in suddenly from the left shoves you to the right—sideways into a hole that will flip you upstream unless you have a strong low brace ready on your left. Upper Stairsteps rapid follows, a wave-train roller coaster on river left. Look out for a large hole in the center halfway down, which gets bigger at higher levels.

Next is Riverwide Stopper (also known as Lower Stairsteps or The Hole). This is a larger Class III–IV wave train. Run it center with a large, river-wide crashing wave midway down. Punch this squarely and with vigor to avoid a fisheye view of the river. At low water you can sneak the hole to the right or left of center.

The next good Class II–III wave train is called Rollercoaster. There are three more Class III rapids. The first is Cliffside: easy on the right and fun on the left. It can be recognized by the cliffs on the left. If you run it on the left, angle right and brace left into a diagonal curler after you enter. Below is Rattlesnake—a long rapid with a rattler on the end. Enter right of the island, and work right for the most conservative route. The last of the trio is Roostertail, which should be run left to avoid a pinning rock on the bottom right.

After a short pool (7.5 miles into the trip), you'll arrive at the top of Pure Screaming Hell (Class IV–V), the last of the major Gauley rapids. This appropriately named rapid starts on a curve to the right and ends on a left turn that is far, far below. The trick to running this rapid successfully is to stay in the center of the main flow. Starting right of center, pass some large holes on your right, then start looking for a larger hole extending out from river left. Skirt the edge of this hole, then cut behind it to avoid hitting an even bigger (almost river-wide) hole just downstream. Although none of these holes are keepers, they play rough! A more serious danger is a bad rock sieve on the outside of the turn, just above the final hole. If you find yourself drifting or swimming in this direction, work back toward the center fast!

Kevin's Folly, the last named drop, appears after a few miles of easy rapids and short pools. A bouncy run at

Scott Gravatt running Koontz Flume on the Lower Gauley. Photo by Court Ogilvie.

release levels, it has some big waves and holes at high water. A mile and a half below, on river right, is Omega Siding, just above the town of Swiss. There are a number of take-out options here.

Access Points for the Upper and Lower Gauley

The first paddlers to run this river assumed that the surrounding area was mostly trackless wilderness. This was never true, and today many of the jeep trails and wagon roads have been rebuilt to provide access for outfitters. Many of these companies permit their use by private paddlers, but remember to follow the directions of outfitter personnel and stay clear of the large trucks and buses that the roads were built to accommodate. Be prepared for some traffic jams on busy fall weekends.

The put-in for the Upper Gauley is easy to find: it's at the base of Summersville Dam (A). Go west on Route 129 from Route 19, about 10 miles south of Summersville. The turn-off to the "tailwaters" of the dam is well marked; during Gauley season, park rangers staff a checkpoint a few hundred yards below it. The huge torrents of water coming from the tubes at the base of the dam have been a humbling spectacle for paddlers since the 1970s. Soon they will be stilled, sacrificed to a hydroelectric project operated by the town of Summersville. Fortunately, the project will not affect fall releases. Private paddlers will run their shuttle on river right, where most of the take-out options are.

A few miles west Route 129 makes a sharp turn at Carnifex Ferry Battlefield State Park. Confederate troops under General Floyd camped here; when probed by a large contingent of Yankee soldiers, they decided they were outnumbered and retreated. Under cover of darkness they traveled down from the heights, across the Gauley, and up the Meadow River Valley. A steep trail leads from an overlook down to the top of Pillow Rock Rapids, and the remains of the old ferry road wind from the heights to a point opposite the mouth of the Meadow. Believe it or not, this was once an important travel route!

Eight miles into the trip, you'll reach the most popular take-out for the Upper Gauley (B). The Mason Branch Road and the Panther Creek Trail are both owned by Class VI River Runners. The road is private, and the trail, while beautiful, is extremely steep. Both are reached via the Panther Mountain Road (WV 22), which turns off Route 129 behind a church a few miles west of Carnifex Ferry Park. American Whitewater and the West Virginia Rivers Coalition work together with the Class VI River Runners to provide a shuttle service during the fall sea-

son. At other times you'll have to carry your boat up the trail or continue downriver. The next access point is Woods Ferry (C), 12 miles into the trip on river right. It can be reached by traveling farther down Panther Mountain Road and taking the left fork. The last half mile is extremely steep and rough.

The Bucklick access (D), owned by Appalachian Wildwater, is 15 miles below the dam. It can be reached by turning off WV 39 at the old Otter Creek School (WV 22), where Peter's Creek turns away from the highway. After the blacktop ends, turn left, then choose the right fork. This winding dirt road is heavily traveled by private vehicles and outfitter trucks and buses; expect delays. After several miles you'll arrive at the top of a well-maintained dirt road dropping into the canyon. Vehicle access is limited during Gauley season, but Imre Szilagyi, the owner, has generously permitted walk-ins at this point for many years. The rules are simple: park where you won't cause problems for the trucks and buses, then carry your boat a half mile down the access road.

The best way to get to the Bucklick access point from Swiss is to use Rusty's Shuttle Service (call 304-574-3475). Rusty meets paddlers at the first parking area and runs them and their boats all the way to the river. The cost in 1996 was $7. You can call to reserve a space or show up and take your chances.

Two miles below Bucklick the Peter's Creek trestle (E) crosses the Gauley. Before other access points were built, paddlers running the Upper Gauley left their boats beside the river here and hiked two miles up the railroad tracks to a muddy clearing in the woods. This walk crosses two other trestles and passes a 20-foot waterfall on Peter's Creek. The trestles have walkways, and this hike is pleasant. To reach the clearing, turn off at Otter Creek School, turn right after crossing Peter's Creek, then take the right fork. The road is badly rutted and requires a high-clearance vehicle.

On the far side of the Peter's Creek trestle the railroad plunges into the 0.9-mile-long Koontz Bend Tunnel, emerging five miles upstream just below Ender Waves. After some boats were stolen from the mouth of Peter's Creek in the mid-1970s, many paddlers decided to shorten the Upper Gauley run and improve security at the same time. They left their boats at the far end of the tunnel and walked the tracks to Peter's Creek. The tunnel was an unpleasant and scary walk even if they remembered to bring flashlights! They stubbed their toes on the ties, splashed through the muddy ditches, and lived with the ever-present fear that a train would come roaring through the mountain. Then they were forced to lie face-down in the filthy ditches while the boxcars clattered past. Needless to say, nobody wanted to do that again! The railroad is now abandoned, but the walk is still unpleasant.

The take-out for the Lower Gauley run is the small hamlet of Swiss (F). Turn left on a side road about eight miles down WV 39 from the Otter Creek School on river right. Several short trails run from the river to the road. During Gauley season a few landowners rent parking spaces in their fields and yards. Because vehicles left just upstream at Omega Siding have been burglarized, it's a good idea to patronize these folks. Be sure to walk from the parking lot to the river so you'll know where to get out. If you do park along the road, all four wheels must be off the pavement or you'll be ticketed. Be sure to park at least five feet from the railroad tracks; the rail cars overhang the rails considerably and can do some serious damage. You can also take out in Jodie, a mile downstream on river left.

River Levels

Flow information on the Gauley River can be obtained from the National Weather Service in Charleston (call 304-529-5127) or from the U.S. Army Corps of Engineers at Summersville Dam (call 304-872-5809). The Belva gauge combines the flows in the Gauley and Meadow Rivers, Peter's Creek, and all other tributaries coming in above Swiss. The Gauley season begins the week after Labor Day and runs Friday through Monday for six consecutive weeks. For more information call the National Park Service in Glen Jean (304-465-0508). American Whitewater's Gauley River Festival is typically on the third release weekend; for more information call them at (301) 589-9453.

Although most paddlers run the Gauley during the fall releases, the river runs over 2,250 cfs 35 percent of the time in May, 10 percent of the time in June, July, and August, and over 50 percent of the time November through March. It runs over 800 cfs, a great level for the Upper Gauley, even more often. To predict the flows, you'll need to know the lake flow and the pool level. If the lake is over 1,575 feet during November–April and over 1,652 feet in May–August, the inflow to the lake is passed through the next day. The Craigsville gauge provides the inflow information. All three numbers are on the Summersville Dam number. But beware: big flows of 6,000 cfs or more with considerable inflow from side streams are not uncommon! If the Meadow River is running over 1,000 cfs, regardless of the dam release, the Lower Gauley is boatable.

Gauley Conservation Efforts

The whitewater of the Gauley River remains available today only because of the efforts of a few private boaters and commercial outfitters with strong support from the West Virginia congressional delegation.

To the U.S. Army Corps of Engineers, which operates the Summersville Dam, the project and the river held great potential for the construction of a hydroelectric power plant. During the early 1980s, the Corps of Engineers made a big political push to build a "long tunnel" hydro project for taking water from Summersville Lake to a powerhouse to be constructed just above Pillow Rock. The project would have dried up several miles of the best whitewater on the Gauley. At the same time, the Corps of Engineers claimed that whitewater releases from the dam were not within the project's authorized purposes, which include flood control and pollution abatement. However, in order to gain the support of river users for its proposal, the Corps of Engineers promised that a hydroelectric power plant would enhance rather than detract from whitewater opportunities on the Gauley.

A group called Citizens for Gauley River, made up of private and commercial whitewater boaters, was quickly formed to fight the Corps of Engineers' proposal and to work for scheduled whitewater releases from Summersville Dam. David Brown of Knoxville, Tennessee, forged this group into an effective and powerful political force, just as he had in an earlier, successful battle to save the Ocoee River in Tennessee. Under Brown's skillful leadership, the Citizens for Gauley River succeeded beyond all expectations.

In early 1984, U.S. Representative Nick J. Rahall of Beckley, West Virginia, threatened to amend a funding bill for the Corps of Engineers with a provision prohibiting any further consideration of the proposed hydroelectric power project and vowed that Congress would never authorize its construction. Almost immediately, the Corps of Engineers withdrew the proposal and ceased further planning for Gauley hydroelectric developments. Rahall proceeded with legislation to authorize whitewater recreation as a project purpose of Summersville Dam. Enactment of this provision later that year set a precedent. The Summersville Dam became the first of many Corps of Engineers water projects to have whitewater recreation as one of its official purposes.

To further enhance whitewater recreation on the Gauley, Rahall also added a provision to the 1986 Omnibus Water Projects Authorization Bill that would guarantee whitewater releases from Summersville Dam at 2,500 cfs for a minimum of 20 days during the six-week period following Labor Day each year. This legislation was enacted by Congress and signed into law in November 1986. In the years that followed, the Gauley became a national river administered by the National Park Service.

New River

The New has a little something for everyone in its three most popular sections. The uppermost section from Sandstone to McCreery (15 miles) is the least paddled and consists of Class II rapids and some seemingly unending pools. It's a good run for open canoes and can be combined with the succeeding Prince to Thurmond run at moderate levels for canoe camping. This latter section sports more continuous Class II and borderline Class III water than the section above and is a longtime favorite of novice and intermediate paddlers in both decked and open boats. Below Thurmond the bottom falls out as the river runs through the celebrated New River Gorge. This is one of the premier Class IV–V whitewater runs of the eastern United States. Contrary to its name, the New is the oldest river in North America and is one of the few large rivers in the world that flows north.

Sandstone to McCreery

The section from Sandstone (A) to McCreery (B) is a very long run consisting of several nice impressive rapids interrupted by very long expanses of flatwater. It is a big powerful river, very beautiful, always up in the summer, with plenty of excellent fishing. Numerous campsites are available for overnight trips. The rapids are mainly long chutes dropping gently over ledges. Although the waves are large, not much maneuvering is required.

Open-boaters and novices will encounter only two places that may cause trouble. The first of these occurs at the top of Horseshoe Bend, which can be viewed from Grandview State Park. The entire river necks down, creating big waves that can swamp open canoes immediately. This one is located about a half mile downstream from the obsolete concrete bridge piers at Glade (the second rapid from there). The river heads to the left and turns sharply back to the right. In this curve you'll find some very heavy water, including a Class III+ stopper. After the rapids have pushed their way to the right, they straighten out and more heavy turbulence is found mid-

stream. Amid these waves is a mean hole that's large enough to eat a whole canoe. You will need a lot of drive to get through this one. Open-boaters or novices may avoid all of the heavy water by maintaining control and staying to the far right.

The second potential trouble spot is a delightfully long Class III rapids at Quinnimont just before reaching the railroad station. It is not difficult, but open canoes might swamp due to its length. Such canoeists should consider dumping excess water halfway down. Near the bottom, a huge drainpipe enters from the right. Just before this there is a powerful hydraulic in the middle of the river, followed by 20 yards of flatwater, and then another very deceptive wave that camouflages a hole deep enough to set a C-2 in. Fun, but surprising!

Access at Sandstone is not ideal, but folks are neighborly and are normally happy to grant you access to the river. To drive to the take-out, take WV 20 out of

Section: Sandstone to McCreery
Counties: Summers, Fayette, Raleigh
USGS Quads: Meadow Creek, Beckley
Difficulty: Class I–III
Gradient: 8 feet per mile
Average Width: 125 feet
Velocity: Slow to moderate
Rescue Index: Accessible to remote
Hazards: None
Scouting: None
Portages: None
Scenery: Generally beautiful
Highlights: Excellent fishing, camping
Gauge: For Hinton gauge information, call Bluestone Dam, (304) 466-0156

Runnable Water Levels:	Minimum	Maximum
Hinton gauge	1.75 feet	2.50 feet

Additional Information: National Park Service, (304) 465-0508

New River • West Virginia

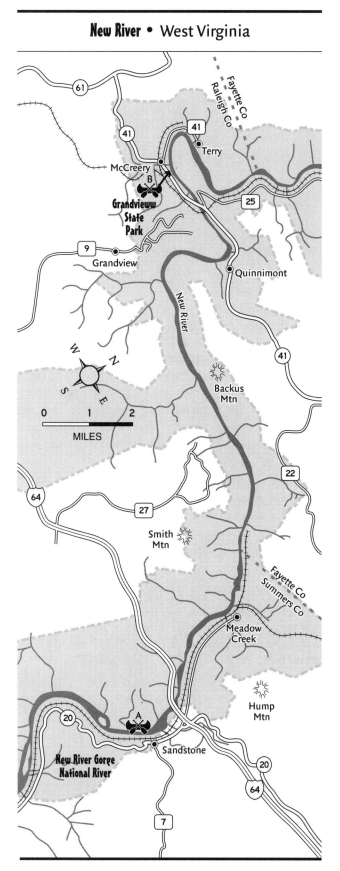

Sandstone to Meadow Bridge, turn left on CR 31 to Danese, and turn left again on WV 41 to McCreery. The take-out is easiest at a very large, sandy beach located on the left, two rapids beyond the WV 41 bridge. It may be reached in a car by turning right off WV 41 onto a dirt road where WV 41 turns left to go up the mountain.

Prince to Thurmond

The stretch from Prince (B, just below McCreery) to Thurmond (C) is characterized by more rapids and more long, flatwater pools. Generally the individual rapids are heavier than those in the upper river. The river is wide and powerful at 2.5 feet on the Hinton gauge, and it would be unwise for novices or open-boaters lacking substantial experience or flotation to proceed at this or higher levels. Each rapid is a long, river-wide stretch of big waves with few obstructions. Occasionally a ledge is encountered at one side or the other, but is always eroded in the heaviest current. Consequently, although large stopper waves and an occasional hydraulic are found, very little maneuvering is required.

Intermediate paddlers with heavy-water experience should encounter no difficulties or unexpected surprises, but this is a tough place for beginners. More than halfway along and after a particularly long flat stretch, four sand silos appear on the right bank of a left-hand turn (the sand in the silos is used for making glass). Just below this, very large Class III+ waves are found along the right bank. Another long, flat stretch, two minor rapids, and a zesty chute over a ledge bring the paddler to the take-out.

You can put in at the McCreery beach mentioned above or at a developed put-in across the bridge over McCreery Creek. The easiest take-out is on the sandy beach 200 yards above a bridge located a mile above Thurmond (the first bridge you'll encounter). This take-out, located on the left side of the river, is reached by a dirt road. The water is pretty flat from this bridge to Thurmond itself, although you'll find a nice Class II rapid right under the Thurmond bridge. Although there is a dirt road connecting Prince to Thurmond, we don't suggest using it when setting shuttle. Take WV 41 from Prince toward Beckley, turn right on WV 61 to Mount Hope, turn right onto WV 16 for about a mile, and then make one more right turn at CR 25 leading to Glen Jean and Thurmond.

For water information call the Bluestone Dam at (304) 466-1234 or (304) 466-0156. The Hinton gauge reading takes into account the output of the Greenbrier; for a computerized reading of this gauge, call (304) 465-1722. The river seldom drops below 1.75 feet and is often at

Section: McCreery/Prince to Thurmond

Counties: Fayette, Raleigh

USGS Quad: Beckley

Difficulty: Class II–III

Gradient: 10 feet per mile

Average Width: 150 feet

Velocity: Slow to moderate

Rescue Index: Accessible

Hazards: None

Scouting: Large waves below four sand silos on river right;
 waves can be avoided on the left

Portages: None

Scenery: Generally beautiful

Highlights: Big river; rapids are mainly waves, the biggest over
 halfway into trip below four sand silos

Gauge: For Hinton gauge information, call Bluestone Dam,
 (304) 466-0156

Runnable Water Levels:	Minimum	Maximum
Hinton gauge	1.75 feet	2.50 feet

Months Runnable: All year

Additional Information: National Park Service, (304) 465-0508

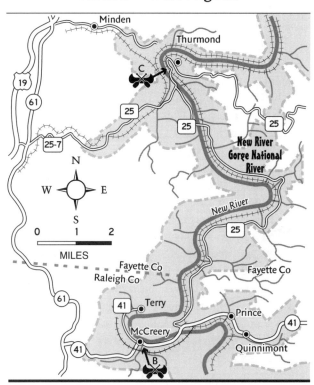

New River • West Virginia

this level in the summer. Approach the entire river with great caution if it's over 2.5 feet.

Thurmond to Fayette Station (The Gorge)

The New River Gorge from Thurmond (C) to Fayette Station (E) contains the biggest whitewater in the southern Appalachians. The river flows through an immense gorge. Steep slopes and rugged cliffs can be seen throughout the run. The first half of this stretch alternates long, flat pools and easy Class II–III rapids that could be run by conventional canoes at low water levels. Below Cunard the drops get bigger and the turbulence increases. Most rapids are straight shots through big waves, with little maneuvering required. There are six drops in the Class III+ to IV+ range. This is a hugely popular commercial raft run and becomes very crowded on summer weekends. A reliable roll is recommended for all hard-boaters.

There's a Class II rapid under the bridge at Thurmond with some medium-sized waves, then several miles of flatwater broken by a small rapid at Buzzard's Bend. About four miles into the trip one particular rapid deserves respect—the famous Surprise Rapid (Class III+). At the top it looks like another straight shot over a gravel bar, but the water rapidly converges toward a huge set of waves. There is a big hole between the first and second

waves that swallows kayaks and sets rafts on end at moderate levels. Hit the left side and angle slightly to the right if you want to punch it, but be prepared to swim out! The hole is easily skirted to either side, with the left side being easier. At high water levels all but the largest rafts opt for the left-hand route.

Three miles below Surprise the National Park Service improved the old four-wheel-drive road to the Cunard put-in (D). People interested in the best whitewater begin their trip here. A half mile away you'll be able to see a railroad trestle downstream. Upper Railroad Rapids starts about 200 yards above the bridge. This rapid has two distinct parts: the top section has a huge hole on river right called the Cunard Stripper. It's a keeper at levels over three feet at Fayette Station, but it can be easily missed on the left. At lower levels there is a tongue that's hard to see from upstream. If you plan to surf this hole, post a lookout upstream to warn off commercial raft traffic and get ready for one hell of a ride. People who swim out of the hole should head for deep water. The second part of the drop features a wave train on the left and a shallow boulder garden on the right.

At the other end of a short pool a horizon line marks the start of Lower Railroad. This steep boulder barrage can be run in several places, but the route is blind and first-timers should scout it. Paddlers typically start one-third of the way over from the left and run right over a big water hump, then work over to the right to miss the hole at the bottom. At low levels (below zero at Fayette Station) there are some deadly undercut rocks in this drop that cannot be seen from upstream. Two boaters have been killed here, so everyone should get out and scout!

Four easy wave rapids, separated by pools, await downstream. These are big fun at high water levels and always offer excellent surfing. The second one is frequently occupied by kayakers playing chicken with oncoming rafts. The third has a nasty hole on the right side that only the most daring boaters will want to try.

After nine miles of paddling you should be warmed up for the big stuff, the Keaney Brothers. Upper Keaney (Class III+) can be recognized by the huge, smooth boulder (Whale Rock) coming in from river left. Run through the waves and angle into the eddy behind Whale Rock to set up for Middle Keaney (Class IV). At higher levels the eddy is hard to get into, so you may want to head directly into the next drop. Middle Keaney has three large, breaking waves in the center channel. The easiest route is just to the left or right of these monsters. At two feet or lower, rafts can aim for a black rock in the bottom right center, while open boats can shoot past a dry, camel-back rock at left center. There are holes on the left and right sides, so don't try to sneak this one! At levels higher than four feet the waves are eight feet high and this rapid merges with the biggest drop of the three, Lower Keaney, which lies downstream.

Even experienced New River paddlers like to get out and scout Lower Keaney (Class IV+) on river left. It cannot be lined or snuck, and it's a nasty carry over giant boulders, so you might as well figure out how to run it. The river has necked down on the left side to one-third its normal width, concentrating the action enormously. The waves at the bottom surge ominously, bombarding a huge rock (Wash-Up Rock) on river left and exploding into a giant wave train. The size of the wave varies with the level; they're big at one foot, wash out slightly at two feet, and come back bigger than ever at three feet. The trick is to start at the center of this huge chute and work quickly over to the right. You can then ease back into the waves if you're looking for a thrill. At certain levels you'll find a roostertail in the center of the chute; you must get to the right of it to avoid being pushed into the rock. There's a small drop about 50 yards below here with a nice surfing wave and an eddy line infested with huge whirlpools. If you have swimmers, pick them up fast.

Dudley's Dip (Class III) follows. Above 0.5 feet on the gauge, begin this rapid left of center. As you enter, look for a pourover rock and run just to the right of it. Below 0.5 feet, enter on the far right and work diagonally to the left; the route is easier to read from this angle. Go between the two pourover rocks on left and right of center. The large, upside-down-canoe-shaped rock on the right side and the slanting rock on the left side are undercut.

Next comes Sunset, or Double **Z** (Class V), the most technical rapid on the river. Over 10 miles into the trip,

Keith Merkel on Lower Keeney Rapid. Photo by Bob Maxey.

Diana Kendrick in Surprise
on the New River.
Photo by Paul Marshall.

it's marked by a chain of rocks extending halfway across the river from the right. First-timers can pull over to the right above this chain of rocks and scout before entering the rapid. Enter the rapid and eddy out behind the rock chain in order to reach the far right channel and avoid a nasty, complex V-ledge and hydraulic in the center. The right channel will take you diagonally to the left, but it tumbles steeply through a field of holes and boulders, ending with a mean pourover and powerful hole below at bottom center. At levels of up to two feet, try to run this rapid close to the right bank. Over three feet, it's best to run left of center down a big V that forms. At levels above four feet, watch for a nasty hole in the middle of the rapid. At all levels, avoid the huge boulder toward bottom left that is undercut and has a powerful current under it.

The next rapid is Old 99 or Hook (Class III). This can be run right, middle, or left. Right gives a sliding-board feeling, middle is a backward S turn, and the left is the straightest. Just below is Bear's Rock or the second part of Old 99 (to some paddlers). Left of center is a smooth chute just to the right of a semidry rock. After running the chute, angle left to pass a large, violent hole on your right.

Work far left or far right after running this rapid because Greyhound Bus Stopper is just below. This aptly named monster could probably stop a bus at high levels and has a dangerous recirculation even at moderate flows. It can be avoided to the far left or right at any level. At levels of 1.5 feet or lower, look for dynamic enders just

right of the rock forming Greyhound. Eddy behind Greyhound Rock and work back up to the spot where the river pours off the right edge. Enjoy!

Next comes Upper Kaymoor or Upper Tipple (Class II), which is easily read. At levels below zero the ledge on the far right side creates a steep, strong hole. Lower Kaymoor or Lower Tipple (Class III) can be run right (following a wave train) or left of the large rectangular rock in the middle (a more technical run). If running left, watch out for the squirrelly curler just to the left of the big rock.

Miller's Folly or Undercut Rock (Class IV+) follows, after 12 miles of paddling. Scout from the left. Avoid the temptation to begin at the far right, but instead begin in the center and paddle toward the left side of the big rock on the right (which is, of course, undercut). Stay in the left of the chute and then cut sharply left before you reach the rock, following the flow of this channel. Just below this you'll encounter some enormous, fun waves. At moderate levels, expect to find large eddies on the left and right that you can use to scout the lower part of the rapid. The best route is just left of center. Watch for an L-shaped hole at the top, run just to the right of it, then angle left to avoid going over Invisible Rock and hitting its accompanying steep, nasty hole. To sneak this lower part, run right. The far left is appropriately called Bloody Nose and should not be run.

Shortly after this rapid you will see two bridges—one crossing the gorge high above. Soon, you will reach Fayette Station Bridge; just below is Fayette Station

Section: Thurmond to Fayette Station

Counties: Fayette

USGS Quads: Thurmond, Fayetteville

Difficulty: Class III–V

Gradient: 15 feet per mile; the first seven miles at 11 feet per mile and the last seven miles at 19 feet per mile

Average Width: 150–200 feet

Velocity: Moderate to fast

Rescue Index: Remote

Hazards: Upper Railroad, big hole on river right; Lower Railroad, pinning rocks on left; Double **Z**, undercut rock at bottom left; Greyhound Bus Stopper, huge hole; Undercut Rock/Miller's Folly, undercut rock on top right and Bloody Nose on lower left

Scouting: Lower Railroad, Middle and Lower Keeney, Double **Z**, Undercut Rock; Fayette Station Rapid

Portages: None at lower levels

Scenery: Generally beautiful

Highlights: Biggest whitewater river in West Virginia, immense gorge

Gauge: Call Bluestone Dam, (304) 466-0516; National Weather Service, Charleston, (304) 529-5127

Runnable Water Levels:	Minimum	Maximum
Fayette Station gauge	-1.5 feet	12 feet

    Though it has been run down to -3 feet, more dangerous, pinning rocks appear; for expert open-boaters, the cutoff is 3–4 feet, although it has been run at 10-foot levels

Additional Information: National Park Service, (304) 465-0508

Rapid (Class IV), which should not be missed. Run right of center. It is a multiholed roller coaster with some deceptively vigorous drops hidden by big waves. Be ready to hit the waves squarely. You can scout from the left. Take out on river left at the National Park Service Fayette Station access point after running this rapid. Other than one or two minor rapids (the second one requiring care to avoid the pourover on the left side) the next four miles to Hawk's Nest Dam are mostly flatwater and seldom run. There is an outfitter's take-out a mile below Fayette Station at Teay's Landing on river right.

The shuttles for the New River Gorge are very straightforward. Fayette Station can be reached from Route 19 via WV 82. This area gets very crowded on summer weekends and parking is at a premium. Thurmond is also reached from Route 19 via Route 12. To find the Cunard access point, take the Main Street/Fayetteville exit off Route 19, drive through town, take the first left past the beer store, and follow signs. The road is steep but very well maintained. Park in the private boater section.

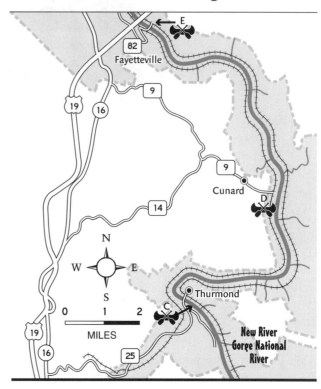

New River • West Virginia

Rusty's Shuttle Service (304-574-3475) will take you to Cunard and drop your car off in Thurmond for $7.

New River Dries

The New River Dries, a five-mile stretch from Cotton Hill to Gauley Bridge, is a little-known but very enjoyable section of whitewater through the most beautiful part of the New River Gorge. The Hawk's Nest tunnel diverts 9,000 cfs of water to the power plant, so the Dries only run when there is water spilling over Hawk's Nest Dam. This happens whenever the New is flowing above 9,000 cfs or when the hydro plant at Gauley Bridge is not running at full capacity. At levels of 1,000–3,000 cfs this is Class II+ open-boatable. From 3,000–10,000 cfs it is suitable for intermediate decked boats and advanced open-boaters. From 10,000–20,000 cfs large holes and standing waves start to form and only paddlers comfortable with big water (like the New River Gorge at four to eight feet) should attempt the run. Above 20,000 cfs the sheer canyon walls constrict the flow into huge exploding waves and holes. At this level, the Dries should be attempted by experts only.

The rapids here are long but readable, with one exception. Entrance Rapid is rocky on the right and sports Broken Paddle Hole at bottom left, but it is easily run down the middle. Then comes Foreplay, a long stretch of smooth surfing waves at levels above 8,000 cfs. The river then bends to the left for Preparation, a half-mile series of Class II–III drops. After a short pool the river turns sharply left for Mile Long, which has the biggest water at high levels. Watch out for Multi-Bender-Bowl-Hole under the overhanging ledge at the bottom right at all levels and for Hatch's Hole at bottom left above 18,000 cfs. A long pool is followed by Landslide Rapid; scout this from river right at low water or river left at higher levels. Enter through the right slot and pick your way through the squirrelly, technical water below. Staying right all the way is safe but other options are possible. The Dries finishes with Afterplay, a series of nice, playable waves and holes.

Due to the unpredictability of water levels on the Dries, it is advisable to check with Hawk's Nest Dam for the most current information before putting in. Efforts are now being made to obtain regular water releases.

New River Gorge High Water Information

When the water gets really high (between 5 feet and 12 feet on the gauge), the New River Gorge dramatically changes. Huge holes, waves and other factors affect many of the rapids, dictating much more scouting and care in running the river. The river is substantially pushier and tougher. The following two examples show how different the gorge becomes.

A new rapid called the Halls of Karma (Class III) only exists between seven and nine feet on the Fayette Station gauge. This is the short narrow section of the river between Double Z and Old 99 (Hook). The sudden extreme narrowing of the river creates some dynamic waves and currents with large waves that are pulsating and moving. Most of the time, luck and quick reactions get paddlers through.

Also, at higher levels Upper, Middle, and Lower Keeney merge to become The Keeney (Class V+). At 10 feet, Whale Rock at Upper Keeney becomes Whale Hole—awesome. Between 8 and 11 feet, is a huge pulsating, crashing wave called The Mouth (downstream of Whale Hole in the center of the river where Middle Keeney used to be). It rises up, opens wide, and crashes down—even eating rafts on occasion. Below this (above seven feet), the rocks at the top right of Lower Keeney become Meatgrinder, a long, nasty hole; the rocks at the bottom left of Lower Keeney create another strong hole called Lollygag (worst between three and seven feet).

The expert paddler should first scout The Keeney. Enter it far right so that Whale Hole does not swallow you. Then run to the right of The Mouth to avoid being eaten. Now start working left, but watch out for two very large, breaking waves angled downstream toward the left. They can easily flip you if you have too much left angle. After this, the river seems to calm down, but not much. Set up for what used to be Lower Keeney. Meatgrinder, the long nasty hole extending from the right, begins fairly small in the center of the river. To avoid it and its downstream companion, Lollygag, run just left or clip the left side of Meatgrinder (where the hole is still relatively small) and angle right. Drive hard to the right so you can miss Lollygag, which extends

New River Gorge Water Level Conversion (correlation) Table

Fayette Station (feet)	cfs
-3	544
-2	1,072
-1	1,704
0	2,440
1	3,352
2	4,436*
3	5,820*
4	7,550*
5	9,550*
6	11,400*
7	14,100
8	17,200**
9	20,200
10	23,800
11	26,800
12	30,000

Source: Dave Bassage

Note: At these levels, the Fayette Station reading is approximately one-half of the cfs level, rounded to the nearest thousand. For example, 4,436 to 5,000 cfs equals 2 feet on the Fayette Station gauge; 5,820 to 6,000 cfs equals 3 feet; 14,000 to 14,100 equals 7 feet.

Note: Calling the Thurmond gauge at (304) 465-0493 gives a system of beeps, which can be converted to Fayette Station equivalents. First, translate the beeps into a reading: you will hear a series of four groups of beeps. A long first beep means zero; a short first beep means one, heavy water. Write down the numbers of each series of beeps, and put a decimal between the second and third numbers, for example, 03.62, or 3.62 feet at the Thurmond gauge. To convert to Fayette Station equivalents, multiply the Thurmond reading by four-thirds (1.33), then subtract 4 2/3 (4.66) from the result. Your answer will show the equivalent reading at Fayette Station.

Example: A Thurmond reading of 3.62 times 1.33 equals 4.81 minus 4.66 gives 0.15 feet as the Fayette Station equivalent. This formula works for levels up to 7 or 8 feet at Fayette Station.

from the left side of the river. Then collapse from exhaustion or enjoy a king-sized adrenaline high in the calm area below.

At levels above eight feet the largest wave on the river is found on the left side of Fayette Station Rapid; it shouldn't be missed. Enter in the left V at the top. Halfway through, a huge, smooth wall of water blots out the sun. If you are good enough to have made it this far, you won't be flipped, and the ride is rivaled only by Hermit rapid on the Colorado River.

Middle Fork of the Tygart River

Look at the rapids under the bridge at Audra State Park (A), look at the lush, sylvan surroundings, subtract the road, bridge, and bathhouse at the park, and then you'll know what to expect for the first 2.6 miles of this run. It's a beautiful, busy, boatbuster. If the water is low, the rapids under the bridge can be run on the right side, heading straight for the retaining wall of the swimming area, then slipping to the left down into the pool. When the water level is high, it is more entertaining to fandango down through the center.

Below the pool the Middle Fork of the Tygart takes off through a delightful mix of ledge and boulder rapids. You

can "read and run" most of them from your boat. At low water, the rapids are scrapy; at higher levels they pack some punch. It's a good place for newcomers to get a feel for technical paddling and prepare for runs like the Big Sandy, Blackwater, and Upper Yough. The water, though polluted with acid, is sparkling clear.

About an hour into the trip you'll paddle through a long rapid ending in a series of well-formed, playable, sliding ledge holes. After you're through messing with them, follow the river as it bends right around a hemlock-covered island. You'll encounter a long slide rapid into a powerful stopper. A rock just downstream makes a flip in the stopper more exciting, and it directs floating debris into an aggressive, left-side, whirlpool eddy. It's easy

Section: Audra State Park to Tygart Junction

County: Barbour

USGS Quad: Audra

Difficulty: Class IV

Gradient: 2.5 miles at 72 feet per mile

Average Width: 35 feet

Velocity: Fast

Rescue Index: Remote

Hazards: Continuous rapids; rocky, steep, technical paddling

Scouting: Last half mile of Middle Fork (three big rapids)

Portages: Possibly one or more of the three big rapids in the last half mile

Scenery: Beautiful

Highlights: Lush, wooded surroundings

Gauge: Visual. The government gauge just upstream of the bridge at Audra State Park has been partially washed away, so you must extrapolate.

Runnable Water Levels: | | Minimum | Maximum |
| --- | --- | --- |
| | 3.3 feet | 5.0 feet |

Additional Information: National Weather Service, (412) 262-5290 (Pittsburgh) or (703) 260-0305 (Washington, DC area); the Belington gauge should be a minimum of 5 feet; Audra State Park, (304) 457-1162; Waterline, (800) 297-4243, #541319

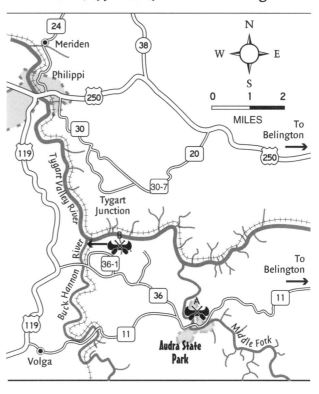

Middle Fork, Tygart Valley River • West Virginia

Jon Wright on the
Middle Fork of the Tygart.
Photo by Charles Walbridge.

enough to avoid the excitement by working right to miss the stopper.

Downstream you'll encounter three rapids that are significantly harder than anything upstream. The first one is a long, boulder rapid culminating in a wickedly sharp left turn around a broken ledge. The ledge can be run, but the channel is narrow and it should be scouted. The next big rapid is easily recognized by a huge boulder on river right. The right side offers a tight but clean run through narrow chutes between huge boulders. The route at the bottom is not obvious from above, but you can scout on the right with little trouble. The final rapid, just above the junction with the Tygart, consists of a steep, sliding ledge backed up by a vertical rock wall. Many people have lost some skin trying to make this move! How you get by depends on water levels, but the obstructed boulder garden on the right is not much better.

The river empties into the Tygart Gorge at about its midpoint, and the only way out is to paddle the remaining four miles to the mouth of the Buckhannon (B). This results in two interesting trips for the price of one. First is the steep, rocky, technical paddling of the lower Middle Fork and then the much heavier, pushy Tygart, with its tripled volume.

Audra State Park can be reached from Belington; take a right turn at the light in the center of town and cross the new bridge over the Tygart. The take-out is the same as for the Tygart Gorge section. The riverside campgrounds at Audra State Park were created during the Depression by hundreds of workers using hand tools. The sites fit perfectly into the riverside environment and offer what is unquestionably the finest riverside camping in West Virginia.

The USGS Audra gauge is about 50 yards upstream from the bridge at Audra State Park on river right. Paddlers often check the water level while running a shuttle from Belington; they head for the Tygart gorge if the Middle Fork flow is insufficient. Because of the beautiful surroundings this section is often run low; I've had a good day on the river with Audra reading 3.2 feet. Conditions at the bridge rapid are pretty indicative of what will be encountered downstream.

Tygart River

The Gorge

The Gorge is the most rugged section of the Tygart, filled with many complex and bodacious rapids. The river runs through an isolated gorge civilized only by a set of worn-out railroad tracks on the right. These tracks have been used many times for walking out. The water is clear, though acid-polluted, and flows through second-growth deciduous forest.

At the Belington put-in, the river is flat, then gradually picks up speed and flows through easy rapids down to an alternative put-in at Papa Weeze's. Immediately below here the river drops over four big ledges. At the first rapid, Keyhole (Class IV), the river tumbles between boxcar-sized boulders separated by four-feet-wide sluiceways. The center slot has been run, but is narrow and nasty. Most paddlers prefer the far right opening, a sharp left turn in a narrow channel. The channel widens and actually becomes easier at moderate flows (5.5 feet at Belington). The next two ledges are clean, but you should scout carefully to find the right chute.

The final ledge, Hartung Falls (Class V), was named for "Crazy Dave" Hartung, the first to run it. The water roars over a 10-foot-high sliding ledge on the left and caroms off the wall behind it to form a huge, nasty-looking diagonal hole. Boaters with enough moxie to run it can brace into the foam and ride it down to the big, exploding wave at the bottom. At moderate levels the ledge can be snuck in the center of the river. The water tends to carry you from right to left, so pick a line that takes this into account. At high water levels this section is very pushy and it may be a good idea to carry the entire section on the tracks at river right.

Below here the river alternates between exciting boulder drops and less obstructed, easier rapids. A few are memorable. Let's Make a Deal (Class IV) is a pushy rapid that culminates in a row of boulders that create three distinct chutes. Take the center door, please; the left goes between undercut rocks, and the right, while open, is a real scramble to reach. Further down you'll see a pyramid-shaped rock that forms part of The Room (Class

IV-). As you run down the left side, the left eddy at the bottom looks tempting, but it tends to throw you out as fast as you come in. Instead, eddy right. Large boulders now surround you on all four sides. Paddle across a boil and leave via the back door.

The river calms down again for a mile or two, then picks up below the mouth of the Middle Fork. The river's volume grows by 50 percent, increasing its power noticeably. After several interesting play rapids the river pools, turns left and drops into a boulder barrage. This is S-Turn (Class V-), which drops 25 feet in its twisting, boiling, 75-yard course. Most paddlers start in the center or far left and pick their way down to a point above a ledge that juts

Section: Belington to Mouth of Buckhannon or Phillippi
County: Barbour
USGS Quads: Belington, Audra, Monongahela National Forest
Difficulty: Class III–V
Gradient: 37 feet per mile; 1.25 miles at 80 feet per mile
Average Width: 100 feet
Velocity: Fast
Rescue Index: Remote
Hazards: Vision limited by huge boulders; undercut rocks; Hartung rapids; Shoulder Snapper has pinning possibilities
Scouting: Keyhole, Hartung, S-Turn, Shoulder Snapper, Hook
Portages: Usually Hartung
Scenery: Pretty to beautiful in spots
Highlights: Big boulders, second-growth mixed forest
Gauge: National Weather Service (Belington gauge), (703) 260-0305

Runnable Water Levels:	Minimum	Maximum
Belington gauge	3.5 feet	7 feet

Months Runnable: Spring (but can be run in the summer after extended rains)
Additional Information: National Weather Service, Pittsburgh, (412) 262-5290; Audra State Park, (304) 457-1162; Waterline, (800) 297-4243, #541471

Tygart River • West Virginia

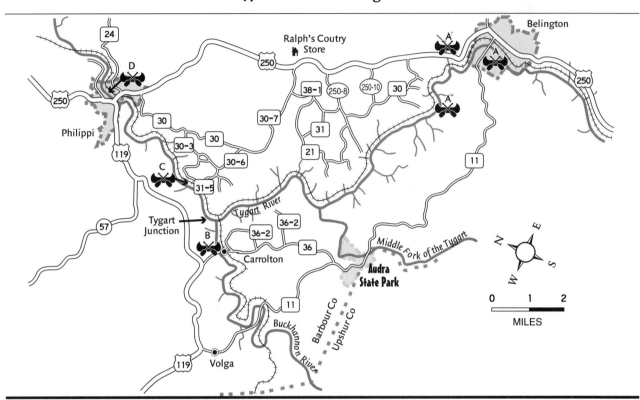

out from river right. Skirt this hole, then sprint for the far right of the bottom chute. This allows you to miss two very powerful pourovers sitting just out of sight at the bottom of the drop. At high water (six feet and higher) the entire drop can be snuck down the far right channel. If someone having a bad day at low to moderate levels, can run down this section and carry the last drop.

On the other side of the pool is the impressive Shoulder Snapper Falls (Class IV+), an eight-foot ledge drop broken out on the right. The name stems from an incident involving John Sweet, one of the strongest paddlers in the late 1960s. Sweet broached against a boulder near the top and dislocated his shoulder, but managed to crawl out on a midstream boulder. Sweet, who hated to swim, was then forced to jump off and float the rest of the drop so his buddies could pick him up. At low water there is a submerged rock in the preferred channel; one boater hit it so hard that he slipped out of his foot brace and impaled his shin. Despite these horror stories, the right center line is a pretty straight shot. The drop is blind, so scout it on river right. At high water, pay attention to the powerful rapid just downstream. A hole at top right pushes hapless boaters left, lining them up for a big stopper hidden between two waves. You can avoid embarrassment by immediately cutting back to the right.

A few miles below here is Hook Rapid (Class IV+), the last major drop. The top of this rapid is full of holes, several of which are capable of stopping a boat and recirculating a swimmer. Then the river curves sharply to the left between two more holes. At low levels a nasty suckhole lies on the inside of the turn. A large rock on river left gives you a good view of the drop; pick a line through the center of the rapid and follow the water as it makes the turn. The next drop is Instant Ender (Class III), a dynamic play spot at levels between 4.0 and 4.3 feet at Belington. From here it's an easy float through moderate rapids to the mouth of the Buckhannon.

For access to this river section, put in at the bridge in Belington (A) or at a pullover spot north of town where the river leaves the road (A'). To avoid three miles of easy whitewater, turn left at the south end of the Belington fairgrounds from US 250, then take the second left down a dirt road to Papa Weese's Paradise, a fishing camp (A''). This is rather time-consuming, and isn't really any faster than paddling the river.

The Mouth of Buckhannon take-out (B) is at the end of a mile-long stretch of railroad tracks that run along the Buckhannon to the covered bridge in Carrolton. It's a tedious hike, exhausting for open-boaters. The tracks are active, so keep your eyes and ears open for trains. To get to Carrolton, turn right at the traffic light in downtown Belington and follow Country Road 11 to Audra State Park. Drive across the Middle Fork, turn right, and 2.5 miles later take the next right onto Country Road 36. Follow this to the covered bridge. It's about five miles from the Middle Fork to Carrolton, a reasonable length for a walking or bicycle shuttle.

There is an alternate take-out (C) for the Tygart River Gorge (one mile below the confluence with the Buckhannon on river right). Head toward Phillipi from Bellington, turn off Route 250 opposite Ralph's Country Store onto Old Route 250 (Country Road 30-7). Take the first right and proceed 3.3 miles to a sharp left turn. Just after the turn, the Union Church will be off to your left. Proceed 0.8 miles to a point where the main road curves sharply to the right at a cinder-block building with a network of outside stairs called the "Garden Apartments" by locals. Take the road to the left here and 0.1 mile later, take a right and keep going right down to the railroad tracks on the river bank. Proceed carefully; it's easy to get lost here.

Below the Buckhannon the Tygart runs a bit over five miles to Philippi (D). The first three miles have several Class II rapids; the last two miles are pretty flat. You can cover this distance quickly at high levels (5.5–7.0 feet), and the shuttle from Belington to Philippi along US 250 is fast and direct. There's a small park on river right where you can leave vehicles and load up afterward.

Arden Section

The Tygart is a big flat river for five and a half miles below Philippi. Then, the first rapids of the eight-mile Arden Section (E) are encountered. This section is strewn with huge boulders and drops over big rock ledges and reefs as the Tygart descends 170 feet before reaching the reservoir behind Grafton Dam. All but the last three miles of the run below Arden may be scouted from a secondary road on the right; this runs from Philippi downstream to the ancient concrete bridge at Teter Creek (F). However, don't take out at Teter Creek unless absolutely necessary because some of the best water is in the remaining three miles to the reservoir (G). At high levels (over 4.5 feet), this eight-mile section becomes expert decked-boater country only.

About a mile below Arden is a ledge channeled on the left. The current continues down the left side for 50 feet, dropping over a boulder and ending in two stoppers. This rapid is called Gallaway by local paddlers and can be scouted from the left. The larger upstream wave must be skirted to the right if one is to maintain the alignment and speed necessary to run a ledge and the second stopper. The second rapid downstream from Laurel Creek (which enters from the right under a steel bridge) is called Deception. Here the river narrows and piles over a rapid succession of three ledges with unavoidable, five-foot, standing waves. Three hundred yards below Deception,

Ollie Fordham running Valley Falls. Photo by Mayo Gravatt.

Tygart River • West Virginia

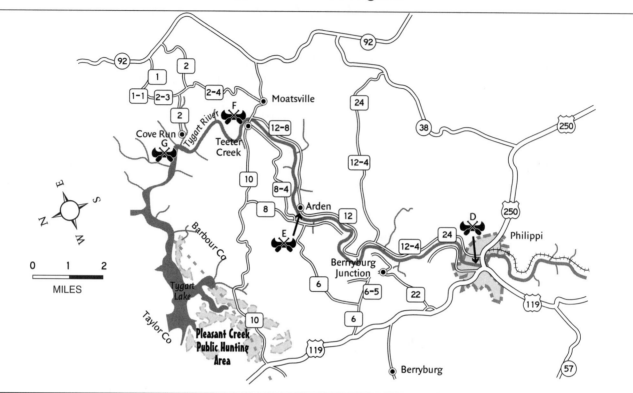

Section: Arden to Cove Run

County: Barbour

USGS Quads: Philippi, Nestorville

Difficulty: Class III–V

Gradient: 27 feet per mile

Average Width: 125–150 feet

Velocity: Fast

Rescue Index: Accessible for the most part

Hazards: Undercut Rock, Moat's Falls, Classic, Wells Falls; very difficult at high water

Scouting: Gallaway, Undercut Rock, Premonition, Moat's Falls, Classic, Wells Falls and rapids below

Portages: Depending on water levels and experience, Undercut Rock, Moat's Falls, Classic, and maybe Wells Falls

Scenery: Pretty in spots, good to fair otherwise

Highlights: Big ledges and large rapids, runnable Moat's Falls, big water at Wells Falls

Gauge: National Weather Service, Pittsburgh (Philippi gauge), (412) 262-5290

Runnable Water Levels:	Minimum	Maximum
Philippi gauge	3.5 feet	7.0 feet

Additional Information: National Weather Service, Washington, (703) 260-0305; Waterline, (800) 297-4243, #541474

the river funnels over a ledge to the left and undercuts a shelf of rock on the left that has a one-foot clearance. This rapid is fittingly called Undercut (Class IV–V depending on water levels) and should be scouted from the right. Be careful when running this rapids to avoid being blown to the left underneath the undercut rock shelf. Expert paddlers can get enjoyable enders here below four feet on the Philippi gauge. A few hundred yards below Undercut is a riverwide three- to four-foot ledge that should be scouted from the right before running it. The right side of this ledge (called Premonition by local paddlers) is a particularly dynamic drop with a curler that forces a quick left turn.

A hundred yards or so farther downstream, the river spills over a good 15-foot riverwide falls called Moats Falls. Very experienced paddlers are now carefully running this falls over the middle—a 15-foot drop into soft suds with a good-sized pool below. Those contemplating running the falls should first scout the launch and landing points carefully. At low water you can go left over the rocks at center. For the squeamish or less advanced boater, an honorable option is to carry along the road on the right and put in just below the falls.

About 500 yards below Moats Falls is a rapid called Classic (Class IV–V at higher water levels) by genteel paddlers and unprintable names by salty boaters. Get over on river left to scout this drop (it can be really nasty at higher levels) and carry it if you have any doubts. The river is narrow and split by a partially submerged, house-sized boulder in a powerful drop. After this rapid, the Tygart is fairly flat until the ancient Teter Creek bridge.

Below Teter Creek bridge is a nice wave train appropriately called Rodeo Rapids. After numerous other good rapids, the river pools behind a natural rock dam, turns left, then immediately right, all the time being necked down considerably. There are big, diagonal stoppers pushing to the right in this turn, and as you regain alignment around the last corner, you are faced with a huge tongue of water called Wells Falls (Class IV at moderate water levels; Class V at high levels), dropping 10 feet over a slide into a formidable stopper. If you slide off the left-side tongue to the right, you will slam into a four-foot wall of water. This is the most powerful of the runnable rapids in the entire Monongahela Basin and should be scouted each time. The next rapid is also mean; it is a sheer drop into another nasty hole. Both Wells Falls and the rapids below are runnable, but they are also easily carried on the right. However, one does have to contend with poison ivy on the portage. The remaining rapids below Teter Creek are nice Class III drops that offer no special problems in low water.

Regarding the shuttle: use the dirt road on the right from Arden because it has been repaired. Drive about two miles upstream to the first rapid for an easy put-in.

Inexperienced paddlers should take out at Arden bridge. One can also take out at Teter Creek for an easy shuttle with a road alongside throughout. To reach the Cove Run take-out, turn right at Teter Creek and go out to the main highway, WV 92, and turn left onto it. Take Cove Run Road "2" to the left, then take a right, another right, and then a left at the succeeding forks. The last part takes you down a very steep, unimproved road to the river. Be sure you recognize this point from the river. You will not find rapids on the lower part until the first of October. Peak drawdown is generally reached about the last of February. At such time there is another 1.8 miles of rapids dropping 30 feet per mile. You then have to paddle another two miles of flatwater before taking out on the left side at Wildcat Hollow Boat Club.

Valley Falls Section

This one-and-a-half-mile section of the Tygart requires careful scouting and close attention to the dam discharge from Grafton. The major difficulty in addition to the 60 feet per mile gradient is the fact that this section of the river has been narrowed by 80 percent as it enters the steep gorge. This is a very heavy descent for such a large volume of water, and the run requires very strong paddling skills.

The put-in for the Valley Falls section of the Tygart is in Valley Falls State Park (H). It's easily found by following signs from Fairmont or Grafton from WV 310 or

Ollie Fordham at Undercut Rock. Photo by Andre Derdyn.

Tygart River • West Virginia

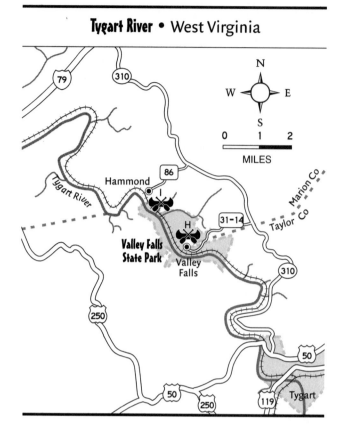

Section: Valley Falls to Hammond
County: Marion
USGS Quad: Fairmont East
Difficulty: Class II–VI
Gradient: 60 feet per mile
Average Width: 150 feet
Velocity: Fast
Rescue Index: Generally accessible
Hazards: First two ledges, Hamburger Helper
Scouting: First two ledges, Hamburger Helper
Portages: None
Scenery: Beautiful
Highlights: Steep gorge and huge drops
Gauge: Grafton Dam, (304) 265-1760

Runnable Water Levels:	Minimum	Maximum
	350 cfs	1,000+ cfs

Additional Information: Valley Falls State Park, (304) 367-2719

Country Road 31/14, respectively. Boaters have negotiated an agreement with park management that specifies the following procedure: First, stop at the park headquarters, a short distance beyond the entrance, and sign in, giving the name, address, and phone number of all members of your party. Next, drive down to the river and make a 200-yard portage from the parking lot, cross a bridge over the railroad tracks, and arrive at the pool above the first drop. Lastly, unlike previous years, boaters are allowed to scout and make multiple runs of the various falls if they wish. Deliberate swimming in the park, with or without PFDs, is not allowed.

Several major drops in this section start just below the put-in. The first ledge is a river-wide, 10-foot drop that at low water levels has three distinct chutes. The sloping right chute and the far left chute can both be run, but scouting is essential. The next Valley Falls ledge of 12 feet is sharp and appears unrunnable. However, at low water it can be run on the left of the right side. The third ledge is called Punk Rock, a Class III rapid with two runnable channels. Both channels require right-angle turns to the left after running tight along the right bank.

The fourth ledge is clearly Class V at even moderate water levels. Aptly called Hamburger Helper, the river here narrows to a single channel and drops eight feet over a boulder with a thin flow at the center and a boiling flume at each side. The fifth rapid (Twist 'n' Shout) is a series of three drops in rapid succession in a 20-foot channel. The last two have huge souse holes up against the undercut right shore. The remaining three ledges (color-

Gauge Conversions

Tygart River at Belington

feet	cfs
3.5	443
4.0	708
4.5	975
5.0	1,250
5.5	1,560
6.0	1,910
6.5	2,260
7.0	2,610
8.0	3,400
9.0	4,270
10.0	5,270

Middle Fork of the Tygart at Audra

feet	cfs
3.0	255
3.5	455
4.0	690
4.5	980
5.0	1,280
5.5	1,620

fully called This, That, and It by local paddlers) are straightforward; the last one can be reached from the take-out.

The Valley Falls section never gets too low to run due to the discharge from Grafton Dam. If several gates are open, however, the rapids would be a nightmare. Always call the Grafton Dam (304-265-1760) before starting. Several outfitters who run summer trips use 750 cfs as a cutoff point. Kayakers will often run at higher levels, exercising caution when running the bigger drops. The Hammond take-out is found at the end of a yellow brick road (CR 86) which leaves WV 310. The road is very rough and several bridges wash out. However, the run is so short that many local boaters find it easier to simply portage their boat back to the park along the railroad tracks.

Laurel Fork of the Cheat River

All things considered, this may be the best intermediate run in the Cheat River basin. It is a long trip through uninhabited and virtually inaccessible country in the high valley between the Middle and Rich Mountains. The remnants of an early logging railroad play tag with the meandering river for the first of a series of two- to four-foot ledges. The ledges continue regularly for the next two miles to the granddaddy of them all, a 12-foot waterfall (runnable by demented experts only!), which you should portage on the left along the tramway bed. A November 1985 flood eroded a big chunk of the left bank below this waterfall, making this portage more difficult. After lunch at the foot of the falls, be ready for seven miles of continuous Class III rapids to the mouth.

There are a total of eight bridge crossings on the run. None of the bridges remain, but the abutments are readily spotted as landmarks. Between the seventh and eighth bridges there is a 50-yard tunnel from one limb of a half-mile loop to the other. The water visible at the mouth is typical of the entire river from the falls down. This is an exhilarating run among some of the least spoiled scenery of West Virginia. After being flushed out into the Dry Fork, it is just a quarter mile to the Jenningston bridge.

Spotting the falls from upstream should be no problem. It takes about one and a half hours of paddling time to reach the falls. You'll see six bridge crossings to the falls; the sixth one is about a mile above the falls. The falls are just around a right turn. Fluorescent strips have been tied in the tree branches on the left above the falls. The only other difficulty is the fatigue brought on by 13 miles of wilderness travel, including 9 miles of continuous maneuvering. Near the end is a cluster of several memorable hydraulics, not far from the Jenningston bridge. At high water levels the hydraulics below many

Section: US 33 bridge to Jenningston
Counties: Randolph, Tucker
USGS Quads: Harman, Monongahela National Forest
Difficulty: Class III–IV
Gradient: 9 miles at 71 feet per mile
Average Width: 50 feet
Velocity: Fast
Rescue Index: Remote
Hazards: Keeper hydraulics in high water; 12-foot falls halfway through trip
Scouting: Several of the larger rapids
Portages: 12-foot waterfall
Scenery: Pretty to beautiful
Highlights: Scenic high valley, 12-foot falls
Gauge: Visual; on the right side of the Route 33 bridge abutment

Runnable Water Levels:

	Minimum	Maximum
	0.3 feet	1.5 feet

Additional Information: National Weather Service, (412) 262-5290 (Pittsburgh), (703) 260-0305 (Washington, DC area); Parsons gauge should be at least 5 feet.

of its ledges become keepers. The Laurel Fork has killed people in its holes, so be careful.

The put-in is at the US 33 bridge (A). The take-out is at the mouth downstream along the left side from the Jenningston bridge (B). The best route from the put-in to the take-out goes west along US 33 four miles to Alpena, then north on "12" by the Glady Fork and Sully. You'll find a gauge painted on the rightside abutment of the US 33 bridge. The water will not be high enough unless the Parsons gauge reads over five feet.

Laurel Fork of the Cheat River • West Virginia

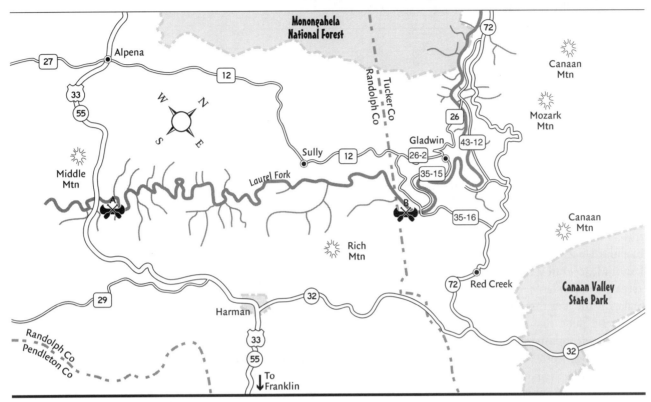

Frank Fico running the
Laurel Fork of the Cheat.
Photo by Bob Maxey.

Blackwater River

Caution: River under construction! The 1985 flood substantially changed the Blackwater River and made it significantly more difficult. Previously, it was a Class IV trip. Now it is a Class IV–V river with numerous rapids like the Upper Yough and somelike the more difficult Lower Meadow in West Virginia. Although the individual drops are not as large, the continuous nature of this river makes it tougher than the Lower Big Sandy (see below). Since the flood many of the drops have become more complex with numerous pinning possibilities, and many rapids change from year to year. Substantial rock slides and fallen trees make this a river for experts only who continually scout and take all safety precautions. Many of the rapids are unstable and continue to change.

The Blackwater from North Fork Junction to Hendricks (seven miles) is West Virginia's longest rapid. It flows through a narrow, steep defile draining the Canaan Valley, a flat, upland swamp on the west side of the Allegheny Front.

Multiple branches of the upper Blackwater funnel the 15-square-mile drainage basin into two main forks that pass the former logging capitals of Davis and Thomas, respectively. Near these nineteenth-century towns, they suddenly leap off the mountain as two falls, 50 feet each, and begin their unrelenting rush to the Dry Fork, eight miles and 1,000 feet below. Its two main headwater streams, the Upper Blackwater and its North Fork, are extreme, steep-creek runs. They join a few miles below their initial drops and slow their descent to a more "realistic" paddling gradient. Here the rhododendron rise 30 feet high along the river, and spruce-topped cliffs tower 1,000 feet above. Both falls, one preserved by a state park and the other on the North Branch are worth seeing.

From the recommended put-in at the junction (A) followed by only minimal veering from left to right, the river is one continuous blind bend—downward. The paddler never sees more than 50 yards ahead before the river disappears over the edge of the world. It has a fantastic 112-feet-per-mile gradient for five miles to Lime Rock, an abandoned community two miles upstream from Hendricks. Fortunately, this descent is generally evenly distributed. It is a gigantic sluiceway between mountains rising 2,000 feet on either side with almost no riverside beach.

Paddling the Blackwater is a constant challenge of reading and negotiating chutes over staircase ledges randomly strewn with 5- to 10-foot boulders. The paddler is constantly maneuvering in the ever-pushing current. Moving side eddies are the only rest or rescue spots along the course. The waters of the river are a nonsilted brown covered with suds—a form of pollution noted since the time of Thomas Lewis, a 1746 explorer who appropriately called this stream the "River Styx." The tannin color is attributed to organic acids from the upland swamps that leach iron oxide from the red shale that lines much of the riverbed.

The action starts immediately, then picks up about 200 yards below the put-in. The first drop, Krakatoa, is a double ledge, each one leading into a large hole. Fortunately this Class V drop is easily carried on the left. At the next major drop the river narrows to about 25 feet and drops over a six-foot ledge into a horrible hole. "The Ledge" can be carried on the left. A number of steep, blind, boulder drops below must be run with precision. One of these, Rock and Roll, is a long, steep Class V rapid created by the 1985 flood. It keeps changing, so scout from a rocky island on the right. A mile and a half into the run the water accelerates for 75 yards over a flat, sloping, red shale ledge. The current reaches incredible speeds before slamming into a hole at the bottom. Most of this rapid is too shallow to paddle, so you have to be on the correct line right from the beginning. Scout and portage on the right. Tub Run, a tributary, enters just downstream on river right.

The river is a bit easier below here, alternating between fast Class III+'s and blind, boulder-strewn Class IVs. Some of these rapids change significantly from year to year. You'll see evidence of recent landslides throughout the run, and downed trees are a continual hazard. At the three-mile point you'll encounter a shallow, 12-foot-high sloping falls. Some people run this mess; others choose to carry on the left. Below these falls is a steep drop that funnels into a big hole. You'll want to look this one over on the right before running it. After about five miles the gradient lets up to about 48 feet per mile. From here it's an easy, two-mile float to the take-out.

Although people traditionally leave the river at the Route 72 bridge in Hendricks, this is private land and there have been complaints about paddlers who park and change in this area. The American Whitewater Affiliation (AWA) recently purchased a piece of land on the Dry Fork, just downstream of the mouth of the Blackwater. Turn right at the first street by the post office as you enter town and drive three blocks to the Dry Fork. You'll see a swinging bridge over the river; the take-out (B) is just upstream of the bridge.

The shuttle is straightforward, but the put-in is a bear! From the take-out, drive out Route 72 to US 219 north. Turn right and follow the road through Thomas, then bear right on a road marked "Douglas 27." You'll start to run along the North Fork of the Blackwater to where the old railroad bed meets the road. Bear left and drive a half mile to a locked gate. Drop your gear, then drive back outside the gate (which closes at 3:30 P.M.) and find a place to park. To reach the river from here you'll have to carry your boat a half mile down the railbed, past the junction of the North Fork, then slide it 300 feet straight down a 300-foot-high, 45-degree incline to the river. There have been several landslides here since the flood and the entire area is steep and unstable. The last 10 to 20 feet are almost vertical, and you'll probably need ropes to lower your boats. The railbed runs alongside on river right all the way to Hendricks. Although high above the river and not visible to paddlers, it provides a fast way out in case of trouble.

An alternate access puts you in below the first big drops. Continue on the Forest Service road past Douglas until you are high above the river on the side of the gorge. You may see a sign marked "put-in" or tape on a tree. Although you'll have to slide your boat farther (almost 400 feet to the tracks), the slope is not as steep and the footing is better. This route was marked in 1986, but may not be easy to follow these days.

An old gauge painted on the bridge at Hendricks was sandblasted off during the 1985 flood. A second gauge painted on the rail bridge upstream was buried a few years later by another period of high water. This area is very unstable and changes from year to year. But because the rapids in the canyon are so narrow, we can safely say that if the take-out looks scrapy but passable, the river

Section: North Fork Junction to Hendricks

County: Tucker

USGS Quads: Mozark Mountain, Monongahela National Forest

Difficulty: Class IV–V, VI

Gradient: Five miles at 112 feet per mile; two miles at 48 feet per mile

Average Width: 30–50 feet

Velocity: Fast

Rescue Index: Remote

Hazards: Continuous technical rapids, trees in chutes, many pinning possibilities

Scouting: Both boat- and land-scouting are continuous

Portages: Several

Scenery: Beautiful

Highlights: West Virginia's longest continuous rapids

Gauge: Visual; levels below refer to Davis gauge on Blackwater

Runnable Water Levels:

	Minimum	Maximum
	2.6 feet	3.5 feet

Additional Information: National Weather Service, (412) 262-5290 (Pittsburgh), (703) 260-0305 (Washington, DC area); Waterline Service, (800) 297-4243 (#541132)

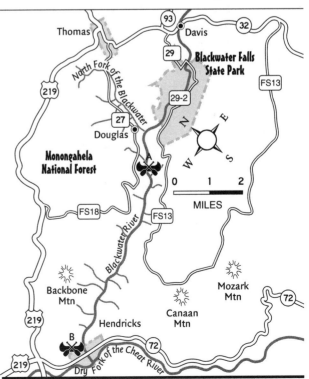

Blackwater River • West Virginia

can be run. If there's plenty of water here, the gorge may well be too high to run. The Davis gauge above the put-in is on the Pittsburgh Weather Service phone. It indicates roughly 50 percent of the flow at the put-in and is a good indicator of the levels on the Blackwater. At 2.6 feet (220 cfs), the river is low and abusive. I've found that 3.1 feet (350 cfs) is a good, medium level, and 3.5 feet (455 cfs) is getting high. The Parsons gauge typically needs to be between 4.5 and 5.5 feet for the Blackwater to be run.

Blackwater River at Davis Gauge Conversion Table

feet	cfs
2.50	197
2.75	257
3.00	320
3.50	455
3.75	527
4.00	605
4.50	780
4.75	867
5.00	960

Big Sandy Creek

Upper Section, Bruceton Mills to Rockville

As this little stream tips down beside Chestnut Ridge to the Cheat Gorge, it provides six miles of progressive slalom training starting at Class I and working up to Class IV. This run is suitable for strong intermediate paddlers at lower water levels, but flotation is recommended for open canoes. Automobile camping is provided at nearby Cooper's Rock State Park or at Cheat Canyon Campground in Albright.

Hazel Run Rapids is the first problem and appears as an impassable barricade of boulders. Try the second passage from the right. Below the mouth of the Little Sandy (on the left), you'll encounter a long slide rapid where the water zips quickly over very shallow rock tables and then terminates in several wide hydraulics. About 500 yards from the confluence with the Little Sandy is six- to eight-foot Falkenstein Falls. It can be recognized easily by the large rock shelf jutting out from the left and forming a dam. The first shelf can be carefully run by cutting hard left below this ledge, then back across to near center for the main ledge. At higher levels you can run straight over the left or far right.

Several long rapids occur just below the falls, and this is where the best action is found. Steep drops over ledges around blind bends require quick decisions and paddle responses. This continues until the take-out. The last rapid is usually a good, Class IV run except in very low water. Intermediates should take out at the rustic cabin on the right just below the mouth of Sovereign Run and Corner Rapids. The approach to the bridge is tricky. At normal water levels, it's easiest to start in the center and then cut sharply to the right. At high levels the far left is no problem.

Put in below the dam at Bruceton Mills (A). To reach the take-out at Rockville Bridge (B), take Route 26 south and turn right on Hudson Road. Drive straight through the four-way intersection at Mount Nebo, pass Glen Miller's house, and follow the road around a sharp curve and across the wooden bridge over Sovereign Run. Take the first left, and follow a rough dirt road down to Rockville. As of this writing the road going out on river right is four-wheel-drive only! Mr. Miller will run your shuttle for a reasonable fee; call him at (304) 379-3404.

Lower Section, Rockville to Cheat River

The Lower Big Sandy is an exciting, beautiful, piquant mistress who shows occasional flares of bad temper to even the most experienced paddlers. However, this five-and-a-half mile trip contains the most scenic and most interesting whitewater in northern West Virginia. The most stunning aspect of the Lower Big Sandy is that it has five of the most distinctive and most memorable Class IV–VI whitewater rapids on the entire East Coast. These are Big Sandy Falls (Wonder Falls), Zoom Flume, Little Splat, Big Splat, and First Island. These rapids are truly unique. Add a pristine mountain setting and you have a truly stupendous trip for expert paddlers. Although the banks are choked with rhododendron, the necessary scouting and portaging is not difficult. If a walkout is necessary, you'll find an old railroad bed on the right to within a mile of the Cheat River. The old railroad bridge is washed out here, but the bed continues on river left to Jenkinsburg.

There are countless difficulties on this trip and numerous Class III–IV rapids not described here. Some drops are hazardous and require scouting or carrying. At 1.5 miles there is a rather difficult sequence terminating in 18-foot-high Wonder Falls. The Class III–IV rapids approaching the falls has a fairly steep, three-part drop on the left into a pool just above the falls. Scout and use safety measures; carry the falls on the right. At normal levels, Big Sandy Falls can be run on the left side of the main current. If running the falls, it is critical that the vertical angle of your boat be 45 degrees as you drop over the falls. Too vertical an angle means you could dive too deep and crunch your bow on submerged rocks below the falls. Too horizontal an angle could mean a very flat landing at the bottom, which could injure your back.

Liz Garland running Wonder Falls. Photo by Mayo Gravatt.

The next series of rapids is busy for a quarter mile, followed by a broad ledge split by a large rock in midstream. This is known as Undercut Rock rapids (Class IV). Run the safe, center slot or scout the gnarly right side. The passage on the right ends in a big curler that throws even good boaters under an undercut rock. Run just to the left of a huge midstream boulder, dropping over a six-foot ledge.

The next biggie is Zoom Flume, a steep, sloped, 8- to 10-foot Class IV drop that is easier than it looks and even more exciting. Scouting on the right is recommended to see the twisting flume. You can enter from river left to avoid being disoriented by the holes and ledges that interfere with a straight shot down the flume. Then work over to catch the flume properly. The cheese-grater rock shelf below has taken off a lot of elbow skin.

Get back out of your boat, if you are still in it, and scout the next rapids, Little Splat. This is one of the most complex and tricky Class V+ rapids anywhere in West Virginia. The upper part can be boat-scouted. At high water you can cut over to the right side. The center route has a reversal that has thrown boats into a nasty pinning rock. At lower levels (below six feet) the easier route on the right dries up and you're forced to run a very tight, twisting channel on the far left.

Big Splat is next. Very aptly named, it is a complex double rapid dropping a total of over 25 feet. Although run by the most skilled boaters, this is clearly a Class VI rapid. If you find yourself wanting to run Big Splat, you should seriously question not only your skills but also

your sanity. The risks are significant and the margin for error is alarmingly small. Several people have been bodily injured here.

The 8- to 10-foot drop guarding the approach to Big Splat falls below is perhaps the most dangerous feature.

Section: Bruceton Mills to Rockville
Counties: Preston
USGS Quads: Bruceton Mills, Valley Point
Difficulty: Class I–IV
Average Width: 60 feet
Velocity: Moderate to fast
Gradient: Four miles at 9 feet per mile; two miles at 45 feet per mile
Rescue Index: Remote
Hazards: 6- to 8-foot falls and long rapids below Little Sandy, trees in river
Scouting: Falls and long rapids below Little Sandy
Portages: None
Scenery: Pretty to beautiful
Highlights: Progressive slalom in wooded setting
Gauge: National Weather Service, (412) 262-5290 (Pittsburgh)

Runnable Water Levels:	Minimum	Maximum
Rockville gauge	5.8 feet	7 feet
Bruceton Mills gauge	0 feet	2.5 feet

Additional Information: National Weather Service, (703) 260-0305 (Washington, DC area)

When scouting from the right bank, the dangers in the Class V+ approach rapid are well concealed. Beginning as a sloping ledge, the current drops directly toward an undercut, partially submerged slab rock. The right side of the chute ends under the downstream corner of another large, undercut boulder. Almost all of the current then drops into a dangerous, horseshoe-shaped hydraulic.

However, one glance at the base of Big Splat falls should convince anyone that swimming here is simply unthinkable. After a short and very fast pool, the entire river drops 16 to 18 feet onto Splat Rock. Some of the water goes through sieves on the right, some underneath Splat Rock, and some pillows off Splat Rock—forming a frightening hole at the base of the falls. This area is fit for neither man nor boat. Fortunately, no one has been trapped in the approach rapids yet and most injuries have been limited to ankles broken by pitoning on Splat Rock. Portage both Big Splat drops on the right, lowering boats and bodies over a ledge.

Below Big Splat are a number of challenging Class IV+ rapids. The first two are steep and obstructed, but can be boat-scouted on the far right. The third drop, Roostertail, starts with a right-hand chute that feeds you into a complex, rocky rapid. Go to the left of the roostertail, then

shoot down the right through a powerful chute and quickly catch an eddy below before getting pushed into a rock jumble. Then you'll have to ferry across the river to finish on the left. After a couple of easier drops you'll encounter a series of medium-sized ledges. You'll have to start on the left, then cut over to run the final drop on the right.

The river eases up a bit until you come to First Island, a Class V drop. This drop is on the right side and should be scouted. It's actually made up of two drops: a steep chute and a ledge where the runout is obstructed by downstream boulders. Angle your boat to the right when going off the top chute to avoid a pinning rock, then scramble downstream and boof the ledge on the far right. This is easier said than done because the current upstream of these drops is often uncooperative. Many people find it useful to catch an eddy (or two) on the way down.

Below First Island is a second island with a slalom boulder garden (Class IV+) that should be run right. Three and a half miles and 272 feet (down) later, the paddler, who may be hiking by now, will reach the Cheat River near Jenkinsburg.

The shuttle is done entirely on rough dirt roads. From the put-in at Rockville (B), drive up on the river-left road, then turn right at the intersection. Drive past Glen Miller's house to the Mt. Nebo intersection. Turn right, pass a large A-frame house on the right, and follow the road

Section: Rockville to Cheat River

County: Preston

USGS Quads: Bruceton Mills, Valley Point

Difficulty: Class IV–V with one Class VI

Gradient: Two miles at 30 feet per mile; four miles at 80 feet per mile

Average Width: 60 feet

Velocity: Fast

Rescue Index: Remote

Hazards: Wonder Falls, Undercut Rock, Zoom Flume, Little Splat, Big Splat, First Island

Scouting: All six of the above rapids, at least

Portages: Possibly one or more of the six major rapids

Scenery: Beautiful

Highlights: Five unusually distinctive rapids in a spectacular gorge

Gauge: National Weather Service, (412) 262-5290 (Pittsburgh)

Runnable Water Levels:	Minimum	Maximum
Bruceton Mills gauge	0 feet	2 feet
Rockville gauge	5.2–5.8 feet	6.5–7.0 feet

Additional Information: National Weather Service, (703) 260-0305 (Washington, DC area); 5.2 feet can be very technical: open-boaters and some decked-boaters prefer a minimum of 5.8 feet.

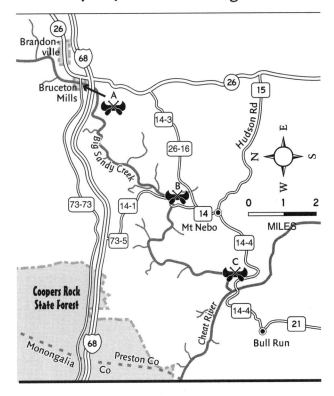

Big Sandy Creek • West Virginia

into the Cheat Canyon. The take-out is at Jenkinsburg Bridge (C) where the Big Sandy meets the Cheat.

The gauge generally used is a government gauge on the bridge at Rockville. The National Weather Service telephone number is (412) 262-5290. The river is rocky and technical from 5.2–5.8 feet. Ideal conditions are 6.0–6.2 feet; over 6.5 feet the river starts to get pushy and powerful. Anything over seven feet is high water; at eight feet and over, some very good paddlers have lost boats.

There is also a paddler's gauge under the Bruceton Mills bridge. The correlation between the two is complex but reliable. Rockville = 3/4 (Bruceton + 1) + 5. The recommended levels for Rockville at Bruceton are zero to two feet. The Lower Big Sandy is often runnable in the spring.

Cheat River

The Cheat River is the largest undammed watershed east of the Mississippi. It passes through steep mountain country where the water runs off quickly. Locals say it got its name by rising without warning, taking away clothing and gear left along its banks. Because the headwaters are so far from the main stem, rain there can cause the river to rise in sunny weather. It's a large river that holds its water well, and it is often runnable well into the summer.

The countryside that the Cheat flows through is unspoiled for the most part. The last major tributary comes in above Parsons. The stretch between Parsons and Rowlesburg is flatwater, passing through unspoiled rural countryside. From Rowlesburg to Cheat Lake outside Morgantown the Cheat remains attractive despite considerable mining and timbering activity. The water quality is pretty good until the first acid stream enters at the take-out for the Narrows. At the mouth of Cheat Canyon two more acid streams, Muddy Creek and Green's Run, enter the river. The acid is not noticeable to most paddlers except at very low summer flows.

In November 1995, the Cheat River drainage was ravaged by a great flood. First, the area received four to six inches of rain on November 4. Late that evening a strong, low-pressure cell stalled at the headwaters, dumping another six to eight inches of rain in a short time. This caused a massive flood that forever altered the river. The entire watershed, including Shavers, Laurel, Glady, Dry, and Blackwater Forks, was scoured by the water. The unprecedented high water in the Cheat, Potomac, and Greenbrier watersheds had tragic results: 40 people dead, 2,600 homeless, and 29 West Virginia counties declared disaster areas. These waters changed the riverbed and rolled giant boulders in Cheat Canyon.

Despite this assault, the river is remarkably scenic. Anyone who runs the Cheat will surely love it! If you want to help with the clean up efforts, Friends of the Cheat is a local group working to restore, preserve, and promote the outstanding natural qualities of this river.

Their current focus is on cleaning up acid-mine drainage. Send $20 to Friends of the Cheat, P.O. Box 182, Bruceton Mills, WV 26525.

The Narrows

The Cheat leaves the town of Rowlesburg quietly but soon becomes narrower and begins to pick up speed. The put-in (A) for the Narrows is opposite a worked-out limestone mine approximately three miles below Rowlesburg. Here you'll encounter the first big waves below Rowlesburg, called Cave Rapids. For the rest of this five-mile trip, the rapids become increasingly more difficult. There are good rescue spots after each rapid, but in high water it's not so easy. After passing several Class II rapids, the paddler enters a long series of harder rapids, properly called the Narrows.

In the first significant rapids, the entire river is necked down by an automobile-sized boulder (Calamity Rock) in midstream. Those unfamiliar with this Class III–IV rapid should scout it. Although this boulder is largely out of the water at roughly 1.5 feet on the Albright bridge gauge, it is completely submerged when the reading is around 2.5 feet. This should give the paddler a healthy respect for what just a few inches' increase in water level means on the Cheat. Usually this boulder should be passed on the right. At very high levels, however, it's best to run along the left bank, whether in boat or on foot. Keep in mind that there are two problems—entering the passage correctly (not always easy due to the combination of waves immediately above it) and managing the powerful drop at the end of the chute. This passage will swamp an open canoe without flotation at any level and flip a raft in high water.

There are three major rapids below this boulder that also pass through narrow confines, creating huge turbulence and powerful crosscurrents. In high water you simply blast through the standing, five-foot waves and try to maintain stability; at lower levels you must be more precise when maneuvering around the exposed boulders.

Paddlers inexperienced with big water might be fooled into thinking that they can "sneak" down the sides of these narrow rapids in relatively calmer water, but they'll usually get sucked over into the big stuff by the high velocity of the main channel (sort of like Bernoulli's principle).

The first of these major rapids (Wind Rapids) is the most difficult in high water and consists of a wide hydraulic before reaching the chute. This hydraulic is best taken on the far left. There is also a severe hydraulic about halfway down the chute on the left, always an interesting scene. The second rapids (Rocking Horse) is the longest narrow passage, 100 yards of turbulence. The last rapid is less severe but still interesting. There is not much left before taking out at Lick Run (B) after an enjoyable five-mile trip. Note that the land at the take-out is private property, but landowners have been cooperative in the past.

The Cheat Canyon

The Cheat Canyon from Albright to Jenkinsburg was explored by John Berry, Bob Harrigan, and Dan Sullivan of Washington, D.C., in the 1950s. Their first run took two days! In the 1960s it was considered one of the most challenging runs in the East. Although it seems less difficult when compared to the hardest rivers being run today, the rapids are still formidable. The hard rapids of the Narrows are like the easier ones in the Canyon. The rafting business in the area has been declining since the late 1970s, eclipsed by the growing popularity of the New

River. The river is now a delightful, uncrowded big-water playground.

Only fools take the Cheat Canyon lightly. The challenges that faced the pioneers of the 1950s must still be dealt with. Low-water runs are tight and technical, with visibility obstructed by huge boulders. The many pools between drops have no current, making the run seem longer. Moderate levels open up the rapids, but the water is considerably more powerful. Really high water brings huge pillowed boulders, boiling eddies, and monster holes. Although the river superficially resembles the Lower Yough, the Cheat has many rapids as difficult as the tough ones on the Yough and five that are significantly harder. A smash-up or injury puts a paddler on foot in very rough country. Walking out of the canyon straight up would take at least two hours, and you would still be miles from the nearest house. There is a good trail on the right, but it is high above the river and intervening cliff bands may make access difficult.

The most challenging aspect of this trip is the number of complex rapids in the inaccessible setting. A detailed description of each rapid is impractical as there are still over 30 (count 'em) rapids rated Class III or higher. Accordingly, scouting is not feasible in many cases. Also, several of the Class IV rapids are separated only by short pools or no pools in higher water. The remoteness of the

Section: Narrows (below Rowlesburg to Lick Run)
County: Preston
USGS Quads: Rowlesburg, Kingwood
Difficulty: Class II–IV
Gradient: 20 feet per mile
Average Width: 100–150 feet
Velocity: Fast
Rescue Index: Accessible
Hazards: Big waves in high water (3–4 feet on the gauge)
Scouting: Calamity Rock
Portages: None
Scenery: Fair to pretty in spots
Highlights: Limestone caves near put-in
Gauge: Visual only; Albright bridge, Route 26
Runnable Water Levels:

	Minimum	Maximum
Albright bridge	0.5 feet	4.5 feet

Additional Information: National Weather Service, Pittsburgh, (412) 262-5290; Parson's reading (see above)

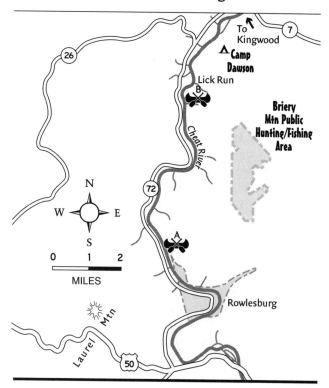

Cheat River • West Virginia

Scot Gravatt entering the
left side of High Falls.
Photo by Ed Grove.

canyon and the cold water in winter and spring make the Cheat a Class IV–V run in high water (over four feet).

The first rapid is Decision (Class III+). It is 1.5 miles below Albright, where the Canyon begins. This rapid starts as a wide rubble bar and gradually narrows as it drops over smaller rocks and ledges, forming several holes. Through this upper part, a left-of-center line is easiest, with an interesting chute on the right. Then move right toward a house-sized boulder through a short pool (or wave train at higher levels) before the river drops over a set of large eroded ledges. This rapid is similar to numerous others in the Canyon and is certainly easier than many. If Decision is too much, please carry out now. Your body and boat will thank you.

After about another mile of pools and three significant smaller drops comes Beech Run (Class III–IV). Enter this long rapid on river right before moving left to dodge rocks or holes depending on water level. About two-thirds of the way through and just below the steepest section, a group of closely spaced rocks obstructs the main channel at levels below about 3.0 feet. Run these on the left.

The next big rapid, and one to sway those who haven't seen any significant changes from the 1985 flood so far, is Big Nasty (Class IV at medium levels and Class IV–V at higher levels). About a half mile and two easier rapids below Beech Run, the river forms a large pool just before a right-hand bend. The left bank is a steep, high mountain here. At water levels above 3.0 feet, first-timers and those with foggy memories should scout from the left bank.

Above Big Nasty, flooding deposited many small and medium-sized boulders, building up the entire riverbed and raising the level of the pool there. The small rapid below Big Nasty has also been obstructed by rubble. In between these pools, the entire river has been channeled toward the right bank and over a ledge. The result is a steep, fast rapid aiming all of the Cheat's water and anything on or in it into one big hole. At 2.0 feet the question "what hole?" seems appropriate, but at 3.0 feet, the hole is hard for decked boats to punch and is fully capable of holding or recirculating floating objects. Around 3.5 feet, it becomes truly nasty, flipping and holding 10-man rafts and recirculating swimmers more than once. At 5.0 feet, Big Nasty becomes a real circus. First, rafts and boaters must take a tightrope line on the approach. Then, for those who slip off the tightrope, the hole pulls repeated stunts like violently flipping and juggling up to three large rafts at once. Finally, the megahole pulls a true disappearing act with swimmers—making them disappear, then reappear up to 50 feet downstream. Above 5.0 feet, the hole is fortunately too violent to recirculate swimmers; it just gets bigger! If this sounds like too much fun, at these levels there's a sneak chute down a side channel on the far left side of the river. Regardless of the water level, successful lines all aim to the extreme left. Still, it is necessary to negotiate several lateral waves or diagonal holes constantly pushing toward the hole. A portage is an honorable option for paddlers looking to avoid joining the chaos.

Even though Maui Wave above Big Nasty is gone, a super surfing wave/hole still remains 200 yards downstream on river left. You'll find it after you cross the cobble rapids forming the pool below Big Nasty. This usually benign hole is called Typewriter because you can easily move back and forth on it. Covering the left half of the river, it is gentle on the right edge, sticky on the left.

After one more rapid, the paddler reaches Even Nastier (Class III–IV). This long rapid is entered just right of center and propels all comers through a respectable wave train leading to the left. From here it is either boiling eddies or ultraquick boat-scouting for the remaining 100 yards to avoid two offset boulders and holes. This rapid can also be entered on river left.

The middle third of the trip (a good three miles) is known as the Doldrums. Here you have Prudential Rock, great playing waves, and lovely scenery. This "flat" section with half a dozen significant lesser rapids ends as you enter the last third of the trip. This last section is the most demanding because it has several complex heavy rapids.

After Cue Ball, a Class III boulder drop with a great surfing wave on the left, the river begins to act more serious. Anticipation, with a fast, narrow chute up against a cliff on river left, is just downstream. After passing

Section: Cheat Canyon, Albright to Jenkinsburg
County: Preston
USGS Quads: Kingwood, Valley Point
Difficulty: Class III–V
Gradient: 25 feet per mile
Average Width: 100–150 feet
Velocity: Fast
Rescue Index: Remote
Hazards: In low water, some undercut and pinning rocks; in high water, heavy water and big holes; the toughest rapids are Big Nasty, High Falls, and Upper Coliseum
Scouting: At least Big Nasty (left), High Falls (right), Upper Coliseum (right), and Lower Coliseum (Pete Morgan's Rapid) at left
Portages: Possibly these same rapids at very high water levels
Scenery: Pretty to beautiful
Highlights: Beautiful gorge marred by acid-stained tributaries near put-in, and the scouring of the November 1985 flood
Gauge: Visual only; Albright bridge, Route 26

Runnable Water Levels:	Minimum	Maximum
Albright bridge gauge	1.0 feet	6.0 feet
Parsons gauge	2.3 feet	

Additional Information: National Weather Service, (412) 262-5290 (Pittsburgh), or (703) 260-0305 (Washington, DC area)

through the chute, work over to the center where the river opens up again. As you move through an easy boulder rapid toward a great surfing hole, notice the high cliffs in the distance on river left. Below here is Teardrop, a deceptive rapid that may lure you into a tricky chute on the far right or trash you in a nasty hole in the center. The easiest run is on the far left, to the inside of the turn.

By now the approaching cliffs and a growing roar signify your arrival above High Falls. Note the high, thin ribbon of water coming in on river left, then get ready for action. This drop is Class IV+ even at moderate levels. Scout from the right shore. There's a sneak route down river right, too shallow at low water, but a good choice when the river is high. There's a tricky route down the far left that flips many boats. The preferred center line is scrapy at low water and rambunctious at higher flows. Start a boat length to the right of a washed-out eddy above the drop. This turns into a small wave at high water. Look for a smooth wave at the lip of the drop and paddle through the left shoulder of the wave, angling your boat left. A few forward strokes will carry you between a huge pourover on the right and a large stopper on the left. Ride the waves over the last ledge into the pool below.

Maze Rapid is just downstream. At low levels the preferred route winds between giant boulders and is tight in

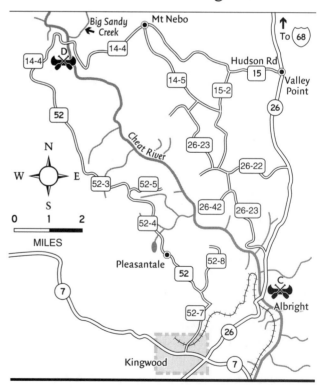

Cheat River • West Virginia

places. Higher water opens up the passages, but huge, pillowed boulders and nasty holes complicate the route. Work from left to right to miss the deviously arranged boulders, then cut right at the bottom to finish. Solve the puzzle and win a chance at a trip down the hardest rapid in the Cheat Canyon: Coliseum Rapid.

Upper Coliseum Rapid (Class V) was formed when the 1985 flood completely filled in the right side of the river. The left chute, formerly a high-water line, now carries the full flow of the river. This wild drop has changed several times in the last decade; don't trust my description or your memory! Eddy out upstream on the right, just above a gorgeous tributary waterfall, and work your way downstream on foot and scout this drop carefully. The best view is from the top from a large rock on river right; the best portage route is on the left.

Here's the way things looked in 1998: Recyclotron, a giant hole that seems to get worse each year, dominates the top of the rapid. There is a clear, left-side route complicated by a breaking wave. After you thread your way between these obstacles you'll confront a powerful chute moving from left to right between two offset holes. The right-hand hole is very dangerous and the left-side pour-over could cause problems at some water levels. Some paddlers like to run to the left of a breaking wave at midstream, then cut to the right. Others like to catch a left-hand eddy, then ferry back out into the chute. The run-out of the drop is fast and powerful and it will be hard to recover swimmers. Boaters might consider setting a safety rope.

Now the river enters Lower Coliseum, cutting left and roaring through a short, complex boulder garden. A huge, pyramid-shaped rock (Coliseum Rock) looms downstream. There are huge holes on the left, but the right side is much easier. The river still does not let up, moving at full speed into Pete Morgan Rapid. This drop honors the owner of the gas station at the Albright bridge; he gave river gauge readings to inquiring paddlers for many years in the 1960s and 1970s. The gas station washed away in the 1985 flood, which also rearranged the rapid. The best route is down the left chute, starting on the right side and cutting left to avoid an aggressive stopper at the bottom. It's easily scouted from a cobble bar on the left. Pause for a moment in an eddy and note the unique fluted sandstone columns on the left side of the run-out before moving downstream.

After Pete Morgan Rapid you'll encounter several long Class III+ drops before the river calms down as it approaches the Jenkinsburg bridge. About a mile from the take-out a clear stream cascades in from river right. The slate outcrops at the mouth of this little stream are a great place to look for fossils and catch some sun. Paddle under the bridge and take out on river right.

There is a painted gauge on Route 26 where it crosses the Cheat in Albright. The river can be run at well below a foot; two to four feet would be considered moderate levels, and anything above that is high water. The gauge readings have fluctuated considerably since the 1985 flood, but we now think that it reads about three inches higher than the pre-1985 level.

After Pete Morgan's gas station washed away in 1985, the Albright bridge gauge could not be reported to the National Weather Service in Pittsburgh. There is a gauge under construction in Jenkinsburg, but it is not available yet. The Parsons gauge, 50 miles upstream, is available by phone. Three and a half feet (900 cfs) at Parsons equals about two feet at Albright; 4.5 feet (1,900 cfs) equals three feet at Albright. The actual flow at Jenkinsburg will be roughly 33 percent greater than at Parsons.

The Albright Power Station Gauge is reported on the flow phone operated by the National Weather Service in Pittsburgh (412-262-5290). This gauge previously gave erratic readings, but it was reset and upgraded in 1997. Steve Ingalls, an Ohio boater, worked with several active Cheat River paddlers to create a conversion formula between the Power Station and Bridge gauges. The formula is: Bridge Level = (1.6 x Power Station Level) + .1. The reliability of this formula for levels under 2.0 feet at the Albright bridge gauge has not been determined. A new gauge was constructed at Jenkinsburg (the Mt. Nebo gauge) but no one has figured out how to use it yet.

Put in at the Albright bridge (C) or, to avoid a mile or two of flat, uninteresting water, at one of the two campgrounds downstream. The take-out at Jenkinsburg (D) is hard to find and involves some travel on rough dirt roads.

Cheat River at Parsons Guage Conversion Table

feet	cfs
3.0	530
3.5	900
4.0	1,350
4.5	1,930
5.0	2,620
5.5	3,440
6.0	4,370
7.0	6,550
8.0	9,440
9.0	12,700
10.0	16,700

From the put-in, take Route 26 north to Valley Point. Turn left on Hudson Road, then take a gradual left turn when you reach the four-way intersection at Mount Nebo. The road turns to dirt, passes to the right of a large A-frame house (the Clarks), crests the hill, then descends steeply into the canyon. It is passable by ordinary vehicles but becomes slippery in wet weather. The river can also be reached from Route 7 in Masontown via Bull Run Road; turning left at the first intersection, right at the second. This road is also steep and rough. The Cheat shuttle takes about an hour and a half to run. Glen Miller (304-379-3404) will pick you up in Jenkinsburg and run you back to Albright for a reasonable fee. It saves time and vehicle wear.

Meadow River

The Meadow River contains several sections of excellent whitewater alternating with long stretches of flatwater. The upper segment is quite isolated and difficult to reach, but contains a long stretch of Class IV rapids. The popular middle section part is easier, with many Class III–III+ rapids leading to a take-out at the Route 19 bridge. Below here is a very dangerous Class V–VI stretch that runs into the Gauley River above Lost Paddle Rapid.

Upper Meadow

The Upper Meadow contains seven miles of continuous Class IV–IV+ rapids in a remote, forested valley that is not easy to reach. Eight miles of flatwater separate Russel-ville and the start of the rapids at Burdette Creek, but an obscure system of dirt roads allows paddlers to bypass the flatwater and get right into the good stuff.

Section: East Rainelle to Russelville
Counties: Greenbrier, Nicholas, Fayette
USGS Quads: Rainelle, Corliss, Winona
Difficulty: Class III–IV+
Gradient: 32 feet per mile
Average Width: 75 feet
Velocity: Fast
Rescue Index: Remote
Hazards: Natural Weir
Scouting: Natural Weir
Portages: Possibly at very high water levels
Scenery: Beautiful
Highlights: Continuous rapids
Gauge: Mt. Lookout gauge

Runnable Water Levels:	Minimum	Maximum
Mt. Lookout gauge	5.2 feet	6.6 feet

Additional Information: Summersville Dam, (304) 872-5809; Huntington District of U.S. Army Corps of Engineers, (304) 529-5127

This run starts to get pretty serious at high water, so caution is advised.

After the lower put-in, the rapids start slowly and begin to pick up speed. They quickly convert to obstructed, Class IV boulder drops, The Rapids, that continue without let-up in unbroken succession for four miles. The drops are often obstructed and frequently contain powerful holes at medium to high water levels. The banks are choked with rhododendrons and mountain laurels, so most scouting must be done from eddies. This technique requires considerable experience, good boat control, and careful spacing between party members. A railroad on river right is convenient when walking out.

One place that should be scouted is Natural Weir, a seven-foot ledge drop plunging between giant boulders. Get off the river when you see the horizon line and take a good look, because all three chutes present problems. Of particular concern is the undercut rock found in the run on the right. Then, as suddenly as the hard rapids started, they end. The remaining three miles to the take-out is a fast run over easy Class II–III rapids.

To reach the put-in (A), take Route 41 to US 60 and head east. At Route 10 (the end of Corliss Road) take a left, then an immediate right onto a paved road. Bear right where the pavement ends, then follow the road through an old strip mine. Continue until you see the river on your left. In the summer, when the leaves are out, you will have to look hard to catch a glimpse of the river. You can also get to the river by following Snake Island Road north from East Rainelle and turning into the City Dump three miles downriver. This does not bypass the flatwater section, but the distance passes quickly at high flows. Take out at the bridge on Quinwood-Nutterville Road (C), which intersects Route 41 a few miles upstream of Nallen.

Middle Meadow

The stretch between Russelville to Nallen is flat as it runs quietly along Route 41. A mile below Nallen, rapids

Section: Russelville to US 19 Bridge
Counties: Nicholas, Fayette
USGS Quads: Winona, Summersville Dam
Difficulty: Class III–III+
Gradient: 39 feet per mile
Average Width: 75 feet
Velocity: Fast
Rescue Index: Accessible to remote
Hazards: Some undercut rocks
Scouting: None
Portages: Possibly at very high water levels
Scenery: Beautiful
Highlights: Miracle Mile
Gauge: Mt. Lookout gauge

Runnable Water Levels:	Minimum	Maximum
Mt. Lookout gauge	5.2 feet	6.6 feet

Additional Information: Summersville Dam, (304) 872-5809;
   Huntington District of U.S. Army Corps of Engineers,
   (304) 529-5127

appear. The river drops through boulder gardens between steep, forested banks, and then moves away from the road after passing a water treatment plant. Locals call this section the "Miracle Mile" because of its accessibility and great play-boating opportunities. The roadside section is a delightful place to hang out, even at low water levels. Interesting Class III–III+ rapids alternate with pools all the way to the take-out. As you travel, the gorge gets deeper and deeper. Soon spectacular, high, sandstone cliffs, fringed with hemlock, appear. Some of these drops develop a bad attitude at high water and must be approached cautiously. The biggest danger is the steep, uphill climb at the take-out (D), just below the Route 19 bridge on river left.

Lower Meadow

The Lower Meadow below the Route 19 bridge may be the most dangerous stretch of whitewater in West Virginia. While the gradient is not severe, the river has a drop-pool character and many of its rapids flow around and under giant undercut boulders and dangerous rock sieves. Even the easier drops have run-outs that push you toward dangerous traps. There have been three fatal accidents on this section claiming the lives of expert paddlers, in addition to several close calls. The last victim was a veteran guide with over 100 successful runs. But the unique challenge and spectacular beauty of the river draws

a small group of paddlers to the run despite its risks. Those who follow them should be very, very careful.

The Lower Meadow was first run by Jack Wright, Tom Irwin, Frank and Bonnie Birdsong, Rick Rigg, and Donna Berglund in the fall of 1972. But while local experts run the river frequently and without incident these days, it is a very serious undertaking for first-timers. You and your party should be in top form and ready for anything. Fortunately, portaging the major rapids via an old railroad bed on the right is not difficult. The abandoned railroad tracks on the left are much higher, but are ideal for walking out. Wear a good pair of shoes to facilitate your carries. It is always wise to go down with someone who knows the river, particularly at higher levels. The following descriptions are taken from notes provided by Donnie Hudspeth, a senior guide for North American River Runners in Hico, West Virginia.

The first hard rapid, Rites of Passage (Class V), can be seen below the Route 19 bridge. A fast approach takes you over a four-foot ledge; the hole tries to shove you under a large rock on the left. The second drop, Hell's Gate (Class V+), trapped a veteran local guide underwater in a deep drain on the left side. Routes vary with water levels, and require you to catch small, guarded eddies to avoid dangerous rocks downstream.

A short distance later you'll encounter three steep, closely spaced drops. In the first, Brink of Disaster (Class V), a messy approach between gnarly pourovers launches you over a 10-foot ledge. The run-out crashes angrily into the left bank and rushes toward an ugly Class VI rapid. The water in between, pushy and dangerous even at low water flows, carried an expert southern paddler to his death at 2,500 cfs. Below is Coming Home, Sweet Jesus (Class V+), where after a tricky approach the river drops seven feet into a powerful ledge hole. The hole breaks right and pushes you into "the box," a huge drain under a giant boulder. A boater swam under the boulder in the 1970s! And Sieve City (Class V+) is just below. At low flows there is a tight left line above horrible sieves. At levels over 650 cfs a "saner" right-hand route opens up. Fortunately, all three drops can be easily portaged via an old railroad grade on river right.

You are now one mile into the run. The river opens up here for a half-mile stretch of good Class IV rapids. There are multiple lines here and the water doesn't always push you into trouble. A short pool lies above Gateway to Heaven. After a tricky series of slots, the river narrows into a steep slide that should be scouted. There are some easier rapids between here and Let's Make a Deal (Class IV+). Here, the river tilts down a long, pushy, Class III+ approach into a strong hole. Below here are three doors;

Meadow River • West Virginia

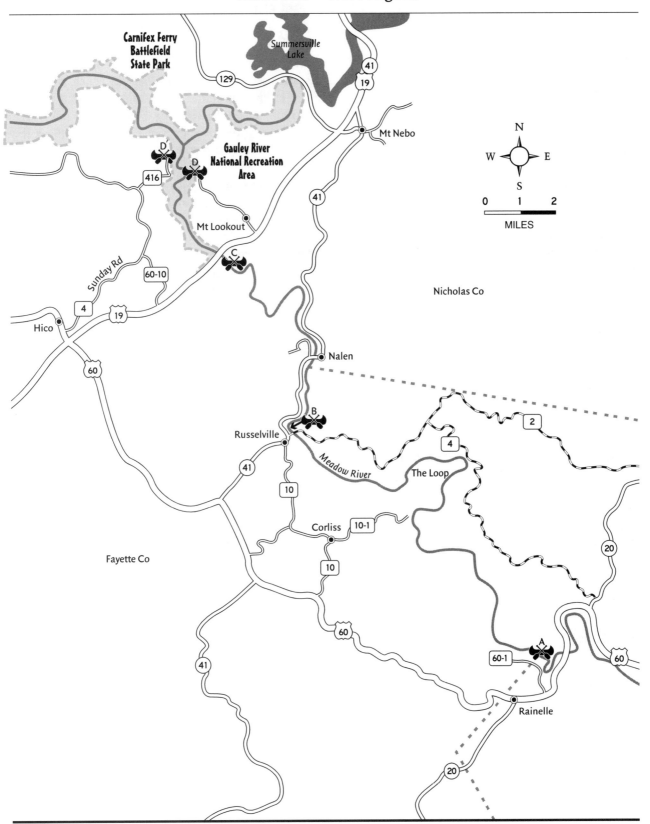

Section: US 19 Bridge to Carnifex Ferry
Counties: Nicholas, Fayette
USGS Quad: Summersville Dam
Difficulty: Class IV–VI
Gradient: 94 feet per mile (two miles at 125 feet per mile)
Average Width: 75 feet
Velocity: Fast
Rescue Index: Remote
Hazards: The entire section
Scouting: The entire section
Portages: Most big drops are often carried
Scenery: Beautiful
Highlights: Outstandingly beautiful canyon
Gauge: Mt. Lookout gauge

Runnable Water Levels:	Minimum	Maximum
Mt. Lookout gauge	4.5 feet	6.0 feet

Additional Information: Summersville Dam, (304) 872-5809;
    Huntington District of U.S. Army Corps of Engineers,
    (304) 529-5127

the left looks tempting, but it's blocked by downstream rocks. The middle door is the best choice, a tight but runnable slot, and the far right is the safest. There's a nice pool below where you can relax and collect your wits before moving on.

Soon a huge bluff on the left marks the beginning of the Islands section. At the first island run right down a long stretch of Class III–IV. At the second island, the center line is blocked. A top expert from the Washington, D.C. area was vertically pinned and killed here, so finish on the left. Immediately downstream you'll encounter a big sliding ledge that tends to shove you left under a nasty undercut. There are a few Class IVs between here and the last big rapid, Double Undercut (Class V+), which can be easily scouted and carried on the left. It consists of a six- to seven-foot horseshoe-shaped ledge into a bad hole. The undercut right side is very hard to avoid. Below here there's a nice stretch of Class III–IV water to the confluence with the Gauley.

To find the put-in (D), take the southbound lane of Route 19 and stop on the north side, about 200 yards above the bridge. On the other side of the guardrail is a steep dirt road down to the river. Most boaters take out at the base of Mt. Lookout Road (E), which turns into a very steep, rough dirt track as it approaches the river. You can also reach the river via Sunday Road (E′), but the approach to the river is even steeper. Both roads leave Route 19 on well-marked roads. Or you could run Lost Paddle Rapid and continue down the Upper Gauley.

The flow of the Meadow is measured at the Mt. Lookout gauge, just above the confluence with the Gauley. The upper and middle stretches are runnable at about 800 cfs, but most people will want 1,000–1,200 cfs for a good run. Anything over 2,000 cfs is considered high and makes the upper section rather pushy. The Lower Meadow is run between 450 and 1,500 cfs; most veterans consider 750 cfs ideal.

Mt. Lookout Gauge Conversion Table

feet	cfs
4.2	200
4.6	500
5.0	720
5.2	840
5.4	940
5.6	1,140
5.8	1,310
6.0	1,500
6.2	1,700
6.4	1,900
6.6	2,120
6.8	2,360
7.0	2,620
8.0	4,100
9.0	5,900
10.0	8,000

Cranberry River

The headwaters of the Gauley River contain many outstanding whitewater streams. The best are collectively referred to as the "fruit basket," and the Cranberry is the sweetest of them all. Born along the state's high mountain backbone, it drains a remarkable wilderness area called the Cranberry Backcountry. The water is crystal clear and flows through an unspoiled Appalachian forest. The South Fork gathers in the Cranberry Glades, a unique, high-altitude swamp filled with rare plants. Part of it can be viewed from a boardwalk accessible via USFS Road 102. A dirt road (USFS Road 76) runs along the river from the Glades to Cranberry Campground, but it is gated and closed to motorized vehicles. Below this seldom-traveled wilderness run is an intense roadside section and a delightful intermediate wilderness stretch.

Section: Above Cranberry Recreation Area to Gauley River
Counties: Pocahontas, Webster, Nicholas,
USGS Quads: Lobelia, Webster Springs SE, Webster Springs SW, Canden on Gauley
Difficulty: Class II–V, depending on section
Gradient: 60 feet per mile
Average Width: 50 feet
Velocity: Fast
Rescue Index: Accessible to remote
Hazards: Steep technical rapids in upper section
Scouting: S-Turn
Portages: None
Scenery: Beautiful
Highlights: Unspoiled wooded surroundings
Gauge: Richwood gauge; Summersville Dam, (304) 872-5809

Runnable Water Levels:	Minimum	Maximum
Above Cranberry Rec. Area	4.6 feet	Flood stage
Below Cranberry Rec. Area	3.5 feet	5.0 feet

Additional Information: U.S. Army Corps of Engineers at Charleston, (304) 529-5127

Wilderness Section

This uppermost "wilderness" section is occasionally run at very high water, but it is difficult to catch up. You'll need high water—over 4.6 feet on the gauge at Richwood Bridge. Park near the locked gate at the end of the Cranberry Glades parking lot (A), shoulder your boat, and carry down the road until a small stream appears on the right. This is the South Fork. Initially the river meanders through a densely vegetated swamp, but it abruptly picks up speed and doesn't let up until the end. Most rapids are straightforward, open Class II–IIIs, but you should keep alert for small-stream tree hazards. Below the Dogway Fork you'll encounter the section known as The Roughs. The water reaches a Class IV rating here; then things calm back down until you reach the Cranberry Recreation Area downstream.

Upper Cranberry

The stretch from Cranberry Campground (B) to the Woodbine Bridge (C) is known as the Upper Cranberry. This is a small, steep, busy stream flowing swiftly around giant boulders. At low water flows the rapids are scrapy and very tight (Class IV), requiring intense maneuvering. At high water the drops open up and become more powerful, a lot like Maryland's Upper Yough. This section can be scouted from the road, where ample pullovers provide a variety of camping and access points.

After a mile of flatwater the river drops over a complex series of ledges; below here one steep drop follows another. Most can be scouted from your boat, but don't be afraid to stretch your legs if necessary. Toward the end of the run you'll encounter a nasty, blind, Class IV+ rapid called S-Turn. A giant boulder marks the top of this drop. The left-side entry looks pretty easy, but once you turn the corner there's no stopping! The water carries you into a second turn where you have to cut precisely between huge boulders. This is a tight and nasty move, so make

Cranberry River • West Virginia

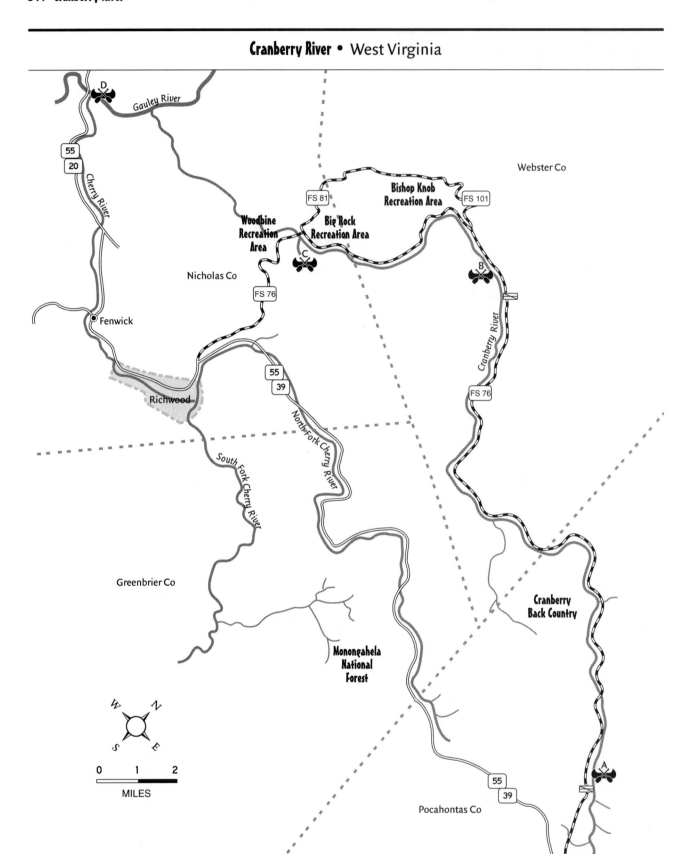

Gauley River

55
20

Cherry River

Webster Co

FS 81

Bishop Knob
Recreation Area

FS 101

Woodbine
Recreation
Area

Big Rock
Recreation Area

Nicholas Co

C

B

FS 76

Cranberry River

Fenwick

FS 76

55
39

Richwood

North Fork Cherry River

South Fork Cherry River

Greenbrier Co

Cranberry
Back Country

Monongahela
National
Forest

W   N
S   E

0   1   2

MILES

55
39

Pocahontas Co

A

sure you look it over first. The river starts to let up below here, but there are still a few more challenging drops before you float under the Woodbine Bridge.

Lower Cranberry

Below Woodbine the river changes character from a tough expert run to something suitable for intermediates. It starts out with two miles of practically continuous Class II–III rapids, then narrows down and picks up speed. The rapids culminate in what was once the Class V Cranberry Split. The infamous Split boulder was pushed aside by a flood, but although the rapid is probably no more than a Class III+, it's still a scramble to get by on the right. Here the river rushes to the right of a brushy island and necks down to about 10 yards wide. The tricky rapids downstream seem easy by comparison.

After five miles of paddling, the Cranberry flows into the Gauley. This is a big, powerful river with many wide-open Class II–III rapids, hidden boulders, and holes. Proceed downstream to the WV Route 20 Bridge at Curtin

for an easy take-out. Because both the Cranberry and the Gauley flow in a westerly direction, the glare of the sun makes it hard to read the water, and sunglasses are recommended for afternoon paddling.

Gauge information is obtained from the U.S. Army Corps of Engineers at the Summersville Dam (304-872-5809) or Charleston (304-529-5127). The latter gives you access to the USGS Richwood Gauge on the Cranberry at Woodbine; 3.5 feet (300 cfs) is the minimum flow; 5.0 feet (1500 cfs) would be considered high water. The Craigsville Gauge, which is listed on both recordings, measures the inflow to Summersville Lake. It should read at least 11.6 feet to justify a trip to the headwaters. The gauge itself is just downstream of Woodbine Bridge on river left.

The shuttle is easy. USFS Road 76 leaves WV 39 just outside Richwood, giving access to Woodbine and Big Rock. There's a nice restaurant at the turn-off. USFS Road 102 leaves WV 39 for the Cranberry Glades about 10 miles further uphill. The Curtin bridge (D) on the Gauley is reached via WV Routes 20 and 46.

Chris Kerr paddling S-Turn on the Upper Cranberry. Photo by Mayo Gravatt.

APPENDICES

Appendix A

Water Level Resources

National Weather Service

The National Weather Service accepts the main federal responsibility for disseminating current, forecast, and hydrological information to the public. The main office in Maryland operates a system of satellites that accepts gauge readings from USGS gauges. Regional river forecast centers collect information from local offices and distribute forecasts and warnings. Local offices are responsible for maintaining a river- and rainfall-reporting network within their hydrological service area and for local distribution of information. You may also access the NWS via the Web at http://www.nws.noaa.gov.

Main Office
National Weather Service
National Oceanic and Atmospheric Administration
Department of Commerce
1325 East West Highway
Silver Spring, MD 20910-3283
(301) 427-7622

River Forecast Centers
Lower Mississippi River Forecast Center
National Weather Service
62300 Airport Road
Slidel, LA 70460
(504) 641-4343

Middle Atlantic River Forecast Center
National Weather Service
227 West Beaver Avenue
Rider Bldg. No. 2, 4th Floor
State College, PA 16801
(814) 234-9701

Ohio River Forecast Center
National Weather Service
1901 South State Route 134
Wilmington, OH 45177
(513) 383-0527

Southeast River Forecast Center
National Weather Service
4 Falcon Drive
Peachtree, GA 30269
(404) 486-0028

National Water Information Center

The National Water Information Center is designed to be a hub for the dissemination of water resources information to all inquirers; call (800) 426-9000. This toll-free number will take your information requests and refer you to the appropriate source of hydrological information. E-mail requests can be sent to h2oinfo@usgs-gov.

National Water Data Exchange

The National Water Data Exchange (NAWDEX) is a group of water-oriented organizations working together to improve access to water data. Its primary objective is to assist users of water data and water information in the identification, location, and acquisition of water data.
National Water Data Exchange
US Geological Survey
421 National Center
Reston, VA 22092
(703) 648-6848

USGS Water Resource Division District Offices

The United States Geological Survey is the principal supplier of hydrological information in the United States. This agency maintains the system of automated gauges reporting river stages (often via satellite) to the National Weather Service and other agencies. The Water Resource

Division District Offices of the United States Geological Survey are NAWDEX assistance centers that can provide the public with water data and answer questions on the water resources of their specific regions.

Alabama

U.S. Geological Survey
2350 Fairlane Drive, Suite 120
Montgomery, AL 36116
(334) 213-2332

Connecticut

U.S. Geological Survey
Abraham A. Ribicoff Federal Building
450 Main Street, Rm 525
Hartford, CT 06103
(860) 240-3060

Delaware

U.S. Geological Survey
300 South New Street
Federal Bldg., Rm 1201
Dover, DE 19901-4907
(302) 573-6241

District of Columbia: See Maryland

Georgia

U.S. Geological Survey
Peachtree Business Center, Suite 130
3039 Amwiler Road
Atlanta, GA 30360-2824
(770) 903-9100

Kentucky

U.S. Geological Survey
9818 Bluegrass Parkway
Louisville, KY 40299
(502) 493-1900

Maine

U.S. Geological Survey
26 Ganneston Drive
Augusta, ME 04330
(207) 622-8208

Maryland

U.S. Geological Survey
8987 Yellow Brick Road
Baltimore, MD 21237
(410) 238-4200

Massachusetts

U.S. Geological Survey
28 Lord Road, Suite 280
Marlborough, MA 01752
(508) 490-5000

New Hampshire

U.S. Geological Survey
361 Commerce Way
Pembroke, NH 03275-3718
(603) 226-7800

New York

U.S. Geological Survey
425 Jordan Road
Troy, NY 12180
(518) 285-5600

North Carolina

U.S. Geological Survey
3916 Sunset Ridge Road
Raleigh, NC 27607
(919) 571-4000

Pennsylvania

U.S. Geological Survey
840 Market Street
Lemoyne, PA 17043-1586
(717) 730-6900

South Carolina

U.S. Geological Survey
720 Gracern Road
Stephenson Center, Suite 129
Columbia, SC 29210
(803) 750-6100

Tennessee

U.S. Geological Survey
640 grassmere Park, Suite 100
Nashville, TN 37211
(615) 837-4700

Vermont

U.S. Geological Survey
361 Commerce Way
Pembroke, NH 03275
(603) 225-4681

Virginia

U.S. Geological Survey
1730 East Parnham Road
Richmond, VA 23228
(804) 261-2600

West Virginia

U.S. Geological Survey
11 Dunbar Street
Charleston, WV 25301
(304) 347-5130

U.S. Army Corps of Engineers Offices

The Army Corps of Engineers builds and operates most public dams and water projects in the United States. Information on Corps projects, dam release schedules, and current releases can be obtained from district offices.

National
Public Affairs Office
U.S. Army Corps of Engineers
20 Massachusetts Avenue, NW
Washington, DC 20314
(202) 272-0010

Division and District
North Atlantic Division
U.S. Army Corps of Engineers
90 Church Street
New York, NY 10007-2979
(212) 264-7500

Baltimore District
U.S. Army Corps of Engineers
10 South Howard Street
Baltimore, MD 21201
(410) 962-2013

New York District
U.S. Army Corps of Engineers
26 Federal Plaza
New York, NY 10728-0090
(212) 264-2188

Norfolk District
U.S. Army Corps of Engineers
803 Front Street
Norfolk, VA 23510-1096
(757) 441-7500

Philadelphia District
U.S. Army Corps of Engineers
100 Penn Square East
Philadelphia, PA 19107-3390
(215) 656-6500

Ohio River Division
U.S. Army Corps of Engineers
P.O. Box 1159
Cincinnati, OH 45201-1159
(513) 684-3010

Huntington District
U.S. Army Corps of Engineers
502 Eighth Street
Huntington, WV 25701-2070
(304) 529-5452

Louisville District
U.S. Army Corps of Engineers
P.O. Box 59
Louisville, KY 40201-0059
(502) 582-6377

Nashville District
U.S. Army Corps of Engineers
P.O. Box 1070
Nashville, TN 37202-1070
(615) 736-7161

Pittsburgh District
U.S. Army Corps of Engineers
Federal Building
1000 Liberty Avenue, Rm 1801
Pittsburgh, PA 15222-4186
(462) 384-4532

South Atlantic Division
U.S. Army Corps of Engineers
60 Forsyth Street, SW, Rm 9m15
Atlanta, GA 30303-8801
(404) 562-5000

U.S. Army Corps of Engineers Support Center
P.O. Box 1600
Huntsville, AL 35807-4301
(256) 895-1691

Charleston District
U.S. Army Corps of Engineers
69 Haygood Avenue
Charleston, SC 29403
(843) 239-8123

Mobile District
U.S. Army Corps of Engineers
P.O. Box 2288
Mobile, AL 36628-0001
(334) 690-2505

Savannah District
U.S. Army Corps of Engineers
P.O. Box 889
Savannah, GA 31402-0889
(912) 652-5270

Wilmington District
U.S. Army Corps of Engineers
P.O. Box 1890
Wilmington, NC 28402-1890
(910) 251-4626

River Services, Inc.

A private company, River Services, Inc., offers a real-time, computer-based, hydrological information service.

River Services, Inc.
3414 Morningwood Drive, Suite 11
Olney, MD 20832
(301) 774-1616

Although the cost of this information service is probably out of the reach of individuals (currently a minimum of $100 per month, including one hour a month of connection time), clubs and outfitters might be interested. Using your personal computer with a modem, a toll-free number, and an access code provided by River Services, you can access a customized computer database of river forecasts and river levels (as well as a wide variety of other information). You should be able to get current readings for every USGS gauge that sends data to the National Weather Service satellite system.

Waterline National River Information Hotline

Waterline is the largest single telephone source of river information available to the public in the United States. Waterline is fully automated, operates continuously, and reports on over 1,100 river levels and flows. Most Waterline reports are updated 6 to 24 times per day via satellite directly from the gauges.

To use the service you need to know the six-digit code for the desired site. These codes are available by mail, fax, or Internet. For codes by mail or fax, call Waterline's customer service number at (800) 945-3376. To have codes and other information mailed to you, press 0 to speak to the operator or leave a message. Staff members are available 9 A.M. to 5 P.M. Eastern Standard Time. To get codes by fax at any time, follow the recorded instructions to fax yourself a state code list. Once you have the list, call back and get the information on the states you desire. The fax system responds within two minutes of your request. Site codes are also available on the Internet at http://www.h2oline.com.

Once you have the desired site code, you can call Waterline's 800 or 900 hotlines from a touch-tone phone. With the 800 line (800-297-4243), you can set up an account and access code to receive information. This line costs 68 cents per minute. A 12-minute block of time is billed to your Visa or MasterCard. Unused time remains for future calls. You can recharge your account anytime by pressing 999 and following the prompts. Time spent setting up or recharging your account is free.

The 900 line (900-726-4243) does not require an account but is available only if you call from home. The cost is $1.28 per minute and will be charged to your phone bill. Federal government rules require that you be 18 years or older or have parental permission to call a 900 number. (At press time, Waterline was working on providing this service free of charge to paddlers)

After the initial messages, Waterline will ask for a six-digit site code. Enter the code whenever you want. You can interrupt the message with a new site code whenever you want. You can also program Waterline to play a list of specified sites whenever you call. The average call time is two billable minutes. Once you are familiar with the system, a one-minute phone call will yield one to four readings for a single river or three to four different river readings.

Waterline also publishes the Waterline Guide to River Levels and Flow Information. This guide contains all the Waterline site codes as well as every known public source, including websites, for current river level information in the U.S. Each copy includes a precharged access card with 12 minutes of time on Waterline's 800 number.

Appendix B

Map Sources

USGS Topographic Maps

Topographic maps are available at many outdoor shops and from other commercial vendors, but for the best prices and selection, you should order directly from the USGS of the Department of the Interior (but see TVA description below). They sell the topographic maps in the standard 7.5-minute (1:24,000) series of quadrangles and in a variety of other sizes as well. Write for the Index to Topographic and Other Map Coverage and the companion Catalog of Topographic and Other Published Maps for each state in which you are interested.

Mapping Distribution
U.S. Geological Survey
Box 25286 Federal Center, Building 41
Denver, CO 80225
(303) 236-5900
(Some of you will remember that the USGS used to have an Eastern and a Western Distribution Branch; that's no longer true.)

County Road Maps

Maine

Department of Transportation
Office of Public Affairs
Transportation Building
State House Station #16
Augusta, ME 04333-2672

New Hampshire

Department of Transportation
John O. Morton Building
1 Hazen Drive
Concord, NH 03302-0483

Vermont

Vermont Agency of Transportation
General Information
133 State Street
Montpelier, VT 05633

Massachusetts

Massachusetts Highway Department
10 Park Plaza, Suite 3510
Boston, MA 02116-3973

Connecticut

Department of Transportation
P.O. Drawer A
Wethersfield, CT 06109-0801

New York

Map Information Unit
New York State Department of Transportation
State Campus Bldg. 4, Room 105
Albany, NY 12232-0415

Pennsylvania

Pennsylvania Department of Transportation
Distribution Services Unit
P.O. Box 2028
Harrisburg, PA 17105

Maryland

Map Distribution Sales
Maryland State Highway Administration
Brooklandville, MD 21022

West Virginia

West Virginia Department of Highways
Planning Division, Attn: Map Sales
1900 Kanawha Boulevard East
Bldg 5, Rm A848
Charleston, WV 25305-0430
(304) 273-8118

Other Map Sources

DeLorme Publishing Co.
P.O. Box 298
Freeport, ME 04032
(207) 865-4171 or (800) 227-1656

Marshall Penn York, Inc.
1538 Erie Boulevard
West Syracuse, NY 13204
(315) 422-2162

Appendix C

Whitewater Schools

The following list includes many of the nation's leading whitewater schools of instruction.

Adventure Quest
P.O. Box 184
Woodstock, VT 05091
(802) 484-3639
www.adventurequest.org

The Kayak Centre
9 Phillips Street
Wickford, RI 02852
(401) 295-4400
www.kayakcentre.com

New England Outdoor Center
P.O. Box 669
Millinocket, ME 04462
(800) 766-7238
www.neoc.com

Riversport School of Paddling
213 Yough Street
Confluence, PA 15424
(814) 395-5744 or (800) 216-6991
www.shol.com/kayak

Saco Bound's Northern Waters School
Box 119-C
Center Conway, NH 03813
(603) 447-2177
www.sacobound.com

Whitewater Challangers Outdoor Adventure Center
P.O. Box 8
White Haven, PA 18661
(570) 443-9532
www.wc-rafting.com

W.I.L.D./W.A.T.E.R.S.
Route 28 at the Glen
Warrensburg, NY 12885
(518) 494-4984 or (888) WILD H2O
www.wildwaters.net

Zoar Outdoor Paddling School
Mohawk Trail
P. O. Box 245
Charlemont, MA 01339
(800) 532-7483
www.zoaroutdoor.com

Appendix D

Organizations

American Canoe Association
7432 Alban Station Boulevard, Suite B-226
Springfield, VA 22150
(703) 451-0141

America Outdoors
P.O. Box 10847
Knoxville, TN 37939
(865) 558-3595

American Rivers
1025 Vermont Avenue NW, Suite 720
Washington, DC 20005
(202) 347-7550

American Whitewater Affiliation
P.O. Box 85
Phoenicia, NY 12464

Friends of the Cheat
119 Price Street, Ste. 206
Kingwood, WV 26537
(304) 329-3621

Environmental Defense Fund
257 Park Avenue S
Ney York, NY 10010
(800) 684-3322

International Rivers Network
1847 Berkeley Way
Berkeley, CA 94703
(510) 848-1155

National Association for Search and Rescue
4500 Southgate Place, Suite 100
Chantilly, VA 20151-1714
(703) 222-6277

The Trade Association of Paddlesports
12455 North Wauwatosa Road
Mequon, WI 53097
(262) 242-5228

River Network
4000 Albemarle Street, NW, Suite 303
Washington, DC 20016
(202) 364-2550

The Sierra Club
85 2nd Street, 2nd Floor
San Francisco, CA 94105-3441
(415) 977-5500

West Virginia Rivers Coalition
801 N. Randolph Avenue
Elkins, WV 26241
(304) 637-7201

Wilderness Society
Department of River Services
900 17th Street, NW
Washington, DC 20006-2506
(800) 843-9453

Appendix E

Web Resources

What follows are the World Wide Web sites and e-mail addresses available on the Internet. All Web addresses should have the http:// prefix. Keep in mind that the World Wide Web is a transient medium and changes often. If a Web address is unavailable, try looking for it through your favorite search engine.

American Canoe Association
Web: www.aca-paddler.org
E-mail: acadirect@aol.com

America Outdoors
Web: www.americaoutdoors.org
E-mail: infoacct@americaoutdoors.org

American Rivers
Web: www.amrivers.org
E-mail: amrivers@amrivers.org

American Whitewater Affiliation
Web: www.awa.org

Environmental Defense Fund
Web: www.edf.org
E-mail: edf@edf.org

Friends of the Cheat
Web: www.cheat.org

Great Outdoor Recreation Page (G.O.R.P.)
Web: www.gorp.com

International Rivers Network
Web: www.irn.org
E-mail: irnweb@irn.org

Kayak.com
Web: www.kayak.com
One of the best resources for release dates of New England Rivers

National Association of Search and Rescue
Web: www.nasar.org
E-mail: info@nasar.org

National Organization of Whitewater Rodeos
Web: www.nowr.org

National Park Service
Web: www.nps.gov

National Weather Service
Web: www.nws.noaa.gov

Northeast River Forecast Center
Web: http://www.nws.noaa.gov.er.nerfc

Professional Paddle Sports Association
Web: www.propaddle.com
E-mail: paddlespt@unidial.com

The Trade Association Paddlesports
Web: www.gopaddle.org
E-mail: info@gopaddle.org

The River Network
Web:www.teleport.com/~rivernet
E-mail: rivernet2@aol.com

Sierra Club
Web: www.sierraclub.org

U.S. Army Corps of Engineers
Web: www.usace.army.mil

U.S. Forest Service
Web: www.fs.fed.us

USGS
Web: water.usgs.gov

Waterline
Web: wwwh2oline.com
E-mail: waterline@readdata.com

West Virginia Rivers Coalition
Web: www.msys.net/wvrc
E-mail: wvrc@msys.net

Wilderness Society
Web: www.wilderness.org
E-mail: tws@wilderness.org